Aron Nimzovich

MY SYSTEM

A Treatise on Chess

Edited by Fred Reinfeld

DAVID McKAY COMPANY, INC.

NEW YORK

Translator's Preface

For nearly twenty years Nimzovich has been the stormy petrel of the chess world. "A law unto himself," "Goes his own way, one, however, not to be recommended to the public," "mysterious," such are typical examples of the kind of criticism which his revolutionary ideas had to meet. And yet this "law," this "way" has governed, has been followed by the whole modern school, call it hyper-modern, or neo-romantic, as you will; they are part and parcel of the game as it is played to-day. For a master, who is one of the four (I include Lasker) who are in common opinion held worthy to challenge the profound and brilliant player who now holds the world's championship, could not have arrived at such a position in the world of chess had his "law" been based on a false philosophy, or his "way" led to barren ground. His post-war record is sufficiently significant. In thirteen Master tournaments he has won outright six times, the most recent occasion being at the important Carlsbad tournament in August 1929. He has also been thrice bracketed 1st, has been 2nd three times, and 3rd once. It is, therefore, a privilege and a pleasure to be allowed to introduce his "System" to the English-speaking public.

The literature of chess is enormous; but the number of books which may claim to reveal something of the spirit of the game, of its philosophy, may almost be told on the fingers of one hand. And while we must never forget what we owe to the writings of *e.g.* Dr. Lasker, Dr. Tarrasch, Capablanca (in his *Chess Fundamentals*), and indeed Mason, yet there is some justification for the claim which Nimzovich makes in his preface to the German edition of this book, to have been "the first to write a real treatise on the *game* of chess, not merely one on the openings," in that he is the first "to reduce a welter of arbitrary ideas to a definite number of inter-related principles"; while he points with legitimate pride to his enunciation of the "five special cases of the 7th and 8th ranks." But no one who has studied his analysis of the principles governing the "blockade," or the pawn-chain, or play in an open file, or his qualitative theory of pawn majorities, or his conception of the "elastic center," will deny the penetration of his thought or the influence which his teaching has had on the chess of to-day, as revolutionary perhaps as was that of Steinitz on his generation.

The difficulties in translating *Mein System* have been not inconsiderable, partly because the novelty of his presentation required a terminology peculiar to itself, for which a suitable English equivalent had to be sought, partly because—but a quotation from his preface will best serve here:—"It is the custom to write text books in a dry, didactic style. It seems to be held that one would sacrifice his dignity did he let a humorous turn creep in, for whatever room is there for humor in a chess manual! This opinion I cannot possibly share; in fact I go further and hold it to be entirely wrong; for true humor often contains more inner truth than the most serious seriousness. As for me, I am an avowed partisan of the humorously drawn parallel, and like to bring in allusions to events in daily life if I may thereby bring greater clarity into complicated situations on the chessboard." A literal translation has, therefore, sometimes been utterly impossible, since not seldom the author's humor (or pun!) would not bear transplanting to foreign soil.

In this English edition several additional games have been inserted, a few passages have, with the concurrence of the author, been omitted, and the arrangement has been slightly altered, *e.g.* for convenience of reference the illustrative games have been collected into one section.

August 29, 1929

PHILIP HEREFORD

Nimzovich's Tournament and Match Record

Tournament	Place	W	L	D
Coburg ("A"), 1904	VI	9—	4—	3
Barmen ("B"), 1905	XV–XVI	3—	8—	6
Munich, 1906	I	8—	0—	3
Ostend, 1907	III–IV	14—	4—	10
Carlsbad, 1907	IV–V	8—	3—	9
Hamburg, 1910	III	8—	3—	5
San Sebastian, 1911	V–VII	3—	2—	9
Carlsbad, 1911	V–VI	11—	5—	9
San Sebastian, 1912	II–III	8—	3—	8
Vilna, 1912 *	IV	6—	3—	9
St. Petersburg, 1914 *	I–II	12—	2—	4
St. Petersburg, 1914	VIII	1—	3—	6
Gothenburg, 1920	XII	1—	5—	7
Stockholm, 1920	II	11—	1—	2
Carlsbad, 1923	VI–VII	8—	5—	4
Copenhagen, 1923	I	6—	0—	4
Copenhagen, 1924	I	9—	0—	1
Baden-Baden, 1925	IX	7—	5—	8
Marienbad, 1925	I–II	8—	1—	6
Breslau, 1925	II	6—	2—	3
Semmering, 1926	IV–V	9—	3—	5
Dresden, 1926	I	8—	0—	1
Hanover. 1926	I	6—	0—	1
New York, 1927	III	6—	5—	9
Berlin, 1927	II–IV	5—	2—	2
Kecskemet, 1927	II	8—	1—	7

* Russian Championship.

Tournament	Place	W	L	D
Niendorf, 1927	I–II	4—	0—	3
London, 1927	I–II	7—	2—	2
London, 1927	I	7—	0—	3
Berlin, 1928	I	8—	1—	3
Berlin, 1928	II	4—	2—	6
Carlsbad, 1929	I	10—	1—	10
San Remo, 1930	II	8—	2—	5
Frankfort, 1930	I	9—	1—	1
Liege, 1930	III–V	3—	2—	6
Winterthur, 1931	I	7—	0—	1
Bled, 1931	III	8—	6—	12
Copenhagen, 1933	I	5—	1—	1
Stockholm, 1934	II	6—	2—	2
Zurich, 1934	VI–VII	6—	3—	6
Totals		281—	93—202	

Matches

		W	L	D
Spielmann, 1906		4—	4—	5
Bogolyubov, 1920		1—	3—	0
Stahlberg, 1934		2—	4—	2
Stoltz, 1934		2—	1—	3
Totals		9—	12—	10
Grand Total:		290—105—212		

Contents

First Part

THE ELEMENTS

Second Part

POSITION PLAY

Third Part

ILLUSTRATIVE GAMES

Introduction

> *Praise, like gold and diamonds, owes its value only to its scarcity*—SAMUEL JOHNSON

> *Ridicule can do much, for instance embitter the existence of young talents*—ARON NIMZOVICH

KNUCKLE-BONES was prehistoric man's favorite diversion. Thousands of years passed before this artless pastime was transformed into chess, and many more centuries were required before the game took on the form in which we now play it.

"It all started with knuckle-bones," writes Dr. Henry Davidson in his fascinating history of chess. "These were elongated bones, originally the phalanges of sheep, which primitive man tossed in the air as a form of amusement. Sometimes it was a game of skill, victory depending on how many you could catch or with what artistry you could toss them. Sometimes it was a game of chance, the surfaces of the bones being marked, and your fortunes depending on what side was face up when the bones fell. From this simple beginning came a long line of games. Knuckle-bones as a game of skill was the parent of juggling. As a game of chance, knuckle-bones fathered a dozen modern forms of play, including backgammon, dice, dominoes, parchesi and chess."

From the "simple beginning" there evolved the most complex of all games, with manifold possibilities that delight the heart of every mathematician. Again I quote Dr. Davidson:

"Kasner and Newman estimate that the total of possible

moves in a game of chess is 10 to the power (10 to the 50th). This is a figure for which we have no name. It is composed first by taking a one with fifty zeros after it, thus: 100,000,000,000,-000,000,000,000,000,000,000,000,000,000,000,000 and then multiplying ten by itself that many times. An ordinary 200-page book accommodates 330,000 letters or numerals; three such volumes would provide space for about a million numerals. To write the number 10 to the 10th to the 50th power would take 30,000,000,000,000,000,000,000,000,000,000,000,000,000,000,000, volumes: all this space being required merely to write down the numeral indicating all the different moves in a chess game."

Luckily only an infinitesimal proportion of all *possible* chess moves possesses *practical* significance; but even this small number gives us a game whose complexity is as disturbing as it is attractive. This explains why the chess world has always had great masters whose ambition it was to analyze the game systematically, to reduce it to a series of *generalized, reproducible* elements, to isolate and enumerate its *basic, inter-related* propositions. These attempts have never been wholly successful, for in chess, as in all activities of living beings, there is always some residue which eludes definition and analysis. Of all the great men who have tried to systematize chess, two stand out above all the rest: Wilhelm Steinitz and Aron Nimzovich.

Steinitz was the great lawgiver and systematizer of chess. He found it a kind of chaos, he left it almost a science. In some ways his great follower Nimzovich had an easier task; in other ways, a more difficult one: for Nimzovich had to sweep away the cobwebs of pseudo-science and excessive simplification.

Nimzovich was born in Riga on the seventh of November, 1886. His father was a well-to-do merchant and a man of considerable culture; something of a poet, a lover of the arts and an excellent chessplayer. One of his games was for many years a favorite item in anthologies of brilliant short encounters. It was played in 1899, and the score follows:

WHITE	BLACK	14 Kt—B7 *ch!*	Q x Kt
S. *Nimzovich*	*Neumann*	15 B x P *ch*	K—Q2
1 P—K4	P—K4		
2 P—KB4	P x P		
3 Kt—KB3	P—KKt4		
4 B—B4	P—Kt5		
5 O—O	P x Kt		
6 Q x P	Q—B3		
7 P—Q3	B—Kt2		
8 Kt—B3	Kt—B3		
9 B x P	Kt—Q5		
10 Q—B2	P—Q3		
11 Kt—Q5	Q—Q1		
12 P—K5	P—QB3	16 Q—B5 *ch!!*	Kt x Q
13 B—KKt5	Q—Q2	17 P—K6 mate	

Nimzovich senior taught his son the moves when the boy
was eight years old. So runs the official account. But it is a good
guess that the child was able to play at a much earlier age; he
must have been present at many a happy session devoted to
casual play and analysis. Much of his aptitude for the game
must have developed and ripened unconsciously on these occasions. He grew up in an atmosphere redolent of chess, as the
players of Riga were noted for their love of the game and their
enthusiastic hospitality to any master who passed through the
town. In later years the Riga players made a great name for
themselves in the chess world for their fine endgame composi-
tions and their impressive success in correspondence play.

Nimzovich was seventeen when he first began to take a really
serious interest in the game. At first his style was purely combinative, as befits a youngster. But in any event, the accent on
combinations was quite logical for that time and place.
Steinitz's theories were still strange to most players, and the
brilliant sacrificial play of Morphy, Anderssen and their more
or less gifted imitators still held the spotlight. Lasker was then,

as always, a lone wolf, whose playing style and philosophy could not be reconciled with the historical development of chess theory. It is true that the positional concepts of the Tarrasch school were beginning to make headway, partly because they were easy to understand; and partly because their regular success in tournament play taught an unforgettable lesson to even the most hidebound admirer of the Golden Age of chess.

In any event, whatever Nimzovich was to learn, he had to learn by himself. Chess books were few in number, good books fewer still. The dashing but aging Tchigorin was still the idol of Russian players, but he was a rebel who loved the chess of the good old days. This much we all know about Tchigorin. What is less well-known is that he was also a profound and original theorist who was in several respects a forerunner of modern tendencies. It was Tchigorin, for example, who popularized the then fantastic notion of answering 1 P—Q4 with 1 . . . Kt—KB3 instead of the almost obligatory 1 . . . P—Q4. It was also Tchigorin who formulated what the modern masters consider the most solid defense to the Ruy Lopez. It was Tchigorin, again, who showed that certain types of cramped positions are quite playable. In this respect, Tchigorin was close to Steinitz and the deadly antithesis of Tarrasch.

However, Nimzovich's familiarity with this side of Tchigorin's play was to come only at a later stage of the younger player's development. At the outset, as we have seen, Nimzovich favored combinative play exclusively. A turning point in his career came when his father sent him to Germany for his university studies. There he came in contact with a large number of players and was able to participate in master tournaments. He was a competitor in the "A" Tournament at Coburg in 1904, and in the "B" Tournament at Barmen in 1905. Here he had his first opportunity to see some of the immortals in action: Schlechter, Maroczy, Tchigorin, Marshall and Janowski. In the tournaments in which he played, he matched wits with other youngsters who were to become famous: Spielmann, Vidmar, Duras, Bernstein, Tartakover, Rubinstein and many others.

Nimzovich's showing in these two early tournaments was not impressive: he did fairly well at Coburg, but he was a miserable failure at Barmen. His enormous gifts for the game were quite obvious, but he was too sensitive, too inexperienced, too unseasoned, too impetuous and, some said, too temperamental.

We are told that these setbacks had a chastening effect on Nimzovich, and that it was at this time that he evolved his system, or the rudiments of it. However, it would be wrong to suppose that the system emerged full-blown at the first attempt: it is reasonable to assume that he realized that lack of positional orientation was his great defect; that he went to work on this weakness with all the determination, all the energy and all the originality for which he later became famous.

Whatever the process, we find that by 1906, when he was only 20, Nimzovich had definitely become a master of the very first rank! That year, playing in a small tournament in Munich, he was first, far ahead of such fine players as Spielmann and Erich Cohn. But it was in 1907 that his genius was displayed in a really impressive manner. At Ostend, in a tournament with 29 players, he tied for third and fourth with Mieses, only half a point behind the winners, Rubinstein and Bernstein. The same year, playing in an even stronger event at Carlsbad, he tied for fourth and fifth with Schlechter.

Although there was now no question of his ability, he had already become notorious for the marked eccentricity of his play. What made his games all the more incomprehensible was his success! He had announced his opposition to the reigning theories of the day (the dogmas of Tarrasch); and he was uncompromising in flaying Tarrasch's easy popularization and simplification of extremely difficult problems. Since Nimzovich's games were generally annotated by his enemies or by people who were horrified at innovation, he fared very badly in the current chess periodicals and newspaper columns.

Smarting over past ridicule and sensitively awaiting future insults, Nimzovich was often overbearing: he felt obliged to go on the warpath in order to forestall attacks by others. Yet we know that basically Nimzovich was a kindly man with a delightful sense of humor. It was a side of his personality which was familiar only to his friends and not to the general public.

Edward Lasker has given us a vivid picture of the Nimzovich of those days: *

> Nimzovich was studying philosophy at the University of Munich. He had had an excellent education, and his keen intellectual faculties were bound to produce some outstanding creative work no matter in what field they were applied. It has been the gain of chess fans throughout the world that Nimzovich happened to concentrate his powers of analytical inquiry on the scientific foundations of the game of chess.
>
> There was a bizarre streak in Nimzovich's makeup, which manifested itself not only in his exotic behavior but also in his thinking. In the last analysis, this probably explains why he was unable to keep up with Alekhine and Capablanca, both of whom coupled a strong practical sense with their fine positional understanding. This practical sense Nimzovich lacked. He also lacked their extraordinary physical endurance.
>
> When I met Nimzovich in Berlin in 1910, I was delighted at the opportunity of discussing with him my principles of "chess strategy," which by that time I had whipped into shape for the manuscript of my first book. While complimenting me on what I had done towards systematizing the knowledge every chess student needed

* Quoted by permission of the author from his forthcoming book *Chess Lessons From the Masters*.

before he could hope to become a strong player, Nimzovich explained with good-natured irony that a master had to understand much more. And after he had shown me some of his new ideas which he proposed to publish under the title *My System*, I thoroughly realized the gap which still separated me from his class. . . .

I saw him once more, in this country, when he was invited to take part in the New York Masters Tournament in 1927. The ironic aggressiveness of his youth was gone. And I was saddened to learn that during the hardships of the First World War and the years following it, his lungs had become affected. Mentally he was as keen as ever. But his nervousness had increased to a degree that was almost pathological. . . .

People who knew Nimzovich only superficially were apt to be repulsed by his abnormally nervous behavior. But those who took the trouble to engage him in conversation on chess or any other subject could not help being impressed with his intellectual honesty and his mental equipment. He was free from personal malice. When he clothed his arguments in sarcasm, and sometimes in rather unfunny jokes, it was nothing but a childlike quality which had persisted in him, as it does in so many chess masters of top rank. I am certain about one thing: Nimzovich was the real father of MODERN CHESS. Alekhine and Reti later contributed a great deal to this subject. But the credit for the original concept, always the hardest step, must go to Nimzovich.

The nervousness and lack of physical endurance to which Lasker alludes kept many a first prize out of reach of Nimzovich's eager grasp. Again and again the tantalizing process was repeated. At Hamburg, 1910, Nimzovich started off brilliantly in a strong field, but losses to Schlechter and Duras pushed him down to third. The following year at San Sebastian (the tourney in which Capablanca made his sensational debut),

Nimzovich tied for fifth, sixth and seventh prizes with the veterans Schlechter and Tarrasch. In the great Carlsbad tournament of the same year, he tied for fifth and sixth prizes with Marshall. The following year, at San Sebastian, he tied with Spielmann for second prize, right on Rubinstein's heels. The outcome of the tournament was decided in the last-round struggle between Rubinstein and Nimzovich. Both players were so nervous that first Nimzovich and then Rubinstein missed a mate in two!

The year 1913 was a milestone in Nimzovich's career, for he published several articles on his system and unleashed a powerful attack on the "modernism" of Tarrasch's *Moderne Schachpartie*. But Nimzovich's views made little impression; some people sneered that he had invented a system in order to conceal his ignorance of chess theory. The public's apathy is all the more remarkable when we realize that young players like Alekhine, Reti and Tartakover, highly sympathetic to the new ideas, were making their mark in tournament play.

Nimzovich's crass failure in the great tournament at St. Petersburg in 1914 was a severe disappointment to him; the elimination feature of the rules called for players with iron nerves, or better still, no nerves at all. The coming of the World War put a stop to Nimzovich's chess activities until 1920. From that time on, he made his residence in Copenhagen, where he was received with heart-warming hospitality. In the following years, he played a great deal of chess in the Scandinavian countries, and undoubtedly made a substantial contribution to the development of a school of great masters in Sweden.

During the period 1920–1924 Nimzovich was again playing himself into form, and in 1925 he began a series of impressive tournament performances which at last gave his system a hearing. Published in the late twenties in German and later translated into English, *My System* has had enormous popularity and profound influence wherever it has appeared.

In the great Baden-Baden Tournament of 1925, Nimzovich resumed international play, and his success was limited to playing several fine games. A few weeks later, however, he played magnificent chess at Marienbad, tying with Rubinstein for first prize. The consensus of expert opinion was that Nimzovich was the moral victor of the tourney. At Breslau the same year, Nimzovich was second to Bogolyubov.

The next year began auspiciously for Nimzovich in one of the greatest tournaments of chess history, held at Semmering. After ten rounds, Nimzovich and Tartakover led the field with the splendid score of 9–1. But in the remaining rounds they both fell off sadly, ending in a tie for fourth and fifth. A short time later Nimzovich went through the Dresden tournament undefeated, securing the first prize ahead of Alekhine. Another (minor) event at Hannover likewise ended in victory for Nimzovich.

His ability was now freely recognized, and the masters and public alike dipped eagerly into the iconoclastic pages of *My System*. Ridicule at long last gave way grudgingly to enthusiasm. Nimzovich's fame earned him an invitation to the great sextangular tournament at New York in 1927. After a fine start, h⌐ dropped to third; the tense nature of the tourney was too much for him. During the same year, he tied for first with Tartakover at Niendorf and London, but it was at Carlsbad, in 1929, that he achieved the great triumph of his career. It was a superb victory against an outstanding field.

Without exception, every great master who achieved success from 1925 on, showed definite traces of the Nimzovich influence. His theories, his innovations, his emphasis on fighting chess all combined to create new possibilities for the game. His novel lines of play in the Nimzoindian Defense, French Defense, Sicilian Defense, Caro-Kann Defense, Nimzovich Defense, Nimzovich Attack, Dutch Defense and other openings have enriched the master play of the last twenty years to a degree which is almost incredible.

Today we know that Nimzovich, by preaching his system all over the chess world, saved chess from the danger of dying out under the "scientific" influence of Tarrasch and Capablanca. Had the views of these two masters not been opposed by Nimzovich, much of the charm and joy of battle would have vanished, perhaps irrevocably, from chess.

What is so remarkable about the system? Look over the table of contents, and every element in it seems so obvious, so logical, so inevitable. But that is precisely the measure of how widespread Nimzovich's ideas have become. The importance of the center and centralization, the usefulness of open files and seventh rank, the strength of the passed Pawn, the proper treatment of end-game play, the utilization of the pin, the significance of the Pawn-chain, the weakness of the doubled Pawn, the value of restraint, prophylaxis, over-protection, maneuvering against weaknesses—"of course" we all knew about those details! Perhaps; but no one had had the great synthesizing genius, the profound absorption in the game, the distinguished teaching ability of Nimzovich; nor had any other chess master had the strength to hold out against the ridicule of the whole world for two decades. This ability of Nimzovich's, to stick to his guns despite almost universal ridicule and condemnation— perhaps this was the most impressive of all the proofs of his genius. Yet Nimzovich, despite the loneliness and bitterness of his position, was able to preserve the delightful sense of humor which peeps out from every page of this book. That is only one of the many unanswerable riddles with which genius likes to mock us.

Nimzovich's death, like his life, was full of tragic irony. He died on March 16, 1935, at the age of 48. His death occurred during the great Moscow Tournament, where many of his dis-

ciples from all over the chess world were distinguishing themselves. He died at a time when he was at last recognized for the
great man that he was. Death snatched him from the reward
that he was just beginning to relish: the universal admiration
and popularity that would have compensated for the many
years of crying in the wilderness. Luckily for us, he left a lasting
heritage, which will give future generations as much pleasure
as it caused him anguish.

FRED REINFELD

New York
February 4, 1947

FIRST PART

The Elements

1. On the Center and Development

Contains a short introduction and what the less advanced student must know about the center and about development.

I N   M Y opinion the following are to be regarded as the elements of chess-strategy:—(1) The center. (2) Play in open files. (3) Play in the 7th and 8th ranks. (4) The passed Pawn. (5) The pin. (6) Discovered check. (7) Exchanging. (8) The Pawn-chain.

Each one of these elements will in what follows be as thoroughly elucidated as possible. We shall begin with the center, which we propose to treat in the first place with the less experienced player in mind. In the second part of the book, which is devoted to position play, we shall endeavor to investigate the center from the point of view of the "higher learning." As you know, the center was precisely the point round which in the years 1911–13 what amounted to a revolution in chess took place. I mean that the articles which I wrote, (*Entspricht Dr. Tarrasch's "Moderne Schachpartie" wirklich moderner Auffassung?*) ran directly counter to the traditional conception, and sounded the call to a revolt which was in fact to give birth to the neo-romantic school. Hence the two-fold treatment of the center which we propose to undertake on didactic grounds, would seem to be justified.

And first a few definitions:

The line shown on Diagram 1 we call the frontier; "line" is of course to be taken in its mathematical, not in its chess sense. The point marked on Diagram 2 is the mid-point of the board, again naturally in its mathematical sense. The mid-point is easy to find; it is the point of intersection of the long diagonals.

DIAGRAM 1

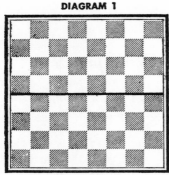

The Frontier Line

DIAGRAM 2

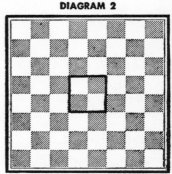

The Mid-Point
The Small Square is the center

§ 1. *By development is to be understood the strategic advance of the troops to the frontier line.*

The process is analogous to the advance on the outbreak of
a war. Both armies seek to reach the frontier as quickly as possible in order to penetrate into enemy territory.

Development is a collective conception. To have developed
one, two, or three pieces does not mean that we are developed.
On the contrary, the situation demands that *all* pieces be developed. If I may so put it, the period of development should
be inspired by a democratic spirit. How undemocratic for instance, it would be to let one of your officers go for a long
walking tour, whilst the others kicked their heels together at
home and bored themselves horribly. No, let each officer make
one move only, and . . . dig himself in.

§ 2. *A Pawn move must not in itself be regarded as a developing move, but merely as an aid to development.*

An important postulate for the beginner is the following:—
If it were possible to develop the pieces without the aid of
Pawn moves, the Pawn-less advance would be the correct one;
for, as suggested, the Pawn is not a fighting unit in the sense

that his crossing of the frontier is to be feared by the enemy, since obviously the attacking force of the Pawns is small compared with that of the pieces. However, the Pawn-less advance is in reality impossible of execution; since the enemy Pawn-center, thanks to its inherent aggressiveness, would drive back the pieces which we had developed. For this reason we should, in order to safeguard the development of our pieces, first build up a Pawn-center.

By center is to be understood the four squares which enclose the mid-point, *i.e.*, the squares K4, Q4 for both sides (see Diagram 2).

The wrecking of a Pawn-less advance is illustrated by the following:—

1. Kt—KB3, Kt—QB3; 2. P—K3. (Since the Pawn has not been moved to the center, we may still regard the advance as Pawn-less in our sense.) 2. . . . . P—K4; 3. Kt—B3, Kt—B3; 4. B—B4 ?, P—Q4. And now the faultiness of White's development may be seen; the Black Pawns have a demobilizing effect. 5. B—Kt3 (bad at the outset, a piece moved twice), P—Q5, and White is uncomfortably placed, at any rate from the point of view of the player with little fighting experience.

Another example is the following:—White without QR, A. Nimzovich; Black, an Amateur. (White's QRP is at R3), 1. P—K4, P—K4; 2. Kt—KB3, Kt—QB3; 3. B—B4, B—B4; 4. P—B3, Kt—B3; 5. P—Q4, P x P; 6. P x P, B—Kt3. Black has now lost the center, and in addition, by neglecting to play 4. . . . . P—Q3, he allows White's center too much mobility; his development may therefore rightly be described as Pawn-less, or, more strictly, one which has become Pawn-less. 7. P—Q5, Kt—K2; 8. P—K5, Kt—K5; 9. P—Q6, P x P; 10. P x P, Kt x BP; 11. Q—Kt3, and Black, who is completely wedged in by the P at Q6, succumbs to the enemy assault in a few moves, in spite of the win of a Rook. 11. . . . . Kt x R; 12. B x P *ch*, K—B1; 13. B—Kt5, *Resigns*.

It follows from the rule given under § 2, that Pawn moves are only admissible in the development stage when they either help to occupy the center, or stand in logical connection with its occupation; that is to say a Pawn move which protects its own or attacks the enemy's center. For example, in the open game after *1.* P—K4, P—K4, either P—Q3 or P—Q4—now or later—is always a correct move.

If then only the Pawn moves designated above are allowable, it follows that moves of the flank Pawns must be regarded as loss of time; with this qualification, that in close games the rule applies to only a limited extent, since contact with the enemy is not complete, and development proceeds at a slower tempo.

To sum up: in the open game speed in development is the very first law. Every piece must be developed in one move. Every Pawn move is to be regarded as loss of time, unless it helps to build or support the center or attack the enemy's center. Hence, as Lasker truly observes: in the opening one or two Pawn moves, not more.

§ 3.   *To be ahead in development is the ideal to be aimed at.*

If I were running a race with someone, it would be, to say

DIAGRAM 3

Typical win of a tempo

the least, inopportune were I to throw away valuable time by rubbing, say, a smut off my nose, although I must not be considered as criticizing that operation in itself. If, however, I can induce my opponent to waste time by some similar action I should then get an advantage in development over him. The repeated moving to and fro of the same piece would be described as an action of this kind. Accordingly we force our opponent to lose time if we make a developing move which at the same time attacks one of his pieces which he has already moved. (See Diagram 3.) This very typical situation arises after *1. P—K4, P—Q4; 2. P x P, Q x P; 3. Kt—QB3*.

§ 4.   *Exchange with resulting gain of tempo.*

The moves just given show in the compactest form a maneuver which we may call a compound one. For why (see Diagram 4) do we take the QP? (*2. P x P*). The answer is, to entice the piece which recaptures it on to a square exposed to attack. This was the first part of the maneuver. The second (*3. Kt—QB3*) consisted in the utilization of the Queen's position which is in a certain sense compromised.

The compound maneuver which we have just outlined is one of the greatest value to the student, and we proceed to give a few more examples. *1. P—Q4, P—Q4; 2. P—QB4, Kt—KB3; 3. P x P !*. And now two variations follow. If *3. . . . . . Q x P*, then *4. Kt—QB3*; and if *3. . . . . . Kt x P; 4. P—K4*; so that in either case White with his 4th move will have made a developing move of full value, which Black will be forced to answer by wandering about. But perhaps the beginner may say in his heart: why should Black recapture? Many a skilful business man displays in chess an altogether unnatural delicacy of feeling; he does not recapture. But the master unfortunately knows that he is

DIAGRAM 4

White to move. The exchange is made in order to entice the recapturing piece on to a compromised square

under compulsion, there's no remedy for it; he must recapture, else the material balance in the center would be disturbed. It

follows from the fact that this is compulsory that the capture retards, for the moment at any rate, the enemy's development, except in the case when the recapture can be made with what is at the same time a developing move. A further example:—
1. P—K4, P—K4; 2. P—KB4, Kt—KB3; 3. P x P !, Kt x P (forced, otherwise Black would be a Pawn down with no equivalent for it); 4. Kt—KB3 ! (stops . . . . Q—R5), Kt—QB3; 5. P—Q3 (the logical complement of the exchange P x P), Kt—B4; 6. P—Q4, Kt—K5; 7. P—Q5, and after 7. . . . . Kt—Kt1 White will have the opportunity of gaining more tempi by 8. B—Q3 or 8. QKt—Q2. The latter contingency must be carefully weighed. The exchange of the time-devouring Knight at K5 for the new-born Knight at Q2 means loss of tempo for Black, since with the disappearance of the Knight there will vanish also the tempi consumed by him; that is to say there will be nothing on the board to show for them. (When a farmer loses a sucking pig through illness, he mourns not only the little pig but also the good food he has gambled on it: the bran, etc.)

An intermezzo is possible in the maneuver: exchange with gain of tempo.

After 1. P—K4, P—K4; 2. P—KB4, P—Q4; 3. P x QP, Q x P; 4. Kt—QB3 !, Q—K3; the exchange maneuver 5. P x P, Q x P ch, comes into consideration for White, since the square K4 must be looked on as an exposed place for the Black Queen. However after 5. P x P, there follows . . . . Q x P giving check, and White is apparently not able to make use of the position of the Black Queen. In reality, however, the check can only be regarded as an intermezzo; White simply plays 6. B—K2 (Q—K2 is still stronger), and after all gains tempi at the cost of the Black Queen by Kt—KB3 or P—Q4; e.g., 6. B—K2, B—KKt5; 7. P—Q4 (not Kt—B3 because of B x Kt !, and no tempo is lost, since the Queen need not move), B x B; 8. KKt x B, Q—K3; 9. O—O, and White has 5 tempi to the good (both Knights and a Rook are developed, the Pawn occupies the center, and the

King is in safety), whereas Black can show but one visible tempo, namely the Queen on K3; and this tempo, too, will later on be doubly or even trebly lost; since the Queen will have to shift her ground more than once (she will be chased away by Kt—B4 etc.), so that White's advantage is equivalent to at least five tempi. Exchange, intermezzo, gain of tempo: the exchange and the gain of a tempo are related, the intermezzo alters nothing.

§ 5. *Liquidation, with consequent development or disembarrassment.*

When a merchant sees that his business is not succeeding, he does well to liquidate it, so as to invest the proceeds in a more promising one. Translated into terms of chess, I mean by this that when one's development is threatened with being held up, one must adopt a radical cure, and on no account try to remedy matters by palliative measures. I will first illustrate this by an example. *1.* P—K4, P—K4; *2.* Kt—KB3, Kt—QB3; *3.* P—Q4, P—Q4 (Black's last move is questionable, for the second player should not at once copy such an enterprising move as *3.* P—Q4); *4.* P x QP, Q x P; *5.* Kt—B3, B—QKt5. For the moment Black has been able to hold his ground, the Queen has not had to move away; but after *6.* B—Q2, Black would still appear to be in some embarrassment (see Diagram 5), for the retreat of the Queen, who is now again threatened, would cost a tempo. The right course, therefore, is to exchange *6.* . . . . B x Kt; *7.* B x B (wholehearted liquidation), and now with the same idea *7.* . . . . P x P (anything but a protecting move, such as, *e.g.,* . . . . B—

DIAGRAM 5

Black liquidates. How?

Kt5, or a flight move, such as . . . . P—K5; in the development stage there is no time for this); 8. **Kt x P;** Black can now proceed with his development with 8. . . . . **Kt—B3,** and has relieved the tension in the center and is in no way behind in development. This relief of tension in the center, taken with the exchange, is a main characteristic of complete liquidation.

After *1.* **P—K4, P—K4;** *2.* **Kt—KB3, Kt—QB3;** *3.* **P—Q4, P—Q4,** White can also embarrass his opponent by *4.* **B—QKt5 !.** (See Diagram 6.) Undeveloped as he is, the latter sees that he is seriously threatened by *5.* **Kt x P.** What is he to do? The protecting move *4.* . . . . **B—Q2** is here as inadequate as *4.* . . . . **B—KKt5.** Both these moves have the common failing that they do nothing towards relieving the tension in the center. *4.* . . . . **B—Q2** loses, after *5.* P x QP, Kt x P; *6.* B x B *ch,* Q x B; *7.* Kt x Kt, P x Kt; *8.* Q x P, a valuable Pawn; while *4.* . . . . **B—KKt5** could here be answered by *5.* P—KR3 (in this case a forcing move). *E.g., 4.* . . . . B—KKt5; *5.* P—KR3 *!,* B x Kt (best do it while he can! If *5.* . . . . B—R4 *?,* then *6.* P—KKt4 followed by Kt x P); *6.* Q x B. From here the Queen exercises a decisive influence on the center. *6.* . . . . Kt—B3; *7.* P x QP, **P—K5** (or a Pawn is lost); *8.* Q—K3 *!,* Q x P; *9.* P—QB4, with decided advantage to White, as Black's game is insecure.

Relatively best for Black would have been (see Diagram 6) immediately *4.* . . . . **P x KP;** and he liquidates thus since his means do not allow him the luxury of maintaining a position of instability in the center. The continuation might be *5.* **Kt x P, B—Q2,** and Black threatens to win a piece by . . . . Kt x Kt. *6.* B x Kt, B x B; *7.* O—O, B—Q3, *8.* Kt x B,

DIAGRAM 6

Black to move. He ought to liquidate in order to relieve the tension in the center. How is he to do it?

P x Kt; 9. Kt—B3, P—KB4, and Black has a satisfactory development and does not stand badly. Or again, 6. B x Kt, B x B; 7. Kt—QB3, B—Kt5; 8. O—O, B x Kt; 9. P x B, and now perhaps 9. . . . . . Kt—K2. After 10. Q—Kt4, O—O; 11. Kt x B, Kt x Kt; 12. Q x P, White, it is true, has a Pawn more, but Black seizes the King's file by 12. . . . . . R—K1, and now after 13. Q—B3, Kt—R4 (the process of development is over and maneuvering begins); followed later by . . . . P—QB3 and the occupation of White's weak squares at his QB4 and Q5 by . . . . Kt—B5 and . . . . Q—Q4, Black stands rather the better. Thus timely liquidation has brought back into the right track the second player's questionable process of development.

Another example is furnished by the well-known variation in the Giuoco Piano: 1. P—K4, P—K4; 2. Kt—KB3, Kt—QB3; 3. B—B4, B—B4; 4. P—B3, Kt—B3; 5. P—Q4, P x P (forced surrender of the center); 6. P x P, B—Kt5 ch; 7. B—Q2, and now the Black Bishop is under the slight threat of B x P ch followed by Q—Kt3 ch, etc. On the other hand the White center Pawns are very strong, and it is absolutely necessary to break them up. However if at once 7. . . . . . P—Q4; 8. P x P, KKt x P, then 9. B x B, either Kt x B; 10. Q—Kt3 and White stands rather the better. The correct play is therefore 7. . . . . . B x B ch (getting rid of the threat to his Bishop); 8. QKt x B, and now the freeing move 8. . . . . P—Q4. After 9. P x P, KKt x P; 10. Q—Kt3, Black makes himself secure by the strategic retreat 10. . . . . . QKt—K2 with about an equal game. White has the freer position, Black has the strong point Q4.

As we have seen, the exchange properly used furnishes an excellent weapon, and forms the basis of the typical maneuvers which we analyzed above: (1) exchange with consequent gain of a tempo; (2) liquidation followed by a developing or freeing move. We must, however, give a most emphatic warning against exchanging blindly and without motive; for to move a piece several times in order thus to exchange it for an enemy piece which has not moved, would be a thoroughly typical beginner's mistake. Therefore only exchange in the two cases outlined above.

An example of a wrong, unmotived exchange:—*1.* P—K4. P—K4; *2.* P—Q4, P x P; *3.* P—QB3 (White offers a gambit), *3.* . . . . B—B4 ?. Curious that this move, which must devour a tempo, should be the beginner's first or second thought. He may consider *3.* . . . . P x P, but having perhaps heard somewhere that one ought not to go Pawn hunting in the opening, rejects it in favor of . . . . B—B4. The continuation, a sad one for Black, will be *4.* P x P, B—Kt5 *ch* (moving the Bishop again!); *5.* B—Q2, B x B *ch* (unfortunately forced); *6.* Kt x B, with an advantage of three tempi. The mistake lay in . . . . B—B4, but (after *4.* P x P) . . . . B—Kt3 would at any rate have been better than . . . . B—Kt5 *ch,* which only led to a disadvantageous exchange.

§ 6.   *The center and its demobilizing force. Some examples as to when and how the advance of the enemy center is to be met. On the maintenance and the surrender of the center.*

As we have already noticed, a free mobile center is a deadly weapon of attack, since the advance of the center Pawns threatens to drive back the enemy pieces. In every case the question is, whether the hunted Knight, losing all control over himself, will have to flit aimlessly from pillar to post, or whether he will succeed in saving himself or the tempi for which he is responsible. An example:— *1.* P—K4, P—K4; *2.* P—Q4, P x P (the White King's Pawn is ready to march and is only waiting for an enemy Knight to show himself on his KB3 to put him speedily to flight); *3.* P—QB3, Kt—KB3 *!.* Black lets what will happen, and this is what every beginner should do in order to gain experience of the consequences of an advance in the center. *4.* P—K5, Kt—K5 *!.* The Knight can maintain himself here, for *5.* B—Q3 will be answered by a developing move of full value,

namely 5. . . . . P—Q4. Not of course a further wandering by
5. . . . . Kt—B4 *?*; for this move, after 6. P x P, Kt x B *ch*; 7.
Q x Kt, would yield an advantage of four tempi to White. On
the other hand after *1.* P—K4, P—K4; *2.* P—Q4, P x P; *3.* P—QB3,
Kt—KB3 *!*; *4.* P—K5, it would not be advantageous to move the
Knight to Q4, for the poor fellow would not find repose here.
E.g., 4. . . . . Kt—Q4; *5.* Q x P (not B—QB4 because of . . . .
Kt—Kt3, and the Bishop in his turn will have to lose a tempo),
P—QB3; *6.* B—QB4, Kt—Kt3; *7.* Kt—B3. White has here six tempi
as against two or one and a half, for the Knight is not better

placed at QKt3 than at KB3, and
the Pawn at QB3 is really not a
whole tempo, since no move of
a central Pawn is here in question. (See Diagram 7.)

Another example: *1.* P—K4,
P—K4; *2.* P—KB4, P x P (loss of
time); *3.* Kt—KB3, Kt—KB3 *!*; *4.*
P—K5, and now we have the
same problem. *4.* . . . . Kt—K5
would not here spell "maintenance"; on the contrary there
would follow at once *5.* P—Q3,

DIAGRAM 7

Black to play. Can he keep his
tempi? Where is the Kt to move?

Kt—B4 *?*; *6.* P—Q4, etc. But here is an exceptional case when
the square KR4 is a satisfying one (as a rule border squares are
not favorable for Knights), *e.g.* (after *4.* P—K5), *4.* . . . . Kt—
R4; *5.* P—Q4, P—Q4 (or . . . . P—Q3 in order to force the
exchange of the White KP for the QP which has only moved
once), and Black does not stand badly. (See Diagram 8.)

In general the Knight seeks to establish himself in the center,
as in our first example (Diagram 7); only exceptionally on the
side. After *1.* P—K4, P—K4; *2.* Kt—KB3, Kt—QB3; *3.* B—B4, B—
B4; *4.* P—B3 (a discomfiting move which plans an assault on
Black's center so as to disturb him in his mobilization), Kt—B3;

5. P—Q4, P x P; 6. P—K5, 6. . . . . Kt—K5 would be a mistake because of 7. B—Q5; but now the Knight can no longer maintain himself of his own strength, so he calls in the aid of the QP, thus: 6 . . . . P—Q4, and if now 7. B—Kt3, then . . . . Kt—K5 and establishes himself there.

An example of how such establishment is maintained: in the
position which we have already
examined, after 1. P—K4, P—K4;
2. P—Q4, P x P; 3. P—QB3, Kt—
KB3; 4. P—K5 !, Kt—K5 !; 5. B—
Q3, P—Q4 !, there follows 6. P x
P, and Black cannot hug himself
with the thought that he is out of
the woods, for a tempo-gaining
attack on the Knight is in the air
(Kt—QB3). Black however de-

DIAGRAM 8

Where is the Kt to move?

velops and attacks at the same time, for instance by 6. . . . .
Kt—QB3; 7. Kt—KB3, B—Kt5 (threatening the QP), or again by

DIAGRAM 9

Which is on principle the right move
for Black, ... P x P, or . . . . P—
Q3? How is . . . . B—B3 met? Why
is . . . . P—B3 bad?

6. . . . . P—QB4, but not by the
illogical 6. . . . . B—Kt5 ch?,
e.g., 6. . . . . B—Kt5 ch; 7. B—
Q2, and Black will be forced to
a tempo-losing exchange.

It is nevertheless more prudent to hold the center intact.
Even should we succeed in
breaking the shock of the advancing mass of Pawns (by a
proper withdrawal of the Knight
as outlined above), yet the line
of play is difficult, and what is
more the "Pawn-roller" need not
advance at once, but may hold

its advance as a continual threat over our heads. Hence, if it can be done without counterbalancing disadvantages, hold the center. (See Diagram 9.)

After *1*. P—K4, P—K4; *2*. Kt—KB3, Kt—QB3; *3*. B—B4, B—K2 (quite playable, though . . . . B—B4 is certainly more aggressive); *4*. P—Q4, Black will do best to support his center by *4*. . . . . P—Q3 and thus hold it intact. After *5*. P x P, P x P; White's center is immobile. In order to maintain the center, support by a Pawn is indicated (of course not by . . . . P—B3; that would be a horrible mistake, the open diagonal—White's QB4 to KKt8—would be decisive), since the Pawn is the born defender. If a piece has to protect any attacked piece or Pawn he feels himself under restraint, whereas in similar circumstances a Pawn would find himself perfectly at ease. In the case under consideration, protection by a piece, *i.e.*, by . . . . B—B3 ?, would only support the KP but not the center considered in the abstract. For instance, *4*. . . . . B—B3 ?; *5*. P x P, Kt x P; *6*. Kt x Kt, B x Kt; *7*. P—B4, and the exchange has occurred in accordance with our rule: Exchange followed by a gain of tempo (by P—B4).

§ 6a. *Surrender of the Center.*

1. P—K4, P—K4; *2*. Kt—KB3, Kt—QB3; *3*. P—Q4, P x P *!* (P—Q3 would be uncomfortable for Black, *e.g.*, *3*. . . . . P—Q3; *4*. P x P, P x P; *5*. Q x Q *ch*, K x Q, else the KP falls, and Black has lost the right of castling, and with it a convenient means of connecting his Rooks); *4*. Kt x P. In the position now arrived at Black can, after mature consideration, play *4*. . . . . Kt—B3, since, after *5*. Kt x Kt, KtP x Kt, possible attempts to demobilize the Knight by, say, P—K5 can be parried by . . . . Kt—K5 (B —Q3, P—Q4). But with this Black will have solved only a part of his problem, namely the little problem of how to develop his King's Knight, but not the larger problem of the center as such. To this end the following postulates are necessary. (1) If one has allowed the enemy to establish a free, mobile center Pawn, the latter must be regarded as a dangerous criminal. Against him all our chess fury must be directed: so that the second postulate follows at once: (2) Such a Pawn must either be executed (*i.e.*, P—Q4, P x P must be prepared for), or be put under restraint. Accordingly we condemn the criminal either to death or to imprisonment for life. Or we can pleasantly combine the two by, say, first condemning him to death, then commuting his sentence to life imprisonment; or, what is the commoner case, we keep him under restraint until he is quite impotent, and then show our manly courage by executing the death sentence (*i.e.*, arriving at P—Q4 and P x P). Restraint would be begun by 4. . . . . P—Q3, and perfected by . . . . Kt—B3, ... B—K2, ... O—O, ... R—K1, ... B—B1; by which procedure any ruffianly advance is kept under close observation. White on his side will do all in his power to make the (criminal) KP mobile, by, for example, P—KB4, R—K1, etc., as occasion offers. The game might run somewhat as follows:— *1.* P—K4, P—K4; *2.* Kt—KB3, Kt—QB3; *3.* P—Q4, P x P; *4.* Kt x P, P—Q3; *5.* B—K2, Kt—B3; *6.* Kt—QB3, B—K2; *7.* O—O,

DIAGRAM 10

The fight in support of and against the White P at K4. White has freedom, Black has pressure

O—O; *8.* P—B4 *!*, R—K1 *!* (not *8.* . . . . P—Q4 because of P—K5); *9.* B—K3, B—B1; *10.* B—B3, B—Q2.

Each side has completed its mobilization, White will try to force P—K5, Black to prevent this advance. This situation (see Diagram 10) gives rise to most interesting struggles, and we recommend the student to practice himself in contests playing in turn for and against the center, for he will thus strengthen his positional insight. Such training will be valuable.

The restraining process is not easy, and to kill off the mobile center Pawn seems simpler, though cases when this is feasible do not very often occur. A few examples follow. *1.* **P—K4, P—K4;** *2.* **Kt—KB3, Kt—QB3;** *3.* **P—Q4, P x P;** *4.* **Kt x P, Kt—B3;** *5.* **Kt—QB3, B—Kt5;** *6.* **Kt x Kt** (in order to be able to make the protecting move **B—Q3**), **KtP x Kt** *!;* *7.* **B—Q3,** and now the second player need no longer lay siege to the KP by, say, ... P—Q3, ... O—O, and . . . . R—K1, since he can at once resort to *7.* . . . . . **P—Q4,** and after the further moves *8.* **P x P, P x P,** the disturber of his peace has disappeared. A like fate overtook the center Pawn in the game Lee—Nimzovich in Ostend (1907): *1.* **P—Q4, Kt—KB3;** *2.* **Kt—KB3, P—Q3;** *3.* **QKt—Q2, QKt—Q2;** *4.* **P—K4, P—K4;** *5.* **P—B3, B—K2;** *6.* **B—B4, O—O;** *7.* **O—O** (see Diagram 11), **P x P** *!;* *8.* **P x P, P—Q4** *!,* and at a blow the proud KP, despite his freedom and mobility, vanishes, is pulverized! After *9.* **B—Q3** (if P x P then *9.* . . . . . Kt—Kt3 with . . . . QKt x P), ... **P x P;** *10.* **Kt x P, Kt x Kt;** *11.* **B x Kt, Kt—B3** (here is our exchange with consequent gain of tempo); *12.* **B—Q3, Kt—Q4;** *13.* **P—QR3, B—B3,** and now Black stands better because of White's rather weak QP. For the continuation see Game No. 4.

As a third illustration take the opening moves of my game against Yates (White) at Baden-Baden (1925): *1.* **P—K4, Kt—QB3;** *2.* **Kt—KB3, Kt—B3;** *3.* **Kt—B3** (or *3.* P—K5, Kt—Q4; *4.* P—B4, Kt—Kt3; *5.* P—Q4, P—Q3; and Black threatens to win back

DIAGRAM 11

Lee—Nimzovich
**Black to play and destroy
White's center**

the 3 tempi he has sacrificed, though perhaps 6. P—K6, P x P might be played with attacking chances for White), P—Q4; 4. P x P, Kt x P; 5. P—Q4, and White has established a free center Pawn. There followed 5. . . . . B—B4; 6. P—QR3, P—KKt3 (the alternative was to restrain the QP by . . . . P—K3, ultimately seizing the Q file and keeping the QP under observation); 7. B—QB4, Kt—Kt3; 8. B—R2, B—Kt2; 9. B—K3, P—K4 !; Black has thus not played to restrain the QP but to kill it. There followed 10. Q—K2, O—O; 11. P x P, B—Kt5; and Black recovered the Pawn with a freer game.

§ 7. *On Pawn hunting in the opening. Usually a mistake. Exceptional case of center Pawns.*

Since the mobilization of the forces is by far the most important operation in the opening stages, it strikes anyone who knows this as comic that the less experienced player should so eagerly plunge into an utterly unimportant side line: Pawn hunting. This eagerness may be more readily explicable on psychological grounds, for the young player wants to give rein to the energy which smolders in him; which he can do by getting the scalps of perfectly harmless Pawns, while the older player is—well, the older player is not loath to show how young he really is. In the event both come to grief. What, therefore, the inexperienced player, young or old, must take to heart is the commandment: *Never play to win a Pawn while your development is yet unfinished!* and to this there is but one exception, which we shall discuss later.

We shall begin by showing the best manner of declining a gambit, which we can do very shortly, since we have already considered some analogous cases. In the Center Gambit, after 1. P—K4, P—K4; 2. P—Q4, P x P !; 3. P—QB3 (Diagram 12), Black can play 3. . . . . Kt—KB3, or any other developing move with the exception of course of 3. . . . . B—B4 ??; thus for instance: 3. . . . . Kt—QB3; 4. P x P, P—Q4; or 3. . . . . P—Q4;

or lastly even 3. . . . . P—QB3; 4. P x P, P—Q4. (It will be noticed that the QBP stands now in logical connection with the center.) If 3. . . . . P—QB3; 4. Q x P, Black still plays 4. . . . . P—Q4; 5. P x P, P x P, to be followed by . . . . Kt—QB3. Again in the Evans Gambit: 1. P—K4, P—K4; 2. Kt—KB3, Kt—QB3; 3. B—B4, B—B4; 4. P—QKt4, we decline the gambit with . . . . B—Kt3 in or-

Black to move

der to avoid being driven about the place, which would happen if we played 4. . . . . B x P; 5. P—B3. Black by playing 4. . . . . B—Kt3 has by no means lost a tempo, since the move P—QKt4, which White was able to throw in gratis without Black being able in the meanwhile to develop a piece, was, in the sense of development, unproductive—unproductive as every Pawn move must be in the nature of things, if it does not bear a logical connection with the center. For suppose after 4. . . . . B—Kt3; 5. P—Kt5 (to make a virtue of necessity and attempt something of a demobilizing effect with our ill-motivated KtP move), Kt—Q5 and now if 6. Kt x P, then 6. . . . . Q—Kt4 with a strong attack.

The beginner should decline the King's Gambit with 2. . . . . B—B4 (1. P—K4, P—K4; 2. P—KB4, B—B4), or by the simple 2. . . . . P—Q3, which move is better than its reputation. For instance: 1. P—K4, P—K4; 2. P—KB4, P—Q3; 3. Kt—KB3, Kt—QB3; 4. B—B4, B—K3 !; after 5. B x B, P x B; 6. P x P, P x P, Black has with good development two open files for his Rooks (the KB and Q files), and in spite of his doubled Pawn, stands rather the better. If after 4. . . . . B—K3; 5. B—Kt5, then perhaps 5. . . . . B—Q2; for since White has wandered about with his Bishop, Black may do the like. The student should notice particularly that after *1*. P—K4, P—K4; *2*. P—KB4, P—Q3; *3*. Kt—KB3, Kt—QB3; *4*. Kt—B3, Kt—B3; *5*. B—K2, the maneuver *5*. . . . . P x P is possible, and if then *6*. P—Q3, P—Q4; timely surrender of the center and a speedy recapture of the same.

DIAGRAM 13

White continues Kt x P, Kt x Kt; P—Q4, in the spirit of § 7a

Acceptance of the gambit is allowable: *1*. P—K4, P—K4; *2*. P—KB4, P x P; *3*. Kt—KB3, Kt—KB3 *!*, not, however, with the idea of keeping the gambit Pawn, but rather to subject the strength of White's center to a severe test (*4*. P—K5, Kt—R4), or to arrive at the counter thrust . . . . P—Q4 (after *4*. Kt—B3).

§ 7a. *A center Pawn should always be taken if this can be done without too great danger.*

For example, *1*. P—K4, P—K4; *2*. Kt—KB3, Kt—QB3; *3*. B—B4, Kt—B3; *4*. P—B3 *?*, Kt x P *!*, for the ideal win (of a Pawn), which the conquest of the center implies, is not dear at the cost of a tempo. It is of less importance to keep the Pawn; it is the ideal not the material gain with which we are here concerned. Put otherwise: the win of a Pawn anywhere on the side of the board brings no happiness in its train; but if you gain a Pawn in the middle, then you really have something to talk about, for thus you will get the possibility of expansion at the very spot round which in the opening stages the fight usually sways, namely the center; in other words you will get elbow room. (See Diagram 13).

With this we close the first chapter, and would refer the reader to Nos. 1 and 2 of the illustrative games at the end of the book.

2. On Open Files

§ 1. *Introductory. General considerations and some definitions.*

THE theory of open files, which was my discovery, must be regarded as one of the pillars of my system. I published the law of the establishment of outposts in open files about fourteen years ago * in the *Wiener Schachzeitung,* but at that time I had not yet arrived at the perception that this maneuver must logically be subordinate to the main objective of any operation in a file, namely the eventual occupation of the 7th or 8th rank. In other words: in order to break down the enemy's resistance in

a file we must establish outposts in it, but without for a moment relaxing our aim at the 7th rank, whose occupation must be regarded as the ideal to be arrived at in such operation. The establishment of an outpost is therefore merely a subsidiary maneuver.

A file is said to be open for the Rook when no Pawn of his is in it; or, if there be one, it is masked as, for example, it is in the KR

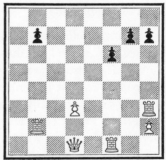

DIAGRAM 14

White's QKt, KB, and KR files are open, the latter from the point KR3. The Q file is closed

file in Diagram 14. This definition implies that in deciding whether a file is "open" or "closed," we are not concerned with the question whether that file gives an avenue of attack on unoccupied, peaceful points, or on living enemy pieces (as a rule Pawns). There is in fact no fundamental difference between

* 1913—Ed.

21

play against a piece or against a point. Let us, for example, imagine a White R on KR1, the Black K on his KKt1 and a Black
P on his KR2. White is attacking the P at his KR7. Suppose
that Pawn removed, White is still attacking the point KR7,
which he wishes to conquer. In either case he will attempt,
with the further material which he has at command (this was
taken for granted: I give only the most important elements of
the position), to establish a preponderance at his KR7, *i.e.,*
bring up more pieces to the attack of this point than the defense can command. Having succeeded in doing this, he will
ultimately play either R x P or R—KR7, as the case may be.
That is to say our procedure is the same whether we are attacking the point KR7 or a Black P at that point; for the measure of the mobility of the Pawn will tend to zero, since every
object of attack must be made as nearly immobile as possible.

§ 2.   *The genesis of open files: By peaceful means. By assault. The objective.*

From the definition of an open file it follows at once that a
file will be opened by the disappearance of one of our own
Pawns. This disappearance will be brought about peacefully if
the enemy feels it incumbent on him to exchange one of our
well, because centrally, posted pieces, and the recapture is
made by a Pawn. (See Diagram 15.) We must here stress the
word "central," for it will be but seldom, and never in the opening, that you will be able to force your opponent to open a file
by the exchange of a piece which you have posted on a flank.
You will gain your object much more quickly if it is centrally
posted; for pieces thus established in the middle of the board,
and exercising their influence in all directions, are those which
will be exchanged.

Diagram 16 from the game Thomas—Alekhine, Baden-
Baden 1925, provides a good example. Black's Knights are cen-

DIAGRAM 15

Black playing . . . . B x B opens
White's KB file for him

DIAGRAM 16

Black's centralized Knights are
strongly entrenched in the center

trally posted, and White finds himself forced to exchange them; so, 1. Kt(B3) x Kt, P x Kt (=opening of the QB file), and after the further moves 2. Kt x Kt, Q x Kt; 3. B—B3, Q—Q2; 4. B x B, Q x B; the significance of this file is considerable. There followed, 5. P—B4 ! (on QB2 the Pawn would have been untenable), P x P *e.p.*, opening the Q file also, since his own obstructing Pawn at Q5 disappears (every Pawn is an obstruction to his own Rooks); and after 6. P x P, Black followed with . . . . QR—B1 and . . . . KR—Q1 with play in both the files. (See Game No. 11.)

Hence post your pieces centrally, so long as you can do so safely, *i.e.* without inviting the advance of the "Pawn-roller." Thus will your opponent be provoked into an exchange which will give you an open file.

Let us in Diagram 15 imagine the continuation, 1. . . . . . B—Kt3; 2. Q—Q2, O—O; 3. O—O—O, P—KR3 ? (see Diagram 17),

DIAGRAM 17

The objective is here Black's PKR3

we shall then get a typical example of an effective opening of a file. Thanks to Black's Pawn at KR3 White can now bring about the speedy disappearance of his KKtP; Black's . . . . P—KR3 was therefore bad; bad, but hardly as a waste of time, for Black had already completed his development; and after all there is a difference between going to sleep after or over our work! The mode of advance against Black's KR3 (the objective or object of attack) is P—KR3, P—KKt4, P—Kt5; on . . . . P x P the P is then recaptured by a piece, whereupon KR—Kt1 takes possession of the file which now is open. True, one of his own pieces is in the way, but this is of no consequence, for it is elastic; it is only a Pawn which is obstinate, and we have our work cut out if we want to induce him to change his state.

As an example for practice let us suppose that in the position shown on Diagram 17, the Bishops at K3 and QKt3 do not exist, and that Black's KRP is at KR2, his KKtP at Kt3. The objective is now Black's KKt3, and the KR file (always the one next to the objective) should be opened. The plan is P—KR4— R5 x P. But in this position, after P—KR4 we must, before going on, first give the Kt at KB3 a dig in the ribs, since he is in the way; perhaps by Kt—Q5, and this done the Pawn can advance to KR5 in all comfort and without any sacrifice. As a last resort the attacked party may attempt to give the Pawn the slip; that is on P—R5 to play . . . . P—KKt4; which, however, here would hardly answer since the square KKt4 is unprotected. If on the other hand the square KKt4 *were* protected and Black could answer P—R5 with . . . . P—KKt4, White would be confronted with a problem of serious proportions: it might ultimately turn out that the opening of a file could not be *forced*. To sum up: no Pawn exchanges, no file-opening; no file-opening, no attack.

§ 3. *The ideal (goal) of every operation in a file. On some accompanying phenomena. Marauding raids. Enveloping operations.*

The ideal which lies at the root of every operation in a file is the ultimate penetration by way of this file into the enemy's game, that is to say to our (White's) 7th or 8th rank.

A very important postulate is the following. Supposing that by operating in the Q file we reach the 7th rank by a round-about way, by, say, the maneuver R—Q1—Q4—QR4—QR7, this cannot be regarded as a direct exploitation of the Q file. A few elementary examples will now be given.

DIAGRAM 18

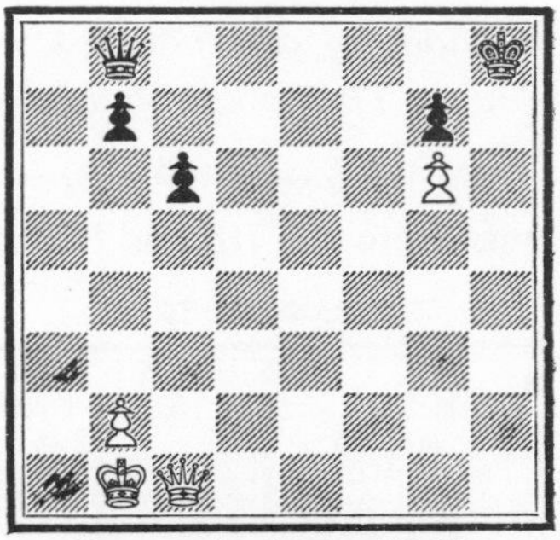

Catastrophe in the KR file

Diagram 18. Line of operation the KR file. This will be seized by *1. Q—R1 ch, K—Kt1;* and now according to rule either Q—R7 *ch* or Q—R8 *ch;* the latter not being feasible, *2. Q—R7 ch,* K—B1, and now *3. Q—R8 ch* followed by a marauding expedition (for so we designate every forking attack on two pieces), which is here not a chance raid, but rather a not untypical concomitant of an entry by force at the 7th or 8th rank. If in Diagram 18 the Black Q were at her Q2 instead of QKt1 our method would be *1. Q—R1 ch,* K—Kt1; *2. Q—R7 ch,* K—B1; *3. Q—R8 ch,* K—K2; *4. Q x P ch,* K—K3; *5. Q x Q ch,* K x Q; *6. P—Kt7,* and the result would be no less unpleasant. We may describe this triangular maneuver of the Q (R7, R8, Kt7) as an enveloping attack. Putting it shortly, we may say: given deficient resistance (that is, no enemy Pawn on his KR3 or KR5), the attacker, after safeguarding the lines of invasion, raids the 7th and 8th ranks, and, doing so, will not seldom be rewarded by the chance of a marauding expedition or of an enveloping attack. So far the operation has been as readily intelligible as it is easily executed. Unfortunately in real life there are often great obstacles to overcome, as § 4 will show.

§ 4.   *The possible obstacles to be met with in the line of operations. The block of granite and how to mine it. The conception of protected and unprotected obstacles (Pawns). The two methods of conducting the attack against obstructing enemy Pawns. The "evolutionary" and "revolutionary" attack.*

We have seen how great may be the significance of a forced entry into the 7th and 8th ranks. This being the case, it is natu-

DIAGRAM 19

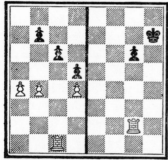

Black's QBP defended by his QKtP is a protected obstacle

The KKtP an unprotected obstacle

ral to presume that nature herself, so to speak, may have done something for the protection of this sensitive area, just as good wise mother nature has given the human heart a place magnificently protected behind the ribs. The characteristic and natural defensive position is shown on Diagram 19. Here the Black P at KKt3 prevents White from invading the 7th rank. The road to the 7th or 8th rank leads only over my dead body, the doughty

peon seems to say.

If, however, this enemy KtP be protected by another Pawn, it would be futile to run one's head up against such a block of granite by, shall we say, tripling our forces in the file. Rather will it be the path of wisdom first to mine it by, for instance, P—KR4—R5, followed by P x P, after which the granite block will have shriveled up to a defenseless pawnling. In Diagram 19, P—Kt5 and P x P has the effect of such a mining operation.

The Pawn, as we have before insisted, is to be regarded as a sure defender. Protection by pieces may almost be called a confusion of terms; the Pawn alone will stand on guard solidly, patiently, without a grumble. Hence a "protected Pawn" means a Pawn protected by one of his fellows. If our Pawn has been enticed away from the confederation of Pawns he will be subject to attack by many pieces.

The obvious idea is then to win the Pawn by piling up our attacks on it; firstly for the sake of the gain in material, but secondly in order to break down the resistance in the file. This will be technically managed by first bringing up our pieces into attacking positions. A hot fight will then be waged round the Pawn. As often as we attack, Black covers; so we now seek to obtain the upper hand by thinning the ranks of the defending forces, which can be done (a) by driving them away, (b) by exchange, (c) by shutting off one of the defending pieces. That is to say we transfer our attack from our opponent to his defenders, a perfectly normal proceeding, often practiced at school (in a rough-and-tumble, I mean). The following end game, see Diagram 20, will illustrate the method, *1.* R—R2, K—R2; *2.* R(K1)—R1. White can pile up the attack since the obstructing P at R6 is without Pawn protection. *2.* . . . . B—B1; *3.* Kt—B5, R—Kt3. Attack and defense balance one another, but by White's next move, *4.* P—Q6, the defending Black R on his Kt3 will be shut out of the fight, and the KRP will fall, while simultaneously the entry into the 7th and 8th ranks via the KR file will be made possible. Had two Black Rooks stood on their 3rd row, the sacrifice of the ex-

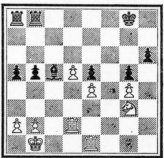

DIAGRAM 20

Converging attack on the Black KRP
(evolutionary attack)

change by . . . . R x P would have been possible, but with the Rooks so placed, such a move as . . . . B x P would have been very bad, for the consequence would have been, after 4. P—Q6, B x P; 5. R x P *ch*. K—Kt1; 6. R—R8 *ch*, K—B2; 7. R (R1) —R7 *ch*, K—B3, and now a waiting move, which after the preceding blows—one R now holding the 7th, the other the 8th rank—is readily intelligible, *i.e.*, 8. R—KKt7, and mate follows next move.

Or take the skeleton position: White R's, KB1, KB2; Kt, Q4; Black having an obstructing P on KB3 protected by the K at KKt2 and BQ1 with R at QB1. The play would be *1.* Kt—K6 *ch*, K any move; 2. Kt x B, R x Kt; 3. R x P, *i.e.*, the ranks of the defenders are thinned by exchange. The maneuver against the obstructing Pawn so far considered is contained in the concept "evolutionary attack." The whole manner of concentration against one point, in order eventually to get superior forces to bear upon it, implies this. The goal, too, was symptomatic; it was, in fact, partly material gain (the win of a Pawn was welcome) which tempted us, partly the ideal hovering before us of conquering the 7th rank. This mixture of motives was significant.

DIAGRAM 21

Break through at KR7—
Revolutionary attack

Quite another picture is revealed in the process employed in Diagram 21 (only the most important actors are shown). Granted that play in the KR file by QR—R1 would be idle because of . . . . Kt—B3 or . . . . P—R3 (with a granite block in the file); how may White otherwise make use of the KR file?

The answer is that he gives up all idea of material profit, and instead does everything, stops at no sacrifice, in order to get the offending Pawn out of the way. Hence *1. R x P ch, K x R; 2. R—R1 mate.* Simple as is this ending, it seems to me to be of the greatest importance as bringing clearly before us the difference between the "evolutionary" and "revolutionary" forms of attack.

DIAGRAM 22

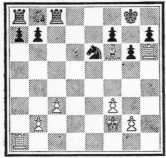

How would the "evolutionary" and "revolutionary" attacks proceed here?

DIAGRAM 23

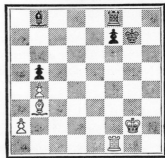

Restricted advance followed by maneuvering the R to another file: 1. R—B5, 2. R x P, 3. R—Kt7

We will therefore give yet another example. (See Diagram 22.) An evolutionary attack would, after *1. QR—R1, Kt—B1; 2. B—K7* (thinning defenders' ranks by exchange), lead to the winning of the objective. The revolutionary attack on the other hand would dispense with the mere win of the Black KRP as follows: *1. R x P, K x R* (there can be no talk of having won the Pawn here for White has given up a Rook for it); *2. R—R1 ch, K—Kt1; 3. R—R8 mate.* The idea of the revolutionary attacks lies, as is here clearly shown, in opening by sheer force an entry to the 7th or 8th rank which had been barred to us. One Rook sacrifices himself for his colleague, that the latter may reach the objective, the 8th rank. Yes, even on a chess board there is such a thing as true comradeship!

In what chronological order are these two methods of attack

to be employed? The answer to this is:—First try the converging attack, *i.e.*, attack the obstructing Pawn with several pieces; by so doing opportunity may be found to force the defending pieces into uncomfortable positions where they will get into one another's way: for the defense will often be cramped for space. Afterwards see whether among other things there is a possibility of a break through by force, in other words of a revolutionary attack.

§ 5. *The restricted advance in one file with the idea of giving up that file for another one, i.e., the indirect exploitation of a file. The file as a jumping-off place.*

In the position shown on Diagram 23 the direct exploitation of the KB file, with eventual R x BP (after, say, first driving off the protecting Rook), would be impossible with the scanty material available. The simple R—B5, however, clearly wins a Pawn, and later R—QKt7 may follow. It is important that we examine this maneuver to see its logical meaning. Since R—B7 was impracticable, there could be no question of a direct exploitation of the KB file in our sense. On the other hand it would be pushing ingratitude to an extreme length if we went on to assert that the KB file had no bearing whatever on the capture of the QKtP, etc. Where then does the truth lie? The answer is:—The file was here used not directly, nor to its fullest extent, but indirectly, as a kind of jumping-off place. See Diagram 24, where another instance of the use of a file in this manner is given.

As a further example consider the skeleton position: White: R, KKt1; B, K3; P, KR2. Black: K, KR2; P, KR3. The maneuver B—Q4, R—Kt7 *ch* would be a direct, and R—Kt3—R3 x RP *ch* would be an indirect exploitation of the KKt file.

DIAGRAM 24

DIAGRAM 25

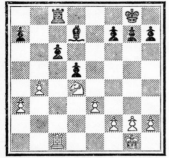

The file as "jumping off" place: a positional example, *cf.* Game No. 11

White establishes an outpost in the Q file

§ 6. *The outpost. The radius of attack. With what piece should one occupy an advanced position on a center file, and on a flank? Change of rôles and what this proves.*

Let us glance at Diagram 25. White has the center and the Q file. Black has a Pawn at his Q3 watching the center, and also holds the K file. In other respects the positions are equal. White with the move will now attempt an operation in the Q file. This presents some difficulties since the protected Black Pawn at his Q3 represents a "granite block." If White, in spite of the rules laid down in § 4, proceeded to assail Black's QP by R—Q2 and R(K)—Q1, not only the esteemed reader but the Black QP himself would deride him; so we had better keep to the rules, and perhaps try to undermine the position by P—K5 (see § 4); but this too proves to be impossible, for the enemy's possession of the K file is a quite sufficient bar to any projected P—K5. Accordingly let us give up the Q file as such, and content ourselves with an indirect exploitation of it by the restricted advance R—Q4, to be followed later by R—QR4, etc., as laid down in § 5. But this maneuver, too, is here somewhat weak, for Black's Q side is too compact. Note that if Black's QRP were isolated it would be wholly in place to bring up by a similar process the KR to the QR file via the Q file. Since all attempts have so far broken down we begin to look round for some other base of operations, and we should be wholly wrong in so doing, for the Q file can be exploited in this position.

The key move is *1. Kt—Q5*, and the Knight here placed we call the outpost; by which we mean a piece, usually a Knight, established in an open file in enemy territory, and protected (of course by a Pawn). This Knight, protected and supported as he is, will, in consequence of his radius of attack, exercise a disturbing influence, and will, therefore, cause the opponent to weaken his position in the Q file, in order to drive him away, by . . . . P—QB3. And hence we may say:—

(a) An advanced post forms a base for new attacks.

(b) An outpost provokes a weakening of the enemy's position in the file in question.

After *1. Kt—Q5, P—QB3* (. . . . R—QB1 would also serve, and in fact in the position given would be the defense adopted by a strong player, but it takes iron nerves to let a Knight so threateningly posted remain in his place for hour after hour! Moreover there may come a time when Black will be *forced* to make the weakening move . . . . P—QB3), there follows: *2. Kt—B3*, and now the Black QP, after White's R—Q2 and KR—Q1, will certainly not laugh derisively any longer.

It is important for the student to know that the strength of an outpost lies in its strategical connection with its own hinterland. The outpost does not derive its strength from itself, but rather from this hinterland, namely from the open file and the protecting Pawn; and if suddenly one or other of these points of contact failed, it would almost entirely lose its prestige and significance. For instance, in Diagram 25 let us suppose a White Pawn at Q3, the Q file would in this case be closed, and then if *1. . . . . . P—QB3; 2. Kt—B3*, the QP would not be weak; for how should a body be weak if it is not exposed to attack?

Or again (Diagram 25), suppose the White Pawn at K3 instead of K4. Contact with the Pawn now fails, as is painfully evident after the moves 1. . . . . P—QB3; 2. Kt—B3, P—Q4 !, and White has achieved nothing; whereas with the White Pawn at K4 the Black QP would remain paralyzed (backward), at any rate for some considerable time. Hence the file to its rear and the protecting Pawn are essential accompaniments to an advanced post.

In Diagram 26, White has the KB file with an advanced post at KB5, Black the Q file with one at Q5. Both files at the moment "bite on granite" (on protected Pawns). To sap this strength White will direct his Knight via K2 and KKt3 to KB5. Arrived there the Knight attacks the point KKt7, and this attack can be still further accentuated by, say, R—B3—Kt3. The obvious course for Black is to drive away

DIAGRAM 26

A position arising from the Giuoco Piano. (We can imagine x other pieces on each side.)

the Knight by . . . . P—KKt3, but by inducing this the strategical mission of White's outpost will have been accomplished; for Black's KBP is now become a weakness. It is important to notice that Kt—KB5 was the starting point of a new attack, namely on Black's KKt2.

Very often the outpost will be exchanged at his station. If the attacking player has proceeded correctly, the retaking piece or Pawn will yield full compensation for the piece which has been taken. Here a conversion of advantages is the order of the day. For instance, if after Kt—KB5 a piece take the Knight, this will be recaptured by the KP, and White now gets the point K4 for a Rook or his other Knight, and in addition some possibility (after P—KKt4—Kt5) of opening the KKt file. Further the

P now at KB5 will effectively render immobile the Black Pawn at his KB3, which is the object of attack. (See Diagram 25, also Game No. 5, v. Haken—Giese.)

In a flank file the advanced post should be occupied by a piece of heavy metal. Flank files are the QR, QKt, KKt, KR; center files the QB, Q, K, KB files.

In Diagram 27 a flank file is in question, and the occupation

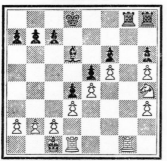

DIAGRAM 27

In a flank file the outpost a Rook
(R—Kt6) not a Knight

of an advanced post in it by a Knight would have little effect, for the attacking range of a Knight at KKt6 would be small (still smaller of course on a R file). R—Kt6 is in fact indicated, since thus we go some way towards gaining control of the KKt file, which so far has been in dispute, or towards getting some other advantage. It should be noted that the file was disputed since neither side could move up or down it unchallenged; freedom to do this is the only sure sign that a file is controlled. It therefore remains for White to find a suitable point on which to double his Rooks. It can be found if we seek it. *1.* R—Kt2 *P,* R x R; *2.* Kt x R, R—Kt1; and Black holds the file. Or, *1.* R—Kt4 *P,* R x R; *2.* P x R, R—Kt1; *3.* Kt—Kt6, and White will hardly be able to make anything of his backward extra Pawn. But *1.* R—Kt6 *!* (outpost), R x R (else QR—Kt1 and the Rooks are doubled); *2.* RP x R, with a giant of a passed Pawn!—and the possibility (after Kt—B3) of R—Kt1—Kt4—R4. So, though because of RP x R White's open file is dead, there has arisen from its ashes a passed Pawn, with possibilities of attack in the KR file. This is a good example of the conversion of advantages referred to above in the case of the exchange of an outpost.

Let us stop for a moment longer at Diagram 27, and we shall come, after *1*. R—Kt6, R x R; *2*. RP x R, R—Kt1; *3*. R—Kt1, on the track of a characteristic exchange of rôles. Before *1*. . . . . R x R the White RP protected the R at Kt6; after the exchange a White R supports this same RP which now has advanced to Kt6. This action, in which gratitude and kindly feeling are beautifully displayed, shows, too, that there is a real strategical connection between the KKt file as such and the Pawn (here the KRP) which protects the advanced post in it.

We shall close this chapter with an example, chosen not for entertainment but for instruction, taken from a game between Nimzovich (White) and an amateur. (See Diagram 28.) *1.* Kt—B4. Development is a principle well worthy of attention right into the end game; is one, however, which is neglected by less experienced players even in the opening. *1*. . . . . QR—KKt1; *2.* R—R7 ! For present purposes we would ask the reader to regard this move simply as the occupation of an advanced post;

DIAGRAM 28

for of course it could also be regarded as an invasion of the 7th rank. *2*. . . . . B—K1; *3*. QR—R1, R x R; *4*. P x R (conversion of the "file" into a "passed Pawn"; *4*. R x R, K—B1; *5*. Kt—R5, with, at an opportune moment, sacrifice of the Knight at B6, would also have been good), R—KR1; *5*. Kt—Kt6 *ch*, B x Kt; *6*. P x B, and the passed Pawn has become a protected passed Pawn. *6*. . . . . K—K3; *7*. R—R5 ! This "restricted" advance stops any attempt of Black to free himself by perhaps . . . . K—K4 or . . . . P—KB4, giving access to White's KKtP. *7*. . . . . P—Kt3; *8*. P—B4 (still more paralyzing would be *8*. P—Kt4, but White follows others plans), P—QB4; *9*. P—R4, P—R4;

10. P—Kt3, P—B3; *11.* K—Q2, K—Q3; *12.* K—K3, K—K3; *13.* K—B4, K—Q3; *14.* K—B5 ! Now White's plan for breaking through is revealed. By *Zugzwang*,* *i.e.*, by exhausting Black's available moves, so that finally his King is forced to break contact with his K4, White is able to play P—K5, whereupon the Black KBP disappears, and the entry of the White Rook at KB7 will become possible. *14. . . . .* K—K2; *15.* P—K5, P x P; *16.* K x P, K—Q2; *17.* R—B5. Now it will be clear that the move R—R5 had all the elements of the maneuver which we have called a restricted advance in a file, since R—R5—B5—B7 must, willy-nilly, despite the time intervening, be regarded as the maneuvering of the Rook from one file to a new one. Black resigned, since R—B7 *ch* and R x KtP would have yielded two united passed Pawns.

* Note on *Zugzwang*. There are combinations in chess (for as such must be regarded any series of moves, however quiet, which stand in a logical relationship to one another) which are based on the fact that to move in his turn is obligatory on a player. This obligation, in general a welcome one, may weigh heavily on him if his pieces are disposed for attack and defense as favorably as the circumstances allow, and when any change in their configuration can only be detrimental. In such a position his condition will get worse step by step until he is forced, by the necessity of making a move, to relax his hold on, or weaken, some key point, and his game collapses. A combination directed to bring about such a catastrophe is called by the Germans *Zugzwang* (compulsion to move), and the player who succumbs under it is said to have got into *Zugzwang*. The ending just examined under Diagram 28 is an excellent example. With 7. R—R5 White announces *Zugzwang*. To prevent White succeeding in his object to break through in the KB file it is vital for Black that his K maintain contact with his K4. To do this he is confined to the squares K3 and Q3. At last compelled to make a move he is forced to give up this contact, and White breaks through. Since the player under *Zugzwang* cannot have the resource of marking time without sensibly altering his position, it will be clear that the opportunity to use the *Zugzwang* weapon will normally present itself only in the end game, and most often when only Kings and Pawns remain on the board.

P.H.

3. The Seventh and Eighth Ranks

§ 1. *Introductory and general. End game or Middle game. The choice of an objective. "Thou shalt not shilly shally !"*

$\mathbf{A}$s w E have seen in the second chapter the entry into enemy territory, in other words into the 7th and 8th ranks, forms the logical consequence of play in a file. I have sought to illustrate this entry by some particularly marked, because catastrophic, examples; but I must here, to offset this, emphasize the fact that, in the normal course of events, it will only be late, when we pass into the end game stage, that the 7th rank will be seized; for catastrophes of whatever nature are, after all, only the result of serious mistakes of our opponent, and consequently cannot be regarded as the normal. We are therefore disposed to regard the 7th and 8th ranks as end game advantages, and this despite the fact that numberless games are decided by operations in these ranks in the middle game. The student should, however, try to break into the enemy's base as early as possible, and if he at first finds that the invading Rook can accomplish nothing, or is even lost, he must not be discouraged on that account. It is part of our system to instruct the student at the earliest possible moment in the strategical elements of the end game. Accordingly, after treating of the "7th and 8th ranks," "Passed Pawns," and the technique of "Exchange," we shall insert a chapter which, though properly coming under the heading "Position Play," must, for instructional purposes, find a place thus early. And after assimilating this, the 7th and 8th ranks will be to the student not merely a mating instrument, but, much more, a keen-edged weapon for use in the end game. As already remarked it is both, but its use as an end game weapon predominates.

It is of the greatest importance to accustom ourselves to carry out operations in the 7th rank in such a manner that we have from the start some settled, definite objective. It is characteristic of the less practiced player that he chooses an opposite course; in fact he shilly shallies, that is, he looks now to the right, now to the left, without any fixed plan. No; settle on your objective is the rule. Such an objective, as we have learnt, may be a Pawn or a point; which, matters nothing. But aimlessly to drift from one to another, this will expose you to a strategical disgrace.

§ 2. *The convergent and the revolutionary attack in the 7th rank. The win of a point (or Pawn) with acoustical echo (i.e. with simultaneous check).*

In the position shown on Diagram 29 White chooses the QBP as his objective. After . . . . R—QB1, attack and defense balance one another; but by a procedure analogous to that used in a file, we now seek to disturb this equilibrium to our advan-

DIAGRAM 29

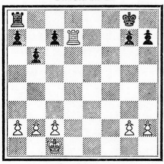

The 7th rank

tage. Accordingly let us suppose White to have a Bishop at K1 and Black a Knight at KKt3, we should then attain our end by B—Kt3; and if our Bishop had been at KB1 (instead of K1), by B—R6 driving away the defending Rook. Next let us suppose the forces on Diagram 29 increased by a White R at Q1, and a Black Knight at KKt3, and that the White KRP is wanting. The logical course would now be R(1)—Q4—QB4, or else *1*. R—Q8 *ch,* R x R; *2*. R x R *ch,* Kt—B1, and White gets back into the 7th row by *3*. R—B8, P—B4; *4*. R—B7, etc. In Diagram 29 as it stands it should be noted that the march of the White King to

his QB6 would be the course to be aimed at, since the point
QB7 is our chosen objective.

The affair takes a similar course in the position on Diagram
30. White's objective is his KR7, since the win of this point
would give the possibility of a deadly enveloping movement.

DIAGRAM 30   DIAGRAM 31

Black to move. Fight for Black's KR2   Forced win of Black's KR2

1. . . . . R—KR3; *2.* Kt—B5, R—R4; *3.* P—Kt4, R x P *ch; 4.* K—Kt2,
R x P; *5.* R—R7 *ch.* He has got there; the defender, the Black
Rook, had to flee; White wins the point KR7 and gives mate.
5. . . . . K—Kt1; *6.* R(B7)—Kt7 *ch* and *7.* R—R8 *mate.* The nature
of a convergent attack on a chosen objective would seem to
have been sufficiently illustrated by this example. Before, however, passing to the "revolutionary" form of attack, we would
underline as important the following rule:—*If the objective
takes to flight, the Rook must attack him from the rear.* For
example, a Rook in the 7th rank holds the Black Pawn at QKt2
under attack. If now *1. . . . .* P—QKt4, then *2.* R—QKt7, and
not a flank attack in the 5th rank. This rule finds its explanation
in the following considerations:—(*a*) The 7th rank is to be
held as long as possible, since it is here that new objectives may
present themselves. (*b*) The enveloping attack (and R—QKt7
was such) is the strongest form of attack (ranged in ascending
scale: i, frontal, ii, flank, iii, enveloping), which (*c*) often

forces the enemy to undertake cramping defensive measures.
It should be noticed that in the case considered above a flank
attack on the QKtP would be comfortably met by R—QKt1.

In Diagram 31 let us "choose" Black's KKt2. The fact that
this point is well protected does not frighten us. We concentrate our attack by means of *1.* Kt—Kt3, P—R6 (the passed
Pawns are very threatening); *2.* Kt—B5, P—R7; *3.* Q—K5 (and
now mate is threatened by R x P *ch*), P—R8(Q); the KKtP is
now protected and White loses; so our objective, Black's KKt2,
was ill chosen. The right one is Black's KR2, and its conquest
follows from a "revolutionary" attack. *1.* **Kt—B6** *ch,* **P x Kt;** *2.*
Q—K6 *ch,* K—R1; *3.* **Q—Q7.** Or, *1.* **Kt—B6** *ch,* K—R1 (Black is
stubborn); *2.* **Q x P** *ch* (White still more so!), **P x Q;** *3.* **R—R7**
mate, and on the chosen spot. This example shows us the idea
of a revolutionary attack applied to the 7th rank. One Pawn is
forcibly got out of the way in order that action in the 7th rank
may be extended to that neighboring point which we had
thought of as our objective.

Another example is shown in Diagram 32. Here the point
KKt7 would be hard to attack successfully, though if White's

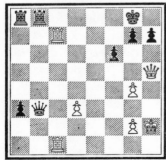

DIAGRAM 32

Win by force of the objective, Black's
KR2. The position calls for "revolutionary" attack

P at KKt4 were absent this
would be easier: for instance by
1. Q—Kt4, P—Kt3; *2.* Q—KR4,
P—R4; *3.* Q x BP, etc. With the
Pawn there, however, matters
are not so easy, for if *1.* R—Q7
(threatening R(B1)—B7), R—
QB1; or if *1.* R(B1)—B4
(threatening Q—B7 *ch*) *1. . . . .*
R—KB1. The right play is *1.* **R x P**
ch (KR7 is our objective), **K x R;**
2. **R—B7** *ch,* K—R1; *3.* **Q x P** *mate.*
The capture at KKt7 extended

the range of action in the 7th row to KR7. If *2. . . . . K—B1; 3.
Q x P* would also have won, since the 7th row could not be held
by Black in any manner. Still more precise, however, would be
the employment of the Queen with gain of tempo; thus: *3. Q—
R6 ch, K—K1; 4. Q—K3 ch, K—B1; 5. Q—K7 ch* (enters the 7th
row with "acoustical echo"), *K—Kt1; 6. Q—Kt7 mate*. This
last maneuver deserves comment; it is typical, since by its
means any approach of the enemy reserves can be prevented.
Take another position. White: K, KB1; Q, KR5; Pawns, Q4, K3,
KB5. Black: K, KKt1; Rooks, QR1, KB1; Kt, KR8; Pawns, KB2,
KB3. White wishes to take the Knight with a check; this he does
by *1. Q—Kt4 ch, K—R2; 2. Q—R3 ch, K—Kt2; 3. Q—Kt2 ch, K—
R3;* and now *Q x Kt ch.* That is to say we drive the King to the
desired side of the board without losing contact with the piece
or point we wish to win.

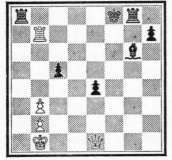

DIAGRAM 33

White mates in four moves

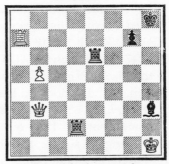

DIAGRAM 34

Example of the first special case

Now see Diagram 33. The point to be won is K7. Either
1. Q—R4 or *1. Q—B2 ch* would fail miserably because of . . . .
P—K6 ch and . . . . *R—R8 mate; e.g. 1. Q—B2 ch, K—K1;
2. Q x P, P—K6 ch,* etc. The right move is *1. Q—B1 ch, K—K1;
2. Q—Kt5 ch, K—B1; 3. Q x P ch, K—K1; 4. Q—K7 mate.* We
could also state the problem as follows:—White to take the

point QB5 with check. After *1.* Q—B1 *ch,* K—K1, *2.* Q—Kt5 *ch,*
White has contact with the point QB5, and, at the same time,
does not lose his driving effect on the enemy King, who is tied
to his own square.

§ 3. *The five special cases in the 7th Rank.*

(1) "7th row absolute" with passed Pawns. (2) Doubled
Rooks give perpetual check. (3) The drawing apparatus
R + Kt. (4) The marauding raid in the 7th rank. (5) Combined play in the 7th and 8th ranks (enveloping maneuver in
the corner of the board).

By "7th rank absolute" we mean that our control is such that
the enemy King is shut in behind it. For example White: R,
QR7. Black: K, KB1; P, KB3. On the other hand were the Pawn
at KB2 control would not be absolute.

(1) The first special case. 7th row absolute with well advanced Pawns wins almost always. An example: White: K,
KR1; R, K7; P, QKt6. Black: K, KR1; R, Q1. White plays
P—Kt7 after which R—QB7 and R—B8 cannot be prevented.
If the Black King had been at KKt3 the game would have been
drawn. In the position on Diagram 34 the following is decisive.
1. Q x B *ch,* R—R3; *2.* Q x R *ch,* P x Q; *3.* P—Kt6, since the 7th row
is now "absolute." If it were not, if the Black KKtP still stood
on his original square, the game would be drawn. In Diagram
35 Lasker in a note points out a win by *1. . . . .* R—R7 *ch; 2.*
K—B1 ?, P—R4; *3.* R x P, P—R5; *4.* R—Kt6, P—R6; *5.* R x BP, R—
QKt7. The rank is "absolute" and Black wins. Interesting on the
other hand would have been, after *1. . . . .* R—R7 *ch,* the attempt to neutralize the "absolute" 7th row by *2.* K—K1 *!.* Lasker
gives the continuation *2. . . . .* P—R4; *3.* K—Q1, P—R5; *4.* K—
B1, P—R6; *5.* K—Kt1 with a draw.

(2) The second special case. Draw by perpetual check,
which has an interest from a psychological error which is

DIAGRAM 35

DIAGRAM 36

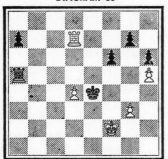

Tarrasch—Lasker, Berlin 1918

Can White draw?

common. In Diagram 36, White, a player of little experience, sees the desperate position of his King and plays for a draw by R(B)—K7 *ch*, quite rightly recognizing that R(Q)—K7 *ch* would lead to the Black King's eventually reaching sanctuary. (*1.* R(Q)—K7 *ch ?*, K—Q1; 2. R—Q7 *ch*, K—B1; 3. R—B7 *ch*, K—Kt1, and White has no checks left.) After *1.* R(B)—K7 *ch*, K—B1; 2. R—B7 *ch*, K—Kt1; 3. R—Kt7 *ch*, K—R1; 4. R—R7 *ch* (if 4. R—Kt1 *? ?*, R—B7 *ch !*), K—Kt1; 5. R(R)—Kt7 *ch !*, K—R1; 6. R—R7 *ch*, K—Kt1, he looks his opponent in the eye; does he really think he can escape?—repeats the checks as above a few times, and then just for variety's sake gives check with the other Rook, 7. R(Q)—Kt7 *ch*, after which his game is lost, since the King reaches sanctuary at his QKt1. From which follows a moral, that variety is not always profitable. The R at Q7 was a sturdy sentinel, and as such should not have been needlessly disturbed.

(3) The third special case. The drawing apparatus (for perpetual check) R + Kt. White: K, KR2; R, QKt7; Kt, KB6. Black: K, KB1; Pawns, QB7, Q7, K7. Black has three embryo Queens; so White seeks to draw by perpetual check. *1.* Kt—R7 *ch*, K—K1; 2. Kt—B6 *ch*, fails because of . . . . K—Q1. The solution is found in *1.* R—Q7, since now after, *e.g., 1.* . . . . . P—K8 (Q) the drawing apparatus works to perfection. Observe

that the key move, *1.* R—Q7, brings R and Kt into strategical contact.

Let us in the same position imagine a Black Rook at his QB1. In this case *1.* R—Q7 would not suffice, but would also be unnecessary, for his own Rook at QB1 stops the Black King's flight and makes a sentinel at Q7 superfluous, so in this case *1.* Kt—R7 *ch,* K—K1; *2.* Kt—B6 *ch,* K—Q1 ? ?; *3.* R—Q7 *mate.* The Black King was a clever fellow; he committed suicide in the middle of the board, when a less talented sovereign would have been satisfied with the corner for this purpose.

(4) The fourth special case is quite simple, but is indispensable in view of the very complicated fifth case. It consists in a driving maneuver. The King will be forced out of his corner, and then will follow a marauding raid. An example.—White: K, KR2; Rooks, QR7, QKt7; Pawns, KKt2, KKt6, KR3. Black: K, KR1; Rooks, QB1, Q1; B, KB8. *1.* R—R7 *ch,* K—Kt1; *2.* R(QR)—Kt7 *ch,* K—B1; *3.* R—B7 *ch,* and wins the Bishop. A necessary condition for success was the protected position of the R at KR7. Had it been otherwise *3. . . . . .* K—Kt1 would have prevented capture of the Bishop. In this fourth case the capacity of the combined Rooks to drive the King from his corner (to KB1 or QB1) must be noted. This capacity provides the basis of the 5th case.

(5) The fifth special case. In the position:—White: R's, QR7, Q7. Black: K, KR1, Q, QKt1, White who designs to seize the 8th rank, tries to do this by low cunning, since the direct road seems to be barred by the Black Queen. He seizes the corner, drives the enemy King out of it, and thus makes room for the enveloping attack of his Rook. *1.* R—R7 *ch,* K—Kt1; *2.* R(QR)—Kt7 *ch,* K—B1; and now *3.* R—R8 *ch,* winning the Queen. The position arrived at after the two checks at KR7 and KKt7 is the typical starting point of all enveloping maneuvers in the 7th and 8th rows. (See Diagram 37.)

The analysis of this position shows us two Rooks each ready

for a turning movement, but also a resourceful King, whose contact with the R at Kt7 protects him from the worst (mate at R8). So long as this contact is maintained mate cannot be given. The King's case is somewhat like that of a pedestrian who is set upon by a foot-pad; the latter raises his weapon to strike, but the former seizes his arm and keeps fast hold of it, knowing that so long as contact is kept up the robber cannot use his arm for the decisive blow. And so the rule runs:—the King who is threatened by an enveloping attack must maintain contact with the nearer Rook as long as possible. The Rooks on their side must seek to shake loose from the contact. The second rule follows directly:—the King who is threatened must struggle towards the corner, the Rooks must and will drive him from it.

DIAGRAM 37

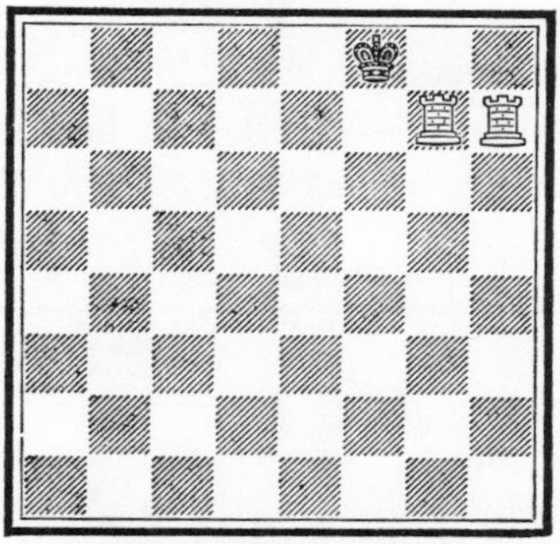

The basis of the enveloping maneuver

Starting from the typical position White can try three maneuvers: (a) for immediate material gain; (b) for a mating combination by breaking off contact between K and R (c) for a tempo-winning combination.

(a) has been already considered. If, say, an enemy Queen stands anywhere in her 1st row there will result from the position R—R8 *ch* with win of the Q for the R at KKt7.

(b) Contact can be broken either through the protection of the R at KKt7 (by Pawn or piece), or by driving away the K by a check from another quarter. For example: White: Rooks KKt7, KR7; B, K1. Black: K, KB1; Q, QR1; R, QR7. There follows *1.* B—Kt4 *ch*, K—K1, and now the Rooks have a free hand to deal the death blow *2.* R—R8 *mate*. Instead of a B at K1 we may imagine a P at K6, and the continuation would be *1.* P—

K7 *ch*, K—K1; 2. R—R8 *ch;* the enveloping operation has been made possible, but the Black King has now a flight square which before was closed to him, *i.e.*, 2. . . . . K—Q2; but this plays no rôle, for the air we have allowed him was alas!—poisoned. 3. P—K8 (Q) *double ch*, and mate is not far off. Now turn to Diagram 38. First White gets the typical position as shown on Diagram 37. 1. R—Kt7 *ch*, K—B1; 2. R—R7 (threatening mate), K—Kt1 (the flight towards the corner); 3. R(B)—Kt7 *ch*, K—B1; and now there follows 4. Kt—Kt5 !, P x Kt; 5. P—B6, with mate at R8. Or, 4. Kt—Kt5 !, P—Q5 !; 5. Kt—K6 *ch*, B x Kt (forced); 6. P x B followed by the driving of the King from B1 by P—K7 *ch*, and history repeats itself. This check at K7, which breaks contact, could only have been parried by . . . .

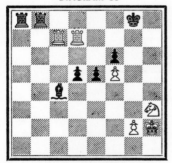

DIAGRAM 38

Triumph of the 7th Rank

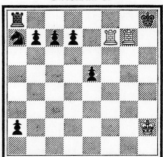

DIAGRAM 39

Win of a tempo. White wins

R—K1, leading to the loss of a Rook, *e.g.*, 6. . . . . R—K1; 7. P—K7 *ch*, R x P; 8. R x R, and White wins easily even if Black has one or two passed Pawns to the good, for there would have been brought into play that capacity which Rooks possess, to which we have called especial attention, of attacking fleeing Pawns from their rear in the 7th rank.

(*c*) See Diagram 39. With 1. R—R7 *ch*, K—Kt1; 2. R(B) —Kt7 *ch*, K—B1, the typical position is reached, but how are we to proceed? Neither (*a*) 3. R—R8 *mate?*, nor (*b*) forcing a break in the contact, seems feasible. Of course, if the White K were already at KKt5, then K—R6 would follow; but as matters stand it would seem as if White must content himself with perpetual check. However, appearances are deceptive. There follows:—3. R x P, threatening mate at R8, so 3. . . . . K—Kt1. Now White repeats the little maneuver, 4. R(Q)—Kt7 *ch*, K—B1; 5. R x P, and again Black is forced to play . . . . K—Kt1; he has no time for the . . . . P—R8 (Q) of his dreams. (If our opponent has no time for something which otherwise would be most advantageous to him because he is forced to make some positional move irrelevant to his purpose, while we advance our project, then we have gained a tempo.) White now plays 6. R(B)—Kt7 *ch*, and the ending runs: 6. . . . . K—B1; 7. R x P, K—Kt1; 8. R(Kt)—Kt7 *ch* (R x Kt would still be a gross error because of . . . . P—R8 [Q]), K—B1; 9. R x Kt, R x R; 10. R x R, and wins the QRP and the game. We may sum this up thus, that in (*c*) we have the case that White gathers new strength by touching the typical starting position, or more simply, by bringing about this position he creates a new mating threat and so a free tempo for gathering loot, *i.e.*, gain of tempo.

DIAGRAM 40

Nimzovich—Bernstein

We have now sufficiently illustrated the five special cases, and have made it clear that the first thing to do is to bring about the "starting point position." We will close with two more end games. Diagram 40 shows the position which White had obtained after 50 moves in the tournament game at Vilna, 1912. My opponent here played 50. . . . . R—KB1, in order, after . . . . P—B3, to reduce the material on the board to such an extent that there would not be enough left to win with. I answered calmly *51.* **R x KtP, P—B3;** for now I manufacture out of its several components my first special case in the 7th rank (passed Pawn and 7th row absolute), which was even at that date known to me. The continuation was *52.* **B—B5, R—B1** (forced; *52.* . . . . R—B2 fails after *53.* R—Kt7, R x R; *54.* P x R *ch,* K x P; *55.* P x P, and Black's Bishop has more work than he can do); *53.* **P x P, R x B;** *54.* **P—B7** (the passed Pawn), **R—B1;** *55.* **R—Kt7** (the 7th row absolute! The extra enemy piece is an illusion), **B—Q6;** *56.* **R—K7** (obviously), **B—Kt4;** *57.* **K—B4** (White avoids *57.* R—K8, B x R; *58.* P—B8 (Q), though thereby he treats himself to the pleasure of getting a new Queen; since after *58.* . . . . B—B3 *ch* and . . . . R x Q, the Queen vanishes and with her also . . . . all joy!), **R—R1;** *58.* **P—R7, B—R5;** *59.* **K—K5, B—Kt4;** *60.* **K—B6, P—K4;** *61.* **K—Kt7,** *resigns.*

DIAGRAM 41

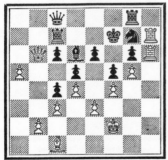

Nimzovich—Eliasstamm
Riga 1910
(White gave odds of QKt)

In the position on Diagram 41 there first occurred *1.* **P—R6, Q—R1** (threatening . . . . R—R2 and . . . . R x P). In this difficult situation White saved himself by the following "subtle trap," as the *Dünazeitung* called it, or by a combination based on a thorough knowledge of the terrain (7th Row!), as we would call it. The game went on. *2.* **P—Kt3, R—Kt1** (better to be sure would be . . . . R—R2); and now followed the Q sacrifice: *3.* **B—R3** *! !,* **R x Q;** *4.* **B x B, R—B1;** *5.* **R x Kt** *ch,* **K x R;** *6.* **B—K5** *ch,* **K any move,** and the Rook gives perpetual check on R8 and R7. It is worth noting that after the Q sacrifice, White has at least a draw in all variations, *e.g., 4.* . . . . . Q x P; *5.* B—K5, K—K1; *6.* R—R8 *ch,* K—Q2; *7.* R(R6)—R7, Q—R7 *ch* (to leave the square R3 open); *8.* K—Kt3, P—B4;

9. R x Kt *ch,* K—B3; *10.* R x R *ch,* K—Kt4; *11.* R x P *ch,* K—R3;
12. R—R8 *ch* winning the Q; or 4. . . . . Q—KKt1; 5. B x R,
R x RP; *6.* P x P, followed by B—K5; or, *4.* . . . . Q—KKt1;
5. B x R, P x P; *6.* B x R, P—Kt7; *7.* R x Kt *ch !,* Q or K x R;
8. R—R1 and White has much the better prospects because of
his strong QRP.

4. The Passed Pawn

§ 1. *To get our bearings. The neighbor who is somewhat disturbing and the vis-à-vis who is wholly unpleasant. The Pawn majority. The "candidate." The birth of a passed Pawn. Rules for "candidates."*

A PAWN is passed if he has nothing to fear from an enemy Pawn in front of him, *i.e.*, in the same file, or from one on a neighboring file, and whose road to Queen is therefore open. (See Diagram 42.) If a Pawn is only checked in his advance (blockaded) by enemy pieces, the fact does not prejudice our conception.

An especial recognition is due to a Pawn from the fact that enemy pieces must sacrifice a part of their effective strength in

DIAGRAM 42

The White QR and K Pawns and the Black QP are passed. The White KP is passed but blocked

order to keep him under observation, and in fact under continual observation. If further, we bear in mind that the Pawn enjoys another advantage over the pieces in that he is the born defender, we shall slowly discover that even on the 64 squares the Pawn, our foot soldier, is worthy of all respect. Who checks an ambitious enemy Pawn best? A Pawn. Who protects one of his own pieces best? A Pawn. And which of the chessmen works for least wages? Again the Pawn; for a steady job, such as protecting one of his own fellows or keeping in restraint one of the enemy's men, does not appeal to a piece at all; moreover, such occupation draws off troops from the active army. When a Pawn is so employed this last applies in very much less measure.

In the position on Diagram 42 neither the QKtP nor the KKtP is free; yet the former seems to be less hampered than the latter, for the QKtP has at any rate no direct antagonist. The *vis-à-vis* might be compared to an enemy, while the Pawn in the next file reminds us rather of a kindly neighbor, who, as we know, can have his drawbacks. If, for instance, we are rushing downstairs to keep an important engagement, and a neighbor suddenly buttonholes us and involves us in a long talk, ranging from the weather and politics to the high cost of beer, he keeps us from our job, just as in Diagram 42 the Black QBP may be a vexation to White's QKtP. Nevertheless a somewhat gossipy chatterbox of a neighbor is far from being a bitter enemy, or to apply the simile to our case, an annoying Pawn on a neighboring file is far from being an antagonist. In our diagram the White KKtP's aspirations to greater things can never be satisfied, whereas the QKtP can always dream of an advance.

Let us now turn to the passed Pawn's family. In this connection we must first consider the question of the majority on one side or the other. At the beginning of the game after the first exchange of Pawns in the center (*e.g.*, after *1*. P—K4, P—K4; *2*. P—Q4, P x P; *3*. Q x P) Pawn majorities loom up. White has now 4 to 3 on the K side, Black 4 to 3 on the Q side. Let us imagine the Black QP standing at Q3 for the purpose of curbing the ambitions of White's KP. The configuration on the K side will then be:

DIAGRAM 43

Majority on the K side

White: Pawns, K4, KB2, KKt2, KR2; as against Black's Pawns at KB2, KKt2, KR2; and on the Q side White has Pawns at QR2, QKt2, QB2, as against Black's Pawns at QR2, QKt2, QB2, Q3. In the course of the game if Black can arrive at . . . . P—KB4, thus killing White's free center Pawn, the majority will be in yet clearer evidence, namely White's Pawns, KB2, KKt2, KR2, as against Black's Pawns, KKt2, KR2.

Rule:—*Every healthy, uncompromised Pawn majority must be able to yield a passed Pawn.* Of the 3 Pawns on the K side in Diagram 43, the KBP is the only one to have no opponent; he is therefore the least trammeled, and accordingly has the greatest claim to become "free" or passed. He is therefore the legitimate "candidate." Put more precisely the rule takes the following shape:—*The spearhead of the advance is furnished by the candidate, the other Pawns are only to be regarded as supports;* so P—B4—B5, then P—Kt4—Kt5 and P—B6. If Black Pawns are at his KKt3, KR4, then White must play P—KB4, P—Kt3 (not at once P—R3 because of . . . . P—R5 and White's majority is crippled), P—R3, P—Kt4, and P—KB5. How simple! and yet how often we see weaker players in this position advancing first with the KtP, to which Black replies with . . . . P—KKt4, and White's majority is worthless. I have often racked my brain to discover why less experienced players begin with P—Kt4, yet the matter bears a simple explanation. The players in question are in two minds whether to begin on the right (P—R4) or on the left (P—B4), and in their perplexity decide, after good respectable custom, to choose the golden mean.

§ 2. *The blockade of passed Pawns. Proof of the obligation to blockade, and why the said proof must be of the greatest importance to the practical player as well as to the theoretician (chess philosopher). The exceedingly complicated, because ever varying, relations between the passed Pawn and the blockader. On strong and weak, elastic and inelastic blockaders.*

In the position shown on Diagram 44 Black has a passed Pawn, which can however be blocked by Kt—Q4 or B—Q4. By blockade we mean the mechanical stopping of an enemy Pawn's advance by a piece, which is brought about by placing our piece directly in front of the Pawn to be blockaded. Here and in all similar cases the question comes up: Does not this

DIAGRAM 44

The problem of the blockade

blockade connote an unnecessary expenditure of energy? Would it not suffice to keep the Pawn under observation (here by the Kt or B bearing upon Black's Q5)? Is keeping up a blockade work worthy of an officer? Will not his mobility, so long as he takes his blockading problem seriously, be to a considerable extent diminished? Is he not thus degraded to the status of a stopped (immobile) Pawn? In a nut-shell, is the blockade economical? I am glad to be able to offer you, as I think, an exhaustive solution to this problem. The mediocre critic would settle the question by laying down quite briefly the general thesis that Pawns must be stopped; but in my eyes this were a proof of poverty of understanding. The why and the wherefore are of extraordinary importance.

There are three reasons which logically make the blockade imperative. In what follows these will be analyzed under § § 2a,

2b, 2c; under § 3 the effective strength of the blockader will be assessed in detail.

§ 2a. *First reason*: *The passed Pawn is a criminal, who should be kept under lock and key. Mild measures, such as police surveillance, are not sufficient. The passed Pawn's lust to expand. The awakening of the men in the rear.*

We return again to Diagram 44. The Black forces, B, R, and Kt, are as we should say, grouped round the passed Pawn, that is to say they conform to a complex of which the QP is the nucleus. Kt and B guard the passed Pawn; the R, however, supplies him with a certain impetus, gives him a supporting impulse in fact. So powerful is the Pawn's desire to press on here, to expand (of which fact indeed visible recognition is given in the way the "officers," laying aside all pride of caste, picturesquely group themselves round this simple "foot soldier"), that our QP often seems ready to advance on his own account, when to do so will cost him his life. So, for instance, *1. . . . . P—Q5; 2.* **Kt** or **B x P** and now of a sudden the Black forces in the rear come to life. The B from QKt2 commands a diagonal bearing on the enemy King, the Rook has a clear file, while the Kt has a new square for himself in the center. Such an advance at the cost of self-immolation, for the purpose of opening a file, is, as a rule, only characteristic of a "Pawn-roller," a compact advancing mass of Pawns in the center (*cf.* the game at odds in I. i. § 2, p. 5), and therefore furnishes a brilliant proof of the lust to expand inherent in a passed Pawn; for the mobile center (the Pawn-roller) is endowed with an almost incredible energy. Again, the clearing of a square for one of his own Knights is a very special characteristic of an advance of this kind. Accordingly we say that the first consideration which logically compels the blockade, is that the free passed Pawn is such a dangerous "criminal," that it is by no means sufficient to keep him under police supervision (by the Kt at QKt3 and

DIAGRAM 45

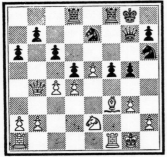

te Kolsté—Nimzovich
Baden-Baden 1925

Black sacrifices a "candidate," and a piece to the rear comes to life. How is this done?

the B at KB2 in Diagram 44); the fellow must be put in prison, so we take away his freedom utterly by blockading him with the Kt at Q4.

The example just considered, we mean the sacrifice of the Pawn (for he intended to die in the advance), is thoroughly typical; although it is not in the least necessary that a whole host of men to the rear should be freed by the operation. It is often but a single piece standing behind it that profits. (Take Diagram 45.)

Black, whose Q side and center seem to be threatened, seeks to turn his "candidate" to account. Since the candidate is 90 per cent a passed Pawn, the same rules apply for him as do for a passed Pawn. Accordingly 19. . . . . P—B5 !; 20. P x BP, P—Kt5 !; 21. B—Kt2, Kt(R3)—B4; *i.e.*, sacrifice of a "candidate" with the result that the square KB4 is cleared for the Kt at R3. The continuation was 22. Q—Kt3, P x P; 23. Q x P *ch*, K—R1; 24. Q—B3, P—KR4; 25. QR—Q1, P—R5; 26. R—Q3, Kt—Q4; 27. Q—Q2, R—KKt1. Black supports his Pawn majority with vigor. 28. B x Kt, P x B; 29. K—R1, P—Kt6; and Black gets the attack. In the game Alekhine—Treybal (see Diag. 46) the following interesting maneuver occurred:—27. P—K4. The mobile Pawn center sets itself in motion. 27. . . . . .

DIAGRAM 46

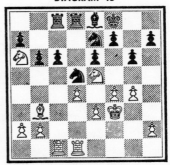

Alekhine—Treybal
Baden-Baden 1925

P—B3 (for . . . . Kt—B2 loses the QBP); 28. **P x Kt, P x Kt.** The passed Pawn which has suddenly come into existence is clearly but as an ephemera, the fruit of some sudden inspiration, and seemingly destined to as speedy a death; but appearances are deceptive, even this creature of a moment knows how to subject itself to the iron laws of chess, and so there followed 29. **P—Q6** *!!.* The purpose of this Pawn sacrifice was not to free the square from which it moved, and yet the advance wholly fulfills the spirit, if not the letter, of our rules. The Pawn intends to lay down its life in advancing, and the main variation would be 29. . . . . **P—K5***ch !* (so as to prevent QP x P which could follow . . . . R x P); 30. **K x P, R x P;** 31. **K—K5** *! !,* **QR—Q1;** 32. **B x P.** Note that the entry of the King into Black's game was made possible only by the Pawn sacrifice.

For a complete game which shows in its full setting the very important operation which we have been discussing, see Leonhardt—Nimzovich, Game No. 12, which the reader is urged to study before proceeding further.

We now pass on to an analysis of our second reason.

§ 2b. *The second reason. Optimism in chess, and the immunity of the blockading piece against frontal attacks. The enemy Pawn as our bulwark. The deeper-lying mission of the blockading piece. The blockading point a weak enemy point.*

In my book on the "Blockade"* I wrote on this point as follows:—"The second reason which we are now to analyze is of great importance from both the strategic and the instructional points of view. In chess in the last resort optimism is decisive. I mean by this that it is psychologically valuable to develop to the greatest length the faculty of being able to rejoice over small advantages. The beginner only 'rejoices' when he can call checkmate to his opponent, or perhaps still more if he can win his Q (for in the eyes of the beginner this is if

* *Die Blockade* von A. Nimzovich, Berlin, Schachverlag B. Kagan.

possible the greater triumph of the two). The master on the other hand is quite pleased, in fact royally content, if he succeeds in espying the shadow of an enemy Pawn weakness, in some corner or other of the left half of the board. The optimism here characterized is the indispensable psychological basis of position play. It is this optimism, too, which gives us strength, in face of every evil, however great, to discover the faintest hint of a bright side to the picture. In the case under consideration we can lay it down as established that an enemy passed Pawn represents an unquestionably serious evil for us, yet even this evil has its tiny gleam of brightness. The situation is this, that in blockading this Pawn we can by good fortune safely post the blockading piece under the shelter of the enemy Pawn itself, so that it is immune from any frontal attack. Thus: —Consider a Black passed Pawn at his K5; a White blockader at his K3 is not subject to an attack from an enemy Rook on the King file (K1 to K6), and hence stands there in a certain measure of security."

So far *Die Blockade*. And to these remarks there is perhaps only this to add, that the relative security here outlined must in truth be at bottom symptomatic of that deeper mission which the blockader has to fulfill. If nature, yes, and even the enemy, too, are concerned about the safety of the blockader, he must have been set apart for great deeds. And in fact we are not out in our reckoning; for the blockading point often becomes a "weak" enemy point.

I can well imagine that the road to a real conception of "weak points" may have led across the blockading field. The enemy has a passed Pawn; we stopped its progress, and now suddenly it appeared that the piece with which we effected this exerted a most unpleasant pressure, and the enemy Pawn actually provided a natural defensive position which the blockader could use as an observation post. This conception once grasped was subsequently widened and dematerialized. Widened, because we now classed as weak every square in front of an enemy Pawn, whether passed or not, if there were any possibility of our being able to establish ourselves on it without risk of being driven off. But the conception of a weak point was also dematerialized. When, for instance, Dr. Lasker talks of White's weak squares in the position on Diagram 47 (from the game Tartakover—Lasker, St. Petersburg, 1909) the presence of an enemy Pawn as a bulwark for the piece occupying a weak square is certainly no longer a *conditio sine qua non.*

§ 2c. *The third reason. The crippling induced by a blockade is by no means local in its nature. The transplanting of the crippling phenomena to the ground in the rear. On the dual nature of the Pawn. On the pessimistic outlook, and how this can be transformed into the blackest melancholy.*

In Game No. 12, Leonhardt—Nimzovich, the White B at Q4 blocked Black's P at QB3, one of the consequences being that Black's B at QKt2 was held a prisoner in his own camp. This state of affairs seems to be typical; only, very often, a whole complex of enemy pieces is sympathetically affected. Large tracts of the board are made impracticable for any maneuvering of the swifter kind. At times, too, the whole enemy position takes on a strangely rigid character. In other words, the crippling effect has shifted from the blockaded Pawn further back to its rear. In Diagram 48 the Black KP and QP are completely blockaded, and the whole of Black's position seems benumbed. B and R are prisoners in their own camp, and White, in spite of his inferiority in material, actually has winning chances.

The state of affairs here sketched need not surprise us in the least. We have often pointed out that any Pawn may be an obstacle in the way of his own pieces, and that to get rid of him may often be our dearest wish, as for instance, if we are

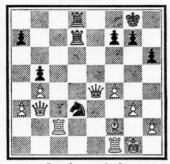

DIAGRAM 47

Tartakover—Lasker
St. Petersburg, 1909
Weak white points

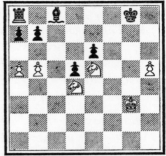

DIAGRAM 48

Transplanting the effects of the
blockade to the region in the rear

planning to open a file or to free a square for a Kt (see § 2a, p. 53). We see then that the blockade is not only embarrassing to the Pawn itself, but much more so really to his comrades in arms, the Rooks and Bishops. In connection, by the way, with the Pawn, it is important for the student to appreciate a certain dual nature which he possesses. On the one hand the Pawn, as we have shown above, is quite willing to commit suicide, while on the other he clings tenaciously to life, for the presence of Pawns, as he knows, is not only of great importance for the end game, but still more helps to prevent the establishment of enemy pieces within his own lines, which but for them might be possible; or to put it otherwise, prevents the creation of weak points in their territory. The mobility of a passed Pawn, particularly of a center one, is often the very life-nerve of the whole position; its crippling must therefore naturally find its echo throughout the whole of that position. We have seen, then, that weighty reasons support the establishment of a blockade at the earliest possible moment, whereas those which seem to tell against it, namely the apparently uneconomical use made of an officer, seemingly degraded to being a mere sentry (=blockader), will be seen on closer examination to carry weight only in certain cases. To be able to recognize these we must now consider the blockader himself.

§ 3. *The blockader's primary and secondary functions. The conception of elasticity. Various forms of the same. The strong and the weak blockader. How the blockader meets the many demands made on him, partly on his own initiative; and why I see in this a proof of his vitality.*

The primary function of a blockader is obviously to blockade in a businesslike manner the Pawn concerned. In exercising this he has himself a tendency towards immobility. And yet, admire his vitality! He very often displays pronounced activity: (1) by the threats which he can exercise from the place where he is posted (see Game 12, Leonhardt—Nimzovich, in which Black's Kt at K3 prepared the way for . . . . P—KKt4); (2) by a certain elasticity which finds expression in the fact that he does on occasion leave his post. He seems to be entitled to a furlough, (*a*) if the journey promise much in results, when the connections must all be made by express, so to speak; (*b*) if he can be sure of returning quickly enough to take up the blockade again on another square, should the Pawn have advanced in the interval; (*c*) if he be in a position to leave a deputy in his place to look after the blockade. It is obvious that such a deputy must be chosen from those pieces which are seconding (protecting) the blockader. This last consideration, for all its apparent insignificance, is of great importance; for it shows clearly the extent to which elasticity, at any rate in the form considered under (*c*), is directly dependent on the degree of weakness or strength of the blockade.

In connection with (*a*) see the end game Nimzovich—Nilsson. (Diagram 67.)

In connection with (*b*) consider the position: White: K, Q1; R, KR4. Black: K, QR1; R, KR1; Pawns, QKt5, KR4. In this simplest of positions the blockading Rook takes a little holiday trip *1.* **R x KtP**. It goes without saying that the passed Pawn will seize the opportunity to advance *1. . . . .* **P—R5;** *2.* **R—Kt2, P—R6;** *3.* **R—KR2**. Master Rook appears in the office, bows to the boss, nods to his fellow employees, and, as if he were fresh as paint and thoroughly rested (though he had to do some bustling to get back in time), takes his seat at his (blockading) desk. He has, however, changed his seat, from R4 to R2. The maneuver here shown may be found repeated in many an example.

In connection with (*c*), see the rôle played by the White B at KB4 in Game No. 15, White's 26th move.

From the above little discussion (under *a*, *b* and *c*), we see that elasticity is slight if the Pawn to be blockaded is far advanced. The maximum elasticity is on the other hand developed when a half passed Pawn in the center of the board is the object of the blockader's attentions; in such a position as, for instance: White: Kt, Q4; Pawns, K3, KB2; Black: B, QKt2; P, Q4. The blockading Kt at Q4 is here very elastic; he can take long journeys from his post and in all directions, and yet not neglect his primary duty which is to prevent the advance of Black's QP. So much on the subject of elasticity. We will now analyze the actual effect of the blockade itself.

§ 3a. *Effect of the Blockade.*

The forces to maintain a blockade should be developed systematically and of set purpose, whereas elasticity often comes of itself without seeking. The blockading effect is intensified by bringing up supports, which, however, in their turn must be safely stationed. Compare Diagrams 49 and 50.

The Bishop in Diagram 49 will for motives of personal safety migrate to Kt3, though to be sure the blockading Rook will thus lose a powerful support. Nevertheless for the B to play about on the long diagonal is a somewhat risky game, for the eye of the law (Q at Q4) is upon him. After *1. . . . .* **B—Kt3**

DIAGRAM 49

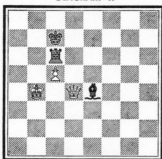

Black to move. Is the R at QB3 a
strong blockader?

DIAGRAM 50

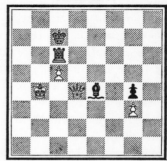

Black to move. Can the blockader
hold his own?

there follows, however, 2. K—Kt5, and now the attempt to re-
store the abandoned strategical connection by 2. . . . . B—K1
fails badly after 3. Q—K5 *ch*, K—Q2; 4. Q x B *ch*, K x Q; 5. K x R.
On the other hand in Diagram 50, the B can go to B6 where he
stands safe and cannot be dislodged, and the R at QB3 thus
gains so much in importance that a draw seems inevitable. We
have shown a similar state of affairs to exist in our study
of outposts. In like manner here the blockader derives his
strength, not so much from himself as from his strategical connection with the country to his rear. A blockader who is insufficiently or imperfectly protected will not be able to hold his
own against the enemy pieces which are hotly pressing him.
He will be put to flight, and either taken or put out of action;
whereupon the Pawn whose road had before been blocked will
resume his advance. In connection with the problem of the
defense, the reader will find extraordinarily valuable the rules
which will be treated in Part II of this book on the over-protection of strategical points. The blockading point is as a rule a
strategically important square, and therefore it is part of wisdom to protect it even more than is absolutely necessary. So do
not wait for attacks to pile up; rather lay up a reserve of defensive force, just as before a dance one lays up a store of sleep.

And so a remarkable fact appears, that whilst the effect of the blockade can only be intensified or even maintained by laboriously bringing up supports, the other secondary virtues of the blockader, elasticity, and the threats he can exercise from his post, prove to be of hard growth; that is to say they come to fulfillment without any particular exertion on his part (like thistles on stony ground). This is explicable, (1) by the state of affairs in which a protecting piece takes the place of the blockader who has gone on his travels; (2) by the fact that, as explained under 2b, the blockading square tends to become a weak point for the enemy. Keeping contact with a strategically important square must according to my system work wonders. This will be considered in greater detail under position play.

We can sum all this up in the following principle:—

Though in the choice of a blockader elasticity and the threats he can exercise must be borne in mind, yet it is often sufficient merely to strengthen the blockade; elasticity and the rest will then not seldom come of themselves.

It must now be clear that an officer in no sense compromises his dignity by answering the summons to act as a blockader, for the post proves itself to be a most honorable one, safe, yet allowing full initiative. The student should thoroughly test the truth of this observation from master games or games played by himself. He should compare the blockaders with one another, their respective merits, their ultimate fate, and how they came to fail or to succeed in their duty, and he will get more benefit out of a thorough knowledge of one "actor" than from a nodding acquaintance with the whole "troupe." It is when working under limitations that the master reveals himself. This true saying applies wholly also to the aspirant to mastership, indeed to every student who is in earnest.

§ 4. *The fight against the blockader. His uprooting. "Changez les blockeurs!" How to get a stand-offish blockader replaced by one who is more affable.*

When we said that the blockader derived his effective strength from his connection with the country to his rear, this was an indisputable truth; yet he can, and should, contribute something of himself to the protection of the blockading rampart. This he does in that, thanks to his attacking radius, he wards off the approach of enemy troops from himself. It is also a merit in him if his origin be humble, the humbler the better. By this we mean that a blockader should have a thick hide. The rather exaggerated sensitiveness displayed by the King or Queen would ill consort with the rôle of blockader. A minor piece (Kt or B) can stand up to an attack—in case of need he has only to call up aid; whereas the Queen reacts to the slightest attack to such an extent, that she at once, though with head proudly erect, leaves the field. In general the King would also be a poor blockader, but in the end game his royal attribute of being able to change the color of his squares stands him in good stead; so that if he be driven away from a black blockading square, he can try at the next halting place to establish a blockade on a white square. For instance:—White: K, KKt4; B, Q1; P, KKt5. Black: K, KKt3; Kt, QR2. The check B—B2 *ch* drives the Black King from Kt3, but now he takes up the blockade again at Kt2.

Since the blockaders as we have seen, may be of varying quality: strong or weak, elastic or inelastic, the obvious thing to do is to get one blockader replaced by another, if this would suit us better. If I take a blockader, the recapturing piece takes over his rôle, and by so doing the command *"changez les blockeurs"* becomes a *fait accompli*. The following combination is typical:—In Diagram 51 the opening moves would be *1.* R—Kt8 *ch*, R—B1, and now the attacking range of the B renders difficult the approach of the White K, which would else be decisive. There follows, however, 2. R x B, R x R; 3. K—Kt7. This new blockader, the R at QR1, now shows himself to be an accommodating fellow, and nothing is further from his thoughts than to stay an attempt at approach, so 3. . . . . R—KB1; 4. P—R8(Q), R x Q; 5. K x R, and the Pawn end game is untenable for Black since (*cf.* Diagram 53) the Black KP's flank will be turned. 5. . . . . K—Kt2; 6. K—Kt7, K—Kt3; 7. K—B6, K—

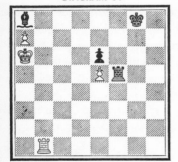

DIAGRAM 51

From one of my games; the blockading Bishop at Black's QR1 will be replaced by the Rook

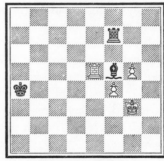

DIAGRAM 52

Changez les Blockeurs!
A startling sacrifice smashes the blockade

Kt4; 8. K—Q7 *!*, K—B4; 9. K—Q6 and wins. On the other hand 1. R—Kt8 *ch*, R—B1; 2. K—Kt6 ? (instead of R x B), B—Q4; 3. K—B7, K—B2; 4. R x R *ch*, K x R; 5. K—Kt8 would fail because of 5. . . . . K—B2; 6. P—R8(Q), B x Q; 7. K x B, K—Kt3; and Black wins. In the position shown on Diagram 52 Black would be perfectly safe if his K were not so far away. White makes the more accommodating Black R take the place of the embarrassing B. Thus *1.* R x B, R x R; 2. K—Kt4, and the White Pawns become mobile and the Black K arrives too late 2. . . . . R—B1; 3. P—Kt6, K—Kt4; 4. P—B5, K—B3; 5. P—Kt7 R—KKt1; 6. P—B6, K—Q3; 7. K—B5, frustrating . . . . K—K3 and wins. The idea is this: The attacking party is prepared to come to an understanding with the blockading company, but wishes first to see its apparently rather unsympathetic spokesman replaced by some one else. This done, negotiations may begin! By "negotiations," I mean the uprooting of the blockader.

How are these "negotiations" to be pursued? Well, we concentrate as many attacks as possible on the blockader concerned. The latter will naturally call up reserves in his support. In the fight now raging round the blockader we seek, following the best practice, to bring to bear a superiority of forces, and this by trying to kill off the defenders by exchanges, or to drive them away, or otherwise to divert them. Finally the blockader will have to retire and our Pawn can move forward. In the end game in the event of a blockade we usually drive away the blockader's supports, in the middle game on the other hand we seek to busy them. A very instructive example of all this is furnished by my game against von Gottschall, Breslau, 1925. See Game No. 13, which the student is advised to study at this point.

§ 5. *Frontal attack by the King against an isolated Pawn as a kingly ideal. The turning movement. The rôle of leader. The tripartite maneuver, made up of frontal attack, the enemy's forced withdrawal, and the final turning movement. The "reserve" blockading point. The superseded "opposition"!*

Many a stout fellow who has grown gray at chess will gasp at this: What? Is the "opposition" also to be abolished now? Yes, I am sorry, but this blow must fall. And first, to get our bearings, let us remark that to conceive the center arithmetically means counting the Pawns standing there, and regarding a numerical majority as giving a guarantee of preponderance. A wholly untenable conception. In reality it is only the greater or lesser degree of mobility which can be counted decisive in passing judgment upon the position in the center. Now if we look deep enough we find that the opposition certainly has a relationship with the center "arithmetically" conceived: and the inner significance of both the one and the other is assessed on purely outward characteristics. In what follows I shall give my entirely new theory, which in eliminating the "opposition" analyzes the inner meaning of what is happening.

In Diagram 53 (right) the creation of a passed Pawn by means of P—R3, P—B3, P—Kt4, would not be sufficient to win, since the White K has lagged behind his passed Pawn. The K must here play the rôle of leader, something like a pace-maker in a bicycle race, and not stay comfortably at home reading the news from the race track. The student, too, must be fully alive to one point, that the King in the middle game and the same King in the end game are two totally different persons. In the middle game the

King is a timid soul, shuts himself up in his fortress (castled position), and only when he feels himself in contact with his Rook, with his own Knights and Bishops attentively grouped around him, does the old fellow feel himself passing well. In the end game the King changes into a hero (not so difficult after all, as the board is swept almost clean of enemies!), and scarcely is it begun than he leaves his castled home and stalks slowly

DIAGRAM 53

Right: White wins one of the enemy Pawns. Left: White, himself threatened with an enveloping movement, turns the enemy position and wins his objective, the P at QB3. How does he do it?

but imposingly to the center—clearly to be in the middle of thing; but of this more in Chapter 6. He shows, however, particular courage in a fight against an isolated Pawn. Such a fight will be started with a frontal attack, as in White: K, KB4; Black: P, KB4. Such a frontal position is an ideal which the

King aims at, and is one in fact well worth striving for, because, given the necessary material, it can be attained, and thus the capture of the beleaguered Pawn facilitated, or, in a pure Pawn ending, it may lead to the eventual turning of the position.

And so, if fighting forces be still available, the Black P at KB4 will be exposed to multiple attacks, which may lead to the protecting pieces having to take up less comfortable positions; while if it comes to a plain duel between the two Kings with no pieces left on the board, the weapon of exhaustion, *Zugzwang*, will be at the disposal of the attacker. As an example suppose on Diagram 53 (right) a White B at KB1, and a Black B at KB2. After 1. K—B3, K—Kt2; 2. K—B4 (the ideal position), K—B3; there follows 3. B—Q3, B—K3, and the difference in value between the active White B at Q3 and the passive Black B at K3, who is chained to the P at KB4, weighs by no means lightly in the scale (see Chapter 6, §2). The pure Pawn end game on the other hand would run somewhat as follows:—See Diagram 53 (right) 1. K—B3, K—Kt2; 2. K—B4, K—B3; 3. P—R4. This is the first stage of the maneuver. Then

DIAGRAM 54

Right: White turns the enemy position. Left: White wins the point QKt5 as a station for his K

comes 3. . . . . K—Kt3, and this is the second stage: the enemy King must willy-nilly go to one side, a direct consequence of the *Zugzwang*. And now follows the third and last stage, namely the White turning movement 4. K—K5 and wins. The frontal attack has developed into a turning movement; an advantage, for an enveloping movement is, as we know, the strongest form of attack (in ascending order: frontal, flank, and enveloping).

That the enveloping attack is very strong in the end game is impressed on us by the examples shown on Diagrams 53 (left) and 54 (right). In the latter there follows *1. K—R6, K—B1; 2. K—Kt6, K—K2; 3. K—Kt7, K—K1; 4. K—B6, K—Q2; 5. K—B7.* Notice the tortuous manner of approach of the White K, who works with *Zugzwang* as his weapon. In Diagram 53 (left) the continuation is *1. K—Q7 !, K—Kt4; 2. K—Q6;* but not *1. K—Q6 ?,* because of . . . . K—Kt4, and White has no good move left, and is in fact himself in *Zugzwang,* in a strait jacket, shall we say? Or finally take the position: White: K, KR5; Pawns, QR4, QR5, KB5. Black: K, Q4; Pawns, QKt2, KB3. *1. K—Kt6, K—K4; 2. P—R6 !, P x P; 3. P—R5.* Here White sacrificed a P in order to throw the unpleasant duty of moving on to his opponent.

Now that we have seen the significance of the enveloping movement, which, by the way, can only succeed against a stationary object (which in its turn limits the movements of its own King!), it will be intelligible to us why we should go to such trouble, in carrying out this tripartite maneuver, to bring off this form of attack.

We will now consider this tripartite maneuver in its three stages in a position where there are no enemy Pawns. (See Diagram 54 [left].) The question at issue here is the win of the point QKt5 for the White K. Why precisely the point QKt5? Because the position of the K at QKt5 would ensure the advance of the passed Pawn as far as QKt6; for if the K occupies this point, he has only to move to one side, say to QB5, and the P whom we imagine as having already reached Kt4 will without question reach Kt6. In the same diagram the square Kt6 is the first unsafeguarded stage on the Pawn's road to Queen; for the points Kt4, Kt5 are already secured by the K at QB4. We therefore institute a frontal attack on the point QKt5. *1. K—Kt4* (this is the first stage), K—R3 or B3 (the forced withdrawal of the K. This is the second stage); *2. K—B5* or R5 (the third stage, the turning movement completed); and now, as he wished to do, the White K reaches Kt5. For instance 2. . . . . K—Kt2; 3. K—Kt5 !. In the position now reached (White: K, QKt5; P, QKt3. Black: K, QKt2), the White King's last move may itself be regarded as a frontal attack on the next halting place Kt6. The tripartite maneuver directed against QKt6 will run an entirely analagous course, namely, 3. K—Kt5, K—R2 or B2; 4. K—B6 or R6, with K—Kt6 to follow.

The application of this method of thought to the defense is still simpler. In the position, White: K, QB4; P, QKt4; Black: K, QB3, Black can draw because the White K has lagged behind. All that Black has to do is to watch that the White K does not assume the rôle of leader, and next to keep well in mind that after the blockading point, the "reserve" blockading point is his safest position. (With a White P on QKt4 Black's QKt4 is his blockading point, QKt3 his "reserve" blockading point.) In the position under consideration Black's reply to 1. P—Kt5 ch, is 1. . . . . K—Kt3 (blockade); 2. K—Kt4, K—Kt2 (reserve blockade); 3. K—B5, K—B2 (but not 3. . . . . K—Kt1 or B1, for that would allow the White K to gain ground); 4. P—Kt6 ch, K—Kt2 (blockade); 5. K—Kt5, K—Kt1 (reserve blockade); 6. K—B6, K—B1; 7. P—Kt7 ch, K—Kt1; 8. K—Kt6 *Stalemate.*

To avoid any possibility of misunderstanding let us repeat that with a White P at his QKt6, Black's QKt1 is the reserve blockading point; if he is at his QKt5 then Black's QKt2 is the reserve point.

In the position, White: K, QB5; P, QKt5; Black: K, QKt2, 1. . . . . K—Kt1 would be a horrible move, for it would leave the whole field open to the White K and give him the chance of assuming the rôle of leader. Thus:—1. . . . . K—Kt1 ? ?; 2. K—Kt6 with a decisive frontal attack on the point QKt7 (our tripartite maneuver).

The theory of the opposition is in its want of clarity only to be described as obscurative; whereas the truth is so clear! The attacking King fights to get into the lead, his opponent strives to prevent this with the aid of the "reserve blockade point."

§ 6. *The privileged passed Pawn: (a) two united, (b) the protected, (c) the more remote. The King as hole-stopper. On preparations for the King's journey.*

As in life, so on the chessboard, the goods of the world are not altogether equally divided, so that there are some passed Pawns who have far greater influence than other, ordinary passed Pawns. Such "privileged" passed Pawns deserve to be highly regarded by the student, who should never miss an opportunity of creating one for himself. In what follows we shall attempt to explain the effect of these "privileged" Pawns by a consideration of their characteristics, from which rules will be deduced for our direction, the pros and cons in the fight with or against the stout fellows we are going to consider.

(a) The typical ideal position of two united passed Pawns is shown on Diagram 55. The relationship between them is one of the truest comradeship, and therefore the position where the two Pawns are on the same rank must be regarded as the most natural one.

The strength of passed Pawns so placed lies in the impossibility of blockading them; for their position (on KR4, KKt4) seems to rule out any blockade on the squares R5 or Kt5. However the march of events will cause the two passed Pawns to give up their ideal position; for though they are, maybe, doing noble work at Kt4 and R4, the innate ambition towards higher things, common to all passed

DIAGRAM 55

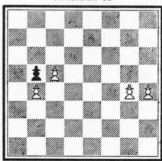

The QBP is a protected passed Pawn, the KKt and KRP's are two united passed Pawns in the ideal position

Pawns, will drive them forward. And the moment one of them moves, possibilities of blockading them will arise. For instance, after P—R5 Black pieces could blockade them at their Kt4 and R3. From this consideration, coupled with the fact that these united passed Pawns can have no dearer wish than to advance together to Kt5 and R5, there follow these rules: The advance of a passed Pawn from the ideal position must take place only at a moment when a strong blockade by enemy pieces is impossible of execution; and further: If the proper Pawn has advanced at the right moment, any blockade which may be attempted will be weak and easily overcome, his companion must then advance as soon as possible, so as to recover the ideal position.

Accordingly (see Diagram 55) at the right moment the proper Pawn, say the KtP, will advance (P—Kt5), a move which affords the enemy the chance of setting up a blockade at his KR4. The blockading piece, which by hypothesis was badly supported (hence the term "weak blockade"), will be driven off, and the move P—R5 will bring about the ideal position again.

Very important service can here be rendered by the White King stepping into the breach which was caused by the advance of the first Pawn. Thus, in Diagram 55, after say 1. P—Kt5, Kt—KR4, the K, whom we imagine to be at hand, with K—Kt4 will slip into the breach and close it. The maneuver here described we shall call hole-stopping; and our King need never be afraid of being out of work, for at worst he can get a job as a traveling dentist and stop cavities! Now for a practical example of hole-stopping.

Diagram 56 shows a position which occurred in a club match in Stockholm in 1921. White played 1. P—Kt6 ch, and thus allowed the Black King to establish an absolute blockade at his QKt2; absolute, because from the nature of things the King can never be driven away. There followed 2. K—Q6 and the K

wandered to his KKt7 and re-
freshed himself with the KRP;
but at that very moment Black
played B—R4, and there was
nothing more for the King to eat
on the K side. Dolefully his Majesty then wandered back to
the other wing, but here, too,
there was nothing for him, since
Black's Bishop, now freed from
guarding the P, made the board

DIAGRAM 56

unhealthy. A fitting punishment overtook White for breaking
the rules by his advance. Correct was *1. P—R6, B—Q6; 2. B—Q4,
B—B8; 3. K—Kt4 ch !* (plans to stop the hole at R5), *K—R1; 4.
K—R5, B—K7; 5. P—Kt6.* Everything according to program: the
QRP advanced first, since the hindrance which can now be
put in White's way (blockade is here almost too strong a term)
can be easily brushed aside; the K stops the hole caused by the
advance; the QKtP moves on in his turn, and the two pals are
again united.

Thus like two trusty comrades on a battlefield, they will
advance together, step by step, and it will be but seldom, and
then only if far advanced, that it may happen that one of them
will push on alone, ruthlessly leaving his friend to be slaugh-
tered. Such an exceptional case is shown in Diagram 57.

(*b*) The difference in value between a protected and an
ordinary passed Pawn is well shown in the following example
(see Diagram 58). White opens fire on the enemy's Pawn
majority. *1. P—R4, K—K4; 2. P x P* (*2. P—B4 ?* would have been
wrong because of *2. . . . . P—Kt5*, with a protected passed
Pawn. The two Kings would then have had the scarcely pleasant job of walking up and down keeping an eye on the Pawns,
hardly an inspiring occupation for a King!), *P x P; 3. P—B4,
P x P ch* (forced, *3. . . . . P—Kt5* would not help, for the

DIAGRAM 57

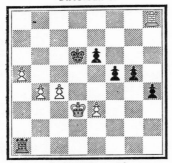

Perlis—Nimzovich
Carlsbad 1911
Black moves. The KKtP shamefully
leaves his comrade the KRP in the
lurch. He gets uppish and forgets the
ties of friendship . . . so *1. . . . .*
P—Kt5 !; 2. R x P, P—Kt6 and wins

DIAGRAM 58

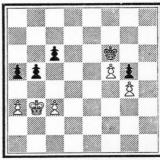

White wins through the difference in
value between a protected and an
ordinary passed Pawn. White's KBP
cannot be undermined, whereas
Black's Queen-side Pawn majority
turns out to be untenable

White Pawns would go on to Queen); and now we have a
position which is characteristic of the difference in value
between the Pawns; for, as is clear, the White King can gob-
ble up the Black passed Pawn without any trouble, whereas
the immunity of the protected KBP from any attack by the
Black King is brilliantly in evidence. True we have in our day
seen how a player of little experience, ignoring this immunity
(in the position White: K, QR1; Pawns, KB5, KKt4. Black: K,
K4; P, KKt4), with a pleased grin on his face and flushed with
the lust of battle, going after the KKtP. After *1. . . . . K—B5;*
2. P—B6, he sees his error and begins in all seriousness to chase
the fleeting Pawn. The last scene of the comedy runs then thus:
—1. . . . . K—B5; 2. P—B6, K—K4 ! !; 3. P—B7, K—K3 ! !; 4. P—
B8(Q), Resigns. We may formulate the case thus: The strength
of a protected passed Pawn lies in his immunity from attack
by the enemy King.

(*c*) In Diagram 59 the KRP is the "remoter" passed Pawn

(that is more remote from the mid-point of the board). After the indirect exchange of the two passed Pawns, *1.* P—R5 *ch,* K—R3; *2.* K—B5, K x P; *3.* K x P, the Black King is out of play, the White King on the contrary is well, because centrally, developed. And this is decisive. The remoter passed Pawn is therefore a trump card (with great power of causing a diversion), but like any other trump card must be hoarded, not played out too quickly; and this must be our rule. The exchange of Pawns which drew off the enemy King, was only the preliminary to the White King's journey which followed. (See Diagram 59.) This journey, however, should be fully prepared for before the Pawn advance takes place. Compare the position: White: K, K4; Pawns, QR4, QB4, KR2. Black: K, Q3; Pawns,

DIAGRAM 59

The more remote passed Pawn, whose capture entices the enemy King away from the middle of the board

QR4, K4, KKt2. White in the QBP has the remoter passed Pawn. His immediate advance would, however, be a mistake; for after *1.* P—B5 *ch,* K x P; *2.* K x P, the King's journey to his Kt7 would be a mere waste of time, for his traveling companion the KRP has been too dilatory. The right move is *1.* P—KR4. The traveling companion reports himself!—and this induces *1. . . . .* P—Kt3. For this obliging advance we have to thank the *Zugzwang* weapon, of which we should make diligent use, particularly in the case of the "remoter" passed Pawn. There now follows *2.* P—B5 *ch !,* K x P; *3.* K x P, K—Kt5; and Black arrives one move too late: *4.* K—B6, K x P; *5.* K x P, K—Kt6; *6.* P—R5, P—R5; *7.* P—R6, etc.

Rules to be observed: **Prepare for the King's journey before** the sacrifice (or exchange) which is to divert the enemy King is made. Make use of the *Zugzwang* weapon whenever possible. Let the traveling companion advance. The impediments to the journey (enemy Pawns on the wing to which the King is to travel) must be enticed forward. All this before the move which is to divert the enemy King out of action is made. (*Cf.* Example 3, Diagram 64, page 81.)

§ 7. *When a passed Pawn should advance*: (*a*) *on his own account*, (*b*) *to win ground for his King who is following him* (*stopping the holes*), (*c*) *to offer himself as a sacrifice to divert the enemy. On the measure of the distance between the enemy King and the sacrifice which is to be offered him as bait.*

It is an old story that the less experienced amateur as a rule lets his passed Pawn advance at the very moment least suitable for it. With two united passed Pawns we saw him in Diagram 56 play *1*. P—Kt6 *ch ?*, and thus allow an iron blockade to be set up. It may therefore be of practical use to note the cases in which an advance is indicated.

We have to ask ourselves: when is a passed Pawn ready to march? We shall differentiate three cases.

(*a*) When the advance brings the passed Pawn nearer to its goal (which will only be when there is a weak blockade), or when the advanced passed Pawn gains in value in that he will then help to protect important points. (See my game against v. Gottschall, No. 13, where *27*. P—Q6 helped to protect the point K7, with the threat Kt or R—K7.) On the other hand it is wrong to push forward a Pawn if he can be hopelessly blockaded, and in his new position will only be protecting unimportant points. It is easy to bring a passed Pawn into the world, it is a much more difficult thing to provide for his future.

(*b*) When the advancing passed Pawn leaves the ground clear for a following piece, and in particular gives his own King the chance of advancing against a new enemy Pawn. See Diagram 60 (right). The game proceeds: *1*. P—B5, K—B2; *2*. K—K5, K—K2; *3*. P—B6 *ch*, K—B2; *4*. K—B5, K—B1. The KBP has no future to look forward to. *5*. K—Kt6 and wins the RP. Here the advance was made simply and solely to drive away the Black King, so that his own King might get near the RP.

(*c*) When the advance takes place with the intention of sacrificing the Pawn, so that the enemy King may be decisively drawn off from the field of battle. (See Diagr. 59.) Another example would be the following:—White: K, KKt3; Pawns, QR4, KR2. Black: K, KR4; P, QR4. Here White's KRP is to be offered as a sacrifice, is to die for King and country. It only remains to decide how and, especially, where. Since the effect of the sacrifice as a diversion varies directly as the distance between the bait to be sacrificed and the enemy King, it would not be advantageous to let the KRP advance, for this distance would become smaller. The right course is rather to play the King at once over to the other wing, thus *1*. K —B4, K—R5; *2*. K—K5, K—R6; *3*. K—Q6, etc. Wholly bad on the other hand would be *1*. P— R4 *? ?*. (Not content with sacrificing him, he actually serves him up on a platter! Which I should call exaggerated politeness.) After *1*. P—R4 *? ?*, there

DIAGRAM 60

Right: advance of the KBP to gain ground for the following King moves.
Left: an affair of tempi

would follow *1*. . . . K—Kt3; *2*. K—B4, K—R4; *3*. K—K5, K x P; *4*. K—Q5, K—Kt4; *5*. K—B4, K—B4; *6*. K—Kt5, K—K3; *7*. K x P, K— Q2; *8*. K—Kt6 (threatening K—Kt7), K—B1; *9*. K—R7, K—B2, shutting in the White King and drawing. After *1*. K—B4 *!*, K— R5; *2*. K—K5, K—R6; his Black Majesty may console himself with the fact that his walk from R4 to R6 has given him an appetite, so that the KRP becomes a pleasant meal after the fatigues of the tour, but this is all the consolation he will get. The student must take this to heart, that though the sacrifice to divert the enemy King is willingly made, it must occur under circumstances which will cause the maximum loss of time to the enemy.

It is not always so easy to recognize the motives of a Pawn advance. See Diagram 60 (left). Play proceeds: 1. P—B5, K— B2; 2. K—Q5, K—Q2; 3. P—B6 *ch*, K—B2; 4. K—B5, K—B1 (reserve-blockade); 5. K—Q6, K—Q1; 6. P—B7 *ch*, K—B1; 7. K—B6. The Pawn advance seems to be quite unmotived, neither cases *a, b,* nor *c,* above, seem to apply; but there follows 7. . . . . P— R4, for Black is now drawn into a *Zugzwang;* he must send forward his Pawn, and with this the curtain rises on an exciting drama. The Black P goes a double stage, he storms ahead full of energy and youthful arrogance; but we choose rather the quiet 8. P—R3 as an answer, in order to prove to our youthful opponent that repose is a very valuable trait. After 8. . . . . P— R5; 9. K—Q6 the game is decided. Suppose that our young friend the Black QRP, recalled and soundly scolded for his impetuosity, now goes the modest stage 7. . . . . P—R3. We then demonstrate to the luckless youth that energy is also a trump card, and we play 8. P—R4. Again after 8. . . . . P—R4; 9. K— Q6 Black is lost. The idea was the following: The stalemating of the Black King forces an advance of his QRP, and then White's QRP will time his advance to meet him so that after the RP's have run their course White has the move. The latter then plays K—Q6 or K—Kt6 and wins. This advance of the QBP may therefore be classified under (*a*). He has advanced on his own account, for the affair of the tempi between the QRP's makes of him a winning Pawn, who otherwise, remembering the backward position of the White King, could only have been considered as a drawing Pawn.

We close this chapter on the passed Pawn with some end

game studies, reminding the reader that the chapter is to be regarded as an introduction to position play.

§ 8. *End Games illustrating the passed Pawn.*

White (see Diagram 61) had the move and sacrificed the exchange. The whole idea of the combination, throughout its weary length (there's no other phrase to use), lay in the one thought; the King must strive to attain the "ideal" position, namely frontal attack on an isolated Pawn (see § 5). I succeeded in carrying out this hidden plan, although it could have been frustrated, because Rubinstein seemed to be handicapped by being not quite familiar with the postulates of my system, which were of course well known to me. I know no other ending in which this struggle of the King to reach the "ideal" posi-

DIAGRAM 61   **DIAGRAM 62**

Nimzovich—Rubinstein
Breslau 1925
The White King's struggle for a frontal attack on an isolated Pawn. Black missed a win at his 7th move

tion is more sharply brought out. The game proceeded:— *1.* **R—K6** *ch,* **K—Q4;** *2.* **R x B, P x R;** *3.* **P x P** (threatening *4.* **P—B4** *ch,* K x P; *5.* **P—Kt6,** etc.), **P—B5,** and now White took the KRP, although for it he had to give up his RP and QKtP. There followed *4.* B x P, R—KR1; *5.* B—Kt7, R x P; *6.* B x P, K—B4; *7.* K—Q2 *!*, the point; all that has happened so far has been simply and solely to one end, to prepare the road for the K to his KB4. (See Diagram 62.) *7. . . . .* K x P *?*, a mistake; Black could have here prevented the White King's contemplated journey by *7. . . . .* R—R3; *8.* B—Q4 *ch,* K x P; *9.* K—K3, R—K3 *ch; 10.* K—B4 *?,* R—K5 *ch,* followed by *. . . .* R x B and wins. The student should observe that *10.* K—B3 (instead of K—B4) would not have saved the game for White either, since Black would then have played at his leisure *. . . .* R—K5; after which the K would have marched to K8 followed by *. . . .* R—K7—Q7, etc.

In the game the continuation was *7. . . . .* K x P *?; 8.* K—K3, K—B4; *9.* K—B4 *!* Now all's right with the world again. *9. . . . .* K—Q4; *10.* P—B3, with a draw in a few moves; since the Black King and Rook cannot both be freed at the same time. If this were possible a double attack on the QBP with consequent sacrifice of the exchange would be feasible. An instructive end game. If you ask why the White King struggled so obstinately for this frontal attack, the answer is that such a struggle responds to an instinct which is innate in him; moreover it must be remembered that in his action he was also obeying the blockade law.

Our second example shows a simple case of a turning movement. (See Diagram 63.) Black played *1. . . . .* K—B2 (he must do something to meet the threat P—B3, which would yield a "remoter" passed Pawn), and the end game took the following very simple but effective course:—
2. P—B3 (if *2.* P—B4, K—Kt3; *3.* P x P, P x P; *4.* K—B2, K—R4 *!*; gaining a tempo), K—Kt3 *!*; *3.* P x P, K—Kt4; *4.* K—B3, K—R5; and the turning movement comes off to perfection despite the loss of a Pawn, a result of the paralysis of White's forces.

The third example illustrates the diversion which can be effected by a remoter passed Pawn. (See Diag. 64.) The score of

DIAGRAM 63

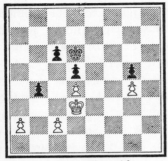

Hausen—Nimzovich
From a simultaneous display in
Randers, Denmark

DIAGRAM 64

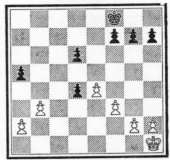

Tarrasch—Berger
Breslau, 1889
The ending is won for White

the game up to the exchange of Queens in the 36th move will be found in Game No. 6. There followed then, 37. K—Kt1, K—K2; 38. K—B2, P—Q4; 39. P—K5 (the simpler 39. P x P, K—Q3; 40. K—K2, K x P; 41. P—QR3, K—B4; 42. P—B4 with eventually the diversion P—Kt4 *ch*, would also have won easily), K—K3; 40. K—K2 (40. P—B4 would be weak because of 40. . . . . P—Kt4; 41. P—Kt3, P x P; 42. P x P, K—B4), K x P; 41. K—Q3, P—R4; 42. P—QR3 (P—KR4 first would be preferable), P—KR5 ! (creates a chance for himself later on); 43. P—QKt4, P x P; 44. P x P, K—Q3; 45. K x P, K—B3; 46. P—Kt5 *ch.* (White neglects the *Zugzwang* weapon which lies to his hand. 46. P—B4 would, after other Black moves had been exhausted, have resulted in an obliging Pawn move being made by Black, which would have furthered the subsequent excursion of the White King and the slaughtering of the Black Pawns), K x P; 47. K x P, K—Kt5 !. Now this diversion has less significance than might have been the case, since after the win of the KKtP and KRP Black will only need a few tempi for his KRP to get home. The ending is interesting because of the mistakes which were made. The position was in the end won by White after Black had overlooked a drawing chance.

DIAGRAM 65

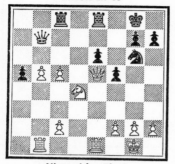

Nimzovich—Alapin
St. Petersburg 1913

The fourth example is significant as illustrating the method of advancing united passed Pawns. (See § 6.) The game proceeded (see Diagram 65) 1. P—B6 ! Here the choice of Pawn to be first advanced rests not on the consideration of greater or lesser danger of a blockade, but on the reason that otherwise the QBP would be lost. 1. . . . . Q—Kt3 (if 1. . . . . R x P; 2. P x R, Q x R; 3. R x Q, Kt x Q; then 4. P—B7 with "passed Pawn and 7th rank absolute," see I. iii. § 3; for instance 4. . . . . Kt—Q2; 5. Kt—B6 and wins); 2. Q—K3, now the problem is to drive away the blockader from QKt6 so that the QKtP who has lagged behind a little may catch up to his friend. (See § 6.) 2. . . . . P—B5 (Kt x BP was threatened); 3. Q—K4, QR—Q1; 4. Kt—B3, R—Q3; 5. P—KR4 ! (holding the center strongly with his Queen at K4. White intends now to prove that Black's defending pieces are somewhat in the air), Q—B4. The idea has worked, the blockader is getting more compliant. 6. Kt—K5 (good and fruitful of results would also have been 6. P—R5, Q x RP; 7. P—Kt6 and the two comrades are happily united again), 6. . . . . R—Q5 (the main variation would be 6. . . . . R—Q7; 7. Kt—Q3, Q x P(7); 8. P—Kt6 !, and heedless of the loss of a piece the Pawns would have marched to Queen); 7. Q—K2, Kt x P; 8. P—Kt6 (all according to book!), R—Kt5; 9. R x R, P x R; 10. P—Kt7, Q—B6; 11. Q—K4, Kt—B4; 12. Kt—Q7, Resigns.

The fifth example shows how impetuous a passed Pawn can become. We do not as a rule regard him as being temperamental, yet knowing his ambitious nature this example will hardly surprise us. (See Diagram 66.) There followed: 1. P—Kt4, B x

DIAGRAM 66

Nimzovich—Amateur
Nuremburg 1904
Odds of QKt. The triumph of the KP

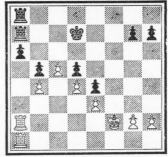

DIAGRAM 67

Nimzovich—A. Nilsson
Northern Masters'
Tournament 1924

KKtP; 2. P x P *ch*, K—B2. The King is here a bad, because a sensitive blockader. The danger of mate makes his blockading effect illusory. 3. B—Q5 *ch !* (in order to give the Rook an effective range, without loss of time; the latter will now support the
passed Pawn with all his might), P x B; 4. Q x R *ch*, K x Q; 5. P—
B7 *ch*, K—B1. The last attempt at a blockade. But now one of
our supports, the QB, comes to life (P—B7 had lengthened his
diagonal), and calls attention to himself in most unpleasant
fashion. 6. B—Kt7 *ch !*, K x B; 7. P—B8 (Q) *mate*. This end game
illustrates most pointedly the ambition of a passed Pawn.

The sixth example (Diagram 67) is characteristic of an elastic blockade, This end game was fully discussed in *Die Blockade,* so that we shall here only consider the more important
points. White intends operations in the KB file, which he could
start by K—Kt3, R—KB1. The breaking-through point, KB6,
he will open by P—R4—R5—R6, and for this reason the
White King's presence on the K side is required. In spite of the
fact that the KB file controls the whole game, White had the
courage to withstand the impulse to exploit it, and calmly
played 1. R—R5 *! !*, only taking up the fight in the KB file later.
The blockade by the R at R5 is here possible, because the

blockader is elastic, that is to say he can at any moment be brought over to the K side by forced marches.

The game proceeded as follows: *1*. . . . . K—B3; *2*. K—Kt3, K—Kt2; *3*. R—KB1, K—B3; *4*. R—B5, R—K2; *5*. P—R4, R(R)—R2; *6*. P—R5, R—K3; *7*. R—B8. The break through, and still the R stands at R5 keeping guard!—faithful, motionless. But the motionless watcher is prepared to intervene at any moment, whether by R—R2—KB2 (proving his elasticity), or by R x RP, if the Black Rook should move away. The possibility of R x RP, it may be noted, should be classed under the threats exercisable from the blockading point. There followed *7*. . . . . P—Kt3; *8*. P—R6, P—Kt4; *9*. R—QKt8, K—B2; *10*. R(8) x P, R x P; *11*. R—R4, R—KB3; *12*. R(Kt5)—R5, K—B1; *13*. K—Kt4, P—R3; *14*. R—R2, R(R) —KB2; *15*. R x P, and won after a further 7 moves.

With this example we have suddenly found ourselves among the blockaders. The reader is asked to loiter for a while in this mixed company and to turn to game Nos. 14 and 15. We know that a blockader ought: (a) to blockade, (b) to threaten, (c) to be elastic, and we shall in No. 14, be introduced to one who performs his manifold duties to perfection, while No. 15 provides an interesting counterpart to this game.

5. On Exchanging

A short chapter whose purpose is to make clear the possible motives for exchanging.

IN ORDER to show the student the danger lurking in indiscriminate bartering, we propose to enumerate the cases in which an exchange seems to be indicated. If an exchange does not come under one or other of these it is bad. With the master the process of exchange is almost automatic. He holds files or safeguards his command of a strategically important point, and the opportunity of exchanging drops like a ripe fruit into his lap. *Cf.* Game No. 11, note to the 35th move.

In Chapter 1 we analyzed the "exchange with consequent gain of tempo." Again we often exchange in order not to be forced to retire, or to make time-losing defensive moves (liquidation with subsequent development). Both cases are in the last resort to be regarded as tempo combinations, though in fact the question of tempo plays an essential part in every exchange. A salient instance is the exchange of a newly developed piece for one which has wasted several tempi. In the middle game the tempo motif finds expression when:

(1) We exchange in order to seize (or open) a file without loss of time. A very simple example. In the skeleton position:—
White: R, K1; B, K4. Black: K, KKt1; B, QKt6; Kt, QB3; Pawns, QKt2, KB2, KKt2, KR2. White wants to seize (or open) a file, in order to be able to give mate in the 8th rank. If to this end he play *1.* B—B3 or R—QR1, Black would have time to take steps against the mate, *e.g.,* . . . . K—B1 or . . . . P—KKt3. The right course is to exchange, *1.* B x Kt. Black has no time to protect the mate, for he must retake; and this "must" may also be taken in the psychological sense.

(2) We destroy a defender by exchanging. We destroy him, that is to say, because we look on him as a defender. In the previous chapters we have made the acquaintance of defending pieces whose functions varied: pieces which protect a Pawn obstructing the road in an open file; pieces which stand by to aid a blockader, and Pawns which help to protect an outpost, etc. The destruction of any one of these is in every single case worth striving for. But by a "defender" we mean something much wider. A stretch of territory can also be defended, as for instance entry to the 7th rank, or a possible enemy approach can be warded off; as in Game No. 14 where the Kt at K3 "protects" the points KKt4, KB5 against a possible .... Q—KKt5 or .... R—KB4. Further it is well known that a Kt at KB3 defends the whole castling wing (preventing, *e.g.*, Q—KR5). So, too, in the case of a centrally posted blockading piece, *e.g.*, in the position: White: Kt, Q4; Pawns, K3, KB3, KKt3, KR3. Black: B, K2; Pawns, Q4, KB2, KKt2, KR2, the attacking radius of the Kt protects and safeguards for White a wide terrain, so that this

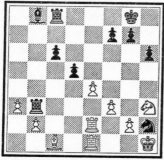

DIAGRAM 68

Series of Exchanges illustrating cases 1 and 2

Kt at Q4 is also to be considered a "defender" in our sense. The rule therefore runs:—Every defender in the narrower or wider sense of the word must be regarded as an object of our destructive wrath. In Diagram 68 where White wins by a series of exchanges, both kinds of motives are exemplified. A glance at the position reveals a Black Kt at KR7 who has more or less gone astray, and his defender the B at QKt1. We play *1.* P x P (opening a file without loss of tempo), P x P; *2.* R—K8 *ch* (the R at QB1 is a defender of the 8th row and must therefore die), R x R; *3.* R x R *ch,* K—R2; *4.* R x B (the arch defender is now fallen). *4.* . . . . R x R; *5.* K x Kt and wins.

(3) We exchange in order not to lose time by retreating. We are here as a rule concerned with a piece which is attacked. If we are faced with the choice whether to withdraw the piece with loss of tempo, or to exchange him for an enemy piece, we choose the latter alternative, especially if we can use to advantage the tempo we have saved ourselves by not withdrawing the piece. Th question of tempo must therefore be an actual one in some form or other. The simplest example would be: White: K, QKt1; R, QKt3; Kt, Q2; P, KB3. Black: K, KR1; B, KB3; Kt, QKt3; Pawns, QR2, QR4. *1.* Kt—K4, P—R5 (a counter attack); *2.* R x Kt (to save a tempo) P x R, *3.* Kt x B; and wins. If a major piece on each side be attacked we have a special variety of this third case and we call it:—

(*a*) "Selling one's life as dearly as possible." In the position: White: K, KR2; Q, QKt2; Pawns, QR2, K5, KR3. Black: K, QKt1; Q, Q3; Kt, QKt2; P, QR5; the second player plays *1.* . . . . P—R6. White is prepared to exchange Q against Q; but if his Q is really condemned to death, the wish to sell her life as dearly as possible is surely very intelligible. Like the soldier who is hemmed in on all sides, is ready to die, but carries on till his last cartridge is gone, wanting to account for as many enemies as possible, to sell his life dearly, in fact; so White plays *2.* Q x Kt *ch !*, in order to get at any rate something for the Queen. For some extraordinary reason such a commercial investment of the Q is less intelligible to the beginner than a thoroughgoing heroic sacrifice. The latter is of common occurrence with him (though perhaps not the sacrifice of the Queen, since for her he has the most abject respect), whereas the former is quite foreign to him. Yet it is really no sacrifice, or at worst only a temporary one, and possibly it is in this amalgamation of sacrifice and sober conservation of material that the psychological difficulty lies, to which the beginner succumbs.

(4) When and how exchanges usually take place.

Lack of space forbids a detailed discussion of this question, and we will only quite briefly point out that (*a*) Simplification is desirable if we have superiority in material. Whence it follows that exchanging can be used as a weapon to force the opponent from strong positions.

(*b*) When two parties desire the same thing a conflict arises. In chess this conflict takes the form of a battle of exchanges. For instance: White: Kt, K4; Pawns, KB3, KKt2, KR2; supported by BQB2, and RK1, and several other pieces. Black: Pawns, K4, KKt2, KR2; Kt, KB3; B, KKt3; RK1; etc. The key point is White's K4. White protects and overprotects the point with every means in his power. Black seeks to clear it, since a White piece on the latter's K4 is an annoyance to him on account of its attacking radius. And in the end it comes to a great slaughter at this point (White's K4).

(*c*) If we are strong in a file, a simple advance in that file is sufficient to bring about an exchange, for our opponent cannot suffer an invasion of his position, and at worst must seek to weaken it by exchanges.

(*d*) There is a tendency for weak points, or weak Pawns to be exchanged, the one for the other (=exchange of prisoners).

DIAGRAM 69   DIAGRAM 70

Dr. Bernstein—Perlis   Rosselli—Rubinstein
1909   1925

The following end game illustrates this. (See Diagram 69.) The game proceeded:—*31*. . . . . R—R1; *32*. R—Kt3, R x P; *33*. R x P. The weak Pawns at QR2 and QKt5 respectively have been reciprocally exchanged and have disappeared, and the same happens to the Pawns Q5 and QKt2. *33*. . . . . R—R4; *34*. R x P, R x P; *35*. R—Kt8 *ch !* The simple exploitation of the QKt file leads to the desired exchanges. *35*. . . . . Q x R; *36*. Q x R *ch*, K—R1. As Dr. Lasker rightly pointed out, it would have been better to maneuver the K to KB3. *37*. P—Kt3, and Bernstein won a brilliantly conducted end game by means of his QKtP.

We close this chapter with two end games. Diagram 70 shows the position in a game between Rosselli (White) and Rubinstein after White's 21st move. There followed:— *21*. . . . . R x R, else White would have doubled his Rooks; moreover Black had really no other sensible move. *22*. B x R, Kt—K1; *23*. R—K2, Kt—Kt2; *24*. B—Q2, Kt—B4 *!*; *25*. R—K1, P—B4; *26*. P x P, B x BP. Now White's Q4 has become the center of interest, and a battle will take place round it. *27*. K—B1, P—R5; *28*. P x P, P—Kt5; *29*. Kt—Q4 *!*, B x Kt; *30*. P x B. (See the last note.) *30*. . . . . R x P; *31*. B—B3, R—R8 *ch*; *32*. K—K2, R—R7; *33*. R—KKt1, Kt—R5; *34*. P—KKt3, Kt—B4; *35*. P—Kt3, K—K3; *36*. B—Kt2, P—R3; *37*. B—B3, Kt—Q3; *38*. K—K3, Kt—K5; *39*.

B—K1. After some fruitless attempts by Rubinstein in the QB file the following position was reached after White's 55th move; White: K, Q3; R, KB1; B, QR5; Pawns, QR4, QKt3, Q4, KB2, KKt3. Black: K, KKt3; R, K2; Kt, K5; Pawns, QR3, QKt4, Q4, KB4, KKt5; and the decisive break-through took place with *55*. . . . . P—B5 *!*; *56*. P x P, R—KR2; *57*. B—Q2, Kt x B *!* (kills the

DIAGRAM 71

Nimzovich—Druwa
Riga 1919

defender of White's KB2 and KB4); 58. K x Kt, R—R6; 59. P—B3, P x P; 60. R—B2, K—B4; 61. K—K3, K—Kt5; 62. P—Kt4 (If 62. P—B5, then 62. . . . . K x P; 63. R x P *ch*, R x R; 64. K x R, P x P; 65. P x P, P—R4; and a successful turning movement against White's K will follow), R—R8; 63. P—B5, R—K8 *ch*; 64. K—Q3, R—K5 and White resigned.

After this classic ending from a tournament game let us give one from a game at odds played in a coffee house, in which the exchange motif took an original shape. (See Diagram 71.) White, who had given the trivial odds of Q for a Kt, "risked" the break-through 1. P—Q5. There followed 1. . . . . P x P (safer . . . Kt x QP); 2. P—K6, P x P (he should have castled); 3. Kt—K5 (here we have the typical advance at the cost of self destruction; the Kt is the "awakened rear-rank man"), Kt x P; 4. B—R5 *ch*, K—K2; 5. Kt x B *ch !*, a surprise, who would ever expect an exchange in the midst of a pursuit of the enemy?! 5. . . . . P x Kt; 6. R—B7 *ch*, K—Q3; 7. Kt x Kt *ch*, P x Kt; 8. R—Q1 *ch*. Now the meaning is clear: the B at B3 was a defender, because of the possibility of . . . . B—Q4 at this point. 8. . . . . K—K4; 9. B—B4 *ch*, K—K5; 10. B—B3 *mate !*

6. The Elements of End Game Strategy

Some General Introductory Remarks

I T I S a well known phenomenon that the same amateur who can conduct the middle game quite creditably, is usually perfectly helpless in the end game. One of the principal requisites of good chess is the ability to treat both middle and end game equally well. True, it lies in the nature of things that the student should gather his first experience in the opening and middle game, but this evil, for such it is, must be rectified as early as possible. It should be pointed out to the beginner at the very start, that the end game does not merely serve up tasteless fragments left over from the rich feast of the middle game. The end game is on the contrary that part of the game in which the advantages created in the middle game should be systematically realized. Now this realization of advantages, particularly those of an immaterial kind, is by no means a subordinate business. Very much the reverse; all the player's qualities as man and as artist are demanded for it. In order to know, and to be able to appreciate, what is happening in the end game, one must be acquainted with the elements out of which it is compounded, for the end game has its elements just as much as has the middle game. One of these elements, the passed Pawn, we have already analyzed thoroughly; there remain to be considered:—
(1) Centralization; with a sub-section on the management of the King, *i.e.*, the "shelter" and "bridge-building." (2) The aggressive Rook position and the active officer in general. (3) The rallying of all isolated detachments. (4) The combined advance, and finally (5) An element already touched upon, the materialization of files; to be understood in the sense that the file, which at first exercised an abstract influence, is narrowed

down to a concrete point (protected by a Pawn), or gains a concrete aspect. The end game would, in fact, be in itself most interesting, even had Rinck and Troitzky never lived.

§ 1. *Centralization.* (*a*) *Of the King,* (*b*) *of the minor pieces,* (*c*) *of the Queen. The journey to the King's castle.*

(a) The great mobility of the King forms one of the chief characteristics of all end game strategy. In the middle game the King is a mere "super," in the end game on the other hand— one of the "principals." We must therefore develop him, bring him nearer to the fighting line. This is brought about by centralizing the King. Accordingly the rule runs:—When the end game is entered let the King set himself in motion, and strive to reach the center of the board, for from this point he can, according to need, make for the right or left, *i.e.*, attack the enemy King, or Queen's wing.

First Example: White: K, KKt1, Black: R, K1 (only the most important actors are indicated) 1. K—B2, pushing towards the center and at the same time protecting his base (the points K1, K2) against the entry of the enemy Rook by . . . . R—K7 or . . . . K8.

Second Example: White: K, KKt1; R, Q2; Pawns, QKt2, KB4, KKt3, KR2. Black: K, KKt1; R, QKt6; Pawns, QKt2, KKt2, KR2. Here, too, the first moves are K—B2—K2, and in this position White chooses the Q side and plays K—Q1—B2, thus protecting the QKtP and releasing the R; who can now undertake something, say by R—Q7.

Third Example: In Diagram 72, White played 33. Kt—B3, since the immediate centralization of the King would have miscarried because of . . . . B—Q4. For instance 33. K—B1, B— B5 *ch;* 34. K—K1, B—Q4, and forces the exchange of pieces or the win of a Pawn. After 33. . . . . B—B5; 34. P—B4, K—K2; 35. K—B2, K—Q3; 36. K—K3, K—B4; the proper moment for

White to get in touch with the point Q4 was passed. If the Kings had been at Q4, Q3 respectively, the win would have been much harder; the game, however, now plays itself. 37. P—Kt4, K—Kt5. This is the point; the central position QB4 is to be regarded as a stepping stone to an attack on the wing, and therein lies the significance of centralization. 38. K—Q4—too late. 38.

DIAGRAM 72

Rubinstein—Nimzovich
Carlsbad 1907

The struggle of the Kings for the center square

. . . . B—Kt6; 39. P—Kt5, P—R5; 40. Kt—Kt1, B—K3; 41. P—Kt3, K—Kt6; 42. Kt—B3, P—R6; 43. K—Q3, P—Kt3; 44. K—Q4, K—B7 !; 45. Resigns. In this example we have been able to look at this advance to the center from another side; and we have seen that it is meant not only to give our own King freedom to move about, but also to restrict the terrain accessible to the enemy King. For this reason the King often fights for a point, as if a kingdom depended on it. The student should bear this carefully in mind, that he must leave no means untried to bring his King as near the center as possible, partly for his own King's sake, but partly also in order to limit the scope of the enemy King, who must not be allowed a place in the sun.

(b) Centralization must not be regarded as a purely royal prerogative. The other pieces also develop a similar tendency. Take the position: White: K, K1; Kt, QKt3; Pawns, QR5, K2, KB2, KKt3, KR2. Black: K, KB1; B, KKt3; Pawns, QR3, Q3, KB2, KKt2, KR2. Here White has two choices: K—Q2—B3—Q4, and Kt—Q4 followed by P—K3. As in the previous example, the centralization of the Kt has here a double effect; (1) He keeps, from Q4, an eye on both wings. (2) He circumscribes the liberty of the enemy King, bars, for instance, his journey via K3 to Q4. If the enemy Rook be still on the board he will provide a rampart for his own King, who will take up a central position behind the Knight. Dr. Tartakover, the witty author of *Die hypermoderne Schachpartie,* would call this an island of pieces; and a very simple example is one which would result from the position White: K, K2; Kt, QB2; Pawns, K3, KB2, KKt2, KR3. Black: K, KB1; R, Q1; Pawns, KB2, KKt2, KR2, namely by *1.* Kt—Q4, followed by K—Q3 with the central island K, Kt, P.

(c) There is no more impressive proof of the importance of centralization than the fact that even the Q, who in truth exerts sufficient influence even if posted on the edge of the board, herself seeks to attain to a central position. The ideal one would be a centrally placed Q defended by a P, and in her turn defending other Pawns. Under such a protectorate her King can undertake long journeys into enemy country. So for example the King at KB3 in Diagram 73 will try to get to QKt6 or KKt6. After many and long wanderings he arrives at length on one of these squares, reaches safety, and wins. (*Cf.* Diagram 86.)

§ 1a. *How his Majesty manages to protect himself against storms. The shelter. Bridge building.*

In order to have protection from the various dangers which may threaten, let the King provide himself in good time with a serviceable shelter. Such a refuge will stand him in good stead should a storm come up. Consider the position in Diag. 74. Here *1.* P—R7 would be an obvious mistake; for after *1.* . . . . R—R7; *2.* K—Kt6 (to free the Rook), the White King would have no protection against the storm, here the series of checks by the Rook, to which he is exposed. The right course would be to consider the point QR7 as a shelter for the K, thus:

DIAGRAM 73

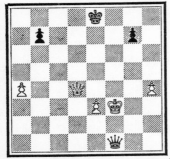

The centrally placed Q, protected and protecting, allows the White K to journey into enemy country. His goal will be QKt6 or KKt6 with a frontal attack on an isolated Pawn

DIAGRAM 74

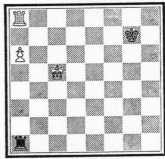

The shelter
A shelter is reserved for White's King at QR7. *1. P—R7 ?* would destroy the shelter, allowing Black to draw

1. K—Kt6, R—Kt8 *ch; 2.* K—R7, R—Kt7; *3.* R—Kt8, R—QR7; *4.* R—Kt6, R—R8; *5.* K—Kt7. The sun is shining again now, so the old King can venture out. *5. . . . .* R—R8; *6.* P—R7 and wins.

Events would take a similar course in the position, White: K, K5; R, KKt1; P, Q5. Black: K, Q1; R, QR7. Here the point Q6 would be the shelter, so this must not be made impracticable by P—Q6. The right move is *1.* K—K6, and if *1. . . . .* R—K7 *ch;* then *2.* K—Q6 and Black has exhausted his checks, and is himself in danger since his King will be forced away from the queening square.

End game technique demands of us in addition that we should be able ourselves to build our own shelter, somewhat as the "pathfinder" builds his tent. In this, bridge-building is useful. (See Diagram 75.) If White plays K—B7, there will follow a series of checks, and in the end the White K will have to return whence he came, his purpose unaccomplished. The key move is *1.* R—K4 *!,* one which at first sight is somewhat incomprehensible. There follows *1. . . . .* R—KKt8, and now the King

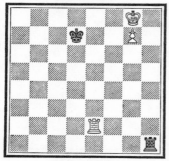

DIAGRAM 75

Bridge building

may venture forth into the light of day again. *2.* K—B7, R—B8 *ch; 3.* K—Kt6, R—Kt8 *ch; 4.* K—B6 *!,* R —B8 *ch; 5.* K—Kt5 *!,* R—Kt8 *ch; 6.* R—Kt4 *!.* The bridge is built; the point KKt5 has become a perfect shelter. After *4.* K—B6 *!,* Black could also have marked time: *4. . . . .* R—Kt7 (instead of . . . . R—B8 *ch*), and then there follows a delicious operation, which every bridge-builder must envy. We transport in fact the whole bridge, with all that pertains to it, from one place to another; and move *5.* R—K5 *! !* and set up the bridge by means of R—KKt5; so that our shelter will now be at KKt6. This charming device belongs to the commonest of every day maneuvers, a proof of the wonderful beauty of chess.

It will be interesting to see whether *1.* R—K5 at once might not serve. This as a matter of fact is the case, *1.* R—K5 also wins; though indeed less convincingly than the "author's solution," *1.* R—K4. After *1.* R—K5 there would follow *1. . . . . .* K— Q3; *2.* K—B7, R—B8 *ch; 3.* K—K8 (not K—Kt6 because of *3. . . . .* K x R; *4.* P—Kt8(Q), R—Kt8 *ch* etc.), R—KKt8; *4.* R—K7, R—QR8; *5.* R—Q7 *ch,* and wins; or *4. . . . . .* R—Kt7 (instead of . . . . R—QR8); *5.* K—B8, R—Kt8; *6.* R—KB7 etc. Bridge-building for the provision of a shelter for the royal traveler is a typical constituent in end game strategy, and is very closely connected with the maneuver which will be treated in § 3. For another example of bridge building see game No. 10, where *38.* ʹϗt—KB5 creates a shelter for the White King at KB3.

§ 2. *The aggressive Rook position as a characteristic advantage in the end game. Examples and argument. The active officer in general. Dr. Tarrasch's formula.*

The advantage of an aggressive Rook position in the end game is a most important one. See Diagram 76 (left). In this

DIAGRAM 76

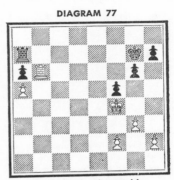

DIAGRAM 77

The White Rook has the aggressive, the Black Rook the passive position

position, assuming that both players still have Pawns remaining on the King's wing, the position of the White R can be made the basis of an advance on the King-side. Still more is this the case in the configuration shown on Diagram 77. White can by means of *1.* P—R4 followed when convenient by P—R5 and P x P lay bare Black's KtP to attacks. And whereas the White R is the very soul of this new operation, the Black R cannot muster up sufficient elasticity to get over to the King-side to oppose a defense against the former's attack. And so we formulate the matter thus:— The weakness of the defending Rook lies in its deficient elasticity in the direction of the other wing, and, further, in this too, that the enemy King wins greater maneuvering freedom (as a rule he is afraid of Rooks, but when the cat's away, etc.!). In Diagram 77, therefore, the threat of the White King's march to QKt6 (naturally by slow stages) is on no account to be underestimated.

It is of daily occurrence in games between masters that one

of the parties will undertake extended maneuvers and go to im-
mense trouble, simply in order, as a reward for all his pains, to
get for himself the aggressive Rook position; that is to say to
force a passive rôle on the enemy

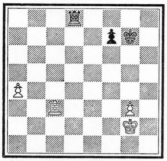

DIAGRAM 78

White to play should make the aggressive Rook move. Black with the
move should find the most enterprising rook position

Rook. On the other hand we
must expect the passive Rook
sometimes to go on strike; as
happens in the following example. White: K, KKt1; R, QB5;
Pawns, QR4, KKt2, KR2. Black:
K, KKt1; R, QKt2; Pawns, QR4,
KKt2, KR2. Black with the move
begs to be excused from the passive rôle intended for his Rook
(*1. . . . . R—R2*) and plays *1.
. . . . R—Kt7 !*; *2. R x P, R—R7.*
The Black Rook is now very mo-

bile and the draw ought to be assured, whereas *1. . . . . R—
R2* would probably have lost. We may then say, that if faced
with the choice of protecting a Pawn with a Rook and of thus
condemning him to a passive, indeed meditative existence, or
of sacrificing the Pawn without further to-do, in order to em-
ploy the Rook in some active capacity, we should decide on the
latter alternative.

When is a Rook's position, taken in regard to his own or an
enemy passed Pawn, to be considered as aggressive?

This question has already been answered by Dr. Tarrasch,
whose excellent formula runs:—The Rook's proper place is behind the passed Pawn, whether it be his own or an enemy one.
(See Diagram 78.) White with the move plays *1. R—R3* taking
up his position behind the passed Pawn. The Rook's influence
is enormous for he breathes into the passed Pawn some of his
own life. On the other hand, if it were Black's move, he must

not post his Rook in front of the Pawn, not *1. . . . . R—QR1 ?;* 2. R—R3 and White wins, but on the contrary behind it, and this he can do by *1. . . . . R—Q7 ch; 2. K—B3, R—QR7.* The Rook position thus gained is aggressive (1) with regard to the White KKtP, who, if opportunity serves, may be gobbled up; (2) having regard to a possible journey of the White King. For instance, should the latter reach his QR6 Black can shut him in by . . . . R—QKt7, or should he venture to QKt8 or QB8, subject him to a series of checks from behind.

It is not only in the case of Rooks but also in that of minor pieces that the difference in value between an attacking or defending piece weighs heavily in the balance. The weakness of a defending Kt lies in the fact that he is uni-operative, he cannot move about and still keep up the defense of the point under his charge. This characteristic favors the *Zugzwang.* In Diagram 79 Black with the move will suc-

DIAGRAM 79

The weakness of the Kt as a defender often leads to *Zugzwang*

cumb under *Zugzwang.* White with the move, on the other hand, suffers only in appearance from a similar disease, for the agile White Kt can develop all manner of threats. White plays *1. Kt—K3* (or *1. K—Q5* with the threat Kt—K5) and the *Zugzwang* weapon is again at Black's throat. If the whole position were moved back one row (White: K, K4, etc., Black: K, K3, etc.) White would still win.

In a defending Bishop, one characteristic stands out, that in the capacity to change front quickly he cannot compete with his attacking colleague. This is brought out in the delightful winning attack in the position on Diagram 80.

The Black B is here defending, and the White B threatens to get to QKt8 via KR4, KB2, and QR7. It looks indeed as if this threat can be comfortably parried by a timely . . . . K—R3. Thus: *1.* B—R4, K—Kt4 *!*; *2.* B—B2, K—R3 *!*; and if now B—R4 with the threat B—Q8—B7, the Black K can get back to B3 in

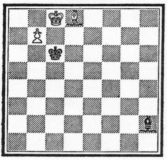

DIAGRAM 80

plenty of time. White, however, plays *3.* B—B5 *!* (in order to cause the Black B to make a move, and at the same time to prevent . . . . B—Q3), B—Kt6. Now White's B goes back to get within range of QB7, thus *4.* B—K7, K—Kt3 *!*; *5.* B—Q8 *ch*, K—B3; *6.* B—R4 *!*, and Black will no longer have time for the resource . . . . K—Kt4 —R3 which he used before, for White has managed to gain

a move; so *6.* . . . . B—R7; *7.* B—B2, and White wins by B—R7—Kt8, *e.g.*, *7.* . . . . B—B5; *8.* B—R7, B—R7; *9.* B—Kt8, B—Kt8; *10.* B—B4, B—R2; *11.* B—K3. A lovely ending.

§ 3. *The rallying of isolated detachments and the general advance.*

Since these two maneuvers are very closely connected, so that the one often merges insensibly into the other, they will here be considered together. To bring single scattered detachments into contact with one another cannot be difficult; one has only to know the bearing one piece has on the other. We know several things; for instance that a Kt is able cunningly to construct a shelter for the King by building a bridge; we know, too, that this officer does not despise the hospitality of a private soldier (Kt protected by a P), and in gratitude is ready to draw his sword if it comes to defending his humble friend from one of his own class, or to an onslaught on an enemy Pawn. See in this connection the White Kt at KB5 in game No. 10 (38th move). We know further that a King stops the holes made by the advance of his own Pawns. And we must not forget that a centrally posted Q can gather far off Pawns into her net. (See Diagram 73.) The contact between the White pieces in the position K, KB3; R, KB4; Pawns, KKt3, QR4 would be by no means bad.

Again the advance must be a collective one. For a passed Pawn suddenly to run wild and rush away from his protectors and friends, as happened say in Diagram 57, is an absolute exception to the rule, which may be stated thus:—The advancing Pawn must stay in close contact with his own people. The place vacated by the advance of a Pawn must be as quickly as possible taken by a "hole stopper." Thus the square K4 left vacant by P—K5 should speedily be occupied by, say, Kt—K4 or K—K4. Instances could be multiplied.

It happens sometimes that an enemy Rook by annoying checks seeks to disturb a combined play, in which case he must be reduced to impotence or driven home (see the game Post—Alekhine Diagram 85, p. 105).

Combined play forms 80 per cent of the whole of end game technique; and the details which we have treated, such as centralization, bridge-building, the shelter, hole-stopping, are all subordinate to one end, combined play. Like a ratchet wheel in a piece of clock work, they see to it that the mechanism gets into motion, they intend to insure a slow but safe forward movement of the serried ranks of the army. A general advance is the order of the day.

The student should note that a "centralization" is possible even on a remote flank. The pieces simply have to group themselves round a Pawn as center, and there can be no question but that "centralization" is effectively carried out. See again the game Post—Alekhine, Diagram 85.

§ 4. *"Materialization" of the abstract conception of file or rank. An important difference between operations in a file in the middle and end game.*

A curious and by no means obvious difference must now be noted. In the middle game the exploitation of a file involves the expenditure of a great deal of energy, in other words is wholly active. We have only to remember the complicated apparatus used: for instance, in particular, the outpost Knight. In the end game, on the other hand, such operations run on simple lines, are in fact of the meditative order. Far and near not a trace of a Kt outpost. The lucky possessor of the file takes his time. At the most he sends forward a handful of men to clean up some position for his advancing Rook. And so we can say that operations in a file are in the middle game active, in the end game meditative, contemplative if you will. And the same applies to a rank. We will illustrate this by some examples. (See Diag. 81.) White holds the clear 5th rank, and by the following sim-

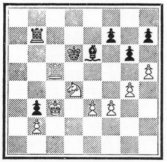

DIAGRAM 81

Nimzovich—Jacobsen
1923
"Materialization" of the 5th rank

DIAGRAM 82

Capablanca—Martínez
Argentina 1914
"Materialization" of the KB file

ple series of moves manages to materialize the rather abstract effect of his possession of this rank, that is to say to condense it to a concrete point. The game proceeded: *42.* R—B6 *ch,* K—Q2;

43. P x P *!*, RP x P; 44. Kt x B *!*, P x Kt; 45. R—B5 followed by R—KKt5 and P—B4. The occupation of the point KKt5 is decisive, the more so since the passive Black Rook will be forced by sympathy to the move . . . . R—Kt2.

Another example is furnished by my end game against Alan Nilsson. (See Diagram 67.) Here scarcely a thing took place, at most the White KRP made a gesture of wishing to advance, and yet the White R succeeded in penetrating to the 8th rank.

The course of the game in the following position is also typical. White: K, KKt5; R, QB1; Pawns, QR2, QKt2, Q4, KB4. Black: K, KKt2; R, Q2; Pawns, QR2, QKt2, KB4, KKt3. White calmly goes for a "walk"; P—Kt4, P—R4, P—Kt5, P—R5, P—Kt6, and finally R—B7. If this threat be parried by . . . . P—Kt3, then the move R—B6 is made possible. So, too, reverting to Diagram 77, after the advance of the KRP etc., the 6th rank was condensed into the concrete point KKt6.

In the position shown on Diagram 82 in which White commands the KB file, and Black tries to defend his 1st and 2nd ranks, Capablanca won almost automatically by the mere deadweight of the file. 27. QR—KB1, KR—K1; 28. P—K4, Q—Kt4; 29.

R—R1 *!* White takes his time, the KB file must in the end crush the opposition by its own weight. 29. . . . . Q—Q2; 30. P—B4, R—B2; 31. R x R, Q x R; 32. R—KB1, Q—Kt2; 33. R—B5, R—KB1; 34. Q—Kt5 *!* winning a Pawn. 34. . . . . Q—R1; 35. Q x RP, Q x Q; 36. R x Q, R—B6; 37. K—Kt2, R x P; 38. R—B5, and Black resigned since the KRP could not be stopped. For example, 38. . . . . R—Kt7 *ch;* 39. R—B2, etc.

The moral application of this

DIAGRAM 83

Nimzovich—Spielmann
San Sebastian 1911
White maintains the initiative

for the student may be thus formulated. If in the end game a file is in your permanent possession, do not worry about an eventual breaking through point, this will come of itself, almost without any assistance on your part.

We will now give a few end games exemplifying the four elements of end game strategy.

First Example. Diagram 83. With *20*. B—B5 *!*, Kt x Kt; *21*. B x B, R x B; *22*. P x Kt, O—O; *23*. P x P, P x P; *24*. Q x P *ch*, Q—B2; *25*. Q x Q *ch*, R x Q; *26*. B x P, White passed into the end game, for which he has to the good a temporary Pawn majority, and more particularly a Bishop permanently posted in the center. There followed *26*. . . . . R—KB4; *27*. P—B4, R x RP; *28*. QR—Kt1, B—K2. Spielmann defends himself with his customary ingenuity. *29*. K—B2 (progressive centralization), P—Kt3; *30*. K—B3, R—R3; *31*. KR—Q1, R—B5; *32*. R—Q7, K—B2; *33*. P—R5, P—Kt4; *34*. R—K1, R(B5)—B3; *35*. B—Q4, R(R3)—K3; *36*. R—KR1, P—R3; *37*. R—Kt7, R(K3)—Q3; *38*. B—K5, R—K3; *39*. K—K4. After the preparatory Rook maneuvers (notice that the R at Kt7 is in close contact with the protected point QKt6, and that the 7th rank is to be materialized) the Black Rooks prove themselves to be "passive" enough actually to invite a further advance of the White King. B, K, and P now form a central island; the B is the bridge builder, the point K4 is our shelter. *39*. . . . . R—B5 *ch*; *40*. K—B5, R—B4; *41*. R—Q1, P—Kt5; *42*. R—Q8, R x P; *43*. R—B8 *ch !*, K x R; *44*. K x R, *Resigns*.

The second Example again shows a centralizing maneuver (Diag. 84). In his difficult situation Black tried *20*. . . . . K—B2; there followed *21*. R—K1 *?* (the right move was *21*. P—KKt4), K—K2; *22*. B—B3, Kt—Q4, and

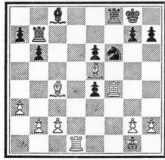

after the further moves 23. R x R, K x R; 24. B—K5, the second
player had overcome the worst of his difficulties. 24. . . . . P—
QKt4; 25. B—Kt3, Kt—B3; 26. K—B1, K—K2. And now Sir George
could not resist any longer the temptation to win back the
Pawn and played 27. B x Kt *ch*, P x B; 28. R x P. Further since
after 28. . . . . P—K4 he exposed his R, by 29. R—KR4, Black
got the upper hand, and by forceful centralization won as follows: 29. . . . . B—B4; 30. K—K2, B—Kt3; 31. B—Q5, R—Kt1;
32. P—B3, P—B4; 33. B—Kt3, K—B3 (observe the collective advance of Black's central forces); 34. B—B2, P—QR4 !; played
because White's majority on this side is really a minority, or if
you will a majority forsaken by all its patron saints (K and R).
35. R—R3, P—K5; 36. R—R4, P—Kt5; 37. RP x P, P x P; 38. R—B4,
K—K4 (stops the hole); 39. R—B1, P—Kt6; 40. B—Q1, P—B5;
41. K—K1, B—B2; 42. P—Kt3, P—B6. White is all sewn up. There
followed the sacrifice 43. B x BP, P x B; 44. R x P, and after a
stubborn fight Black won through his superiority in material.

The third Example. An ending rich in combinations. The
gifted, imaginative Franco-Russian seems in this game to wish
to sweep away the rules of my system with the hurricane of
his seething inspiration. This, however, is only apparently the

case; in reality everything is
done in the spirit of the system
and of centralization. (See Diagram 85.) 40. . . . . P—Kt5 *ch*;
the "candidate" (P, KB4) stays
behind, but we are here concerned with a sacrificial combination. 41. K—Kt2 (41. K—B4 ?,
K—B3 with mating threats), K
—B2; 42. Kt x P, R—K8; 43. P—
KR4, K—Kt3 !; 44. Kt—Kt4, P—B5 !
(this is the winning idea); 45.
P x P, R—Kt8 *ch*; 46. K—R2, P—

DIAGRAM 85

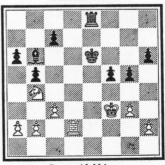

Post—Alekhine
Mannheim 1914
A combinative ending

Kt6 *ch; 47.* K—R3, B—B7. Now P, B, and R are united into one whole, but this whole has, at any rate for the moment, small possibility of expansion. *48.* K—Kt4 (the threat was . . . . R—R8 *ch;* K—Kt4, R x P *ch !*), R—KR8; *49.* P—B5 *ch,* K—B3; *50.* Kt—Q5 *ch,* K—K4; *51.* K—B3, K x P; *52.* Kt x P, R x P; *53.* Kt x P. Black has given up his whole Q side. With what justification? Well, because with the fall of White's KRP the capacity for expansion which was somewhat lacking before (see note to the 47th move) is now present in rich measure: the two united passed Pawns, with the King there to stop the holes, demolish all resistance. *53.* . . . . R—B5 *ch; 54.* K—Kt2, P—R4 *!; 55.* R—Q8, P—R5 *!; 56.* R—B8 *ch* (the R wants to stop the combined attack), K—Kt4; *57.* R—Kt8 *ch* (*57.* R x R P, K x R followed by . . . . K—Kt5), K—R4; *58.* R—R8 *ch,* K—Kt3; *59.* R—K8 (in order after . . . . B—B4 to safeguard his base which would be threatened by . . . . R—B7 *ch*), B—B4; *60.* R—K2, K—B4 (the hole-stopper draws near!); *61.* P—Kt4, B—Kt3; *62.* K—R3, R—B7; *63.* Kt—Q6 *ch,* K—B5; *64.* R—K4 *ch,* K—B6; *65.* K x P, B—Q1 *ch ! !; 66.* K—R5, R—R7 *ch; 67.* K—Kt6. The White pieces are all "away," the house stands deserted and desolate. *67.* . . . . P—Kt7; *68. Resigns.*

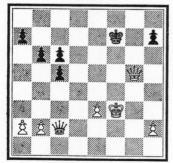

DIAGRAM 86

E. Cohn—Nimzovich
Munich 1906
Black's King will reach Q6

As the fourth Example let us follow a King in his wanderings, which interests us inasmuch as they take place under the watchful eye of a centrally placed Queen. (See Diagram 86.) The game proceeded:—*39.* Q—K5, Q—Q8 *ch; 40.* K—B2, Q—Q4. The fight for the mid-point of the board. *41.* Q—B4 *ch,* K—Kt3 ! Beginning of the wandering, ... Q—B4 is now threatened. *42.* K—K1, Q—B4 *!; 43.* Q

—Kt3 *ch*, K—R4; *44.* Q—Kt7, Q—K5 *!* The Black King is preparing to go either to KR7 or K5. (*Cf.* Diag. 73.) *45.* Q—B7 *ch*, K—Kt5; *46.* Q—Kt7 *ch* (or *46.* Q—Q7 *ch*, K—R5 *!*), Q—Kt3; *47.* Q—Q7 *ch*, K—B6; *48.* Q—R3 *ch*, K—K5 *!* Our ideal frontal position. *49.* K—K2, K—K4 *!* After the K has gone to great pains and trouble to get to the point K5, he retires with the threat . . . . Q—B7 *ch*. This is the point of the maneuver; namely to get time for the move . . . . P—B5, which forces the White Q perpetually to protect the point Q3. How the Black King, in order to be free of checks, now flees to his K2, and the Q side pawns carry out their irresistible advance, is as interesting as it is instructive. *50.* K—Q2, P—B5; *51.* Q—B1, Q—K5; *52.* Q—K2, K—Q3; *53.* Q—B1, K—K2 *!*; *54.* Q—K2, P—Kt4; *55.* Q—B1, P—QR4; *56.* Q—KKt1, Q—K4; *57.* K—B2, P—Kt5; *58.* Q—B2, Q—K5 *ch*; *59.* K—B1, P—R5; *60.* Q—Kt3, P—Kt6; *61.* P x P, BP x P; *62.* Q—B7 *ch*, K—K3; *63.* Q—B8 *ch*, K—Q4; *64.* Q—Q7 *ch*, K—B5; *65.* Q—B7 *ch*, K—Q6; *66. Resigns.*

7. The Pin

§ 1. *Introductory and General. Tactics or Strategy. On the possibility of reintroducing a pinning motif which has had to be abandoned.*

A F T E R the difficult sixth chapter, difficult at any rate in the positional sense, the present one may appear very easy. And the question may perhaps be asked, whether the pinned piece can really be spoken of as an element in our sense, since a game may be laid out on the basis of an open file or a passed Pawn, but surely never of a pin! This point of view we cannot share. True, pins as a rule occur in purely tactical moments as, for instance, in the pursuit of the fleeing enemy; on the other hand, however, a pin foreseen in the planning of a game may quite logically influence its whole course. In connection with this possibility Game No. 5, v. Haken—Giese* is of special interest. The move 25. . . . . B—KKt3 signifies a resuscitation of the pin motif which had been dead since the 7th move, for now there is threatened an advance, when occasion serves, against the objective, White's P at KR3, by . . . . P—KR4 and . . . . P—Kt5. The original White move P—KR3 was, however, conceived as a parry to the threatening pin, and hence stands in logical connection with that motif. Consequently the attack on White's KRP should also be reckoned as a logical variation on the same theme, the pin motif; and this despite the fact that in the game as played Black did not pursue the adventure involved in or rather restarted by the move 25. . . . . B—KKt3, but contritely returned to his K file, whereupon virtue found its reward. But this is quite immaterial, for it could easily have

* Page 268.

happened otherwise. What is of importance is that we should have learnt the great strategic range of the pin motif.

§ 2. *The conception of the wholly, and half pinned piece. The defense a pinned piece can give is but imaginary. Exchange combinations on the pinning square (= the square on which the pinned piece stands), and the two distinct motives for such combinations.*

To a pin there belong three actors, (1) the pinning piece, (2) the pinned enemy piece, and (3) the piece standing behind the pinned piece. The first attacks the third across the second, that is to say the pinned piece stands in the way of the capture of the piece behind it by the pinning piece, and for shortness we shall call them the "pinning," the "pinned," and the "screened" piece. The screened piece is usually of noble blood, that is King or Queen, for otherwise it would not be likely to hide itself behind another piece. All three actors stand either in the same file or the same diagonal. (See Diagram 87.) The pinned piece dare not move since if he did the piece behind him would be exposed to the attack from which it had previously been screened. If this immobility is absolute, that is, if the pinned piece dare make no move whatever, he is said to be wholly pinned. If on the other hand the pinned piece has any squares at his disposal in the line of the pin to which he can move, he is said to be only half pinned. In Diag. 87 the pin by the Rook is only a half pin since the move . . . . P—R4 is pos-

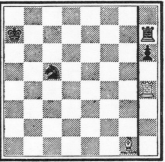

DIAGRAM 87

White's R at KR4 half pins Black's P at R3; White's B at KKt1 wholly pins Black's Kt at QB4. The screened pieces are the R and K respectively

sible. A pinned Kt is always wholly pinned. Of other pieces we may say that a piece can only half pin one of its own kind. For instance, White: B, KR1, Black: B, QB3; K, QKt2. Here the Black B at B3 is only half pinned; he can move anywhere in the diagonal QR1 to KR8. A Pawn can only be wholly pinned by a diagonally moving piece; if the pin is in a column the pinning piece must block the pinned Pawn (*e.g.*, White: R, KKt6. Black: P, KKt2; K, KKt1), in order to enforce complete immobility. But such immobility has really no connection with the pin: it could equally be the result of the blockade.

A pinned piece's defensive power is only imaginary. He only makes a gesture as if he would defend; in reality he is crippled and immobile. Hence we may confidently place our piece *en prise* to a pinned piece, for he dare not lay hands on it. An example will be found in Diagram 88. The winning moves *1.* Q x P *ch* or *1.* Q x P *ch* are easy to find. All we have to be sure of is that the Black B at B5 or P at Kt2 is pinned; if this be the case, the points (KKt3, QR6) which seem to be protected are really at our mercy. And so we may seek out such points which make a pretense of being protected, and at once rightly declare them to be free as air. How simple! And yet the less experienced amateur would rather put his head in the lion's jaws than put his Queen *en prise!*

DIAGRAM 88

Right: *1.* Q x P *ch*, and wins Q. Left: *1.* Q x P *ch* and mates next move

It is very often profitable to play for the win of the pinned piece. To us, who know that every immobile, or even weakly restrained, piece tends to become a weakness, this fact will not appear surprising. But parallel

with the problem of winning the pinned piece runs that of preventing its unpinning; for on this its mobility would be restored,
and with that all its strength also.

Apart from the fact that the possibility of an unpinning must
always be kept in view, the fight to win a pinned piece proceeds
on the usual lines, namely by multiplying attacks, and in the
case of adequate protection by thinning the ranks of the defenders. (See also I. ii. § 4.) A clear profit may, however, sometimes be recorded, namely in the case when a pinned piece can
be attacked by a Pawn, for then this attack on it will be decisive. That this must be so follows from the consideration that
a piece can only evade a Pawn attack by flight. If, however, the

DIAGRAM 89

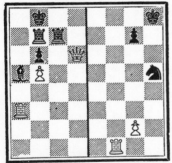

Two elementary examples of the win
of a pinned piece by a Pawn attack

DIAGRAM 90

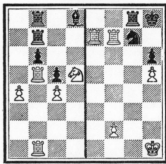

Pawn attack after an anterior
investment carried out by pieces

piece is pinned, he is defenseless against an attacking Pawn,
since flight is denied him. (See Diagram 89.) On the right the
course will be *1.* R—KR1, P—Kt3; and then up will come the
Pawn *2.* P—Kt4. On the left things are not made quite so easy
for the Pawns, there are one or two interferences to brush
aside, and this is done by *1.* R x B, P x R; *2.* P—Kt6 and wins.

In general, the plan of attack against a pinned piece calls
for a great effort to secure that preponderance in material

which we have on various occasions particularized, that is to say a majority of attackers over the defenders of our objective, which in this case is the pinned piece; but the ideal to be aimed at is the Pawn attack, which not infrequently will crown the whole enterprise. For example: In Diag. 90 (left) it is plainly visible that a close investment of the pinned Black P at Kt3 has been instituted. We may remark that the ideal result of this siege may be registered in the passive state to which the Black defenders are reduced. But now the RP moves forward, and this advance leads to a more tangible result.

In the same diagram (right) the Black Kt at Kt2 is in a pitiful state of pin. The screened piece is represented here by the mating threat at White's KR7. By the advance of the KRP White prevents any unpinning of the Kt by . . . . K—R2—Kt3. The pressure exerted on the pinned Kt by the pieces alone is right grievous here, yet does not lead to any immediate result. But now the BP comes up with a dagger under his cloak, and decides matters. And so while the officers may put on pressure (at times this suffices for the win of the piece, and after all an officer is not one to joke with), the proper person to execute the death sentence will always be the private soldier.

§ 3. *The exchange combination on the pinning square.*

The first motive. See Diagram 91 (right). In this position the capture of the pinned Black P at Kt2 may be our object. We pile up attacks (the preponderance 3:2 has here already been achieved), and then find to our disappointment that the Pawn jauntily advances; the beggar was not even pinned, or at best only half pinned, for though a capture by the KKtP would not be feasible, ... P—Kt3 is. The problem of how to win our objective, is, nevertheless, easy of solution, and this by *1.* Kt ⤢ P, B x Kt; *2.* P—B6. The idea is that White substitutes the wholly pinned Bishop for the half-pinned Pawn at Kt2. A substitution of this kind is our first motive.

There is, however, still a knotty question to answer, namely how White, notwithstanding the surrender of one of his attacking pieces, can yet maintain his preponderance against the point KKt7. The answer, of course, lies in the fact that though Black still has two of his original defenders (K and B) on the board, the B can no longer be regarded as a defender of the threatened point, but has him-

DIAGRAM 91

The exchange combination. Right: the 1st motive. Left: the 2nd motive

self become the pinned object of our attack at that point, whereas White still has his R and the KBP which, close at hand, is ready to plunge into the fray; so that the operation *1.* Kt x P, B x Kt puts out of action a piece on each side and the relative preponderance of White is unchanged.

The second motive. In the famous game, Morphy—Duke of Brunswick and Count Isouard, after the moves *1.* P—K4, P—K4; *2.* Kt—KB3, P—Q3; *3.* P—Q4, B—Kt5 ?; *4.* P x P, B x Kt; *5.* Q x B, P x P; *6.* B—QB4, Kt—KB3; *7.* Q—QKt3, Q—K2; *8.* Kt—B3, P—B3; *9.* B—KKt5, P—Kt4; *10.* Kt x P, P x Kt; *11.* B x KtP *ch*, QKt—Q2; the position of the pinned Black Kt at Q2 was a very critical one. There followed *12.* O—O—O (the quickest way to unite the Rooks for an attack in the Q file against the point Q7), R—Q1. (See Diagram 92.) In this position the simple doubling of the Rooks in the Q file would win the Kt: *13.* R—Q2, Q—K3; *14.* KR—Q1, B—K2; *15.* B x Kt; but Morphy has a much stronger maneuver at his command. There followed: *13.* R x Kt, R x R; *14.* R—Q1. This exchange combination on the pinning square deserves our notice. Did it take place in order to substitute a wholly pinned piece for one which is half pinned? No, for the Kt at Q2 as it was, was wholly pinned. Would it have taken place if the White R had already stood at Q2? No, for in that case doubling the Rooks would have sufficed. The exchange combination was evidently carried out in order, in the struggle for the point Q7, to gain a tempo.

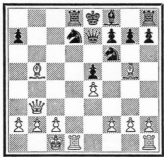

DIAGRAM 92

The 2nd motive

Let us dispassionately consider the state of affairs before and after R x Kt. Before this capture White had two attackers against two real defenders, for the Kt at B3 is half dead, and the Q is too great a personage, and would cut a poor figure in a rough and tumble with minor pieces. After R x Kt White loses one attacker, whom he, however, at once re-places by a fresh R; whereas the defending R which previously stood at Q1 is irrevocably lost to Black. (*Cf.* our "knotty question" above.) Accordingly White has profited to the extent of a fighting unit, and has thus a preponderance of forces in his fight for the pinned piece. The 2nd motive, therefore, is the gain of a tempo. After *14. . . . . Q—K3; 15.* B x Kt would have won easily; but Morphy preferred the prettier method *15.* **B x R** *ch,* Kt x B; and now the Kt is in its turn pinned because of the mating threat at Q8. The Kt is, however, forced to move, whereupon mate follows: *16.* **Q—Kt8** *ch !,* Kt x Q; *17.* **R—Q8** *mate.*

In the position on Diagram 91 (left) the pinning R is attacked; to withdraw him would mean giving the enemy the tempo he needs to get rid of the pin. For instance, *1.* R—Kt2, K—R2; *2.* R(Q)—QKt1, Kt—Q3. The correct play is *1.* **R x Kt,**

R x R; and now *2. R—QKt1* wins. Since the sacrifice at Kt7 was made only to avoid the loss of a tempo, our second motive is obviously present.

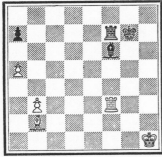

DIAGRAM 93

The 1st and 2nd motives appear together, enabling White to gain a decisive tempo

DIAGRAM 94

From a game at odds by Dr. Tarrasch. The pin exploited by means of *Zugzwang*

The two motives can also appear together in one combination. (See Diagram 93.) Here a general exchange is clearly indicated. However, after *1. B x B ch, R x B; 2. R x R, K x R; 3. P—Kt4, K—K4,* the Black K would arrive on the scene just at the right moment. We must therefore bring about the exchanges more cleverly. This we can do by *1. R x B !, R x R; 2. P—Kt4;* for now Black will have to lose a tempo with a K move. Thus *2. . . . . K—B2; 3. B x R, K x B; 4. P—Kt5* and now the P cannot be overtaken. A tempo-winning combination, you will say. Quite true, but the gain of a tempo was only attained because we were able to replace the half-pinned B by the wholly pinned R. Taking one thing with another therefore we see that in this case we have an amalgamation of the two motives.

We will close this section with an example which will show us the utilization of the pin combined with the justly popular *Zugzwang* motif. That a pin may easily lead to a dearth of available moves is obvious, for often enough the elasticity of

the defending pieces is very small; in fact, it not infrequently
happens that the defense is uni-operative, *i.e.*, cannot shift its
ground and still maintain the protection of the threatened
point. So in Diagram 94, after the initial sacrifice which we
have so often discussed (first motive), after the moves *1.*
R x B, R x R; there followed *2.* P—Kt3 *!*. But for P—Kt3 Black
could have given his K air by means of . . . . P—B5; but now
this move would fail after *3.* P—Kt4, and Black succumbs owing to the uni-operative quality of his defense of the R at K4.
After *2.* P—Kt3, P—Kt5 Black is equally "in the soup," and for
the same reason.

We have now, in essentials at any rate, exhausted the subject of play against a pinned piece and will pass on to that of
unpinning.

§ *4.   The problem of unpinning: (a) The "question"; its
character and the dangers involved. (b) Ignoring the pin. (c)
Unpinning by bringing up reserves. (d) Maneuvering and
holding choice of policy in suspense. (e) The "corridor" and
the defensive alliance of the beleaguered.*

After the moves *1.* P—K4, P—K4; *2.* Kt—KB3, Kt—QB3; *3.* B—
B4, B—B4; *4.* Kt—B3, Kt—B3; *5.* P—Q3, P—Q3, White can set up
a pin by *6.* B—KKt5; and curiously enough this simple little pin

DIAGRAM 95

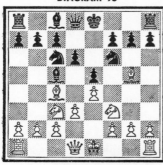

The problem of unpinning

evokes a whole forest of possibilities. (See Diagram 95.)
Should Black immediately put
the "question" to the bold Bishop
by *6.* . . . . P—KR3; *7.* B—R4,
P—KKt4; *8.* B—KKt3, or should
he put the strictest restraint upon
himself and with an unembar-
rassed smile play *6.* . . . . B—
K3? Or should he even risk a
counter-pin with . . . . B—KKt5?

Again may he not consider it reasonable to ignore the threat involved in the pinning move B—KKt5 (namely 7. Kt—Q5, with consequent disorganization of his King-side Pawn position, by B or Kt x Kt), in order with 6. . . . . Kt—Q5 quietly to "centralize"? There is further 6. . . . . Kt—QR4 to be considered, while 6. . . . . O—O must not be dismissed with a mere shrug of the shoulders.

(a) The "Question."

It will be clear without further remark that the premature advance of the wing Pawns must have a compromising effect. In the Scotch Game, to give an example, after 1. P—K4, P—K4; 2. Kt—KB3, Kt—QB3; 3. P—Q4, P x P; 4. Kt x P, Kt—B3; 5. Kt—QB3, B—Kt5; 6. Kt x Kt, KtP x Kt; 7. B—Q3, P—Q4; 8. P x P, P x P; 9. O—O, O—O; 10. B—KKt5, P—B3; 11. Kt—K2, there can follow 11. . . . . P—KR3; 12. B—R4, P—Kt4? but now after 13. B—Kt3 White has at his command the attacking move P—B4, and also the possibility of occupying the squares KB5 and KR5, which have been weakened by the advance of the KtP, for neither point can ever be attacked by . . . . P—Kt3. The "question" was therefore ill-timed.

On the other hand, there are occasions when the "question" is very opportune. For instance, in the following opening of a tournament game, E. Cohn—Nimzovich: 1. P—K4, P—K4; 2. Kt—QB3, B—B4; 3. Kt—B3, P—Q3; 4. P—Q4, P x P; 5. Kt x P, Kt—KB3; 6. B—K2, O—O; 7. O—O, R—K1 (Black has given up the center, but has pressure on White's KP). 8. B—KKt5 ? (B—B3 was his right move), P—KR3 !; 9. B—R4, P—KKt4 !; 10. B—Kt3, Kt x P. It was to win this important Pawn that Black put up with the disorganization of his own position, in the spirit of Chap. 1. § 7a. The continuation was 11. Kt x Kt, R x Kt; 12. Kt—Kt3, B—Kt3; 13. B—Q3, B—Kt5 !; 14. Q—Q2, R—K1; and after . . . . Kt—B3 and . . . . Q—B3, Black's position was consolidated; the P at Q3 has in particular a stabilizing effect. Black won easily.

We have purposely taken two extreme cases in order to see what is at stake if the "question" be put; and we have found that the "question" is disorganizing, and therefore should not be put unless there be compensation in another direction. Such compensation usually lies in the fact that the Bishop which has been driven off finds himself in a "desert." Such a desert will, however, at once be changed into a flowering garden if the center can be opened. The following examples will make this point clear:

After the moves *1.* P—K4, P—K4; *2.* Kt—KB3, Kt—QB3; *3.* Kt—B3, Kt—B3; *4.* B—Kt5, B—Kt5; *5.* O—O, O—O; *6.* B x Kt, QP x B; *7.* P—Q3, B—Kt5; *8.* P—KR3, B—R4; *9.* B—Kt5 (*9.* P—Kt4 at once would be bad because of *9.* . . . . . Kt x KtP; *10.* P x Kt, B x P; followed by . . . . P—KB4), Q—Q3; *10.* B x Kt, Q x B, it is perfectly correct to play *11.* P—Kt4, for the Black B on arriving at KKt3 will find nothing to "bite upon" but the unshakeable mass of center Pawns. It should be noted that if Black still had his QP, *i.e.,* a P at Q3 instead of P at QB3, this "desert" could have been given life by . . . . P—Q4. True the Black B can eventually be brought to KB2, after . . . . P—KB3, but that takes time. White on the other hand has nothing to fear, for with a compact center a disorganized King's wing is easily defensible. And more than that, these disorganized King-side Pawns will become a slowly but surely advancing instrument of attack (of the "tank" order), especially with a Kt to help at KB5. (*Cf.* Game No. 16, Nimzovich—Leonhardt, of which the above are the opening moves.)

DIAGRAM 96

The "question" and its "consequences"

And now, having shown more or less definitely the logical connection between a "desert" and the "center," it will be profitable to analyze the position referred to at the beginning of this section. (See Diagram 96.) After the moves: *1.* P—K4, P—K4; *2.* Kt—KB3, Kt—QB3; *3.* B—B4, B—B4; *4.* Kt—B3, Kt—B3; *5.* P—Q3, P—Q3; *6.* B—KKt5, P—KR3; *7.* B—R4, P—KKt4; *8.* B—KKt3, it will be interesting to see whether the desert into which the B has been forced can be made hospitable or not. To this end we must minutely examine White's possibilities of attack in the center.

There are, as will be seen, two such possibilities, the one B—Kt5 followed by P—Q4, the other Kt—Q5 with P—B3 and P—Q4 to follow. (In passing it may be remarked that the position of the Kt at Q5, as a diagonal outpost in the diagonal of the B at QB4, is analogous to that of an outpost in a file.) After *8. . . . .* P—R3 (to remove the first possibility), White could play *9.* Kt—Q5; for example, *9. . . . .* B—K3; *10.* P—B3, B x Kt; *11.* P x B, Kt—K2; *12.* P—Q4, P x P; *13.* Kt x QP, and now Black can pocket a Pawn, but after *13. . . . .* KKt x P; *14.* O—O, White's game is to be preferred, for the B at KKt3, now come to life, will by no means have to kick his heels in idleness any longer.

After *8.* B—KKt3 (see Diagram 96) Black can also play *8. . . . .* B—KKt5, in order in some measure to curb White's aspirations in the center. In a game (see No. 17, Nimzovich—Fluss) the continuation was *9.* P—KR4, Kt—KR4 (. . . . R—KKt1 or even . . . . K—Q2 was possible here; . . . . Kt—KR4 takes too many troops from the middle of the board); *10.* P x P (Tempting as this move looks—for is it not the natural consequence of the Pawn advance?—it is not good here; the right move was Kt—Q5. The argument is this: *9.* P—KR4 has had *9. . . . .* Kt—KR4 as a result, so that White has now attained a preponderance in the center which he can exploit by *10.* Kt—Q5), Kt—Q5. This transposition of moves loses, since White has a surprising combination in reserve. With *10. . . . .* Kt x B; *11.* P x Kt, Kt—Q5, Black could have launched a lovely attack. Thus: *12.* R x P,

R x R; *13.* P x R, B x Kt; *14.* P x B, Q—Kt4. Or *12.* Kt—Q5 (this attempt to exploit the center comes too late), B x Kt; *13.* P x B, Q x P; *14.* P—KKt4, P—QB3; *15.* R—R5, P x Kt *!* , and wins, since the Q has as her traveling companions to the next world all White's pieces.

It is therefore of the utmost importance for the student to realize that the "question," though seemingly only a matter concerning the wing, is fundamentally a problem affecting the center. Later under (*c*) we shall demonstrate the reality of this connection by another example.

(*b*) Ignoring the threat, or, in other words, permitting our Pawn position to be broken up.

This method may be chosen if we can in return secure greater freedom of action in the center, and by this we mean not merely a passive security such as was considered under (*a*) above; we must here have a guarantee that we shall get active security. For instance, after the same opening moves, *1.* P—K4, P—K4; *2.* Kt—KB3, Kt—QB3; *3.* B—B4, B—B4; *4.* Kt—B3, Kt—B3; *5.* P—Q3, P—Q3; *6.* B—KKt5 (see Diagram 95), Kt—Q5 threatens unpleasantness. Nevertheless we can ignore the threat, thus *6.* . . . . O—O; *7.* Kt—Q5, B—K3. And now the break up of our King-side Pawns by *8.* Kt x Kt *ch,* P x Kt; *9.* B—KR6, R—K1; *10.* Kt—R4, K—R1, would yield a game with chances and counter chances, yet White can by no means claim any striking advantage, for Black has the desired freedom of action in the center (the possibility of . . . . P—Q4), and there is no more effective parry to an operation on a flank than a counter-thrust in the center. White has let his troops create a diversion, which has in fact made them lose contact with the center. This diversion would only find real justification if it led to the permanent possession of the point KB5, and this seems questionable. After *8.* B x Kt (instead of Kt x Kt), P x B; *9.* Kt—R4, the outcome would also be uncertain.

Best for White, after 6. . . . . O—O; 7. Kt—Q5, B—K3, would be 8. Q—Q2, which keeps up the pressure. After the further moves 8. . . . . B x Kt; 9. B x B, the unpinning by means of the "question" is impracticable (9. . . . . P—KR3; 10. B—R4, P—KKt4 ?; 11. B x Kt, P x B; 12. Kt x KtP), and White stands slightly better.

(c) Bringing up reserves in order to effect the unpinning by peaceful means.

For all who love the quiet life, this is a very commendable continuation. We have excellent examples of it in the Metger Defense to the Four Knights Game, and in Tarrasch's match game (a Petroff) against Marshall.

The Metger Defense is this:—1. P—K4, P—K4; 2. Kt—KB3, Kt—QB3; 3. Kt—B3, Kt—B3; 4. B—Kt5, B—Kt5; 5. O—O, O—O; 6. P—Q3, P—Q3; 7. B—Kt5, and now Metger plays 7. . . . . B x Kt; 8. P x B, Q—K2, intending . . . . Kt—Q1—K3, and if the White B then goes to KR4, Black persistently follows him up by . . . . Kt—B5—Kt3 on which if B—Kt5 again, Black at last plays . . . . P—KR3. It is again evident that such a lengthy time-wasting maneuver is only feasible if the position in the center is solid. In reply to 8. . . . . Q—K2 the usual continuation is 9. R—K1, Kt—Q1; 10. P—Q4, Kt—K3; 11. B—B1, P—B4 (or B3) with about equal chances.

In the Petroff, Tarrasch, after the moves 1. P—K4, P—K4; 2. Kt—KB3, Kt—KB3; 3. Kt x P, P—Q3; 4. Kt—KB3, Kt x P; 5. P—Q4, B—K2; 6. B—Q3, Kt—KB3; 7. O—O, B—Kt5, is wont to get out of the pin by the quiet maneuver R—K1, QKt—Q2—B1—Kt3 and then P—KR3 (sometimes he plays P—KR3 first), and he has won some fine games thus. The logical framework, which seems to justify him in a maneuver taking up so much time as this does, is based on the two following postulates: (1) the unpinning must be brought about as quickly as possible, (2) to the troops thus hurried up in support there is offered, as a kind of reward for the aid they bring, a favorable position with possibilities of getting contact with the enemy (*e.g.*, by Kt—KB5). I should like to add the remark that, incidentally, the moderns are not disinclined to put up with the unpleasantness of a pin for some considerable time; we are no longer quite convinced that a pin must be shaken off without any delay. Our plan of action may be seen from (*d*).

(*d*) Maneuvering and holding the choice of (*a*), (*b*), or (*c*) in reserve.

Such a line of action is difficult, and makes great demands on our technical skill. As an example, in the position shown on Diag. 95, Capablanca played 6. . . . . B—K3, and the continuation was 7. B—Kt5, P—KR3; 8. B—KR4, B—QKt5 !; 9. P—Q4, B—Q2. This advance of the QP which Capablanca provoked leaves White's KP lacking protection. 10. O—O, B x Kt; 11. P x B (B x KKt could have been played first here), P—Kt4; 12. B—Kt3, Kt x KP (Black had postponed the unpinning until a suitable moment occurred); 13. B x Kt, B x B; 14. P x P, P x P; 15. B x P (Kt x KP was possibly better), Q x Q; 16. QR x Q, P—B3; 17. B—Q4, K—B2; 18. Kt—Q2, KR—K1 with a favorable end game for Black. His opponent, the author of this book, had to lay down his arms on the 64th move.

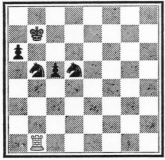

DIAGRAM 97

Unpinning by occupying one of the points in the "corridor"; here QKt7 to 5 and QKt3. Thus: Kt—Kt3 or Kt5

(*e*) The corridor and the need for the defenders to maintain effective contact.

In an advanced stage of the game, particularly in tactical operations, the process of unpinning presents an entirely different aspect. In Diagram 97, for instance, Black plays . . . . Kt—Kt5 or Kt3. We call the space between pinning and pinned pieces and that between the pinned and the screened pieces the "corridor." By placing a protected piece in such a corridor the pin can be raised. Another possibility lies in the removal of the screened piece out of the line of the pin. Thus in Diag. 97 either . . . . K—B3 or

DIAGRAM 98   DIAGRAM 99

The beleaguered troops get in touch
Black releases the pin

. . . . K—B2 would put an end to the pin. If the screened piece is not too valuable, we may achieve the same end by giving it adequate protection; but in this case we must be careful to maintain contact between the pieces concerned in the pin, whether directly or, as defenders indirectly. (See Diag. 98.) White intends with R(R2)—Kt2, and B—Q3 to make the threat P—R4 an actuality. How can Black anticipate this maneuver? By transferring his R from QKt3 to QKt2, and then safeguarding him by . . . . B—B3; after which, for all he cares, P—R4 may be played at any time. Notice, too, how the unpinning is effected in Diag. 99 by *1*. . . . . R—Kt8 *ch;* 2. K —Kt2, R—Kt7 *ch,* followed by *3*. . . . . B—Q5. In this position by establishing contact between B and R, the B, which otherwise would have been lost, is saved.

Another example of the pin. (See Diag. 100.) In the game White played 22. R—Kt1, on which Black countered by . . . .

DIAGRAM 100

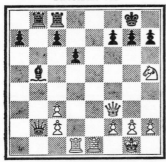

Position from the game
Nimzovich—Vidmar
Carlsbad 1911

R—K1; but as I afterwards showed, 22. R—K4 would have won. The main variation runs: 22. R—K4, B—B3; 23. Kt—B6 *ch*, P x Kt (If 23. . . . . K—R1; 24. R—KR4, Q x P [B7]; 25. Kt x P *!*), and now we come to a direct pursuit of the Black K, who will be driven to flight, but by no means to an untroubled flight, rather one in which some disagreeable pins lie in wait for him; for, as we observed at the beginning of this chapter, the pin is characteristic of a pursuit; there follows 24. R—Kt4 *ch*, K—B1; 25. Q x P, B—Q2 *!*; 26. R—Kt7, B—K3; 27. R x RP, K—K1; and now comes pin No. 1, namely 28. R—K1, threatening Q x P *ch !*. To escape this Black must play 28. . . . . K—Q2; but now the KBP is pinned (No. 2) and 29. Q x B *ch* wins easily. Let us, for the sake of practice, dwell a moment on the position after 25. Q x P, B—Q2. Here 26. R—KB4 would also win, for . . . . B—K3 will not do because of Q x B; 26. . . . . B—K1 fails against 27. R—K1; and if 26. . . . . K—Kt1, then 27. Q x P *ch*, K—R1; 28. Q—B6 *ch*, K—Kt1; 29. R—B3 decides matters.

The reader is advised to study now Games Nos. 16, 17, and 18, which illustrate the connection between the pin and the center.

8. Discovered Check

A SHORT chapter, but rich in dramatic complications.

§ 1. *The degree of relationship between the pin and the discovered check is more closely defined. Where should the piece which discovers the check move to?*

Diagram 101 gives a clear picture of the degree of relationship between the pin and discovered check, and we see from it that the pinned piece, tired of eternal persecution, has changed his color. This change has had the effect of transforming the once sickly youth into a doughty warrior; and so we can describe a discovered check as a pin in which the pinned piece has passed over with colors flying into the enemy camp. Further, in the discovered check, as in the pin, we have to do

with three actors, namely: (1) the piece threatening a check which is now masked by one of his own fellows; (2) the masking piece; (3) the piece standing behind the masking piece; or more shortly (1) the threatening piece, (2) the masking piece, (3) the threatened piece. But whereas in the pin the immobility of the pinned (masking) piece is the source of all his troubles, in the discovered check the masking piece enjoys quite uncanny mobility; any and every square within his reach is open to him; he can even seize a point subject to multiple

DIAGRAM 101

In the discovered check on the right the Rook is the "threatening," the Knight the "masking," and the King the "threatened" piece

enemy attacks, for his opponent, being in check, cannot touch him.

If we examine the possible moves open to such a masking piece, we find that he can do three things:

(*a*) He can take anything within reach with impunity since the enemy cannot recapture him.

(*b*) He can attack any major enemy piece, not letting himself for one moment be disturbed by the thought that the square on which he so haughtily alights by right belongs to the enemy, that is to say one which is under heavy enemy fire.

(*c*) He can exchange his square for another one, if for any reason this appears more favorable to him than the one he has left.

DIAGRAM 102

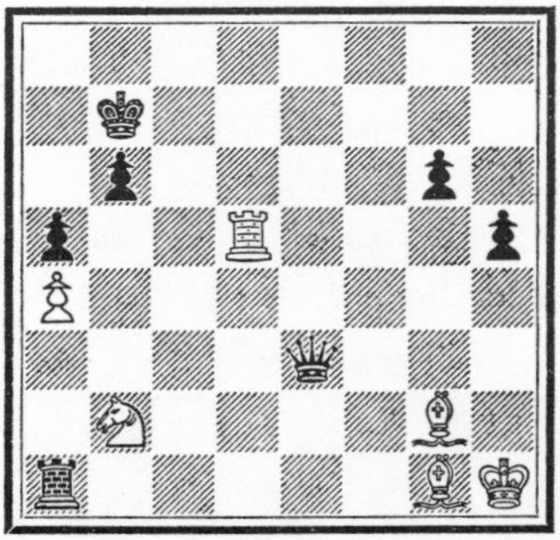

Thus in Diagram 102 (*a*) could be carried out by R x QRP, or KRP *ch*. Notice that the R can make either capture quite fearlessly. If he chooses to follow the course outlined in (*b*) he will play R—K5 *ch* or R—Q3 *ch*; while we find (*c*) followed, if he feels the reproach that his B is pinned, a fact which dulls his lordship's usually healthy appetite, and we have *1*. R—Q1 *ch*, K any move; *2*. B x Q, etc.

The (*c*) group has naturally a very wide range, but no purpose would be served by further elaboration, for the reasons why a piece is more effective placed "here" than "there" are manifold. We may refer, however, to yet another example in the following section.

§ 2. *The see-saw. The long range masking piece can move to any square in his line of motion without spending a tempo, that is to say, wholly gratis.*

DIAGRAM 103

Two See-saws.

Right: after 1. B—R7 *ch*, K—R1; 2. B—K4 *ch*, K—Kt1; and save that the B is on another, perhaps better, square, the position is unaltered; White still has the move

In Diagram 103 (right) White plays *1.* B—R7 *ch*, whereupon the Black K has only one move, ... K—R1, and now the terrible weapon concealed in the discovered check is revealed. If White now plays 2. B—Kt1 *ch*, Black with 2. .... K—Kt1 escapes the discovered check, but with 3. B—R7 *ch*, White beckons him back again to the fatal square, since the Black King has but this move at his disposal, and only has this because the B by B—R7 *ch* has masked the attack of the threatening piece. This stalemate position which we have described gives us thus a kind of see-saw, with the great advantage that the masking piece can occupy any square in the line of his withdrawal (here the diagonal KR7 to QKt1), without the maneuver costing him a tempo, for White again has the move. In actual play the see-saw leads to richly comic effects whose humor, however, does not appeal to the losing player.

The see-saw can be the cause of frightful devastation. In Diagram 104 the game would proceed, *1.* B—R7 *ch*, K—R1; *2.* B x P *ch*, K—Kt1; *3.* B—R7 *ch*, K—R1; *4.* B x P *ch*, K—Kt1; *5.* B—R7 *ch*, K—R1; *6.* B x Kt *ch*, K—Kt1; *7.* B—R7 *ch*, K—R1; *8.* B x Kt *ch*, K—Kt1; *9.* B—R7 *ch*, K—R1; *10.* B x R *ch*, K—Kt1; and now White gives back of his superfluity, somewhat like a usurer who has grown very rich and in his old age at small outlay turns benefactor. So *11.* R—Kt6 *ch*, P x R; *12.* B x B *ch*,

DIAGRAM 104

The See-saw
Great slaughter, the conciliatory sacrifice, and to crown all, mate

DIAGRAM 105

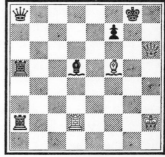

White wins
The see-saw is applied in more re-
fined manner

and mate next move. The B has eaten his way to QKt1, in
order, after the preparatory R sacrifice, to seize the diagonal
QR2 to KKt8.

A similar but finer picture is shown in Diagram 105. Here
the problem is to entice Black's B at Q4 from the defense of
his KBP, and this will be done by *1.* B—R7 *ch*, K—R1; *2.* B—B2
ch ! (the "better place" in the sense of (*c*) above), K—Kt1; *3.*
R—Kt2 *ch !*, B x R; and now again *4.* B—R7 *ch*, K—R1; *5.* B—Kt6
ch, K—Kt1; *6.* Q—R7 *ch*, K—B1; *7.* Q x P *mate*.

Another example of the see-saw is seen in the game (Diagram 106) which Torre won against Lasker. In this threatening position (his R at K1 is directly, and his B at Kt5 indirectly,
attacked), Torre hit upon the move *21.* P—QKt4 *!*; there followed *21. . . . . .* Q—KB4, (not . . . . Q x P, because of R—
QKt1; better than the text move would however have been *21.*
. . . . . Q—Q4); *22.* R—KKt3, P—KR3; *23.* Kt—B4 (this intervention of the Kt would have been impossible had the Black
Q been at Q4), Q—Q4; *24.* Kt—K3 (Torre fights like a lion to
break the pin, but without a point for his B to fall back upon,
he could not have succeeded) *24. . . . . .* Q—Kt4; *25.* B—B6 *!*
(That this might have real effect it was necessary to entice the

Diagram 106

Torre—Lasker
Moscow 1925

DIAGRAM 107

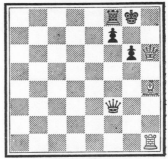

Double check
Startling effects are achieved

Q to an unprotected square, which was the object of 24. Kt—K3), Q x Q; 26. R x P *ch*, K—R1 (and now we have a see-saw); 27. R x P *ch*, K—Kt1; 28. R—Kt7 *ch*, K—R1; 29. R x B *ch*, K—Kt1; 30. R—Kt7 *ch*, K—R1; 31. R—Kt5 *ch*, K—R2; 32. R x Q, K—Kt3; 33. R—R3, K x B; 34. R x P *ch*, and wins.

§ 3. *Double check. Is brought about by the masking piece also giving check. The effectiveness of a double check lies in the fact that of the three possible parries to a check, two are nugatory, namely the capture of the piece giving check and the interposition of a piece. Flight is the one and only resource.*

See Diagram 107. Here the choice lies between *1.* Q—R7 *ch,* and *1.* Q—R8 *ch.* The former yields only an ordinary discovered check (*1.* Q—R7 *ch*, K x Q; 2. B—B6 *ch*) and allows the parry 2. . . . . Q x R or . . . . Q—R4. *1.* Q—R8 *ch,* however, leads to a double check, and these parries are now automatically ruled out. Therefore *1.* Q—R8 *ch !,* K x Q; 2. B—B6 *double ch,* K—Kt1; 3. R—R8 *mate.* So again in the well known position, White: Q, KB6; B, QKt2; Kt, K5. Black: K, Kt1; R's, K1, KB1; Pawns, KB2, KKt3, KR2. White mates in three, thus: *1.* Q—R8 *ch,* K x Q; 2. Kt x BP *double ch,* K—Kt1; 3. Kt—R6 *mate.*

The double check is a weapon of a purely tactical nature, but of terrible driving effect. Even the laziest King flees wildly in the face of a double check.

We close this chapter with three apposite examples:

DIAGRAM 108

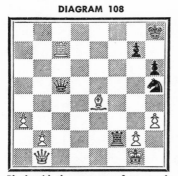

Black with the move can force a win

(1) In a game played some years ago between v. Bardeleben and Nisnievich there occurred the amusing position shown in Diagram 108. White's last move had been R(QKt7)—QB7 (obviously not R—Kt8 *ch* because of . . . . R—B1 *ch* and . . . . R x R). To R—QB7 Black replied . . . . Q x R and the game was drawn. I subsequently pointed out the following win:

1. . . . . R—B8 *double ch;* 2. K x R, Kt—Kt6 *ch;* 3. K—K1, Q—K6 *ch;* 4. K—Q1 (observe the driving effect; the King is already at Q1 and only a move or two ago he was sitting snugly at home!), Q—K7 *ch!;* 5. K—B1, Q—K8 *ch!;* 6. K—B2, Q x B *ch;* 7. K—B1, Kt—K7 *ch!*, and wins the Q and the game. Note that on the double check there was built a line of play, which is well known, and only strikes us as unusual because it takes place in a diagonal, and not as is usual in a file. This line of play (a tactical maneuver) consists in breaking a link in the defense, by forcing a third piece between two mutually protecting pieces. In the position under consideration the K was enticed on to his QB2 between the Q at QKt1 and the B at K4.

(2) The following well known little game was played between Réti (White) and Dr. Tartakover (Black). *1.* P—K4, P—QB3; *2.* P—Q4, P—Q4; *3.* Kt—QB3, P x P; *4.* Kt x P, Kt—B3; *5.* Q—Q3 (a most unnatural move), P—K4 ? (the rather theatrical gesture of the first player, the move Q—Q3, has worked; Black has in mind a brilliant refutation of it, but his idea proves im-

possible of execution; for Q—Q3 was not as bad as all that!
And so White gets the better game. The right move was 5.
. . . . Kt x Kt; 6. Q x Kt, Kt—Q2; followed by . . . . Kt—B3
with a solid position); 6. P x P, Q—R4 *ch*; 7. B—Q2, Q x KP; 8.
O—O—O, Kt x Kt *?* (a mistake; he should have played . . . .
B—K2); 9. Q—Q8 *ch !*, K x Q; 10. B—Kt5 *double ch*, K—B2; 11.
B—Q8 *mate*. If 10. . . . . K—K1, then R—Q8 *mate*. The clos-
ing combination is really very pretty.

(3) In December, 1910, I gave a simultaneous display in
Pernau (on the Baltic), on which occasion the following pretty
little game was played. White: Nimzovich. Black: Ryckhoff. 1.
P—K4, P—K4; 2. Kt—KB3, Kt—QB3; 3. B—Kt5, Kt—B3; 4. O—O,
P—Q3; 5. P—Q4, Kt x P *?*; 6. P—Q5, P—QR3; 7. B—Q3, Kt—B3
(7. . . . . Kt—K2 would have saved the piece, but not the
game. For instance: 8. B x Kt, P—KB4; 9. B—Q3, P—K5; 10.
R—K1, P x B or Kt; 11. Q x P, with a strong attack); 8. P x Kt,
P—K5; 9. R—K1, P—Q4; 10. B—K2 *! !* (By forcing Black to protect his KP, White got time to remove his pieces from the fork
unhurt; but instead he played his B to a square which allowed
the capture of the Kt), P x Kt (Black sees no danger and un-
concernedly pockets the piece). 11. P x KtP, B x P (if 11. . . . .
P x B; then simply P x R(Q) for the KP is pinned); 12. B—Kt5
double check and *mate*.

9. The Pawn-Chain

§ 1. *General remarks and definitions. The base of the Pawn-chain. The conception of the two distinct theaters of war.*

A FTER *1.* P—K4, P—K3; 2. P—Q4, P—Q4; 3. P—K5, a Black and White Pawn-chain has been formed. The Pawns at Q4, K5, and K3 and Q4 are the several links in the chain. The P at Q4 is to be regarded as the base or foot of the White chain, while the P at K3 plays a like rôle in Black's. Accordingly we call the bottommost link of the chain, on which all the other links depend, the base.

Every Black and White Pawn-chain, in other words, two consecutive series of Pawns abutting on one another in consecutive diagonals, divides the board diagonally into two

DIAGRAM 109   **DIAGRAM 110**

The Pawn-Chain

halves. For convenience we shall call such a Black and White Pawn-chain simply the Pawn-chain. (See Diagrams 109, 110.)

Before the student tackles what now follows, he should make perfectly sure that he has grasped the principles of the open file and the blockade of the passed Pawn; if he has not he should read through again Chapters 2 and 4, for they are indispensable to a proper understanding of what we have now to consider.

The question is this: After 1. P—K4, P—K3; 2. P—Q4, P—Q4; so long as White's P remains at K4, he can if he wishes, open the K file with P x P, in order to start more or less permanent operations in the file, by planting, say, an outpost Kt at K5. By playing 3. P—K5 he renounces this chance, and in addition he relieves the tension in the center, and this for no visible reason. Why then does he do this? Now I do not believe that the attacking energy latent in White's position before the move P—K5 can suddenly disappear as a consequence of P—K5; it must be present as before, though in a modified form; for 3. P—K5 above all things checks the movement of the Black Pawns, and therefore implies a blockade. But we know that Pawns, especially those in the center, are consumed by an enormous desire for expansion, *i.e.*, to press forward, and we have consequently inflicted on the enemy a not inconsiderable hurt. Moreover, thanks to P—K5 there are now two theaters of war on the board, of which the one is Black's King wing and the other the center.

On the King's Wing.

See Diag. 111. The P at K5 may here be described as a detachment which has been pushed forward to form a wedge in enemy territory, and to act as a demobilizing force. The P at K5 robs a Black Kt of the square KB3, and thus allows an easy approach of the White storm troops (Q at Kt4). Black's King wing which is cramped by the same Pawn is also a target for bombardment by other pieces, *e.g.*, B at Q3, Kt at KB3, and B at QB1. If Black seeks to defend himself by opening communications in his 2nd rank, by a timely advance . . . . P—B4, and eventually posting a Rook at his QR2, our P at K5 will prove

DIAGRAM 111

The K's wing as theater of war. The troops engaged are Q, B and Kt. The R is held in reserve ready for the possible enemy counter . . . . P—B4; P x P, R x P, when he will attack in the K file

himself an excellent wedge-driver; what we mean is that when White attacks the point KKt7, Black will play . . . . P—B4 in order to use his second rank for the defense of the threatened point. This otherwise excellent defensive idea would, however, fail because the P at K5 would protest violently. The reply to . . . . P—B4 would be P x P, e.p. and White, after the recapture . . . . R x P, would use the K file, including the point K5 in it, for bringing pressure on the backward enemy P at K3. In the first case (*i.e.*, King's wing as theater of war) a White P at KB4 would on the whole be a hindrance to White, since its negative effect (as an obstruction to the QB and to any other of his pieces wishing to use the square) would overshadow any positive advantage it might have.

In the center.

Beside that of cramping the enemy King's wing White's P at K5 pursues other and quite different ends. White, in fact, intends by P—K5 to fix the Black P at K3 at his post, in order later to open fire on him with P—KB4—B5; for . . . . KP x P would then imply the surrender of the base of Black's Pawn-chain. Should Black abstain from this move, White can either form a wedge by P—B6, or play P x P, P x P; R—B7—K7, which would mean the beginning of the end of Black's P at K3.

In order the better to understand the association of ideas, it will be well to examine more closely the germ-cell of a flank, or enveloping, attack. In Diagram 112 left we see the Rook in

DIAGRAM 112

Left: frontal attack in simplest form.
Right: Flank or enveloping attack in its simplest form

a frontal attack, in which the objective is bombarded at White's leisure. To the right a frontal attack being out of the question, the maneuver R—Kt6 x P or R—Kt7—B7 x P is planned. It is important for our purpose to emphasize the fact that the White P at KB5 in this position is a necessary element of the problem, for if this were absent, a frontal attack against the Black KBP would not only be possible, but by far our easiest course. Moreover, the attack against the point KB6 if this had not been pinned down, would have no strategical sense, in conformity with the principle: the objective must first be reduced to immobility. It follows that the position shown in Diag. 112 (right) represents the true germ-cell of the flank or enveloping attack.

This being established, the plan of action shown in Diag. 113 is seen to be logically justified, for its end is a preparation for such an attack as we have seen in germ in Diag. 112 right, and if this operation can be called an attack, as indeed it is, we can with a good conscience ascribe to the maneuver P—K5 (chain building) followed by P—KB4—B5 a like significance. Accordingly the center, in other words the Black P at K3, is to be taken as a second theater of war.

DIAGRAM 113

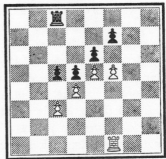

Skeleton representation of a central theater of war. The two opponents attack the respective bases of the Pawn-chain. The Rooks keep on the alert ready for the break-through

To recapitulate: P—K5, that is to say the formation of a Pawn-chain, always creates two theaters of war, of which the enemy wing, cramped by the advance, forms one, and the base of the enemy Pawn-chain the other. And further, P—K5 is inspired by the desire to attack. The attack on Black's P at Q4 which was present before the advance of our KP has been transferred to Black's P at K3, which has been reduced to immobility by our P at K5, so as to be exposed to a flank attack by P—KB4 —B5.

§ 2. *The attack against the Pawn-chain. The Pawn-chain as a blockade problem. The attack against the "base."*

There was a time, before 1913, when it was the firm conviction that a Pawn-chain, with the disappearance of one of its links, must give up all pretension to a happy existence. To have shown this conviction to be based on pure prejudice is a service for which I may take credit, since as early as the year 1911 I had proved by some games (against Salve, Carlsbad, 1911, Game No. 46, against Levenfish, and against Dr. Tarrasch, in 1912, Game No. 20) that I was inclined to conceive of the Pawn-chain as a purely cramping problem, and that the question was not whether the links of the chain were complete, but simply and solely whether the enemy Pawns remained cramped. Whether we effect this by Pawns or pieces, or indeed by Rooks or Bishops at long range, is immaterial. The main thing is that they, the enemy Pawns, should be cramped. This conception of mine, to which I had arrived through an intensive study of the blockade problem, did not fail, in those days, to arouse a storm of protest. To-day, however, everyone knows that all the things which I then said about the Pawn-chain are incontestable truths.

It was disputed at that time (see in particular a violent article by Alapin in the *Wiener Schachzeitung*, 1913), that after *1.* P—K4, P—K3; *2.* P—Q4, P—Q4, any attack on Black's Q4 existed at all; but we, that is the friendly readers of my book, know well enough that such an attack does very much exist. Alapin did not know it, since he was not acquainted with the theory of the open file, which I originated. So, too, to take another disputed point, everyone recognizes to-day that in positions characterized by the advance P—K5 (at the 3rd or at a later move), the thrust P—KB4—B5 may well be, and often is, the logical sequence. We can learn a lot by a closer investigation of the question, why after *1.* P—K4, P—K3; *2.* P—Q4, P—Q4; *3.* P—K5, the Black attack . . . . P—QB4 should hold the field rather than an immediate White attack by P—KB4—B5. As we have already insisted, the disposition of both the White and Black links in the chain is directed towards cramping the opponent. The White Pawns wish to blockade the Black, and vice versa. Now after *1.* P—K4, P—K3; *2.* P—Q4, P—Q4; *3.* P—K5, it is the Black Pawns who are held up on their road to the center, whereas the corresponding White Pawns have already outstripped the middle of the board (compare the relative positions of the two KP's); hence we are justified in regarding the White as the cramping, the Black as the cramped Pawns. And since the Pawns' desire to expand is naturally greatest when directed towards the center, we see that Black is more justified in the attack . . . . P—QB4 than White is in the corresponding thrust on the other wing (P—KB4—B5). The threat of the advance of the KBP exists, however, in spite of everything; and when Black's attack has burnt itself out, White's turn then comes for the thrust with his KBP.

That this threat fails in many games to be translated into action only goes to prove that White has plenty on his hands in meeting the attack . . . . P—QB4, or else that he has chosen the first of the two theaters of war (*i.e.*, Black's cramped King's wing) for his operations.

As to what concerns the transference of our attack from Black's Q4 to his K3, the student will soon see how wide is the bearing of this proposition of mine. But let us proceed systematically.

§ 3. *Attack on the "base" a strategical necessity. The clearing away of the links in the enemy chain is only undertaken with the idea of freeing our Pawns which they had been cramping. Accordingly the problem of the chain is in essentials reduced to one of blockade.*

To recognize an enemy Pawn-chain as an enemy and to go for it is one and the same thing; this may be formulated thus:—
Freeing operations in the region of a Pawn-chain can never be set on foot soon enough.

This war of liberation will, however, be conducted thus:—
We first direct our operations against the base, which we attack with a Pawn, and, by threats or otherwise, seek to cut off the base from its associates in the chain. This done, we turn our attention to the next opponent, namely the link which is now become the new base. For instance, after *1.* P—K4, P—K3; *2.* P—Q4, P—Q4; *3.* P—K5, the Black Pawns (K3, Q4) appear to be checked. The attack on the cramping White chain should, by our rule, be launched without any delay, and note, by *3.* . . . . P—QB4, not by *3.* . . . . P—KB3; for the link P—K5 corresponds to an architectural adornment to our building (the chain), whereas the P at Q4 is the very foundation of the whole structure. If we wish to sap a building, we should not begin with its architectural ornaments, but we should blow up its foundations, for then the destruction of the ornaments with all the rest will automatically follow.

White has several replies to *3.* . . . . P—QB4. The plan of the second player will stand out clearest if White plays ingenuously, as if he had no conception of the problem of the Pawn-chain, therefore, in some such way as this: *4.* P x P, B x P; *5.* Kt—QB3 *?*, P—B3 *!*. Events have taken their logical

course. The Hetman, the P at Q4, was first put out of action,
and then the P at K5 got it in the neck. All things decently and
in order, but we must always begin with the Hetman, the base
of the Pawn-chain. To continue our game: after 5. . . . . P—B3

there would follow 6. P x P
(which is as artless as ever. Kt—
B3 was certainly better), Kt x P;
7. Kt—B3, Kt—B3; 8. B—Q3, P—
K4 ! and thanks to White's faulty
strategy, Black's freeing operations, which as a rule take up
some 20–25 moves, may already
be regarded as ended. Black first
caused the links in White's chain
voluntarily to disappear one after the other, beginning with the
base (by the captures P x QBP,
P x KBP) and thereupon let his

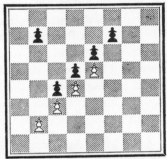

DIAGRAM 114

Here the right procedure for Black
is to attack the chain by . . . . P—
Kt4—5 in order to provoke BP x P.
. . . . P—B3 would be wrong

own Pawns advance in triumph, with . . . . P—K4. This advance, so eagerly sought after, affords the explanation of the
energetic measures taken by Black with his third and following
moves, namely the recovery of their mobility for his cramped
Pawns. This was all that Black sought or desired. Accordingly
it often happens that Pawns thus advanced are filled with a
particularly war-like spirit; we get the impression that they
wish to take bitter vengeance for the humiliation they have
suffered by being hemmed in.

Diagram 114 shows another example. Here White's P at B3
is the base of the White Chain, not his P at Kt2, be it well
noted, for this Pawn has not yet been attached to the association in the Black and White Pawn chain, since a Black colleague is wanting at White's QKt3; and against this base we
send forward the QKtP to storm it; accordingly . . . . P—Kt4

—Kt5. Having provoked BP x P, the P at Q4 is now promoted to the base, but, unlike his predecessor, is not protected. The unprotected base (*i.e.*, undefended by a Pawn) is, however, a weakness, and hence gives occasion for a lasting siege, such as we propose to consider in § 5. In the above example . . . . P—B3 (instead of, correctly, ... P—Kt4—Kt5) would have to be labeled a mistake, for after the fall of the KP White's chain would still remain intact.

We are now on the road to a true understanding of the matter. The freeing operations in the domain of the Pawn-chain are analogous to the fight against a troublesome block-ader (Chapter 4) and accordingly our present problem is re-duced to one of blockade.

§ 4. *The transference of the blockade rules from the "passed Pawn" to the "chain." The exchange maneuver (to bring about the substitution of a more amenable enemy blockader for a strong one) applied to the Pawn-chain.*

It is clear to us, after studying Chapter 4, that every enemy piece which holds in check a Pawn which would otherwise be mobile, must be conceived of as a blockader. Nevertheless it must cause surprise that, after the moves *1*. P—K4, P—K3; *2*. P—Q4, P—Q4; *3*. P—K5, we should agree to regard the P at Q4 and P at K5 as proper blockaders in our sense; and the surprise lies in seeing a Pawn so described, for in general we think of Pawns as being blockaded, and the rôle of a blockader we imagine to be reserved for an officer. This is in general true, but the Pawns in a chain are Pawns of a higher order, and in their functions differ from the common herd. To conceive of the Pawns in a chain as blockaders would then appear to be quite correct.

Recognizing this, let us now try to apply the "exchange ma-neuver on the blockading square," with which we became acquainted in Chapter 4, to the chain. The exchange, we said there, could only be justified if the new blockader proved himself to be weaker than his predecessor. The same applies to the chain.

An example: After 1. P—K4, P—K3; 2. P—Q4, P—Q4; 3. P—K5, P—QB4 !; 4. Kt—QB3, Black can try to get the blockader (the P at Q4) replaced by another (the Q at Q4). In fact, after the further moves 4. . . . . P x P; 5. Q x P, Kt—QB3, the Q turns out to be a blockader whom it will be difficult to maintain at her post, and hence the exchange is proved to be correct; and this in spite of a possible 6. B—QKt5, for after 6. . . . . B—Q2; 7. B x Kt, P x B; Black has two Bishops and a mobile mass of Pawns in the center, and has the advantage.

On the other hand this exchange maneuver would be weak after 1. P—K4, P—K3; 2. P—Q4, P—Q4; 3. P—K5, P—QB4; 4. P—QB3, Kt—QB3; 5. B—K3, for after 5. . . . . P x P (. . . . Q—Kt3 is better); 6. B x P, the B would be a tough customer to deal with, and a further exchange, so as to be rid of him, i.e., say 6. . . . . Kt x B; 7. Q x Kt, Kt—K2; 8. Kt—B3, Kt—B3; 9. Q—KB4, would lead to the driving off of the blockading troops, but only at the cost of loss of time caused by the moves of the Black KKt.

In this position White stands quite well; his pieces are placed as they would be for a King-side attack, but have also a sufficient bearing on the center. For example: 9. . . . . P—B3 (to roll up White's chain); 10. B—Kt5, P—QR3; 11. B x Kt ch, P x B; 11. O—O, and Black will never succeed in making his P at K3 mobile, for if . . . . P x P, then Kt x P, and the establishment of the Kt at this point, K5, would follow.

With this we have got further towards an understanding of the Pawn-chain. All exchange operations in the region of a chain only take place with the object of replacing a strong enemy blockader by a weaker one, and the experience we have got from Chapter 4 will be of great help here. We have, I mean, to decide in a given case whether the blockader in question is strong or weak, elastic or inelastic, and the faculty of discriminating rightly in such cases will be of enormous service to us. See for example Diag. 115. Here Q—B2 would be a weak move in spite of the sharp threat of B x Kt and B x P. The mistake lies in the fact that White had much better have done something towards the defense of his blockading wall, *e.g.*, Kt—Q2, O—O; Kt—B3. On the other hand if *1*. Q—B2 *P*, the continuation might be *1.* . . . . O—O; *2.* B x Kt, R x B; *3.* B x P *ch*, K—R1; *4.* B—Kt6 (or Q3), P—K4 *!*. White, it is true, has won a Pawn, but Black has overcome the blockade, and now stands ready to march in the center. White should lose.

In Diag. 116, the maneuver *15.* B—Q4, Q—B2; *16.* Q—K2 might be considered, with the intention of following with *17.* Kt—K5. However, this plan to widen the blockading ring is

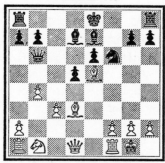

DIAGRAM 115

Permanently to occupy the points K5 and Q4 is White's immediate problem. Which move is the better to this end, Kt—Q2, or Q—B2?

DIAGRAM 116

To attain a permanent blockade of Black's P at K3 and P at Q4, which is the better: *15.* B—Q4, Q—B2; *16.* Q—K2, or at once *15.* Q—K2?

impracticable, for, after *16.* Q—K2, Kt—Kt5 *! !*; *17.* P—KR3, P—K4 *!*, the Black Pawns assert themselves whatever counter-measures be taken. The right move is rather *15.* Q—K2; and there follows *15.* . . . . QR—B1 (or *15.* . . . . B x B; *16.* Kt x B,

QR—B1; *17*. P—B4 *!*); *16*. **B—Q4** *!* , **Q—B2**; *17*. **Kt—K5**, and
Black is seriously blockaded. We may say therefore that the
line of play *15*. B—Q4, Q—B2; *16*. Q—K2 was bad because the
reserve blockader who was keeping watch (the Kt at KB3)
would have but slight blockading effect, that is to say would
never succeed in reaching K5. In the notes to my game against
Salve (No. 46, from which this example is taken) we shall
prove our theory of exchanges by further examples.

§ 5.   *The conception of a war of movement and that of siege
warfare applied to the region of the chain. The attacking party
at the parting of the ways.*

If the attacking party has played in the spirit of the explana-
tions given in this chapter (that is to say, attack on the "base,"
and the correct application of the exchange operation on the
blockading point), it will often happen that the full freedom
of his hampered Pawns will be
his reward. There will be times,
however, when the fight he has
waged with the measures here
indicated will reach a dead point,
and in such cases the use of
some new plan becomes necessary. As an example we will take
the position given in Diag. 117.
The opening moves of the game
were: *1*. P—K4, P—K3; *2*. P—Q4,
P—Q4; *3*. P—K5, P—QB4; *4*. P—
QB3, Kt—QB3; *5*. Kt—B3, Q—Kt3
(Black seeks by hook or by crook
to induce White to give up his
base, the P at Q4. An attack with
this purpose, one which aims at
the rolling up of the chain, we

DIAGRAM 117

Black with the move is at the parting
of the ways between the war of
movement and positional warfare.
The former would take the course:
. . . . B—Q2 in order finally to
cause White to make the move P x P
which Black desires; the latter takes
the form . . . . P x P; P x P followed by a long siege of White's
Pawn at Q4

class as a war of movement, of which the move . . . . Q—Kt3 must be regarded as a part. Q moves in the opening are as a rule out of place; here, however, the weal or woe of the Pawn-chain dictates all our actions); 6. B—Q3 (See Diag. 117), B—Q2. A very plausible move; and since White still hesitates to make the capture P x P, Black proposes to make his decision easier by 7. . . . . R—B1. The right move, however, was 6. . . . . P x P; 7. P x P, and with it to adopt other methods, namely siege or positional warfare. These were the opening moves of the game No. 46, Nimzovich—Salve, played at Carls-bad in 1911. From first move to last it is highly instructive; moreover, I regard it as the first game to be played in the spirit of the new philosophy of the center, which I originated. The student is advised to play through this game before proceeding further.

We have already said, and the course of the game shows, that at his sixth move (see Diag. 117) Black could, and should, have sought a quieter channel by playing 6. . . . . P x P; 7. P x P, B—Q2; with eventual . . . . KKt—K2—B4. He preferred, however, to play for the complete capitulation of his opponent (in the region of the chain, I mean). His plan was (1) to force White to play QP x QBP and KP x KBP, (2) to drive off any blockading pieces that might take their place, (3) triumphantly to advance his center Pawns, now freed. His plan failed because the substitute blockaders were not to be driven away, that is to say they had a strong blockading effect. The two fol-lowing postulates are here of importance: (a) It makes no dif-ference whatever to the strangled (*i.e.*, hemmed in) Pawns whether they are strangled by Pawns or by officers; the opera-tion is as painful in one case as in the other; whence it follows that (b) the destruction of the cramping Pawns in the chain does not in itself imply a more or less complete liberating op-eration, for the substitute blockaders, the pieces, have still to be driven away. How and in what measure this last is possible is the question of really decisive importance.

The following, taken from my article, *"The surrender of the center—a prejudice,"* written in 1913, may serve to throw light on the relations between Pawns and pieces:—"True, the Pawns are best fitted for building up the center, since they are the most stable; on the other hand pieces stationed in the center can very well take the place of Pawns." Moreover, as we shall see later, the center can often be effectively held at long range by Bishops and Rooks, so that the actual occupation of the center by a Pawn or Pawns does not necessarily mean its control. The greater part of this article is reprinted in II. i. § 7 below; at the moment we would only remark that we are inclined to regard as most dangerous any liberating operation which is begun *but not completed* (as in Salve's attempt in the game under consideration—No. 46), dangerous that is to say, to the one ostensibly freeing himself. And now to return to the position on Diagram 117.

§ 5a. *Positional warfare: the slow siege of the unprotected base. Repeated bombardment. The defending pieces get in one another's way. How can we maintain the pressure? The genesis of new weaknesses. The base as a weakness in the end game.*

Since in the position shown on Diagram 117 the move 6. . . . . B—Q2 seems to give little promise of profit, Black, as we have several times insisted, had much better have played 6. . . . . P x P. What does this move signify? The White base (P at Q4) has thereby been made immobile, has been fixed at Q4. Before . . . . P x P took place White's QP could, whether for good or evil, at any rate leave his place (by QP x P); but now this is no longer possible. We must be quite clear on one point, that by playing 6. . . . . P x P Black has had to resign himself to renouncing his ambitious dreams of forcing his opponent into complete capitulation in the chain area; these are now gone to their grave. But Black does retain certain small yet real possibilities. For instance: White's P at Q4 will be attacked by several pieces, not so much for the reason that the conquest of White's base is likely, but rather in order to force upon the defending enemy pieces a passive, because purely defensive, rôle. Black's aim is, in fact, an ideal one, the advantage of the aggressive position for his pieces discussed in I. vi. The continuation could be 6. . . . . P x P; 7. P x P, B—Q2 (threatening . . . . Kt x QP, which, of course, could not be done before because of 7. . . . . Kt x QP ? ?; 8. Kt x Kt, Q x Kt; 9. B—Kt5 *ch* winning the Q); 8. B—K2 (if 8. B—B2 Black could obtain the two Bishops with 8. . . . . Kt—Kt5), KKt—K2 !. Whether it be slow or quick, Black chooses the development which puts pressure on the base. And rightly, for in close games, those characterized by the presence of Pawn-chains, the chain is the one true guide post. 9. P—QKt3, Kt—B4; 10. B—Kt2 (see Diagram 118), B—Kt5 *ch* !; this check shows up, and in the most glaring light, so to say, the dark side of an enforced defense by many pieces. The defending pieces are in one another's way. 11. K—B1 (for either 11. Kt—B3 or QKt—Q2 would rob the base of a defender), B—K2. Tarrasch's idea, the student should ponder the argument on which this move is based. If he is to keep up the pressure on White's P at Q4 Black must never allow the equilibrium of attack and defense (now 3:3) to be disturbed to his disadvantage. The attacking pieces must strive to maintain their attacking positions. To effect this 11. . . . . P—KR4 could be played (to prevent P—KKt4); the text move attains the same end by other means. If now 12. P—KKt4 the answer would be 12. . . . . Kt—R5; an attacker and a defender would disappear together and the *status quo* would be maintained.

The typical strategy appropriate to the various cases which may arise is made clear by the following postulates:

(*a*) The enemy base, being fixed to one spot, should be attacked by several pieces.

(*b*) By these means we shall at least obtain the ideal advantage of the aggressive position for our pieces. Worth mentioning in this connection is the slight elasticity (capacity for maneuvering), possessed by the defending pieces; for instance, in the case of a sudden attack on another wing, they will not be able to equal the attacking pieces in rapidity of motion, and will lag behind.

DIAGRAM 118

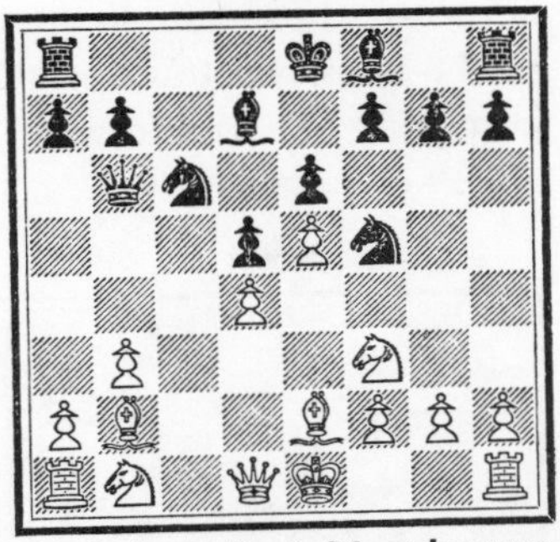

White's base, P at Q4 under pressure. The typical siege of an "unprotected" base

(*c*) We must seek to keep up the pressure on the base for as long as possible, at any rate until the appearance of new weaknesses in the enemy camp, which will follow as the logical consequence of his difficulties in development.

(*d*) When this occurs our plan of action will be modified; the original weakness, the base, will be let alone, the new one attacked with the greatest energy. And only much later, perhaps not until the end game, will the weak enemy base be again "promoted" to the dignity of being our objective.

(*e*) The weak base is, when all is said and done, to be regarded as, in particular, an end game weakness; since the specific attacking instrument, the open adjoining file (in this case the QB file) only comes completely into its rights in the end game (. . . . R—B5 x P at Q4, or . . . . R—B7—Q7 x P at Q4).

(*f*) The attacking party must never forget that he on his side has a base to defend. If his opponent succeeds in making his part of the chain region healthy, *i.e.*, in shaking off the pressure on his base (the P at Q4 in our case), an entirely new and disagreeable turn may be given to the game by his playing P—KB4—B5, with attack on the base (PK3), or on the other hand launching an attack with his pieces on the King's position which is cramped by his P at K5.

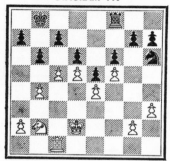

DIAGRAM 119

The application of (*a*) will hardly present any difficulties to the student. Take for instance Diagram 119: The chain we have to do with is formed of the KP's and QP's on both sides. Black's base is the P at Q3. White now plays *1.* P x QP, P x P; *2.* R—B6, Kt—B2; *3.* Kt—B4, R—Q1 (if . . . . R—QB1 then *4.* P—Kt5, R x R; *5.* QP x R with the superior end game); *4.* P—QR4 ! (to maintain the attacking Kt at B4 on this square); White has now put the base P at Q3, under pressure, and consequently has the advantage referred to of the more aggressive position for his pieces. The Kt at B4 is more aggressively placed than Black's Kt at B2, etc. This advantage could be exploited either by *5.* P—Kt5 followed by, say, K—B3 and P—QR5, or by play on the King's wing: P—KR4, and then K—K3—B3—Kt4—R5 followed by P—Kt4—Kt5; when the parry . . . . P—KR3 would allow the King's entry at KKt6.

It is much more difficult for the student to assimilate the points made in (*c*) and (*d*). The direct exploitation of a Pawn weakness is not, properly speaking, a matter for the middle game; see point (*e*). All that we may hope to attain is to cause our opponent to suffer for a considerable period under the disadvantage of the duties of defense which have been forced on him. If, as a result of these difficulties, a new weakness be induced in the enemy camp (as is by no means improb-

able), it is not merely *permissible* for the attacking party to re-
lease the base from pressure, in order to devote his attention to
the new weakness; such a course is *absolutely indicated.* The
further removed (geographically and logically) the two weaknesses are from one another, the better for us! This connection
of ideas was more or less unknown to the pseudo-classical
school. Tarrasch, for instance, was wont with relentless persistence to keep under continual attack the base which he had once
selected as his objective, or at least to remain true to the wing
of his first choice. (See Game No. 19, Paulsen—Tarrasch.)

In opposition to this we lay stress on the principle that the
weakness of the enemy base cannot be completely exploited
until the end game—*cf.* (*e*); or,
more accurately: in the end
game our aim is the direct, that
is to say actual, conquest of the
base which serves as our objective; in the middle game the
bombardment of this base can
and should only help to yield us
indirect advantages. For example, suppose Black to be attacking the enemy base in the middle game; White's pieces will get
in one another's way, difficulties
of development will arise, and

DIAGRAM 120

Black to move. How is the pressure
on White's Q4 to be kept up? The
position of the K at KB1 is a disadvantage. How can this be exposed?

White will find himself forced to create a new weakness in his
own camp, in order to remove those difficulties. On this Black
now concentrates his attack, and only in the end game may he
find it profitable to take up again the attack on his first objective, the enemy base.

As an example of this indirect exploitation of a weakened
enemy base we may study the position shown on Diagram 120

taken from Game No. 19, Paulsen—Tarrasch. After the moves
1. P—K4, P—K3; 2. P—Q4, P—Q4; 3. P—K5, P—QB4; 4. P—QB3,
Kt—QB3; 5. Kt—B3, Q—Kt3; 6. B—Q3, P x P; 7. P x P, B—Q2; 8.
B—K2, KKt—K2; 9. P—QKt3, Kt—B4; 10. B—Kt2, B—Kt5 *ch*, White
saw himself forced to forego castling by having to play K—B1;
thus the pressure on his P at Q4 has taken tangible shape.
Black's problem, therefore, no longer consists in keeping up the
pressure on the QP (which could be done by 11. . . . . P—
KR4 or 11. . . . . B—K2 as we have already indicated (see
Diagram 118); he should rather give up the attack on White's
base, and do everything he can to expose and exploit the weakness of White's K at B1. This, indeed, is only possible by means
of a hidden sacrifice of the exchange. In this position in reply
to 11. K—B1, I play 11. . . . . O—O. If then 12. B—Q3 to lessen
the pressure on the QP, there would follow 12. . . . . P—B3;
13. B x Kt, P x B; with advantage to Black in his two Bishops.
The main variation, after 11. K—B1, O—O ! !, lies in the continuation 12. P—Kt4, Kt—R3; 13. R—Kt1, P—B3; 14. P x P, R x P !;

DIAGRAM 121

The position after the exposure of
White's disadvantage in the position
of his K at B1. In spite of his material superiority White stands badly

15. P—Kt5, R x Kt; 16. B x R (or
P x Kt, R—B2), Kt—B4; 17. R—
Kt4. (See Diagram 121) White's
desolate King's wing and the
weakly defended points in the
KB file ought, in my opinion, to
lead to a lost game. I give one
possible continuation: 17. . . . . .
B—K1 (. . . . R—KB1 is also
good enough); 18. Q—K2,
QKt x P; 19. R x Kt !, Kt x R; 20.
Q—K5 (the last chance), B—Kt4
ch; 21. K—Kt2, Kt—B4; 22. B x P
(if 22. Kt—B3 then 22. . . . .

B x Kt; 23. B x B, P—Q5, etc.), P x B; 23. Q x Kt, R—KB1; 24.
Q x QP *ch*, R—B2 ! (a self-pin for the purpose of safeguarding

his KKt2 against a possible Q—Q4); 25. Q—Q4, B—B4, and White must resign. The decision took place, as was logical, on the King's wing; the second player was able to exploit to the full the new weakness without any regard to the old one. The student will do well to note most carefully the transfer of the attack from the center (the base, P at Q4) to the King's wing which had been weakened by K—B1. The transfer called for resolute attacking play.

As an antithesis to the maneuver we have just demonstrated we would emphasize the fact (see Diagram 120) that *11. . . . . B—K2*, after *12. P—Kt3* and *13. K—Kt2*, with the subsequent safeguarding and relieving of the P at Q4 would give White good chances, for after his position had been consolidated White would be well able to turn the tables on his opponent as outlined in (*f*): by an attack on Black's King's wing which is cramped by the P at K5. (See Game No. 20, Nimzovich—Tarrasch.)

Before we proceed further, we impress upon the student that he should practice so as to be able to take advantage of a weak enemy base in the end game. We recommend the study of Game No. 15 and further the application of the following method. Set up a Pawn-chain on the board, *e.g.*, White: Pawns at Q4 and K5; Black: Pawns at Q4 and K3; give to each side some more Pawns (White: QR2, QKt2, KB2, KKt2, KR2. Black: QR2, QKt2, KB2, KKt2, KR2) and try to take advantage of the weakness of White's P at Q4 in an end game with Rooks on the board or a Rook and a minor piece on each side.

§ 6. *The transfer of the attack.*

In the position on Diagram 117 Black had the choice, as we have often pointed out already, of two different lines of play, namely between *6. . . . . B—Q2* with a war of movement, or *6. . . . . P x P* with positional or siege warfare directed against White's fixed base, the P at Q4. It will be granted that a moment must come when Black will be forced to make his choice. It is not possible to keep open at will the choice between two lines of play, least of all when we are concerned with a Pawn-chain, for the simple reason that the defending party, relying on the state of suspense in the position, and the possibilities arising out of it, can threaten an attack to free himself. Once this enemy threat becomes actual, we are forced to make an immediate decision. Another crisis which compels a decision occurs when our opponent threatens us on another wing, when we shall have to decide on as sharp a counter as possible, since any further flirting with two different plans would no longer be opportune.

Whereas we have up to now considered only the choice between two methods of attack, while the objective (White's P at Q4 in the example we have taken) remained fixed, and was therefore not in doubt, it will be shown in what follows how painful even the choice of an objective can sometimes be. We are concerned with a Pawn-chain which is to be attacked. "What can there be doubtful in such a case?" the reader will ask. "We must of course direct our attack against its base?" But what if the base is not to be shaken; would it not be better to direct our attack against a new base? How this is done will be seen from the strategem of the transference of the attack which will not be sketched.

DIAGRAM 122

Black can play . . . . P x P or he can push . . . . P—B5, changing the base of White's Pawn-chain

Let us consider the following chain resulting after 1. P—K4, P—K4; 2. Kt—KB3, Kt—QB3; 3. B—B4, B—K2; 4. P—Q4, P—Q3; 5. P—Q5, Kt—Kt1. White now chooses the center as the theater of war, and plays say B—Q3 and P—B4, with the idea of eventually P—B5. (He could as an alternative have decided on an attack with his pieces—without playing P—B4—on the enemy Q's wing which is cramped by the P at Q5.) Black tries to make possible . . . . P—KB4, in order to shake White's base, the P at K4. The pseudo-classical school held . . . . P—KB4 to be a refutation of White's P—Q5. This is, however, not the case, as I proved in my revolutionizing article on Dr. Tarrasch's *Moderne Schachpartie;* . . . . P—KB4 is only a natural reaction to White's P—Q5, and as such every bit as endurable as P—QB4—B5. In essentials the position arrived at could be that shown on Diagram 122. Black's attack on the base P at K4 does not look as if it promised much; for if at any time . . . . BP x P, the answer would be either P x P, and the base is well defended, or Kt (or B) x P with a good "substitute center." Hence Black plays . . . . P—B5, thus changing White's base from P at K4 to P at KB3. True the latter can be sufficiently defended (against . . . . P—KKt4—Kt5 x BP which Black plans), but White's King's position seems then to be threatened and is certainly cramped. In other words White's King's position marks out the P at KB3 as a weaker base than the P at K4.

And there are other circumstances which may make one base appear weaker than another; hence the switching over of the attack from one base to the next is not a mere matter of chance (as Alapin and other masters seemed to think before the appearance of my essay to which reference has just been made); it is in fact an additional weapon in the fight against a Pawn-chain. A judgment on the strength of a Pawn-chain as a whole must run something like this: "The base K4 is difficult of attack, the base KB3 (after . . . . P—KB5) is for such and such reasons sensitive to attack, etc., hence it will pay to transfer our attack to the new base, KB3." This formulation of the case I may claim as my discovery.

We must content ourselves with the above concise suggestions else this Chapter would stretch to too great a length. This transference of attack is typical, and we could give endless examples from games. We will, however, only show the following opening here. *1.* P—K4, Kt—QB3; *2.* P—Q4, P—Q4; *3.* P—K5, B—B4; *4.* P—KB4, P—K3; *5.* Kt—KB3, Kt—Kt5; *6.* B—Kt5 *ch*, P—B3; *7.* B—R4, P—QKt4; *8.* P—QR3 *!*, Kt—R3; *9.* B—Kt3, P—B4; *10.* P—B3. Since White's base, the P at Q4; seemed actually to be over-defended, Black quite rightly played here *10. . . . .* P—B5, transferring the attack from White's Q4 to his QB3. After the further moves *11.* B—B2, B x B; *12.* Q x B, Kt—K2 (*cf.* II. ii. on Restraint), Black put under restraint White's King's Wing which was ready to attack, by making the natural advance P—B5 impossible, and then by means of . . . . P—QR4 and . . . . P—QKt5 finally launched the attack on the new objective, White's base at QB3.

Before closing this chapter and with it the discussion of the "elements" we should like to point out quite briefly how difficult it is to conduct the play in the Pawn-chain correctly. Very soon after the formation of the chain we have to choose whether a wing or the base shall be our objective; then later, incidental to an attack on the base, we have to make the difficult decision between a war of movement and siege warfare; and, as if that is not enough, we have always to reckon with a possible transference of the attack to the next link of the chain. In addition to all this we must never forget, in spite of all these possibilities of attack, that we, too, have a vulnerable base.

A difficult chapter, but one in which the inherent obscurity of its subject matter will, we hope, now have largely disappeared, thanks to our treatment of it.

It will have been seen that my laws governing Pawn-chains have grown logically from those applying to "open files" and "play against the blockader." The reader will find a further discussion of the subject in Part II, Chap. ii on the "Center" and "Restraint"; he is urged at this point to play over Games No. 19 to 24 and No. 46, which illustrate the subject of the Pawn-chain.

SECOND PART

Position Play

1. The Conception of Position Play and the Problem of the Center

Sets forth as introduction my conception of position play and carries further the treatment of the problem of the center.

§ 1. *The mutual relations between the treatment of the elements and of position play.*

As the reader will soon see, my conception of position play is based for the greater part on the knowledge we have laboriously wrung from our consideration of the elements. Especially is this true of the devices of Centralization and of Restraint which we have outlined. The connection which thus exists has the advantage, that it must give to this book a certain unity of structure, which can only be of benefit to the reader. It would, however, be an error on his part to indulge in the expectation that the exploration of the spirit of position play cannot now afford him any further difficulties worth mentioning. For firstly, position play contains other ideas than those we have met so far, as for instance the law of "over-protection," which I discovered, or the very difficult strategy of the center; while secondly, the actual transference of the ideas which we have learned from the elements on to a new field, that of position play, is difficult enough. The degree of difficulty is much the same as that which faces a composer who wishes to adapt a violin sonata for a full orchestra. However unchanged the theme, the motives, may be, the whole must gain in depth and breadth. Let us explain this by a concrete case in chess, for instance "restraint." In the "elements" this touches a comparatively small field; a passed Pawn is to be checked, or an enemy Pawn-chain which has become free to move is to be prevented from advancing. In position play on the other hand the restraint theme makes a much more impressive appearance; now it is often a whole wing which must be held in check. In games in which the player who is putting restraint on his opponent is "scoring" his theme very heavily (I have in mind for instance my game against Johner, No. 35), we have the whole board, both wings, every corner taking up the theme, and blaring it forth.

The second case is even worse for the student; for here the theme appears in epic breadth, with a series of seemingly purposeless moves, to and fro, mixed with it. This kind of maneuvering corresponds in a way to the accompaniment in music. Many people hold both this maneuvering and accompaniment as things which may be dispensed with; many lovers of chess go so far as to characterize this moving to and fro as a fruit of decadence. In reality, however, this maneuvering often enough provides the only strategical—be it noted strategical, not merely psychological—way of throwing in the scale a slight advantage in terrain and the consequent capacity of moving our troops more quickly from one wing to the other.

§ 2. *On certain noxious weeds which choke a proper understanding of position play, namely (a) the obsession to be for ever doing something which haunts so many amateurs, and (b) the overrating of the principle of the accumulation of small advantages which may inspire the Master.*

There are, it would seem, a number of amateurs to whom position play appears to mean nothing. Twenty years' experience in teaching chess has, however, convinced me that this trouble can be easily removed, since it results from a faulty presentation of the subject. I maintain that there is nothing inherently mysterious in position play, and that every single amateur who has studied my "elements," in the first nine chapters of this book, must find it an easy matter to penetrate into the spirit of this style of play; he has only (1) to destroy the weeds which perhaps choke his understanding, and (2) to carry out the precepts laid down in the rest of the book.

A typical and very wide-spread misconception is the assumption of many amateurs that each single move must accomplish something directly; so that such a player will only seek for moves which threaten something, or for a threat to be parried, and will disregard all other possible moves such as waiting moves, or moves calculated to put his house in order, etc. Positional moves as I conceive them, are in general neither threatening nor defensive ones, but rather moves designed to give to our position security in the wider sense, and to this end it is necessary for our pieces to establish contact with the enemy's strategically important points or our own. This will be brought out later when we are considering "over-protection," and the fight against enemy freeing moves.

When a positional player, that is one who understands how to safeguard his position in the wider sense, engages one who is a purely combinational player, the latter who has only attack in his thoughts, is preoccupied with but two kinds of counter-moves, and looks only for a defensive move from his opponent, or calculates on the possibility of a counter-attack; and now the positional player dumfounds him by choosing a move which will not fit into either of these categories. The move somehow or other brings his pieces into contact with some key point, and this contact has miraculous effects; his position is thereby imbued with strength, and the attack on it comes to naught. A similar disconcerting effect is also often produced by a move which protects a point which is under no sort of attack. The positional player protects a point not only for the sake of that point, but also because he knows that the piece which he uses for its defense must gain in strength by mere contact with the point in question. This will be considered further under "over-protection."

And now I will take a game which is an admirable illustration of the very widespread misconception to which I have referred. I had the White pieces against a very well known and by no means weak amateur, who, however, was under the impression that a proper game must take some such course as this:—One side Castles K-side, the other Q-side, a violent Pawn attack is launched on both sides against the respective castled positions, and he who gets in first wins! We shall see how this amateurish conception was reduced ad absurdum.

The game was played in Riga in 1910 and ran:—*1.* P—K4, P—K4; *2.* Kt—KB3, Kt—QB3; *3.* P—Q4, P x P; *4.* Kt x P, P—Q3 (this move is quite playable but only in conjunction with a strong defensive structure, attainable by say . . . . Kt—B3, B—K2, O—O, and R—K1 with pressure on White's KP); *5.* Kt—QB3, Kt—B3; *6.* B—K2, B—K2; *7.* B—K3, B—Q2; *8.* Q—Q2, P—QR3; *9.* P—B3, O—O; *10.* O—O—O, P—QKt4. The attack seems hardly in place here, so that my opponent's expression, "Now we're in for it," charged as it was with the lust of battle, struck one as all the prettier. I understood him at once; he clearly expected the answer P—KKt4 with a consequent race between the Pawns on both sides, according to the motto "who gets in first wins." See Diagram 123. What did happen however was *11.* Kt—Q5. With this move, by which an outpost station in the Q file is occupied, White obeys another principle of position play, namely that premature flank attacks should be punished by play in the center (=break-through in, or occupa-

DIAGRAM 123

The attempted attack by . . . . P—QKt4(?) is to be defeated by a positional move. What is this to be?

tion of, the center). There followed *11. . . . . KKt x Kt; 12. P x Kt, Kt x Kt; 13. B x Kt*, and White has very much the better game. He has a centralized position which cannot possibly be taken away from him by, say, *13. . . . . B—KB3; 14. P—KB4, R—K1; 15. B—KB3* followed by *KR—K1*; and moreover Black has a disorganized Q wing which exposes bad weaknesses for the end game. And the moral of the story is: Do not be always thinking of attack! Safeguarding moves (in the higher sense), indicated by the demands made on us by the position, are often much more advisable.

Another erroneous conception may be found among Masters. Many of these and numbers of strong amateurs are under the impression that position play above all is concerned with the accumulation of small advantages, in order to exploit them in the end game. This mode of play is said to demand the finest intelligence and also to be aesthetically most satisfying.

In contradiction to this we would remark that the accumulation of small advantages is by no means the most important constituent of position play. We are inclined rather to assign to this plan of operation a very subordinate rôle. Moreover the difficulty of this method is very much overestimated, and lastly it is not quite easy to see how the petty storing up of values can be called beautiful. Does not this procedure remind one in some sense of the activities of some old pinchpenny; and who would think of calling them beautiful? And so we here note the fact that there are quite other matters to which the attention of the positional player must be directed, and which place this "accumulation" wholly in the shade.

What are these things, and in what do I see the idea of true position play? The answer is short and to the point:—in a "prophylactic."

§ 3. *My original conception of positional play as such: the well known idea of the accumulation of small advantages is only of second or third significance; of much greater importance is a prophylactic applied both externally and internally. My new principle of over-protection, its definition and meaning.*

As I have several times observed, neither attack nor defense is, in my opinion, a matter properly pertaining to position play, which is rather an energetic and systematic application of prophylactic measures. What it is concerned with above all else is to blunt the edge of certain possibilities which in a positional sense would be undesirable. Of such possibilities, apart from the mishaps to which the less experienced player is exposed, there are two kinds only. One of these is the possibility of the opponent making a "freeing" Pawn move. The positional player has accordingly so to arrange his pieces that enemy freeing moves may be prevented. In connection with which it is to be noticed that we must examine every case that arises to see whether the freeing move in question really is freeing. For as I pointed out in my article on Dr. Tarrasch's *Die moderne Schachpartie*, the saying, "all is not gold that glitters," applies to freeing moves. Many there are which only lead to an unfavorable, premature opening up of the game, whereas other freeing moves should be considered as normal reactions, and as such must be calmly accepted; for it were a presumption to wish to fight against natural phenomena! In spite of the fact that freeing moves will be considered in detail in another place under "restraint," it will not be amiss to give here two illustrations. From these examples we shall see that not every freeing move need be prevented.

For an example of an incorrect freeing move see Diagram 124. In similar positions the move . . . . P—K4 would properly be classed under freeing moves; for it opens up Black's otherwise cramped game, and in addition stands for the action in the center, positionally indicated as a counter-measure to the encircling movement which White is striving for on the Q's wing. Nevertheless White rightly plays here P—QKt4 ! (instead of

DIAGRAM 124

White by playing P—QKt4, allows his opponent to make the freeing advance . . . . P—K4. Was he right in so doing?

R—K1), as will be seen. *1.* P—QKt4 *!,* P—K4 *?; 2.* P x P, Kt x P; *3.* B—KB4 *!,* Kt x Kt *ch; 4.* Q x Kt, Q—Q1; *5.* P—R3 followed by QR—Q1 and the occupation of the square Q4 (blockading point) by B or Kt, with superior game for White: Black was, to start with, behind in tempi; hence the failure of his freeing maneuver.

Our second example, Diagram 125, shows us that it is not possible permanently to hold up a freeing advance for which in the nature of the things the time is ripe; our object must therefore in similar cases be limited to making the freeing maneuver as difficult of execution as possible, nor must we under any circumstances persist in the attempt, impossible of achievement from the start, to stop such an advance. The position in Diagram 125 was reached after the moves *1.* P—K4, P—K4; *2.* Kt—KB3, Kt—QB3; *3.* B—B4, B—K2; *4.* P—Q4, P—Q3; *5.* P—Q5, Kt—Kt1. The Pawn-chain made up of the KP's and QP's will make White strive for P—QB4—B5, Black for . . . . P—KB4. Forcible measures, such as say *6.* B—Q3, Kt—KB3; *7.* P—KR3,

DIAGRAM 125

Black "threatens" . . . . P—KB4

O—O; *8.* P—KKt4 *?* would not be in keeping with the position; on the other hand *6.* B—Q3, Kt—KB3; *7.* P—B4, O—O; *8.* Kt—B3, Kt—K1; *9.* Q—K2 would seem to be indicated; in order in reply to *9. . . . .* P—KB4, to undertake the operation *10.* P x P, B x P; *11.* B x B, R x B; *12.* Kt—K4 (*cf.* the remarks on Diagram 122).

We note then, that the prevention of freeing Pawn moves (as far as this appears necessary and feasible) is of great importance in position play. Such prevention is what we wish to be understood as an exterior prophylactic. It is much more difficult to grasp the idea of an interior prophylactic, for here we have to do with an entirely new conception. We are in fact now concerned with the warding off of an evil, which has really never been understood as one, yet which can, and in general does, have a most disturbing effect on our game. The evil consists in this, that our pieces are out of, or in insufficient contact with our own strategically important points. Since I conceived of this condition as an evil, I was led to advance the strategical proposition that one must over-protect his own strategically important points, that is, provide defense in excess of attack: lay up a store of defense. My formulation of this argument runs as follows:—*Weak points, still more strong points, in short everything that we can include in the collective conception of strategically important points, ought to be over-protected.* If the pieces are so engaged, they get their reward in the fact that they will then find themselves well posted in every respect.

There are two explanatory remarks to be made here; firstly, that as we have incidentally shown in our discussion of the passed Pawn, we have the enigmatical circumstance that blockading squares prove themselves as a rule to be in every respect good squares; and the pieces detailed for dull blockade duty find, unexpectedly, their reward in the possibility of a heightened activity from their blockading station, just as in a fairy tale where good deeds are always rewarded. The idea of over-protection is in a certain sense no other than that above sketched though in an expanded form, as we may see from the following example. (See Diagram 126). Here we over-protect the strong P at K5 which has been pushed forward. The defense afforded by the QP is insufficient, since White plans to reply to . . . . P—QB4 by P x P (=surrender of the base of his chain and occupation of the point Q4 now become free.) We over-protect the KP by pieces thus: 9. Kt—Q2, and the game (Nim-zovich—Giese) continued 9. . . . . Kt—K2; 10. Kt—KB3 !, Kt—KKt3; 11. R—K1 !, B—Kt5 (to get the B finally to B2, and then,

DIAGRAM 126

Nimzovich—Giese
White to move. What point must be over-protected?

DIAGRAM 127

The career of the "over-protector": White's Kt has left KB3 for a men-acing post at KKt5

despite the over-protection of White's KP, to play . . . . P—B3); 12. P—B3, B—R4; 13. B—B4 ! (the third over-protection), O—O; 14. B—Kt3, B—B2; 15. Kt—Kt5 (and now the inner strength of over-protection is manifested in a drastic manner; the seemingly lifeless over-protectors, the Kt at KB3, the B at B4, and that old blade, the R at K1, suddenly raise a consider-able hubbub), KR—K1; 16. Kt—B4, Kt—R1; 17. Q—Kt4, Kt—B1; 18. R—K3 (the old soldier sniffs a fight and rejoices), P—QKt3 (rather better was . . . . B—Q1); 19. Kt—R5, Kt(R)—Kt3; 20. R—B3, R—K2 (See Diagram 127); 21. Kt—B6 *ch*, K—R1; and now White could win right off by 22. Kt(B6) x RP, Kt x Kt; 23. Kt x P *ch,* R x Kt; 24. R x R. The idea was the following: It was a good deed to over-protect a strategically important point; the reward came in the form of a large radius of activity for the pieces engaged on that service.

Just one more example, for later on a whole chapter will be devoted to over-protection in all its bearings. (See Diagram 128) After 15. QR—Q1, QR—K1; there followed a maneuver which seemed most surprising, namely 16. R—Q2 and 17. KR—Q1. Why? Because the Q at Q3 (and perhaps too the P at Q4) is the key stone of White's position, and hence over-protection is indicated. And in fact after a few moves the two Rooks prove to be most serviceable combatants (they protect their own King excellently). After 16. R—Q2 the continuation

DIAGRAM 128

Nimzovich—Alekhine
Baden-Baden 1925
Alekhine's last move was 14. . . . . Q—B4 ! there followed 15. QR—Q1, QR—K1. Which point now calls for over-protection?

was 16. . . . . Q—Kt4; 17. KR—Q1, B—R2 ! !; 18. Kt—B4, Kt—B4; 19. Kt—Kt5, B—Kt1 and now R—K2 and KR—K1 ought to have been played, when the over-protectors would have reaped their merited reward.

Secondly, the rule for over-protection applies, as is natural, most particularly to strong points, to important squares in the center, which are likely to come under heavy fire, to strong blockading squares, or to strong passed Pawns, etc. Ordinary weak points should under no circumstances be over-protected, for this might very well lead to the defenders getting into passive positions (*cf.* I. vi. § 2). However, a weak P that forms the base of an important Pawn-chain may and should be well

over-protected. To illustrate this let us return to our old friend
the Pawn-chain made up of the QP and KP on each·side. See
Diagram 129 and compare it with Diagram 130. In the former

DIAGRAM 129

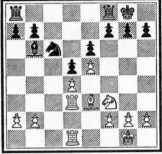

The safeguarded base Q4 increases
the importance of the attacking
(wedge) P at K5. The heaping up of
Rooks acts therefore as a deliberate
over-protection

DIAGRAM 130

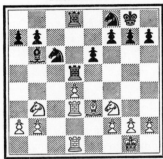

Here the piling up of White's Rooks
does not have the effect of over-
protection, but, absolutely, that of a
passive defensive position which is
classed as an evil

the Rooks protect the weak base of the Pawn-chain (every such
base is in a certain sense to be classed as weak since the one
sure defense, by a Pawn, is wanting). Yet this protection stands
the strong P at K5 also in good stead; for, as we know, the
strengthening of the base involves at the same time a strengthening throughout the whole chain. The reader is advised to
play over again my game (see No. 20) against Dr. Tarrasch, in
which, after first laboriously over-protecting the point Q4, having achieved my purpose, I got a strong attack which led to victory. The soul of that attack was, however, the P at K5, who
could so to speak trustfully lean up against the P at Q4, who by
that time was thoroughly healthy. On the other hand in the position shown on Diagram 130 the P at K5 is wanting, and hence
the rôle which the R at Q1 and R at Q3 would otherwise have
had to play, is much restricted. In fact, of the once so respon-

sible rôle nothing really remains but the tedious obligation of preventing the P at Q4 from going under. In other words, the disposition of the over-protection in the case of Diagram 130 does not carry with it any sort of plan of attack for the future (in marked contrast to the case of Diagram 129), and consequently we get nothing but that passive disposition of defending pieces, against which we had to register so emphatic a warning. To recapitulate:—*The law of over-protection applies in general only to strong points. Weak points can only lay claim to over-protection in such cases where they help to support other and strong points.*

§ 4. *Side by side with the idea of prophylactic, that of the collective mobility of a Pawn-mass is a main postulate of my teaching on position play.*

In the last resort position play is nothing other than a fight between mobility (of the Pawn-mass) on the one side and efforts to restrain this on the other. In this all-embracing struggle the intrinsically very important device of the prophylactic is merely a means to an end.

It is of the greatest importance to strive for the mobility of our Pawn-mass; for a mobile mass can exercise a crushing effect in its lust to expand. This mobility is not always injured by the presence of a Pawn that has possibly remained behind in the general advance *i.e.*, by a backward Pawn, who can perhaps be used as a nurse to tend his fellows at the front. In the case of a mobile Pawn-mass we must therefore look for collective and not individual mobility, each Pawn for itself. For instance in Diagram 131 we should expect sooner or later the leveling advance P—Q4, in order to be rid of the backward Pawn. In the game, however, there was played more correctly 17. P—B4, Q—K2; 18. P—K4 *!*, B—B3; 19. P—KKt4 (see Diagram 132), and White won easily. See Game No. 25.

DIAGRAM 131

DIAGRAM 132

Nimzovich—Prof. Michel, Semmering 1926

White establishes a mobile Pawn-mass and leaves one of them at home as nurse. How does he do it? Which Pawns advance, which Pawn remains at home?

The Pawns at K4, KB4, and KKt4, in conjunction with the diagonal QKt2 to KR8 lurking in the rear, form the storm troops. The backward QP safeguards the QBP and KP after P—Q3

Again in my game against Rubinstein (Black) in Dresden 1926 (see No. 33) I was in no hurry to get rid of my backward Pawn. Thus if after the opening moves *1.* P—QB4, P—QB4; *2.* Kt—KB3, Kt—KB3; *3.* Kt—B3, P—Q4; *4.* P x P, Kt x P; *5.* P—K4, Kt—Kt5; *6.* B—B4, P—K3; *7.* O—O, Black had played 7. . . . . . P—QR3, I should not have been in any hurry to advance the backward QP, for *8.* P—Q4, P x P; *9.* Q x P, Q x Q; *10.* Kt x Q, B—B4; *11.* B—K3, B x Kt; *12.* B x B, Kt—B7 !; *13.* QR—Q1, Kt x B; *14.* R x Kt, Kt—B3; *15.* R—Q2, P—QKt4, followed by . . . . B—Kt2 and . . . . K—K2 would have only led to an equal game. I should rather, after *8.* P—QR3, Kt(Kt5)—B3 have chosen *9.* P—Q3 and after B—K3 and marshaling my major pieces I should have been well prepared to attack. In the game he played 7. . . . . QKt—B3 (instead of . . . . P—QR3) and after *8.* P—Q3, Kt—Q5 (else *9.* P—QR3); *9.* Kt x Kt, P x Kt; *10.* Kt—K2, White got, after P—B4, a mobile Pawn-mass, effectively supported by the B at B4.

We will now turn our attention to that terrible region in which the amateur (and on occasion also the Master) only too often trips up, namely the center.

§ 5. The center. Insufficient watch kept on the central territory as a typical and ever-recurring error. The center as the Balkans of the chess-board. On the popular, but strategically doubtful diversion of the attack from the center to the wings. On the invasion of the center. The occupation of central squares.

It may be taken as common knowledge that in certain positions it is necessary to direct our pieces against the enemy center; for instance in positions characterized by the presence of White Pawns at K4 and KB4 and of Black Pawns at Q3 and KB2 (or White at Q4 and QB4; Black at QB2, and K3). On the other hand it is not so well known that it is a strategical necessity to keep the center under observation even if it be fairly well barricaded. The center is the Balkans of the chessboard; fighting may at any moment break out there. Take the position, already discussed under Diag. 96; which from the point of view of the center seems harmless enough, yet after the moves *1.* P—K4, P—K4; *2.* Kt—KB3, Kt—QB3; *3.* B—B4, B—B4; *4.* Kt—B3, Kt—B3; *5.* P—Q3, P—Q3; *6.* B—KKt5, P—KR3; *7.* B—R4, P—KKt4; *8.* B—KKt3, Black's center is threatened by two raids, (i) B—Kt5 and P—Q4, (ii) Kt—Q5 followed by P—B3 and P—Q4. Another example is furnished by the opening of the game Capablanca—Martínez (1914). After *1.* P—K4, P—K4; *2.* B—B4, B—B4; *3.* Kt—QB3, Kt—KB3; *4.* P—Q3, Kt—B3; *5.* B—KKt5, P—KR3; *6.* B—R4, P—KKt4; *7.* B—KKt3, P—KR4; *8.* P—KR4, P—Kt5; *9.* Q—Q2, P—Q3; *10.* KKt—K2, Q—K2; *11.* O—O, Black thought that he could treat himself to a move like *11. . . . .* P—R3. See Diag. 133. The loss of time involved weighs the more heavily in the scale since the position is only in appearance a closed one, and in reality can be opened at any moment. (The same applies to

90% of all closed central positions.) There followed 12. Kt—Q5, Kt x Kt; 13. P x Kt, Kt—Q5; 14. Kt x Kt, B x Kt; 15. P—B3, B—Kt3; 16. P—Q4, P—KB3 !, and as I first pointed out White could get a decisive advantage by 17. KR—K1 (Capablanca played the weaker QR—K1), e.g., 17. . . . . B—Q2 (if 17. . . . . O—O, then 18. P x P, BP x P; 19. R x P, B x P ch; 20. Q x B, Q x R; 21. B x Q, R x Q; 22. K x R, P x B; 23. R—K1, and wins; but not 23. P—Q6 ch P,

DIAGRAM 133

Capablanca—Martínez

White punishes the waste of time involved in Black's last move (. . . . P—R3) by an invasion of the center

K—Kt2; 24. P x P, P—Kt4, followed by . . . . R—R2); 18. P—R4, O—O—O; 19. P—R5, B—R2; 20. P—Kt4, followed by R(K1)—QKt1 and P—Kt5 with a winning attack. After the first six moves Black by a little more skillful strategy in the center could have got the initiative, thus:—6. . . . . P—Q3 (though 6. . . . . B—K2 would be simplest), and if 7. Kt—Q5, P—KKt4; 8. B—Kt3, then 8. . . . . B—K3; with the well known threat 9. . . . . B x Kt; 10. P x B, Kt—K2; 11. B—Kt5 ch, P—B3; 12. P x P, P x P; and Black would dominate the center. Another possibility was 6. . . . . Kt—Q5 (instead of . . . . P—Q3). e.g., 7. Kt—Q5, P—KKt4; 8. B—KKt3, P—B3 !; 9. Kt x Kt ch, Q x Kt; 10. P—B3, Kt—K3; 11. P—KR4, P—Q3, followed by . . . . B—Q2, ... O—O—O, and when opportunity occurred, ... Kt—B5. Black's text continuation was inferior.

All these examples teach us that the function of a Kt at QB3 does not solely consist in holding up a Pawn advance to Q4. No, the Kt so posted is under obligation, the moment the enemy gives him the chance, of undertaking an invasion of the center by Kt—Q5. Such a chance is often given by amateurs, who

DIAGRAM 134

White's last move P—B5 does nothing in the sense of observation of the center, but is rather a movement directed away from the center. How is this faulty strategy to be punished?

show a preference for starting a maneuver on a wing before it is justified, unfortunately without giving much thought to the question whether they may perhaps be taking too many troops away from the center: else how could such a line of play as the following persist for so many years, yes and even in Master tournaments! 1. P—K4, P—K4; 2. Kt—QB3, Kt—KB3; 3. B—B4, B—B4; 4. P—Q3, Kt—B3; 5. P—B4, P—Q3; 6. P—B5 ? ? (Diag. 134; naturally 6. Kt—B3 is the proper move), and now by 6. . . . . Kt—Q5 followed by . . . . P—B3, ... P—QKt4, ... P—QR4, ... Q—Kt3, and, if possible . . . . P—Q4, Black gets a strong game in the center and on the Queen-side which yields him a pronounced advantage. This would demonstrate the premature character of 6. P—B5.

Another example, though this time a mild one, of the evils which follow an unwarranted change of front from center to flank, against which the student cannot be sufficiently warned. 1. P—K4, P—K4; 2. Kt—KB3, P—Q3; 3. P—Q4, Kt—KB3; 4. P x P, Kt x P; 5. B—Q3, Kt—B4; 6. B—KB4, Kt x B ch (Black had the opportunity here, by . . . . Kt—K3 and . . . . P—Q4, to build up his position on scientific principles; the Kt at K3 would have been our strong, elastic blockader); 7. Q x Kt, Kt—B3; 8. O—O (8. Kt—B3 followed by O—O—O would please us better), B—K2; 9. P x P, B x P; 10. B x B, Q x B; 11. Q x Q, P x Q. See Diagram 135; there followed 12. R—K1 ch ?, B—K3; 13. Kt—Kt5 (the change of front characteristic of non-positional players), K—Q2; 14. P—QB3, and White does not stand particularly well. The right course was 12. Kt—B3 (instead of R—K1 ch ?), and, after *13*. Kt—QKt5 and *14*. QKt—Q4, he would be centralized and have the superior game.

It will be instructive to give here an example characteristic of the disregard so often shown even by strong players for central strategy; it is from a game played in 1920 in a Swedish

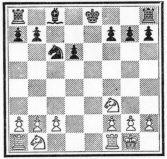

DIAGRAM 135

White, after R—K1 *ch*, B—K3, executed the popular change of front Kt—Kt5. What central strategy was indicated here (instead of R—K1 *ch* ?, etc.)

DIAGRAM 136

Black to move. A typical example of a fight for a central point. Here White's K5 is the square for whose control both sides will struggle

tournament between K. Berntsson (White) and S. J. Bjurulf (Black). *1*. P—Q4, P—Q4; *2*. Kt—KB3, Kt—KB3; *3*. B—B4, P—K3; *4*. P—K3, P—B4; *5*. P—B3, P—QKt3 (the following line of play seems best here: *5*. . . . . Kt—B3 *!*; and if now *6*. QKt—Q2, B—K2; *7*. P—KR3, anticipating . . . . Kt—KR4, then *7*. . . . . B—Q3 *!*; *8*. Kt—K5, B x Kt; *9*. P x B, Kt—Q2; *10*. Kt—B3, and now a fierce fight will be waged round the point K5. See Diagram 136. We strongly recommend the would-be positional player to exercise himself in such central fights. In the present position a good plan would be *10*. . . . . P—QR3 *!*; *11*. B—Q3, P—B3 *!* [not *11*. . . . . Q—B2 because of *12*. O—O, Kt x P *?*; *13*. Kt x Kt, Kt x Kt; *14*. Q—R5 and wins]; in order after *12*. P x P, Q x P; to seize the hotly disputed point K4 by . . . . P—K4. We advise our readers to study this position. The move 5.

. . . . P—QKt3 is a typical error in that it seems to disregard the fact that there is such a thing as a central theater of war); 6. QKt—Q2, B—Q3; 7. Kt—K5 (this move pleases me well, although here there is by chance a tactical possibility which is

DIAGRAM 137

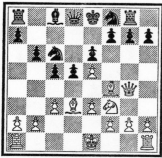

White to move. The point K5 is in his undisputed possession. But where should the attack be directed, on the right, or the left, or in the center?

DIAGRAM 138

Black to move. How shall he best punish his opponent's neglect to keep the center (K5) under observation in his last moves?

perhaps objectively preferable, namely 7. B—Kt5 *ch*, B—Q2 ?; 8. B x B, B x B; 9. P x P. But 7. Kt—K5 is the more logical move, since owing to the loss of time involved in Black's . . . . P—QKt3, the center was ripe for an invasion), B x Kt; 8. P x B, KKt—Q2; 9. Q—Kt4, R—Kt1; 10. Kt—B3, Kt—QB3; 11. B—Q3, Kt—B1. (See Diagram 137.) 12. Kt—Kt5 (White commits the strategical error of underestimating the importance of the point K5, the key point of his whole position. Under no circumstances should the attack be so conducted as to endanger its safety. On the contrary, as we know, over-protection of this point would here be indicated. The right course to adopt was to remain passive on the K's wing, to advance P—K4 in the center and on the Q's wing P—Kt4 and P—QR4, and in some such order as this: 12. O—O, B—Kt2; 13. P—Kt4 *!*, P—B5 [not . . . . P x P;

14. P x P, Kt x KtP because of B—Kt5 winning a piece or causing some other similar unpleasantness]; *14.* B—B2, Q—Q2; *15.* P—QR4, P—QR3 ! [if *15.* . . . . O—O—O, then *16.* P—R5, P x P; *17.* P—Kt5 !, with a winning attack]; *16.* P—K4 !, O—O—O; *17.* B—K3, K—B2; *18.* P—R5 !, with a decisive attack), **Q—B2 !; *13.* B x P, R—R1; *14.* B—B2.** (See Diagram 138.)

14. . . . . **B—Kt2 ?** (Black must seek to conquer the point K4, dangerous as this may appear. So simply *14.* . . . . Kt x P !; and he would have got a satisfactory, in fact the better, game. For instance: *14.* . . . . Kt x P !; *15.* Q—Kt3, P—B3; *16.* Kt—B3, Kt x Kt *ch;* *17.* Q x Kt, P—K4 !; *18.* Q x QP, B—Kt2; *19.* B—R4 *ch,* K—K2, and Black wins a piece. Or, *14.* . . . . Kt x P !; *15.* B—R4 *ch,* K—K2, with the threat . . . . Kt—Q6 *ch;* on the other hand the reply *15.* . . . . B—Q2 would have been bad, for White by means of *16.* B x B *ch,* Kt(B1) x B; *17.* Kt x KP !, P x Kt; *18.* Q x KP *ch,* K—Q1; *19.* Q x QP, would get a strong attack, with three Pawns for his sacrificed piece. But, as suggested, with *14.* . . . . Kt x P !; *15.* B—R4 *ch,* K—K2, Black could have got an excellent game. The strategical events in this game present themselves as follows: *5.* . . . . P—QKt3 had no bearing on the center, and in consequence White waxed strong and mighty there [Kt—K5]; but at his 12th move he did not pay sufficient regard to the key point [K5] and this, if Black had made the proper reply, could have led to his losing all his advantage. We see then what a dominating influence central strategy exercises); *15.* **Kt—B3, P—Kt3;** *16.* **B—Kt5 ?** (Scarcely had he by luck escaped the dangers in the center, than the leader of the White forces, always on the lookout for a combination, again sacrifices his chief possession from a strategical point of view, the point K5. The over-protectors, the Kt at B3 and the B at B4 should have remained at their posts. His proper course was indicated in the note to move 12), **Kt x P !** (now he shows courage!); *17.* **Kt x Kt, Q x Kt** (see Diagram 139).

18. P—KR4. (It is absolutely essential for White to recover the point K5. Accordingly, *18.* B—B4 *!* and if in reply *18. . . . .* Q—R4, then *19.* Q—Kt3, P—KB3; *20.* B—Q6, and Black could hardly succeed in consolidating his position, which is threatened in every nook and corner. After the text move Black, on the contrary, could make himself fully secure), P—Kt4 *?* (not only spells loss of time but also weakens the P at QB4 and al-

DIAGRAM 139

White can and must win back the point K5. How?

lows P—QR4. The right move was *18. . . . .* Kt—Q2, and if *19.* B—R4, then *19. . . . .* P—B3; *20.* B—B4, Q—K5 *!*; *21.* B—QKt5, P—Kt4, or *21. . . . .* O—O—O, and Black stands well); *19.* O—O, Kt—R2; *20.* B—B4, Q—R4; *21.* Q x Q, P x Q; *22.* P—R4 and White won the ending which he conducted very cleverly.

The moral of this game runs thus. (i) Watch the center; *cf.* Black's 5th move, White's 12th and following moves, Black's 14th move. (ii) Over-protect the key point; *cf.* White's 12th and 16th moves. (iii) Do not divert your attack prematurely; *cf.* White's 12th and 16th moves. (iv) After the Pawns are gone the key points must be occupied by pieces; *cf.* White's 18th move.

§ 6. *The leitmotif of correct strategy is the over-protection of the center with, further, a systematically carried out centralization of our forces. Wing attack met by play in the center.*

In the very characteristic game which has just been quoted we saw how the diversion of the attack from the center to a wing, and, what is in principle the equivalent, the disregard of the central key points, led to some curious situations. This "diversion" sometimes appears also in games by Masters. We need only remind the reader of Game No. 22, Opocensky—Nimzovich, in which in the position shown on Diag. 140 there occurred the following moves: *13.* Kt—K2 *P,* Kt—R4; *14.* Q—Q2, P—Kt3; *15.* P—Kt4, Kt—Kt2; *16.* Kt—Kt3, P—QB3 *!.* The diversion of the Kt, now completed, has so altered the situation that Black, though much cramped on the Q's Wing, can venture to proceed to the attack!

Centralization is ever a characteristic of Master play—and the talented Czech Master Opocensky is of course no exception. Alekhine makes use of this strategy with special predilection, and this (with play against enemy squares of a particular color) forms the leitmotif of all his games. Even when the knife seems actually to be at his King's throat in a King-side attack, he

DIAGRAM 140

White maneuvers the Kt at QB3 over to the King-side, though his true business was to look out for Black's . . . . P—B3. Another example of an unseasonable diversion

yet finds time to mass troops in the center. A typical example is furnished by his game with me at Semmering in 1926 (see No. 43), in which after the moves *1.* P—K4, Kt—KB3 (Alekhine was Black); *2.* Kt—QB3, P—Q4; *3.* P—K5, KKt—Q2; *4.* P—B4, P—K3; *5.* Kt—B3, P—QB4; *6.* P—KKt3, Kt—QB3; *7.* B—Kt2, B—K2; *8.* O—O, O—O; *9.* P—Q3, Kt—Kt3, he got into some trouble through having omitted to play *9.* . . . . P—B3. There followed *10.* Kt—K2, P—Q5; *11.* P—KKt4 (the beginning of a violent attack), P—B3; *12.* P x P, P x P (else would follow the centralization of the White Kt, by Kt—Kt3—K4); *13.* Kt—Kt3, Kt—Q4 *!*; *14.* Q—K2, B—Q3 *!*; *15.* Kt—R4 (see Diag. 141), Kt(B3)—K2 *!* *16.* B—Q2, Q—B2; *17.* Q—B2, and now the inner strength of the centralized structure of Black's position was made clear by

DIAGRAM 141

Nimzovich—Alekhine
Semmering 1926

White's P at KKt4 and Kt at KR4 point to a diversion having been started. His Kt at KKt3 has a fairly clear conscience in the centralizing sense, but he also has his eye on KR5. Black as against this has in his P at Q5 and Kt at Q4 the kernel of a beautifully centralized structure, which he completes in the sequel

DIAGRAM 142

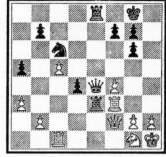

Yates—Nimzovich
Semmering 1926

Possession of the open center file, the Pawn at Q5, and in particular the position of the Queen at K5 stamp Black's structure as being centralized to a high degree. But White's formation lacks character: it gives the impression of being improvised with no special aim in view

the surprising continuation *17. . . . . P—B5 !; 18. P x P, Kt—K6 !* and Alekhine had equalized the game.

I too, both theoretically and in practice, am absolutely on the side of centralization. Examine, say, my game against Yates (Semmering, 1926), in which I had the Black pieces. *1. P—K4, P—K3; 2. P—Q4, P—Q4; 3. Kt—QB3, B—Kt5; 4. P x P, P x P; 5. B—Q3, Kt—K2; 6. Kt—K2, O—O; 7. O—O, B—Kt5; 8. P—B3, B—KR4; 9. Kt—B4, B—Kt3; 10. Kt(B3)—K2, B—Q3; 11. Q—K1.* (Here B x B followed by Kt—Q3 would have comported with the spirit of centralization, and the points QB5 and K5 would then have been kept under perpetual observation.) *11. . . . . P—QB4 !; 12. P x P, B x P ch; 13. K—R1, QKt—B3; 14. B—Q2, R—K1; 15. Kt x B, RP x Kt !* (creates a central point at KB4); *16. P—KB4* (the normal development of things would have been *16. Q—*

R4, Kt—B4; *17.* Q x Q, QR x Q; and Black has a slight advantage for the end game), *16. . . . .* Kt—B4; *17.* P—B3, P—Q5 *!;* *18.* P—B4, Q—Kt3; *19.* R—B3, B—Kt5 (to occupy the central point K6); *20.* P—QR3, B x B; *21.* Q x B, P—R4 (= restraint); *22.* Kt—Kt1, R—K6; *23.* Q—KB2, QR—K1; *24.* R—Q1, Q—Kt6 *!;* *25.* R—Q2, Kt—Q3; *26.* P—QB5, Kt—B5 *!;* *27.* B x Kt, Q x B (White's QBP is weak, the blockading B at Q3 has been got out of the way, and the central pressure is more burdensome to White than ever); *28.* R—B2, Q—Q4 *!;* *29.* R—B1, Q—K5 *!.* (See Diag. 142.) With this move centralization is completed. White sacrificed a Pawn, by *30.* P—B5, in order to defend himself against the ever increasing pressure in the King file, but lost the ending after *30. . . . .* R x R; *31.* Kt x R, Q x P. Further striking examples of centralization will be found in great plenty in the games of the Masters; we will only mention Alekhine—Treybal, Baden-Baden, 1925, and Nimzovich—Spielmann, San Sebastian, 1912. (See Game No. 49)

We now proceed to the analysis of play in the center vs. play on a wing. The game Nimzovich—Alekhine, just given, furnishes an example of how such a struggle usually proceeds. The "central player" always has the better prospects, and very especially in the frequently recurring positions which we are about to outline. One party has undertaken a diversion against his opponent's King's wing which in itself promises a reward. All would be in the most perfect order, but that (there's always a "but"!) his opponent holds an open center file, and with as-

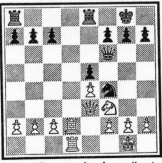

DIAGRAM 143

Plan to illustrate the theme "center file vs. flank attack." The Black Kt is the mainstay of the latter, but is not too formidable

180 MY SYSTEM

tounding regularity the flank attack is shipwrecked on this rock. This state of affairs is not accidental: it has its own inner logic.

We will first note (see Diag. 143) the ground plan of such a situation. In the position shown Black's attack must always fail, because his Rooks are under the unpleasant obligation to guard their base (their first and second ranks) against an inroad of the White Rooks who are all ready for the adventure. In addition his K4 is insufficiently protected, and this again is not accidental, since the White Kt is centralized in harmony with the rest of the White structure. As the whole matter is of extraordinary importance to an understanding of the spirit of the theory of the center, we will illustrate it by a complete game, Rubinstein—Nimzovich, San Sebastian, 1912.

1. P—Q4, Kt—KB3; *2.* P—QB4, P—Q3; *3.* Kt—KB3, QKt—Q2; *4.* Kt—B3, P—K4; *5.* P—K4, B—K2 (probably there is nothing against . . . . P—KKt3 and . . . . B—Kt2); *6.* B—K2, O—O; *7.* O—O, R—K1; *8.* Q—B2, B—B1; *9.* P—QKt3, P—B3 (here, as Lasker very rightly pointed out, the sounder line of play was . . . . P—KKt3, ... B—Kt2, then . . . . P x P and . . . . Kt—K4); *10.* B—Kt2, Kt—R4 ?; *11.* P—Kt3, Kt—Kt1; *12.* QR —Q1 (the center file looms up!), Q—B3; *13.* Kt—Kt1 !, B—R6; *14.* KR—K1, Kt—B5; (that I should be able to get the Kt to KB5 under any circumstances, I had foreseen when I played *10.* . . . . Kt—R4, a misfortune, for else I would have withstood the temptation to undertake this diversion). See Diagram 144. *15.* P x P, P x P; *16.* Kt x P, R x Kt; *17.* B—KB1 (After *17.* B x R, Kt x B *ch;* *18.* Q x Kt, Q x B; *19.* R—Q8—the center file! White would also have the advantage), Kt—Q2; *18.* Q—Q2 (now the Black pieces embarked on their diversion are in the air), B x B; *19.* R x B, Kt— R6 *ch;* *20.* K—Kt2, Kt—Kt4 (threatening mate in two); *21.* P— B4, Q—Kt3; *22.* P x Kt, R x KP ? (After *22.* . . . . Q x P *ch,* *23.* K—R3, R—K2; *24.* R(Q1)—K1 would have won a piece. Relatively best was *22.* . . . . R—K2; the win then could only

have been attained by *23.* B—
R3 *!,* P—QB4 *!* [not *23.* . . . . Q
x P *ch;* because of *24.* K—Kt1,
P—QB4; *25.* R(B1)—K1]; *24.*
Kt—B3; for after *23.* . . . . P—
QB4, which is forced, there is
no possibility of playing . . . .
Kt—B4, while on the other hand
White has his Q5 as a base for
his operations); *23.* Q x Kt, R—
K7 *ch; 24.* R—B2, and White won.
See also Game No. 28, Kline—
Capablanca for another variation
on the same theme.

DIAGRAM 144

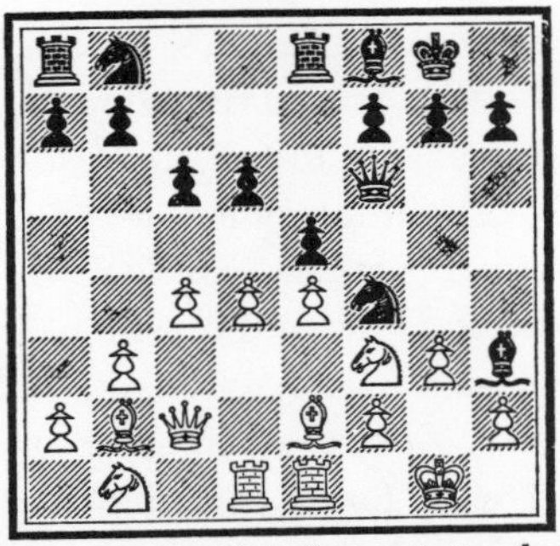

White (Rubinstein) demonstrates by
clever play the weakness of Black's
diversion on the King-side

§ 7.   *The Surrender of the Center.*

As early as 1911 and 1912 I had published some notes on
games, in which I put forward what was then an entirely new
idea, that the center need not necessarily be occupied by
Pawns; that centrally posted pieces or even lines bearing on the
center could, as I maintained, take the place of Pawns; the
main point being to place the enemy center Pawns under restraint. This idea I embodied in an article in 1913 which, by
the courtesy of the *Wiener Schachzeitung,* I am allowed to re-
produce here, and do so, because in this the age of the "neo-
romantic school" it is in a high degree pertinent. The article
ran as follows:—

When Black in the much disputed variation of the French
Defense *1.* P—K4, P—K3; *2.* P—Q4, P—Q4; *3.* Kt—QB3, plays
3. . . . . P x P, he gives up, according to the current opinion,
the center. This view seems to me to rest upon an incomplete
grasp, in fact a misconception, of what the center is. In what
follows the attempt will be made, (i) to show that this view is
based on a prejudice, (ii) to set out its historical development.

And first the definition of the concept "center." Here we have simply to abide by the meaning of the word. The "center" consists of the squares in the middle of the board, *squares*: not Pawns. This is fundamental and must never under any circumstances be lost sight of.

The importance of the center, that is to say the complex of squares in the middle of the board, as a base for further operations, is beyond question; and a note of Emanuel Lasker's to a game is worth recalling. "White," he wrote, "does not stand well enough in the center, to undertake an operation on the wing." This is finely conceived, and at the same time illustrates the close relationship between the center and the wings, the center being the dominating principle, the wings subordinate to it.

That control of the center must be of great significance, is, other considerations apart, clear from one thing, that if we have built up our game in the center, we have from thence the possibility of exercising influence on both wings at one and the same time, and of embarking on a diversion should opportunity offer. Without healthy conditions in the center, a healthy position is definitely unthinkable.

We spoke of a control of the center. What are we to understand by this? How is this conditioned?

Current opinion holds that the center should be occupied by Pawns; P at K4 and P at Q4 is the ideal, but in fact the presence of one of these two Pawns postulates occupation of the center, provided the corresponding enemy Pawn is wanting.

But is this really the case? Is the P at Q4, after the moves *1.* P—K4, P—K3; *2.* P—Q4, P—Q4; *3.* Kt—QB3, P x P; *4.* Kt x P, justified in speaking of a conquest of the center? If, in a battle, I seize a bit of debatable land with a handful of soldiers, without having done anything to prevent an enemy bombardment of the position, would it ever occur to me to speak of a conquest of the terrain in question? Obviously not. Then why should I do so in chess?

It dawns upon us then, that control of the center depends not on a mere occupation (placing of Pawns), but rather on our general effectiveness there, and this is determined by quite other factors.

This thought I have formulated thus:—With the disappearance of a Pawn from the center (*e.g.*, 3. . . . . P x P; 4. Kt x P as above) the center is a long way from being surrendered. The true conception of the center is a far wider one. Certainly, Pawns, as being the most stable, are best suited to building a center; nevertheless centrally posted pieces can perfectly well take their place. And, too, pressure exerted on the enemy center by the long range action of Rooks or Bishops directed on it can well be of corresponding importance.

We meet this last case in the variation 3. . . . . P x P. This move, so wrongly described as a surrender of the center, as a matter of fact increases Black's effective influence in the center very considerably; for with the removal by . . . . P x P of the P at Q4, which is an obstruction, Black gets a free hand in the Q file, and the long diagonal QKt2 to KR8, which he will open for himself by . . . . P—QKt3. Obstruction! that is the dark side of the occupation of the center by Pawns. A Pawn is by nature, by his stability, his, so to speak, conservative spirit, a good center builder, but, alas, he is also an obstruction.

That effective influence in the center is independent of the number of Pawns occupying it, appears from many examples, and of their abundance we will take one or two.

Pieces in the center. (1) Black's P at K3 and P at Q4 held under restraint by the White Kt at K5 and P at QB3 *e.g.*, Diagram 145 from the game Nimzovich—Levenfish, Carlsbad, 1911. (2) the isolated Pawn couple (see II. iii. § 6) at Q4 and QB3 rigidly blockaded by White pieces as in Diagram 146. The two cases quoted show us a blockade. But blockade is an elastic term and often a slight restraint induced by an annoying Rook whose primary function was to hold up the advance of

184 MY SYSTEM

the enemy center may be the prelude to a complete crippling, which culminates in its mechanical stoppage.

The cases in which pressure is exerted on the enemy center are without number. See, *e.g.*, Diagram 147 where the course

DIAGRAM 145

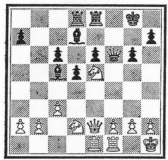

DIAGRAM 146

DIAGRAM 147

of events will lead either to a blockade with consequent destruction of the KP (for movement is life), or to uncomfortable positions for the defending pieces, which will lead to the downfall of the "lucky possessor" of the center.

All this teaches us that by counting the heads of the Pawns in the center, nothing, literally nothing, is gained. To make mere arithmetic the starting point of a philosophy of the center can only be characterized as a mistaken proceeding. I am sure

that in a very few years no one will regard 3. . . . . P x P as a
"surrender" of the center; and with the disappearance of such
a prepossession, the way will be clear for a new and brilliant
development in chess philosophy—and strategy.

A word on the genesis of this prejudice, which is closely
bound up with the history of position play. . . . First came
Steinitz; but what he had to say was so unfamiliar, and he
himself was so towering a figure, that his "modern principles"
could not immediately become popular. There followed Tarrasch, who took hold of Steinitz's ideas and served them up
diluted to the public taste. And now to consider the application
to our case. Steinitz was, we repeat, deep and great, but deep-
est and greatest in his conception of the center. When in his
defense to the Ruy Lopez (. . . . P—Q3) he was able to
transmute the enemy P at K4 which was to all appearances so
healthy, into one whose weakness was patent to every eye,
this was an unsurpassable achievement. Nothing lay further
from his thoughts than a formalistic, arithmetical conception
of the center. . . .

So far the article. For illustrations we would refer the reader
to I. iii. on the Pawn-chain, and to Game No. 26 (Tarrasch—
Mieses). The reader is also urged to study before proceeding further Games No. 25–30 inclusive, which bear on this
chapter.

2. The Doubled Pawn and Restraint

§ 1. *The affinity between a "doubled Pawn" and restraint; the former should favor the execution of enemy plans for restraint. What does it mean to labor under the disadvantage of doubled Pawns? The conception of passive (=static) and active (=dynamic) weaknesses. When does the dissolution of enemy doubled Pawns seem to be indicated? The one real strength of doubled Pawns.*

RESTRAINT is conceivable without the presence of enemy doubled Pawns; but a really complete restraint, which extends over large tracts of the board and makes it difficult for

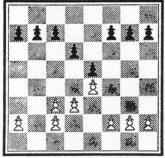

DIAGRAM 148

Skeleton position. After White has played P—Q4, any further advance by P—Q5, P—QB4—B5 is stopped by . . . . P—QKt3, which would not be the case if White's QKtP were present

the enemy to breathe, is only possible when the opponent labors under the disadvantage of doubled Pawns. What do we mean exactly by laboring under this disadvantage? Chiefly this, that in the event of an advance in close formation certain paralyzing phenomena may intervene. See, for example, Diagram 148. If a White P had been at QKt2 instead of QB2 the close advance P—Q4—Q5, followed by P—QB4, P—QKt4, and P—QB5 would have been possible. But in the position on the diagram the QKtP is wanting, and hence any attempt at a transference of attack (see above I. ix on the Pawn-chain) will be vain. To P—Q4—Q5 and P—QB4

the answer will be . . . . P—QKt3, and the further advance
P—QB5 we had planned is shown to be impossible of execution. What we have just learnt about the chief weakness of
compact (easily defendable) double Pawns (which we would
class as active, or dynamic, weaknesses) enables us to formulate this rule, that it pays to incite the possessor of a Pawn-
mass, whose attacking value is lessened by the presence of
doubled Pawns, to an advance. Acting in this spirit Black in the
case under consideration should, if White has played P—Q4,
endeavor to induce his opponent to continue his action in the
center. So long as he can stop at Q4, the defect of the doubled
Pawn will be as little in evidence as is a limp in a sitting person.
It is only in the advance that the weakness will appear.

We must differentiate an active and a passive (static) weakness. The latter is, in contradistinction to that in our last example, revealed when we send forward our own Pawns in a
storming party against the doubled Pawns. Let us imagine in
Diagram 148 the White QP at Q5 instead of Q3, a White K at
KKt1 and R at K2, and a Black K at KB1 and R at QB1. Here
the static weakness of the dou-
bled Pawn is great; for after *1.*

DIAGRAM 149

. . . . P—QB3; *2.* P x P, R x P;
or *1.* . . . . P—QB3; *2.* P—
QB4, P x P; *3.* BP x P, R—B6,
followed by . . . . R—QR6,
Black will in either case get the
advantage. The rule is therefore:
Given a passive weakness in
doubled Pawns, an advance
against these Pawns is indicated,
whereby the dissolution or undoubling of the enemy doubled
Pawns need cause us no fear.
The evil is in fact only half dis-

The indirect exchange of his QP for
White's P at K4 seems to Black to
be worth striving for. How should
Black seek to bring this about? He
has a choice of procedures

sipated, a part of the weakness is got rid of; but for what remains behind, the player has to suffer the heavier penance.

Let us turn now to Diagram 149. Black, the author of this book, let his opponent (E. Cohn) take the initiative in the hope that the resulting play would in the end lead to a simplification, after which in the end game it could not be very difficult to take advantage of the doubled Pawns. The game proceeded: *16*. . . . . Q—Q2; *17*. Q—K1, Kt—Kt3; *18*. B—Q3, B—B3; *19*. Q—B2, B—K4 (Black relies on the solid strength of his K4); *20*. R—B2, R—KB1; *21*. K—R1, P—Kt3; *22*. Q—B3, QR—K1; *23*. R(B2) —B2, Kt—R1; *24*. Q—R5, P—KB3; *25*. P—KKt4, P—B3; and now Cohn let himself be carried away by the idea of an interesting attack, which, however, in the end only resulted in the simplification of the game, and the exposure of the hopelessness of his Pawn position, P at K3 and P at K4. He played *26*. P—B5, and after *26*. . . . . B x Kt; *27*. R x B, QP x P; *28*. B—B4 *ch*, Kt—B2; *29*. P—Kt5, R—K4; *30*. R—B5, R x R; *31*. P x R, the win could be forced by *31*. . . . . K—R1; for the answer to *32*. P—Kt6 would have been . . . . Kt—R3, and to *32*. B x Kt it would be *32*. . . . . Q x B; *33*. P—Kt6, Q—Q4 *ch*, followed by . . . . P—KR3. Black was therefore right in choosing a waiting strategy, for the wing attack must fail against the center file, with Black's strength at K4, and the end game is hopeless for White. Although the waiting strategy was correct, yet the advance was also possible, for White's doubled King Pawns, are here a static weakness. This advance could be executed somewhat as follows:—*16*. . . . . Kt—Q2 (instead of . . . . Q—Q2); *17*. B—B3, Kt—B3; *18*. Q—QB2, P—B3 ! He "sacrifices" the QP in order at once to get in its stead White's P at K4. After *19*. QR—Q1, Q—K2, we get our "exchange" and then White's P at K3 can be bombarded in comfort.

The full rule, therefore, runs: To isolated doubled Pawns, and to "compact" doubled Pawns, or those which are advancing, the "question" should be put (=be attacked by

Pawns). An enemy doubled Pawn complex which has not started its advance, should, before the "question" is put to it, first be incited to action.

§ 1a.   *The one real strength of the doubled Pawns.*

As we have seen, a Pawn-mass which is afflicted with doubled Pawns has in it a certain latent weakness, which makes itself felt when the time comes to make use of that mass by advancing it. We characterize this, as we have said, as a dynamic weakness. This mass, if at rest (holding its configuration), may be very strong. Turn back to Diagram 148. After White has played P—Q4, a position is reached out of which he can be driven only with the greatest trouble. We mean by this that Black hardly possesses the positional means to be able to force his opponent to a decision to play P x KP or P—Q5. On the other hand this would be much more possible if White's Pawn were at QKt2 instead of QB2. The doubled Pawns in fact make holding out easier. Why this should be so it is difficult to explain: perhaps it is due to an equalizing act of justice, an attempt to compensate for dynamic weakness by static strength; it may be that the QKt file enters into the question; at any rate experience has shown that the doubled QBP does favor holding out.

In this tenacity we see the one real strength of the doubled Pawns; *cf.* my game against Haakanson in the next section and further those against Rosselli and Johner (No. 34 and 35). Unfortunately, in all these games, the player with the doubled Pawns failed to make the best use of them. However, in each case the proper procedure has been pointed out.

§ 2.   *The most familiar doubled Pawn complexes (for short double-complexes) are passed in review. The double complex as an instrument of attack.*

See again Diagram 148. The strongest formation for White is the one reached after he has played P—Q4; and this formation should be preserved for as long as possible. However, after P—Q5 White's weakness will make itself felt; so that it is a strategical necessity for Black to force White to this move, and if possible without the aid of . . . . P—QB4. For after . . . . P—QB4; P—Q5 the possibility of putting the question (by . . . . P—QB3) will have gone, as also the chance of occupying the point QB4 with a Kt.

In the same position (Diagram 148) many players, having Black, make the mistake of letting loose at once with . . . . P—Q4, a course which runs counter to our rule, according to which an enemy double complex must first be incited to action. Then and only then may the active (dynamic) weakness of the double complex be exploited.

We shall now give some examples which will illustrate the struggle between a defense which is trying to hold out in its position and an attacking force which is seeking to force a decision, and first one in which the defending party (in this case White) by one thoughtless move throws away all the trumps in his hand.

Haakanson—Nimzovich. Played in 1921. *1.* P—Q4, Kt—KB3; *2.* P—QB4, P—K3; *3.* Kt—KB3, P—QKt3; *4.* B—Kt5, P—KR3; *5.* B x Kt, Q x B; *6.* P—K4, B—Kt2; *7.* Kt—B3, B—Kt5; *8.* Q—Q3, B x Kt *ch; 9.* P x B, P—Q3 (and now after . . . . P—K4, the double complex we have been discussing will have arisen); *10.* Q—K3, Kt—Q2; *11.* B—Q3, P—K4; *12.* O—O, O—O; *13.* P—QR4, P—QR4; *14.* Kt—K1. White stood well, for it is improbable that Black would have been able to force him to a decision (*i.e.*, to

P—Q5), but the rather ponderous text-move creates difficulties in his own camp. His right course was *14.* Kt—Q2 and P—B3; his Queen who is rather exposed at K3 would then have had a flight square at KB2, and nothing would have stood in the way of further holding out in his formation. After *14.* Kt—K1 *?* there followed *14. . . . .* QR—K1; *15.* P—B3, Q—K3 *!*, and now White ought to have eaten the bitter fruit, *i.e.,* played P—Q5, but he moved instead *16.* Kt—B2, and after *16. . . . .* P x P *!*; *17.* P x P, P—KB4 *!*; *18.* P—Q5, Q—K4; *19.* Q—Q4, Kt—B4; *20.* KR—Q1, P x P; *21.* P x P, Kt x B; *22.* R x Kt, Q x KP, lost a Pawn and the game.

DIAGRAM 150

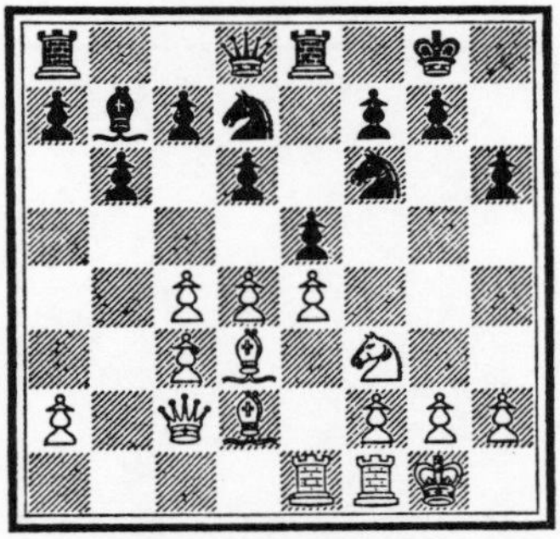

Janowsky—Nimzovich
Black with the move fights against
White's persistence in holding to his
Pawn formation

The next example is of much heavier metal and is taken from the game Janowsky—Nimzovich, St. Petersburg, 1914. *1.* P—Q4, Kt—KB3; *2.* P—QB4, P—K3; *3.* Kt—QB3, B—Kt5; *4.* P—K3, P—QKt3; *5.* B—Q3, B—Kt2; *6.* Kt—B3, B x Kt *ch*; *7.* P x B, P—Q3; *8.* Q—B2, QKt—Q2; *9.* P—K4, P—K4; *10.* O—O, O—O; *11.* B—Kt5, P—KR3; *12.* B—Q2, R—K1; *13.* QR—K1. (See Diagram 150.) Black was now faced with the difficult problem of how to induce his opponent to take action in the center. He tried to solve it by playing . . . . Kt—R2—B1—K3. Another possibility was *13. . . . .* Kt—B1; *14.* P—KR3, Kt—Kt3; *15.* Kt—R2, R—K2 *!*; and if now *16.* P—B4, then . . . . P x BP; *17.* B x P, Q—K1; and White has no way of comfortably defending his PK4. In the game, however, there was played, as already said, *13. . . . .* Kt—R2; and the continuation was *14.* P—KR3, Kt(R2)—B1; *15.* Kt—R2, Kt—K3 *!*; *16.* B—K3 (he holds on!), *16. . . . .* P—QB4 (because he sees no other way of breaking his opponent's obstinacy); *17.* P—Q5, Kt—B5 *!*; *18.* B—K2, Kt—B1, and the weakness of White's P at QB4 and possession of the point KB5 offer Black chances of attack on both wings.

Since, as we have seen, it is often very difficult to induce an opponent who is hanging on to this "crouching" position to take action in our sense, it is obvious that we ought only to bring about an enemy double complex if it seems likely that we shall succeed in forcing him out of it. In this connection the following opening will be found extremely instructive.

DIAGRAM 151

Nimzovich—Rosselli

White with the move refrains from bringing about by B x Kt *ch*, P x B, a double complex in the enemy position, since he recognizes the impossibility of inducing him to advance his QP to the 5th; for in reply to P—K4 he would merely stay where he is

Nimzovich—Rosselli, Baden-Baden, 1925. After the first 7 moves. *1.* Kt—KB3, P—Q4; *2.* P—QKt3, P—QB4; *3.* P—K3, Kt—QB3; *4.* B—Kt2, B—Kt5 ?; *5.* P—KR3 *!*, B x Kt; *6.* Q x B, P—K4; *7.* B—Kt5, Q—Q3; White had the opportunity of giving his opponent doubled Pawns by *8.* B x Kt *ch*, P x B; *9.* P—K4. But what would he have gained by this? How was Black to be forced into playing . . . . P—Q5? So White played *8.* P—K4 (see Diagram 151), renouncing the idea for

the time. *8.* . . . . P—Q5; but now with the advance . . . . P—Q5 already made the double complex would be a consummation devoutly to be wished; so to this end White played *9.* Kt—R3 (threatening Kt—B4, Q—B2; B x Kt *ch*, P x B), and the game proceeded *9.* . . . . P—B3 *!*; *10.* Kt—B4, Q—Q2; *11.* Q—R5 *ch*, P—Kt3; *12.* Q—B3, Q—QB2 (if *12.* . . . . O—O—O; then *13.* Kt—R5, KKt—K2; *14.* Q x P); *13.* Q—Kt4, and the diagonal KKt4 to Q7 very soon led to Black's resigning himself to the doubled Pawns in order to be rid of other unpleasantnesses. For the whole game see No. 34.

If saddled with a double complex, the player has to take into account the fact that its mobility is very limited, and hence must suit his moves to the occasion, artfully contrived to bear on both sides. What is meant by this will appear from the next examples.

Nimzovich—Sämisch, Dresden, 1926. After the moves *1. P—QB4, P—K4; 2. Kt—QB3, Kt—KB3; 3. Kt—B3, Kt—B3; 4. P—K4, B—Kt5; 5. P—Q3, P—Q3; 6. P—KKt3, B—Kt5; 7. B—K2, P—KR3; 8. B—K3, B x Kt ch; 9. P x B, Q—Q2;* White was fully conscious of the dynamic weakness of his double complex; and accordingly he made his plan to let the QP persist at Q3 or at most at Q4. Observe the artful little moves of the White pieces, which suit the conditions created by the Pawn configuration in the center; for with small working capital (and the slight mobility of White's Pawns is analogous to this), the greatest economy is necessary. The continuation was *10. Q—B2 !, O—O; 11. Q—Q2 !* (if he had at once played *10. Q—Q2,* the answer would have been . . . . O—O—O, and the White Q would have been very awkwardly placed at Q2. After *10. Q—B2, 10. . . . . O—O—O* would have been answered by O—O and KR—QKt1, and White would have had a fine

DIAGRAM 152

White's attacking position in the center has here, *inter alia*, to help conceal his own dynamic weakness (the doubled Pawns); hence it must more rightly be regarded as a "crouching" one

ensemble, the Q at B2 being not the least contributing factor), *Kt—R2; 12. P—KR3 !, B x P; 13. Kt—Kt1, B—Kt5; 14. P—B3, B—K3; 15. P—Q4,* and White won a piece and the game.

We have now submitted the doubled Pawn complex to a very searching analysis. Seen in the light of this analysis many incidents of daily occurrence appear under a new aspect. In the position on Diagram 152, reached after the moves *1.* P—K4, P—K4; *2.* Kt—KB3, Kt—QB3; *3.* Kt—B3, Kt—B3; *4.* B—Kt5, B—Kt5; *5.* O—O, O—O; *6.* P—Q3, P—Q3; *7.* B—Kt5, B x Kt; *8.* P x B, Q—K2; *9.* R—K1, Kt—Q1; *10.* P—Q4, White is said, according to the current view, to have the attacking position in the center. This is not true, as I see it. It would be true if a White P were at QKt2 instead of QB2. But, as it is, the apparently attacking position of the P at Q4 has but the deep purpose of hiding the weakness in his own camp, namely the doubled Pawns. Once P—Q5 has taken place this (dynamic) weakness would be evident. Hence the Pawn configuration which we have in Diagram 152 will be regarded by one who has thought the matter out as a crouching position. The game proceeded *10.* . . . . Kt—K3; *11.* B—QB1, P—B3 (. . . . P—B4 was the right move here: *11.* . . . . P—B4; *12.* P x KP, P x P; *13.* Kt x P *?*, Kt—B2; etc.); *12.* B—B1, R—Q1; *13.* P—Kt3, Q—B2; *14.* Kt—R4, and White intends to play P—KB4. So had White after all the initiative in the center?! No, the situation is rather this:— Since Black at his 11th move did not take the opportunity to bother his opponent, White could, out of his crouching position, build up an attack, but originally it was in fact but such a position. The continuation was (we follow the excellent game Spielmann—Rubinstein, Carlsbad, 1911) *14.* . . . . P—Q4; *15.* P—KB4 *!*, P x BP; *16.* P—K5, Kt—K5; *17.* P x P, P—KB4 *!*; *18.* P x P e.p., Kt x P(B3); *19.* P—B5, Kt—B1; *20.* Q—B3, and Spielmann won in brilliant style: *20.* . . . . Q—B2; *21.* B—Q3, B—Q2; *22.* B—KB4, R—K1; *23.* B—K5, P—B4; *24.* K—R1, P—B5; *25.* B—K2, B—B3; *26.* Q—B4, Kt(B1)—Q2; *27.* B—B3, R—K2; *28.* R—K2, R—KB1; *29.* R—KKt1, Q—K1; *30.* R(K2)—Kt2, R(B1)—B2; *31.* Q—R6 *!*, K—B1; *32.* Kt—Kt6 *ch,* a brilliant break-through

combination. 32. . . . . P x Kt; 33. Q—R8 *ch*, Kt—Kt1; 34. B—Q6.
Black who is hemmed in and pinned all round has nothing to
oppose to an invasion at his KKt1 via the KKt file. 34. . . . .
Q—Q1; 35. R x P, Kt(Q2)—B3; 36. R x Kt *!*, R x R; 37. R x P *!*,
Resigns.

We now pass to a consideration of the next species of double
complex. See Diagrams 153 and 154; which as will be seen are
very similar, the White center P being at K4 or Q4 according

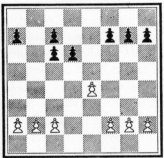
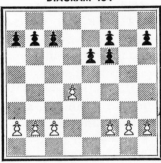

DIAGRAM 153   **DIAGRAM 154**

as Black's double complex is on the Queen- or King-side. The
import of this Pawn configuration lies in this, that Black may
regard his P at QB3 (or P at KB3) as compensation for his lost
center, since either Pawn has an action towards the center. This
action finds expression in the fact that White, *e.g.*, in the case
of 154, cannot use his K5 as an outpost station; further in the
threat of . . . . P—K4, and again in the possibility of . . . .
P—KB4, ... R—KKt1 (White: P—KKt3), ... P—KR4,
. . . . P—KB5, and . . . . P—KR5. In other words the mass P
at K3, P at KB3, P at KB2, which in the first instance is defensive in its action, can deploy and be thrown forward to the attack. Its weakness lies in the isolated KRP. White will seek to
neutralize the attack we have outlined (. . . . R—Kt1, ...
P—KB4, etc.) by posting his Pawns at KB4, KKt3, and KR2

with perhaps Kts at KB3 and KKt2. The game would then be equal. It is, however, extremely difficult for Black to decide on the fitting moment to emerge from the defensive with . . . . P—KB4. We give an example:—

Nimzovich—Dr. Perlis, Ostend, 1907. *1.* P—K4, P—K3; *2.* P—Q4, P—Q4; *3.* Kt—QB3, Kt—KB3; *4.* B—Kt5, P x P; *5.* Kt x P, B—K2; *6.* B x Kt, P x B; *7.* Kt—KB3, Kt—Q2; *8.* Q—Q2, R—KKt1 (this move might perhaps have been postponed); *9.* O—O—O, Kt—B1 (protects the weakness, the isolated P at KR2); *10.* P—B4, P—B3; *11.* P—KKt3, Q—B2; *12.* B—Kt2, P—Kt3; *13.* KR—K1, B—Kt2; *14.* K—Kt1, O—O—O (Dr. Perlis has very skillfully turned the defensive strength of his "complex" to good account, and will soon see the moment ripe to let his double complex appear as an attacking weapon); *15.* Kt—B3, K—Kt1 (see Diagram 155); *16.* Q—K3 (White feels the want of the outpost station K5 painfully), Kt—Kt3 (already . . . . P—KB4—B5 is threatened, for the Kt now is looking after the point K4); *17.* P—KR4, P—KB4; *18.* Kt—K5 (at last!), P—B5 *!*; *19.* Q—B3, Kt x Kt; *20.* P x Kt, P x P; *21.* P x P, B—Kt5, with an equal game. *22.* P—QR3, B x Kt; *23.* Q x B, P—QB4; *24.* B x B, Q x B; *25.* R—Q6, R x R; *26.* P x R, R—Q1; *27.* R—Q1, Q—K5 *ch*; *28.* K—R2, R—Q2, and the game was abandoned as a draw two moves later. In this game Dr. Perlis, who was an adept in such positions, took splendid advantage of his double complex, both defensively and in attack.

The treatment of the problem was less convincing in the game Yates—Dr. Olland, Scheveningen, 1913.

1. P—K4, P—K3; *2.* P—Q4, P—Q4; *3.* Kt—QB3, Kt—KB3; *4.* B—Kt5, P x P; *5.* B x Kt *?* (Kt x P first was better), P x B; *6.* Kt x P, P—KB4 *?* (the moment for the advance does not seem to me happily chosen. The construction of the characteristic position [= Pawn skeleton] by means of . . . . P—Kt3, ... P—B3, ... Kt—Q2, ... Q—B2, ... B—QKt2, and . . . . O

—O—O, as in the previous game, was more congruent with the position); 7. Kt—QB3, B—Kt2 (this Bishop now undertakes the protection of the point K4, but the P at KB3 was a more reliable watchman); 8. Kt—B3, O—O (the answer to 8. . . . . . Kt—QB3, which in 1913 I recommended as better in the *Wiener Schachzeitung*, could be. 9. B—Kt5, O—O; 10. B x Kt, P x B; 11. Q—Q3 *!*, R—Kt1; 12 O—O—

DIAGRAM 155

Black has exploited his Pawn complex defensively. White cannot use his K5 as an outpost station

O, and all Black's attempts to get an attack would probably fail because of the possibility of a White invasion by Kt—K5, for instance 12. . . . . Q—K2; 13. Kt—K5, Q—Kt5; 14. P—QKt3, etc.); 9. B—QB4 *?* (9. Q—Q2 and O—O—O was here indicated), P—Kt3 *?* (9. . . . . Kt—B3; 10. Kt—K2, P—K4 *!*; 11. P x P, Kt x P; would have given the Bishops space to move in: 12. Kt x Kt, B x Kt; 13. P—QB3, B—K3 and Black stands well. The important point for us to observe is that the possibility of playing . . . . P—K4 did after all arise; *cf.* our introductory remarks on the complex under consideration); 10. Q—Q3, B—Kt2; 11. O—O—O, Kt—Q2; 12. KR—K1, Q—B3; 13. K—Kt1, KR—Q1; 14. Q—K3, P—B4 *?* (. . . . P—B3 seems better, in order on the one hand to nail White's QP down, and on the other to prepare for . . . . P—Kt4 and . . . . Kt—Kt3. The affair with the KBP [. . . . P—KB4] has not turned out well; the Pawn mass did not become a weapon of attack, and the thrust P—KKt4 is already in the air); 15. P—Q5, P—K4; 16. P—KKt4 (the game now passes beyond the region of exact calculation. White ought to have been satisfied with getting a passed Pawn, and against the pair of Pawns [K and KB] a maneuver of restraint would be in place, started say by Kt—Q2 and P—B3. White would then not stand badly), P x P; 17. Kt—KKt5, B—KR3; 18. Kt(B3)—K4, Q—Kt3; 19. P—B4, KP x P; 20. Q x KBP with tremendous complications. After some further mistakes on Black's part White won on the 44th move.

In the game just given Black's double complex did not make itself felt as an instrument of attack; quite otherwise in the following game, in which it is true we have to do with the complex P at QB2, P at QB3, P at Q3 against P at QB2, P at K4 (Diagram 153 and not 154). We may regard the skeleton positions in these two diagrams as wholly identical in their main characteristics.

Teichmann—Bernstein, St. Petersburg, 1909. *1*. P—K4, P—K4; *2.* Kt—KB3, Kt—QB3; *3.* Kt—B3, Kt—B3; *4.* B—Kt5, P—Q3; *5.* P—Q4, B—Q2; *6.* O—O, B—K2; *7.* R—K1, P x P; *8.* Kt x P, O—O; *9.* B x Kt, P x B; *10.* P—QKt3, R—K1 (in addition to the problem of how to take proper advantage of his double complex, Black has another problem to solve, namely the restraint of the free enemy center); *11.* B—Kt2, B—KB1; *12.* Q—Q3, P—Kt3; *13.* QR—Q1, B—Kt2; *14.* P—B3 (he forgoes the chance of attaining, by P—B4, to an aggressive development of his center, and rather strives after a secure position), Q—Kt1 (the last measures are taken to make the effect of the intended . . . . P—B4 a powerful one); *15.* B—B1, Q—Kt3 (better according to Dr. Lasker was 15. . . . . P—QR4 [threatening . . . . P—R5]; *16.* Kt—R4 *!*, P—B4; or if *16.* P—QR4, then 16. . . . . P—B4; *17.* KKt—Kt5, B—B3 followed by . . . . Kt—Q2 with a good game for Black); *16.* Kt—R4, Q—Kt2; *17.* Kt—Kt2 *!*, P—B4; *18.* Kt—K2, B—Kt4; *19.* P—QB4, B—B3; *20.* Kt—B3 (the configuration P at QR4, P at QKt3, P at QB4 leaves in similar positions a sick child at QKt3, and thus robs White of all winning chances; that in the text aims at preventing the advance . . . . P—QR4—R5 without recourse to weakening Pawn moves; Black would then also have on his hands his own weakness, the QRP), Kt—Q2; *21.*

B—K3, Kt—Kt3; 22. R—Kt1, P—
QR4; 23. B—B2. And now 23.
. . . . Q—B1 should be played,
see Diagram 156, for then . . . .
P—R5 would threaten. The re-
ply to 24. Kt—Q5 would be
. . . . Kt x Kt; 25. BP x Kt, B—
Q2; followed by . . . . P—R5.
Other trumps, except Kt—Q5,
White hardly possesses. The im-
pression we gain is this: . . . .
P—B4 frees the square for
White's Kt—Q5, and is therefore
to be regarded as somewhat two-
edged. But if the primary condi-

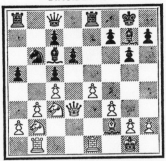

DIAGRAM 156

Aggressive utilization of the complex. White can after all get his outpost station at Q5. Observe the appropriate measures taken in support
of and against . . . . P—R5

tion be satisfied, namely if the KP is kept in a certain measure
of restraint, and if an effective parry is in readiness to meet a
possible Kt—Q5, then the thrust . . . . P—B4 may be held
justified. The counter-structure chosen in this game, namely
White's P at QB4, P at QKt3, P at QR2, with Kt at QB3 and
Kt at Kt2, we regard as sound, but a win for White we consider
impossible. Games played on these lines, *cf.* those of the match
Lasker—Schlechter, lead in fact always to a draw.

On the other hand we hold the development . . . . P—Q4
to be bad, since it may easily provoke sinister restraints. In this
connection the game Billecard—Dr. Bernstein, Ostend, 1907,
is very instructive. After the moves: 1. P—K4, P—K4; 2. Kt—KB3,
Kt—QB3; 3. Kt—B3, Kt—B3; 4. B—Kt5, P—Q3; 5. P—Q4, P x P;
6. Kt x P, B—Q2; 7. O—O, B—K2; 8. B x Kt, P x B; 9. P—QKt3,
O—O; 10. B—Kt2, P—Q4; there followed: 11. P—K5, Kt—K1; 12.
Q—Q2 ! (White rightly thinks that Black's doubled Pawns will
not get any stronger by advancing), P—QB4; 13. Kt(Q4)—K2,
P—QB3; 14. QR—Q1, Q—B2; 15. Kt—B4, Q—Kt2 (Kt x P was
threatened); 16. Kt—R4 (this move ushers in a blockade by the

occupation of the point QB5. It would be still worse for Black were his Pawns at QB2, QB3, Q4. The effect, then, of a Kt at QB5 would be simply crippling. This game is intended to help bring out the affinity between the doubled Pawns and restraint to which allusion was made at the beginning of this chapter), P—B5; *17.* B—Q4, P x P; *18.* RP x P ? (BP x P seems more logical), Kt—B2; *19.* Kt—Q3, Kt—K3; *20.* Kt(Q3)—B5, Q—B2; *21.* Kt x B, Q x Kt; *22.* Q—K3, Kt x B; *23.* Q x Kt, QR—Kt1; *24.* Kt—B5, Q—B4; *25.* Kt—Q3. White dominates the point QB5; but had he on his 18th move played BP x P, the pressure in the open QB file would have been appreciably strengthened. With this *10.* . . . . P—Q4 seems to be refuted. The student who is interested in the deeper logical connections will now say to himself: "How easy the complex P at QB2, P at QB3, P at Q4 must be to blockade! for Black succeeded in undoubling the Pawns, in addition White made a serious mistake (*18.* RP x P instead of BP x P), and yet the mobility of Black's P at QB3 and P at Q4 remained as slight as it was before!" This calculation is in fact correct. The P at QB2, P at QB3, and P at Q4 are very susceptible indeed to blockade infections; in other words the "affinity" between the doubled Pawns and restraint which we emphasized at the beginning of this chapter may already be accepted as probable. As we go on, the probability is likely to be turned into a certainty (*cf.* Game No. 12, Leonhardt—Nimzovich).

§ 3. *Restraint. The "mysterious" Rook moves. On true and spurious freeing-moves, and how they are to be combated.*

In Diagram 157 White clearly intends to play P—Q4 at any moment when this move seems feasible. Black's . . . . R—K1 is intended to help make this freeing move difficult of execution for all time. We have here therefore to do with a preventive action. Hence it is only the outer form of the move which is mysterious (a Rook to seize a file which is still closed), its strategical end is not. To demand of a piece only direct attacking activity is the stamp of the mere "wood-shifter." The keener chess mind quite rightly demands of the pieces that they also undertake preventive action. The following situation is typical: A freeing action (usually a Pawn advance) planned by our opponent would in the result give us an open file. This potential file, to open which does not lie in our power, we nevertheless seize, and in advance, with the idea of *giving our opponent a distaste for the freeing action.* The "mysterious" Rook move is an indisputable ingredient of a rational strategy. We will give some examples:

DIAGRAM 157

Blackburne—Nimzovich 1914
Black makes the "mysterious" Rook move . . . . R—K1. The Rook's function is here to act as a preventive against P—Q4

White: K, KKt1; R's; QB1, KB1; B, K2; Kt, KB3; Pawns, QR2, QKt2, Q4, K3, KB2, KKt2, KR2. Black: K, KKt1; R's, Q2, KB1; B, QKt2; Kt, KB3; Pawns, QR4, QKt3, QB3, Q4, KB2, KKt2, KR2. The position is a constructed one, in the opening stage of a game, and White plays KR—Q1; that is to say he expects

. . . . P—B4 to be played at an opportune moment, and intends in this case, after P x P, P x P, to take advantage of the QB and Q files to bring pressure on the resulting hanging Pawns (QB4 and Q4).

The "mysterious" Rook move is generally an affair of the opening, though in the early stages of the middle game it also plays an important rôle. In Diagram 158 Black plays coolly 1. . . . . R—R2. If White now plays 2. P—QR3 then 2. . . . . KR—R1. And now White can only realize his plan, to play P—QKt4 and P—QB5, at the cost of certain concessions to his opponent. The continuation might for instance be: 1. . . . .

R—R2; 2. P—QR3, KR—R1; 3. Q—Kt2, Q—Q1; 4. P—QKt4, P x P; 5. P x P, Q—Kt1; 6. R x R *P*, Q x R, and Black keeps control of the QR file. Or. 6. KR—Kt1, K—B1; 7. P—B5, KtP x P; 8. R x R, R x R; 9. P x P, Q x Q; 10. R x Q, R—R6; 11. R—QB2, B—B1 !; 12. P—B6 ! (best; not however 12. P x P, P x P; 13. Kt—Kt5, R—R8 *ch;* 14. K—B2, B—R3; and the game is about equal), Kt—K1 followed by . . . . P—B4 with some counter play.

DIAGRAM 158

Black tries by . . . . R—R2 and . . . . KR—R1 to prevent White's plan of P—QR3, P—QKt4, and P—QB5; or at worst to lessen the effect of White's advance

DIAGRAM 159

Black (Capablanca) starts a preventive action against White's P—KKt4, and carries it out with great virtuosity. His "mysterious" Rook moves are masterly

A further example (see Diagram 159) is taken from an actual game, Kupchik—Capablanca, Lake Hopatcong, 1926. After White's 19th move the position shown in the diagram was reached. The Pawn-chain calls for a Black attack on its base the White P at QB3 by . . . . P—QR3, ... P—QKt4, ... P—QR4, and . . . . P—Kt5. But it is necessary for Black to safeguard himself against P—KKt4. With this idea Black played 19. . . . . . P—KR4 !; 20. R(K1)—KB1, R—R3 ! ! (the "mysterious" Rook move, for Black sees White's P—KR3 and P—KKt4 coming, and wishes when this happens to be ready to attack in the KR file); 21. B—K1, P—Kt3; 22. B—KR4, K—B2 !; 23. Q—K1, P—R3 (now timely!); 24. B—R4; P—QKt4; 25. B—Q1,

B—B3; 26. R—R3 (a defensive move on the Queen wing was here indicated), P—R4; 27. B—Kt5, KR—R1; 28. Q—R4, P—Kt5; 29. Q—K1 (or B—B6, B—K2), R—QKt1; 30. R(R3)—B3, P—QR5, and Black pushed his attack home; 31. R(B3)—B2, P—R6; 32. P—QKt3, BP x P; 33. B x KtP, B—Kt4; 34. R—Kt1, Q x P; etc. The Rook maneuver in this game . . . . R—KB3—R3—R1 stands out with plastic effect and must give pleasure to any one who plays over the game.

In the position of Diagram 160 Black wanted to take advantage of his majority on the K side by the maneuver . . . . K—Kt3—B4, followed by . . . . P—K4. However on . . . . K—Kt3 White would play P—KKt4; therefore I chose the "mysterious" Rook move 28. . . . . . R—R1 *!*, and after the further moves 29. R—Q1, K—Kt3; 30.

DIAGRAM 160

R—Q4, K—B4; 31. B—Q2, there again followed a "mysterious" Rook move 31. . . . . R—KB1, which we might more accurately call semi-mysterious, for whereas . . . . R—R1 followed merely preventive ends, ... R—KB1 has this essential difference that its nature is purely active; there followed 32. B—K1, P—K4; 33. P x P, P x P; 34. R—R4, P—KKt4; 35. R—QKt4, K—K3 *ch;* 36. K—

v. Gottschall—Nimzovich
Hanover 1926

K2, P—K5; 37. B—B2, R—B6. The passed Pawn, the penetration of the Rook into the enemy position, and a certain weakness in White's QBP slowly wrought the destruction of White's game. See II. vi. § 3, where the interesting ending of this game is given, interesting because of the tactics employed to break down White's resistance by maneuvering against both flanks.

The "mysterious" Rook move places a Rook in a closed file, which can only be opened by the enemy himself, and if he does not do so our Rook is standing there with "nothing doing"; such a move must never be made, except consciously and with the intention of sacrificing something of the Rook's effective strength. This sacrifice is made in order to prevent an enemy freeing maneuver, or at any rate to render it difficult. If, however, we recognize a freeing move planned by our opponent as illusory (as not really having a freeing effect), then it would be in the highest degree uneconomical to make such a sacrifice. In the game which was quoted above, Blackburne—Nimzovich, the difference between a true and an illusory freeing move leaps to the eyes; and as it is also pertinent to our conception of prophylactic strategy we give it in full in the Games Section. (See No. 32.) The student is recommended to play it over before proceeding further.

The following postulate I regard as of the utmost importance: *There is no such thing as an absolute freeing move.* A freeing move in a position in which development has not been carried far always proves to be illusory, and, vice versa, a move,

DIAGRAM 161

Black's "freeing-move" . . . . P—B4 leads, owing to his backward development, to a premature opening up of his game which becomes in consequence compromised

which does not come at all in the category of freeing moves, can, given a surplus of tempi to our credit, lead to a very free game.

Consider for instance the position on Diagram 161, White has obviously a substantial plus in tempi, and in these circumstances the freeing move . . . . P—B4 only leads to a premature opening of Black's undeveloped game. For example *1. . . . . P—B4; 2. KP x P, KtP x P; 3. Kt—R5* followed by *P—B4* with a strong attack. This association of ideas was unknown to the pseudo-classical school, which knew only absolute freeing moves. Black's . . . . P—B4 in a position with the central Pawn configuration as in the diagram, was reckoned as such by it, and in 80 per cent of cases was held worthy of commendation. We have reduced the proportion to about 60 per cent; for even after the defensive White move P—B3 (after 1. . . . . P—B4; 2. P x P, P x P) the strength of the pair of Black Pawns at K4 and KB4 must not be rated too high. And now we suddenly find ourselves facing the germ-cell of restraint action, to which because of its importance a separate section will be devoted.

§ 4.   *The germ-cell of restraint action directed against a Pawn majority is developed. The fight against a central majority. The qualitative majority.*

I find it impossible to present the germ-cell of restraint by means of diagrams, so I will adopt another method. Black, shall we say, has a majority: P at QR4 and P at QKt4 against White's P at QR3; or P at K4 and P at KB4 against P at KB3. In both cases Black threatens to make a passed Pawn, and in the second to attack White's castled position by the wedge . . . . P—KB5 in conjunction with . . . . R—KB4—KR4, etc. The idea of the restraint now lies in the plan of neutralizing the enemy's Pawn plus by means of the open K file and two different blockade points. In the position under consideration, besides "Knights, halberdiers, and archers," the possessor of the Pawn majority has two threats at his disposal; the one lies in the advance . . . . P—K5, the other in the wedge . . . . P—B5, supplemented perhaps by the diversion . . . . R—KB4—KKt4 or KR4, or . . . . P—KR4, etc., and at the same time the establishment of a Black Kt at his K6 will be planned.

In what does the restraint idea now consist? In the case of

. . . . P—K5, in P—KB4 with an eventual B—K3 to blockade Black's KP at that point, and on the other hand if Black should advance his KBP (. . . . P—KB5) to stop any further advance by Kt—K4. This Kt, thanks to his radius of action, will help to make Black's diversion difficult to carry out. It follows that we must look for the germ-cell of restraint action in an open file combined with a two-fold possibility of setting up a blockade.

A central majority must not be allowed to advance too far, otherwise the wedge threat would have a much too painful effect. For example in the position White: K, KKt1; Pawns, KB2, KKt2, KR2. Black: Pawns, K5, KB5, KKt2, KR2. (Imagine any number of pieces added.) Black with . . . . P—B6 (the wedge) threatens to cut the White lines of communication between his KR and KKt Pawns and the rest of his 2nd rank (a White R on his QR2 could no longer protect either of these Pawns), and Black's attack must, *ceteris paribus,* be reckoned as very strong. Hence it is necessary to fix an enemy central majority on its 4th rank, *i.e.,* with the configuration Black: Pawns at K4, KB4. White: P at KB3.

The conception of the qualitative majority is an easy one to assimilate by any one who has mastered the Pawn-chain. In the position, White: Pawns, K5, Q4, QR2, QKt2, QB3, KB4, KKt4, KR3. Black: Pawns, K3, Q4, QB4, QR2, QKt2, KB2, KKt2, KR2, White has the qualitative majority of the King's Wing, Black on the Queen's. That is to say *that majority which is the more advanced towards the enemy base is naturally regarded as qualitatively the superior one.* It stands to reason that the further advanced a wing majority is, the sooner will lines be opened in that sector for exploitation by the possessor of the qualitative majority.

§ 5. *The different forms under which restraint is wont to appear are further elucidated. (a) The fight against mobile center Pawns. (b) The restraint of a qualitative majority. (c) Restraint of double-complexes. (d) My "special variation" and its restraint motif.*

(a) The mobile center Pawn. White with a Pawn at K4 against Black's P at Q3 and P at KB2 (or P at Q4 against P at K3 and P at QB3). Such a Pawn can result from say *1.* P—K4, P—K4; *2.* Kt—KB3, Kt—QB3; *3.* B—Kt5, P—Q3; *4.* P—Q4, P x P; *5.* Kt x P, B—Q2. Black's restraint operation will be begun by .... Kt—B3, ... B—K2, ... O—O, ... R—K1, ... B—KB1. Another important aid towards the crippling of White's center is the more passive Pawn structure P at Q3 and P at KB3. The position White: P at K4; Black: Pawns, Q3, KB3 is typical and I call it the "sawing" position, since White's KP is to be sawn up between these Pawns.

The sequence of events in a maneuver directed against a mobile center is usually: (i) the passive "sawing position," then (ii) the more aggressive hindering action of a Rook exerting pressure on it; (iii) making backward or isolated a once mobile center Pawn; (iv) mechanical stopping of the same by a blockading piece; (v) winning the Pawn.

The aim of the restraining party in a game may be sufficiently summed up thus: *First restrain, next blockade, lastly destroy!* To carry this out is difficult but remunerative, and the process is instructive for the student. Hence the analysis of the position reached after *1.* P—K4, P—K4; *2.* Kt—KB3, P—Q3; *3.* P—Q4, P x P; *4.* Kt x P is excellent training, and as such cannot be too strongly recommended to the aspiring student.

The following illustrative game is apparently complicated, but only in its motives; in reality it is the fight against White's P at K4 which dominates. Shoosmith—Nimzovich, Ostend, 1907. *1.* P—Q4, Kt—KB3; *2.* P—QB4, P—Q3; *3.* Kt—KB3, QKt—

Q2; *4.* Kt—B3, P—K4; *5.* P—K4, B—K2; *6.* B—Q3, O—O; *7.* O—O, P x P *!* (If 7. . . . . R—K1, then *8.* P—Q5 and Black will be cramped for a long time to come. For instance, *8.* . . . . Kt— B4; *9.* B—K3, Kt x B; *10.* Q x Kt, Kt—Q2; *11.* P—QKt4, P— QR4; *12.* P—QR3, etc.); *8.* Kt x P, R—K1; *9.* P—QKt3, Kt—K4; *10.* B—B2, P—QR3 (this advance will soon be intelligible); *11.* B— Kt2, B—Q2; *12.* P—KR3, B—KB1; *13.* P—B4, Kt—Kt3; *14.* Q—B3, P—B3; *15.* QR—K1, P—Kt4 (now the situation is clear: Black keeps an eye on White's KP and seeks at the same time to be rid of the disturbing QBP, since the latter makes his P at Q3 backward); *16.* Q—Q3, Q—B2; *17.* K—R1, QR—Q1; *18.* B— Kt1, P—Kt5 *! !* (We are dealing with a chain formation, certainly rather an unusual one. The links of the chain are White's P at QKt3 and P at QB4, Black's P at QKt5 and Kt at QB4[!], for why as an exception should not an officer be allowed to play the rôle of a Pawn in a chain? The plan consists in playing . . . . B—B1, ... Kt—Q2—B4 and . . . . P— QR4—R5 attacking the White enemy base the P at QKt3. Accordingly . . . . P—Kt5 involved the transference of the attack from the White P at QB4 to his P at QKt3); *19.* Kt— Q1, B—B1; *20.* Q—KB3, Kt—Q2; *21.* Kt—B5, Kt—B4; *22.* P— Kt4 ? (a mistake which leaves his P at KB4 insufficiently defended for a moment; but this short moment is long enough to allow Black to break through brilliantly), Kt—K3 *!* (exploiting White's mistake); *23.* Q—Kt3, B—Kt2; *24.* P—KR4, P—Q4; *25.* P—K5, P—B4; *26.* P x P, R x P; *27.* K—Kt1 (B—K4 ?, R x Kt *!*), R—Q7; *28.* Kt(B5)—K3, Q—B3; *29.* *Resigns.*

The reader may here be referred to my games against Teichmann and Blackburne (Nos. 2 and 32).

(*b*) The fight against a qualitative majority. Let us imagine that in Diagram 158 the Black Kt is at QB4 instead of KB3; we should then have a typical case of the restraint of a qualitative majority. If now Kt x Kt, then . . . . KtP x Kt and White's advance is crippled. If however *1. P—QR3* intending to follow with P—QKt4, then *1. . . . . P—R5 !; 2. P—QKt4, Kt—Kt6 !;* and this strongly posted Kt is compensation for a possible White P—QB5. The student should notice that the action of Black's flanking Pawn is made up of equal parts of passive and aggressive effect, for this Pawn, or the P at KR4 in Diagram 162, is the true prop of our whole restraint maneuver. In both positions White's P—R3 will be answered by P—R5.

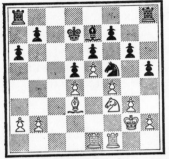

DIAGRAM 162

White's qualitative majority appears to be held in restraint. 1. P—KR3 will be effectively answered by . . . . P—R5, and 2. P—KKt4 by . . . . Kt—Kt6

Another typical example is shown in the following end game. (See Diagram 163.) Here the advance in close formation planned by White, namely Q—Kt3, P—KR4, P—Kt5, cannot be held up permanently. This advance (let us imagine for a moment that Black's inevitable . . . . P—B3 has taken place) would expose the base of Black's Pawn-chain (after P x BP, P x P). But the King's side attack involved in White's advance would be much worse for Black. His right plan will, therefore, be to hold up White's P—KR4 and P—Kt5 long enough for the King to escape by flight. With this idea Black played *21. . . . . Kt—R2,* and then followed *22. Kt—B3,*

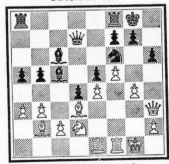

DIAGRAM 163

Van Vliet—Nimzovich

Q—K2; 23. Q—Kt3, KR—K1; 24. P—KR4, P—B3; 25. R—R1 (White, too, has weaknesses), Q—Kt2; 26. R(B1)—K1, K—B2 !; 27. R—K2 (If 27. P—Kt5, then . . . . RP x P; 28. P x P, K—K2 ! with a tenable game), R—R1 ! (the "mysterious" Rook move!); 28. K—B2, Kt—B1; 29. P—Kt5, RP x P; 30. P x P, Kt—Q2; (White's K side attack may be said to have spent itself, for after 31. P x P, P x P; 32. Q—Kt6 *ch*, K—K2; 33. Q—Kt7 *ch*, K—Q3, Black would have a splendid game). The game proceeded: 31. P x P, P x P; 32. Kt—R4, QR—KKt1; 33. Kt—Kt6, R—R4; 34. R—KKt1, R—Kt4; with advantage to Black. The resource here demonstrated is worth the attention of the student.

(*c*) Restraint of double complexes. Side by side with the dynamic weakness of such a complex, which we have often emphasized, we have to characterize the following points as often decisive: (1) the imprisoned Bishop, (2) cramped terrain and consequent difficulties in finding a defense.

DIAGRAM 164

The "dead" Bishop (KKt2) a prisoner in his own camp. The QB is in not much better state

Bird's Opening and the English Opening will give us an example of (1).

I. *1.* P—KB4, P—Q4; *2.* Kt—KB3, P—QB4; *3.* P—Q3 (somewhat unusual) Kt—QB3; *4.* Kt—B3, B—Kt5 *!*; *5.* P—KKt3, B x Kt *!!*; *6.* P x Kt, P—K3; *7.* B—Kt2, P—B4 *!*; *8.* O—O, P—Q5 (delightful play; the B at KKt2 is now a prisoner in his own camp. Black's weakness at his K3 is easily protected; see Diagram 164); *9.* Kt—Kt1, P—QKt4; *10.* P—QR4, P—Kt5; *11.* Kt—Q2, Kt—R4; *12.* Q—K2, K—B2; *13.* R—K1, Q—Q2; *14.* Kt—B4, Kt x Kt; *15.* P x Kt, Kt—B3; and Black (Dr. Edman) dictated the tempo.

II. *1.* P—K3, P—K4; *2.* P—QB4, Kt—KB3; *3.* Kt—QB3; Kt—B3;

4. Kt—B3, B—Kt5; 5. B—K2 (to be considered was 5. P—Q4, P x P; 6. P x P, P—Q4; 7. B—K2 with an equal game), O—O; 6. O—O, R—K1; 7. P—QR3, B x Kt; 8. KtP x B, P—Q3; and White labored through the whole game under the difficulty of making use of his QB. (From the game Nimzovich—Réti, Breslau, 1925.)

Diagrams 165 and 166 are given to illustrate (2). The latter shows us a blockading Kt whose effect on the double complex is simply enormous: for not only is Black's majority in its collective value illusory, but each single component of that majority seems individually to have its life threatened. Under these conditions White's majority will win, almost at will. Even with Rooks present on both sides, *e.g.*, White, R at QR4; Black, R at Q1 or R at QKt3, the game would be untenable for the second player. This shows to what degree restrained double Pawns may cripple a position.

DIAGRAM 165

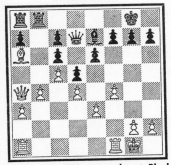

DIAGRAM 166

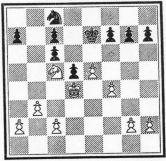

If his P at QB2 were absent Black would have freedom to move about; as it is—bearing in mind the threat B—Kt7—he is almost stalemated

The effect of a Kt who is blockading enemy doubled Pawns is crushing. Sooner or later, Black will succumb to *Zugzwang*

(*d*) My "special variation" with its restraint motif. The line of play in question is *1.* P—QB4, P—K4; *2.* Kt—QB3, Kt—KB3; *3.* Kt—B3, Kt—B3; and now *4.* P—K4. As early as 1924 I had tried after the moves *1.* P—KB4, P—QB4; *2.* P—K4, Kt—QB3; *3.* P—

Q3 (originated by Dr. Krause), P—KKt3, the move 4. P—B4, whose motif I visualized as a blockade spanning half the board, and in *Kagans Neueste Schachnachrichten* for 1925, p. 10, I made the following note to this move:—"Since this move is not inspired by the hope of preventing or even of making more difficult . . . . P—Q4, a special explanation is needed. Black wishes to build up the configuration P at K3, P at Q4. This done, he will consider the extension of his attack formation on the Queen's wing, *i.e.*, by . . . . Kt—Q5 when opportunity offers, in order after Kt x Kt, P x Kt; to bring pressure in the QB file on White's Pawn at QB2. The text move is made to forestall this possible extension of play on the Queen's wing. The hole at Q4 does not seem to be a serious matter."

When I to-day ask myself whence I got the moral courage, for it takes moral courage to make a move (or form a plan) running counter to all tradition, I think I may say in answer, that it was only my intense preoccupation with the problem of the blockade which helped me to do so. To this problem I was ever seeking to bring new aspects, and so it came that, as Black in Dresden, 1926, after the moves 1. P—K4, P—QB4; 2. Kt—KB3, Kt—QB3; 3. Kt—B3, I ventured the move . . . . P—K4, which at that time caused a great sensation. My special variation given above, is to be considered merely a further step on a trail which had already been broken. Moreover the able Danish theorist Dr. O. H. Krause, has pursued an original inquiry into the possibility of a combination of P—K4 and P—QB4, in which, independently of my analysis, he has arrived at much the same conclusions as I did.

The student is advised now to study Games No. 33 to 35, and in addition is referred to the investigation of the idea in my brochure, *Die Blockade*.

3. The Isolated Queen's Pawn and His Descendants

§ 1. *Introductory.*

THE problem of the isolated QP is in my opinion one of the cardinal problems in the whole theory of positional play. We are concerned with the appraisal of a statically weak Pawn, who, however, notwithstanding his weakness, is imbued with dynamic strength. "Which preponderates, the static weakness or the dynamic strength?" So put, the problem gains in significance, in fact it strays in a sense beyond the circumscribed boundaries of chess.

DIAGRAM 167

The isolated QP. Notice White's outpost station at his K5, Black's at his Q4

DIAGRAM 168

Skeleton diagram of the isolated QP. 1 = White outpost. 2 = Black outpost

It is indispensable that the student should face this problem himself, that is to say have personal experience of it. He should try as White to get the so-called normal position in the Queen's Gambit: *1.* P—Q4, P—Q4; *2.* Kt—KB3, Kt—KB3; *3.* P—B4, P—K3; *4.* P—K3, P—B4; *5.* Kt—B3, Kt—B3, and then, alternately, in one game 6. B—Q3, P x QP; 7. KP x P, P x P; 8. B x P and White has an "isolani," in the other, 6. P x QP, KP x P; 7. P x P, B x P; and now White has to fight against the isolani. It will do him good to realize in his own person how dangerous an enemy isolani may be, and how difficult it is to save his own from an untimely end.

§ 2. *The dynamic strength of the isolated QP.*

The strength of an isolani (see Diagram 168) lies in its lust to expand (=the tendency P—Q5), and in addition to the circumstance that this Pawn protects, indeed creates the White outpost stations at K5 and QB5. As opposed to this, the Black outpost station at Q4 has not, at any rate in the middle game, the full equivalent value, for quite apart from any arithmetical preponderance (two outposts to one), White can point to the fact that a Kt at K5 (see Diagram 167) must have a sharper effect than is ever possible to an opposing Kt at Q4; for it is clear that a Kt at K5 seconded by two powerful Bishop diagonals (Q3 to KR7 and KKt5 to KB6) must exert pressure on Black's King's wing, and what can be "sharper" than an attack on the King? The linear investigation yields therefore an undoubted plus to the first player.

On the other hand our Pawn, as is well known, tends to become a weakness in the ending. How are we to understand this? Is the difficulty only this, that the P at Q4 is hard to defend, or are there other calamities in store?

§ 3. *The isolani as an end game weakness.*

Our judgment on the problem which we have sketched must be influenced by the circumstance that to the points K5 (White) and Q4 (Black) a different valuation must be assigned in the end game than was the case in the middle game; for in the ending attacks on the King are not in question, and so White's K5 loses much of its glory, while Black's Q4 gains in importance. And if White has not already got through to QB7, or lacks other trump cards earned in the middle game to point to, his position will not be particularly enviable. White will suffer not only under the want of protection felt by his isolani, but also from the fact that the white squares such as Q5, QB4, K4 can easily become weak. Imagine in Diagram 168 a White K at QB4 and B at Q2, and a Black K at QB3 and Kt at K2. Black by a check with the Kt drives the White K from QB4, plays then . . . . K—Q4, and pushes further forward with his King via QB5 or K5. In every pertinent case that may arise Q4 must be regarded as the key point of Black's position. With this point as base he will blockade, centralize, maneuver. Black's Q4 will provide a gate of entry into the enemy position, (*cf.* the above example) and also a point of junction in all possible troop movements, as for instance (imagine now Diagram 168 enlivened by the presence of Rooks and Knights) in the case of Black's . . . . R(Q1)—Q4—QR4, or . . . . Kt(KB3)—Q4—QKt5, or finally . . . . Kt—Q4—K2—KB4 x QP. A Black Kt posted at Q4 exercises an impressive effect on both wings; a Bishop at Q4 not seldom forces a decision even with Bishops on opposite color (*e.g.,* if there be Rooks remaining on each side). Obviously White may have counter-balancing, or even apparently preponderating, compensation for these trumps of Black's; for instance, should one of his Rooks have penetrated to his QB7; but such cases can only be considered as exceptions to the rule. To recapitulate: White's weakness in the end game rests on the fact that his P on Q4 seems to be threatened, while Black's Q4 is extraordinarily strong; further, that the white squares, his QB4, Q5, K4, tend to become weak, whereas much of the one-time importance of his K5 is spent. White's Pawn position was in fact not "compact," and other disadvantages to which we have called attention, such as a weakness pervading a complex of squares on a given color, must necessarily attach themselves to a Pawn position which is not compact (which is broken up). We earnestly recommend to the student, as extremely profitable, that he sharpen his sense for compact positions and the reverse. He must also bear carefully in mind that it is not only the isolani itself that tends to become a weakness, *but also the complex of squares surrounding it.* In this the principal evil is to be found.

§ 4. *The isolani as a weapon of attack in the middle game.*

Solidity of construction and purpose should at the first sign of neglect on the part of the opponent (*e.g.*, if he has withdrawn his pieces from the K's wing) give place to a violent attack. Many players with an isolani proceed much too violently, but it seems to me that there is no objective motive for "plunging" into a desperate attack. At first the utmost solidity is called for. The attack will come of itself in good time, for instance when Black has withdrawn his Kt at KB3, which he will at some time naturally do, since the Kt wants to get to Q4. In the development stage (see Diagram 167) we would therefore recommend the solid construction, B at K3 (not KKt5), Q at K2, R's: QB1 and Q1 (not Q1 and K1), further B at Q3 or QKt1 (not QKt3); and the first player cannot be too strongly warned against attempting surprise attacks in the early stages, started by perhaps Kt(K5) x KBP (a B being at QR2) or by a Rook sally (R—K1—K3—KR3). A solid position aimed at maintaining the security of the P at Q4 is the one and only right course, and it must ever be remembered

DIAGRAM 169

Nimzovich—Taubenhaus
Black with the move played . . . .
Kt—K1 (to get to Q3). This is the
trumpet call for the attack for White.
How will the attack be started, and
what will be its course?

that the B at K3 belongs to the P at Q4 as does a nurse to a suckling child!

It is only when Black has withdrawn his pieces from the K's side that White may sound the attack, and this, if he will, he may carry out in sacrificial style. (See Diagram 169.) White has developed his pieces in the spirit of this section, and the text move (. . . . Kt—K1) gives him the chance which, as in all similar cases, he avidly seizes to launch a direct attack on the enemy King. The result in the present case is doubtful, but since the whole manner of conducting the attack is characteristic of "isolani positions," we give a few variations: *19. . . . . Kt—K1; 20. Q—R5, P—Kt3* (if *20. . . . . P—B4*, then *21. B—KKt5*); *21. Q—R6, Kt—Kt2* (or *21. . . . . P—B3; 22. Kt—Kt4*); *22. B—KKt5 !* (the pieces now come out of their reserve), *P—B3; 23. B x KtP, RP x B; 24. Kt x P*, and now two variations arise according as the Queen retreats to Q2 or Q3. If the former, White has two courses open to him, either *25. B—R4 !* or the more combinational *25. B x P; 24. . . . . Q—Q2; 25. B x P, Kt x B; 26. Q—R8 ch, K—B2; 27. Kt—K5 ch, K—K1; 28. Kt x Q, R x Q; 29. Kt x Kt ch*, with three Pawns for the piece sacrificed. If Black plays *24. . . . . Q—Q3* (instead of . . . . *Q—Q2*), White can carry on with *25. Q—R8 ch, K—B2; 26. Q—R7, P x B; 27. Kt—K5 ch*, and the continuation could be *27. . . . . K—K1; 28. Q x Kt, Q—K2; 29. Q—Kt6 ch, K—Q1; 30. R—B6* with wild complications. So once more, build up a solid position, support the isolani (*B—K3 !*) and only attack when opportunity really offers.

§ 5. *Which cases are favorable for White and which for Black?*

In general it may be said that the two following cases are worth striving for by White.

(i) When White has effected P—Q5, KP x P; a piece x P, and thereby gets the better, because a centralized position (as in the game Rubinstein—Tartakover, at Baden-Baden, 1925).

(ii) When White has built up a position in the QB file (*cf.* Game No. 36, Nimzovich—Taubenhaus).

For Black the following are desirable.

(i) All cases (*ceteris paribus*) of a pronounced end game character.

(ii) Those where Black has played . . . . Kt(Q4) x Kt (QB3); KtP x Kt, with the idea of pinning down White's P at QB3 from the start and of laying siege to it (*cf.* Game No. 11, Thomas—Alekhine and see § 7 below on the isolated Pawn couple).

§ 6.   *On the possible genesis of reflex weaknesses among the Queen side Pawns of the player with an isolani.*

An index of the weakness of the isolani appears in the possibility which is not seldom offered to the opponent, of transferring his attack from the QP to the Q's wing; such a case of "reflex weakness" may be seen in game No. 23 (Rubinstein—Duras); a similar picture is presented in the following game (Rubinstein—Dr. Lasker, Moscow, 1925). After the moves *1.* P—Q4, P—Q4; *2.* P—QB4, P—QB3; *3.* P—K3, Kt—B3; *4.* Kt—QB3, P—K3; *5.* Kt—B3, QKt—Q2; *6.* B—Q3, P x P; *7.* B x BP, P—QKt4; *8.* B—K2, P—QR3; *9.* O—O, B—Kt2; *10.* P—QKt3, B—K2; *11.* B—Kt2, O—O; *12.* Kt—K5, P—B4; *13.* B—B3, Q—B2; *14.* Kt x Kt, Kt x Kt; *15.* Kt—K4, QR—Q1; *16.* R—B1, Q—Kt1; *17.* Q—K2, P x P; *18.* P x P, R—B1; *19.* P—Kt3, Q—R1; *20.* K—Kt2, KR—Q1; *21.* R x R, R x R; *22.* R—B1, R x R; *23.* B x R, P—R3, Black took a strategically most interesting advantage of the weakness of White's P at Q4. The continuation was: *24.* B—Kt2, Kt—Kt3; *25.* P—KR3 (since he wants to avoid the exchange of Queens, Q—B2, Q—QB1 would be of no use), Q—QB1; *26.* Q—Q3, Kt—Q4 *!* (threatening . . . . Kt—Kt5); *27.* P—R3, Kt—Kt3 *! !* (Now White's QKtP has become weak); *28.* K—R2, B—Q4; *29.* K—Kt2, Q—B3; *30.* Kt—Q2, P—QR4 *!*; *31.* Q—B3 (in his trouble he decides after all to submit to the exchange of Queens; but succumbs to the reflex weaknesses which have now arisen), B x B *ch* !; *32.* Kt x B (Q x B would fail because of . . . . Q—B7; Q—Kt7, Kt—Q4 *!*), Q x Q; *33.* B x Q, P—R5 *!* (and now the weakness of White's Q side is evident); *34.* P x P, P x P, and White lost since the attempt to save himself by *35.* B—Kt4, failed against *35.* . . . . B x B; *36.* P x B, P—R6; *37.* Kt—Q2 and now *37.* . . . . Kt—Q4, whereby the approach of the White K via K2, Q3, and QB4 is prevented (the answer to K—K2 after *38.* P—Kt5 would always be . . . . Kt—B6 *ch*). What is remarkable in this fine ending, in addition to the transference of the attack, is the masterly and varied use made of the point Q4.

On the manner of laying siege to an isolani I would make this additional remark, that today we no longer consider it necessary to render an enemy isolani absolutely immobile; on the contrary, we like to give him the illusion of freedom, rather than shut him up in a cage. (The principle of the large zoological garden applied to the small beast of prey.) How this is done is shown in the following game: Lasker (whom we class under the moderns)—Tarrasch, St. Petersburg, 1914. *1.* P—Q4, P—Q4; *2.* Kt—KB3, P—QB4; *3.* P—B4, P—K3; *4.* P x QP, KP x P; *5.* P—KKt3, Kt—QB3; *6.* B—Kt2, Kt—B3; *7.* O—O, B—K2; *8.* P x P, B x P; *9.* QKt—Q2, and now the isolani has the choice whether he will become weak on Q4 or Q5. Tarrasch chose the latter and there followed *9.* . . . . P—Q5; *10.* Kt—Kt3, B—Kt3; *11.* Q—Q3, B—K3; *12.* R—Q1, B x Kt; *13.* Q x B, Q—K2; *14.* B—Q2, O—O; *15.* P—QR4, Kt—K5; *16.* B—K1, QR—Q1; *17.* P—R5 *! !*, B—B4; *18.* P—R6, P x P (if . . . . P—QKt3, then Q—R4 threatening P—QKt4 in addition to Q x Kt); *19.* QR—B1. And now all the pieces defending the P at Q5 are in the air. There followed *19.* . . . . R—B1; *20.* Kt—R4, B—Kt3; *21.* Kt—B5, Q—K4; *22.* B x Kt, Q x B; *23.* Kt—Q6, winning the exchange. Taking everything into consideration the isolani is not an ineffective weapon in the middle game, but it can become very weak in the ending.

§ 7.   *The isolated Pawn couple.*

In the position on Diagram 170 Black can exchange at his QB6; if in the sequel he succeeds in holding back White's

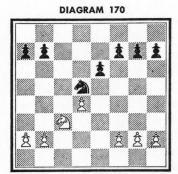

DIAGRAM 170

The genesis of an isolated Pawn couple, P at QB3, P at Q4, (1. . . . . Kt x Kt; 2. P x Kt)

P at QB3 and P at Q4, and finally in blockading them absolutely, his otherwise rather doubtful strategy (. . . . Kt x Kt) will have been justified, for to have the Pawns tied down in their own camp and close to the frontier will worry White not a little. The one trouble, namely the obligation to keep the P at QB3 and P at Q4 protected, will be aggravated by the other, a cramped terrain. The Pawns blockaded on QB3 and Q4, and only these, are what I call the isolated Pawn couple. A good example is met with in Game No. 11 (Thomas— Alekhine).

An essentially different picture is met with when the beleaguered player succeeds in advancing his QBP. We then have the P at QB4 and P at Q4. These Pawns we no longer call an "isolated Pawn couple," but designate them as "hanging" Pawns.

It will not be difficult to decide where the preference lies between the isolated Pawn couple, which has as a rule but slight mobility, and the two hanging Pawns. It stands to reason that hanging Pawns are much to be preferred, if only for the reason that they imply threats. And even if these should prove to be only apparent threats, which is after all what we might expect, nevertheless a doubtful initiative is always better than a passivity which is dead beyond all manner of doubt, as we have discovered in the case of a blockaded isolated Pawn couple in Game No. 11. We have then the following postulate for our guidance: The possessor of an isolated Pawn couple (Diagram 170, after the moves . . . . Kt x Kt; P x Kt) must do everything in his power to make P—QB4 possible; he must not at any cost allow a blockade. He must regard the awkward formation P at QB3, P at Q4 as a transition stage to the mobile structure P at QB4, P at Q4, with its eternal threat of P—B5 or P—Q5.

We will now give an example of the case where Black (who is saddled with an isolated Pawn couple) struggles to advance . . . . P—QB4. (Nimzovich—J. Giersing and S. Kinch, Copenhagen, 1924.) *1.* P—QB4, P—K4; *2.* Kt—KB3, Kt—QB3; *3.* P—Q4, P x P; *4.* Kt x P, Kt—B3; *5.* Kt x Kt, KtP x Kt; *6.* P—KKt3, P—Q4; *7.* B—Kt2, B—Kt5 *ch;* *8.* B—Q2, B x B *ch;* *9.* Kt x B, O—O; *10.* O—O, R—Kt1; *11.* Q—B2 (White avoids P—Kt3, since he designs to maneuver over QKt3: Kt—Kt3 or Q—R4), R—K1; *12.* P—K3, B—K3; *13.* P x P (*13.* Kt—Kt3, P x P; *14.* Kt—Q4 was also to be considered), P x P (Black has now the isolated Pawn couple in question: for the formation P at QB2, Q4 deserves the designation "isolated" even more than does P at QB3, Q4: he therefore quite rightly tries to make . . . . P—B4 possible); *14.* Kt—Kt3, Q—Q3; *15.* KR—B1, KR—QB1; *16.* Q—QB5, Q x Q; *17.* R x Q, Kt—Q2; *18.* R—R5 (in order on the next move, by R—QB1, to establish an enduring blockade), P—QB4 *! !;* *19.* R x RP, P—B5; *20.* Kt—Q4, R x P *!;* *21.* Kt x B, P x Kt; *22.* R x Kt, P—B6 (Black has purchased the mobility of his QBP at the cost of a piece! White cannot force a win); *23.* B—R3, P—B7; *24.* B x P *ch,* K—B1; *25.* R—B7 *ch* (B—B5 was also possible), K—K1, *26.* B x R, R—Kt8 *ch;* *27.* K—Kt2, R x R (or *27.* . . . . P—B8[Q]; *28.* R x R, Q x R; *29.* R—B4); *28.* R—B7, P—B8(Q); *29.* R x Q, R x R; and the game was drawn on the 42nd move.

§ 8.   *Hanging Pawns. Their pedigree and what we can learn from it. The advance in a blocked position.*

The evolution, or the story of the genesis of hanging Pawns will be found illustrated in the trio of diagrams 171, 172, 173. A glance at this shows that we are minded to trace the descent of the hanging Pawns from the isolani, and the "family tree" shows very clearly the generations: Isolani, the founder of the family. Isolated Pawn couple. Hanging Pawns.

This view, the soundness of which is demonstrable, serves us in good stead, for it will enable us to compare the hanging Pawns with their anything but distinct motives, with their grandpapa the Isolani whose motives are more plain. In short a study of their family history should help us to a better understanding of one particularly "difficult" member of that family. From their grandpapa the hanging Pawns have inherited one essential trait, namely that *curious mixture of static weakness and dynamic strength.* But whereas in the case of an isolani both strength and weakness stand out clearly, with hanging Pawns both are masked. In these highly problematical creatures two things only may be held to be established: (i) that the two hanging Pawns (as, say, in Diagram 173) are "unprotected" (are not defended by any Pawns), and that the bombardment to which, being in open files, they are subjected, will be all the more harassing on that account; (ii) that the possibility of attaining to a comparatively secure position, *i.e.*, one in which one of the two hanging Pawns protects the other (P at Q4, P at QB5, or P at QB4, P at Q5), often presents itself.

The problem, however, is this: If this possibility, to attain to relative security, is only to be bought at the cost of all initiative in the center, if the Pawns in getting this "security" can be blockaded, is it not more advisable to forego this offered security and to remain "hanging"?

The answer to this is not easy. It depends entirely on the

The Isolani and his Descendants:
A family tree from the game
Rubinstein—Nimzovich, Carlsbad, 1907.

DIAGRAM 171

The Isolani

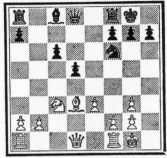

DIAGRAM 172

The isolated Pawn-couple

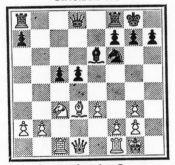

DIAGRAM 173

The two hanging Pawns

particular circumstances; namely on the manner and the details
of the resulting blockade. That to talk of the "security" in which
such a blockaded complex can rock itself is greatly to stretch
the meaning of the word, this I concede in advance, for blockaded Pawns all too easily tend to become weaknesses. Nevertheless, it would seem to be entirely fitting, in certain cases, to
let the hanging Pawns advance in a blocked position. These

cases are the following:—(i) When the Pawns in the enemy blockading ring are themselves attackable, as is the White P at QKt2 in Diagram 173. (ii) When the blockade would cost the enemy too much, either because the blockading apparatus is too great, or because the blockaders at his disposal prove to be for some reason unfitted for their task whether for lack of elasticity or as having insufficient threat effect from their positions (*cf.* I. iv. § 3). As an antithesis to this we may point to Diagrams 174 and 175. Here the "blockaded" security is shown

DIAGRAM 174

E. Cohn—Duras
Carlsbad 1911
The "security" achieved by the
hanging Pawns is a very relative
one. The P at B4 is weak, though it
is true that the P at Q5 is passed

DIAGRAM 175

The P at Q5 is the product of two
hanging Pawns. Many moves ago
there occurred . . . . P—Q5; KP x
P, BP x P. The P at Q5 will now be
blockaded by K—K2—Q3. White
gets the advantage

to be deceptive; the advanced Pawns become weak. And again the reason for this lies in the quality of the blockading forces: in Diagrams 174 and 175 the Kt at Q3 and the K at Q3 are respectively excellent blockaders, which sufficiently accounts for the miscarriage of the attempt to save the situation.

The truth seems, therefore, to lie in the following statement of the case:—Just as our judgment on the isolani P at Q4 depended on the greater or lesser degree of initiative to which he could lay claim (of course the outpost station which he supports must have some value), so, too, we consider that we have the right to expect some measure of initiative in hanging Pawns which have attained to a "blockaded" security. Dead passivity has no prospects before it.

We will now give some examples:

In the position Rubinstein—Nimzovich, Diagram 173, there followed 15. Q—R4, Q—Kt3 (Black holds tight); 16. Q—R3, P—B5 ! (steps into "blockaded" security, but here White's blockading ring is attackable in the P at QKt2. Black's advance was therefore justified); 17. B—K2, P—QR4; 18. KR—Q1, Q—Kt5; 19. R—Q4, KR—Q1; 20. R(B1)—Q1, R—Q2; 21. B—B3, R(R1)—Q1; 22. Kt—Kt1 (A waiting measure would be better here, e.g., R(Q4)—Q2, etc.), R—Kt1; 23. R(Q1)—Q2, Q x Q !; 24. Kt x Q, K—B1; 25. P—K4 (leads in the end to the loss of a Pawn, but White in any case stood unfavorably. The equilibrium which still existed at the 21st move—the weaknesses of the P at Q4 and the P at QKt2 balanced one another—has been clearly disturbed; the P at QKt2 is now become really weak, whereas the P at Q4 seems to be actually over-protected), P x P; 26. R x R, Kt x R; 27. B x P, Kt—B4; 28. R—Q4 (or 28. B—B6 !, R—Kt5; 29. B—Q5, Kt—R5; with advantage to Black), Kt x B; 29. R x Kt, R x P; 30. Kt x P, R—Kt5; 31. Kt—Q6, R x R; 32. Kt x R, B x P; and Black won. For the concluding moves see I. vi. § 1, p. 93.

In master practice the move P—Q5 (from the hanging Pawn position P at QB4, P at Q4) occurs much more frequently. It leads quite prettily to the closing of the somewhat original circle from isolani through the hanging Pawns to isolani. The whole point now is whether the isolani which has newly come into existence can maintain itself or not. An example taken from the game Nimzovich—Tartakover, Copenhagen, 1923:—1. Kt—KB3, P—Q4; 2. P—QKt3, P—QB4; 3. P—K3, Kt—QB3; 4. B—Kt2, B—Kt5; 5. B—K2, Q—B2; 6. P—Q4, P x P; 7. P x P, P—K3; 8. O—O, B—Q3 (we have now a Queen's Gambit Declined with colors reversed); 9. P—KR3, B x Kt; 10. B x B, Kt—B3; 11. P—B4 !, P x P; 12. P x P, O—O; 13. Kt—B3 (the construction Kt—Q2—Kt3,

Q—K2, QR—B1, KR—K1 would here have been in the spirit of a holding tight policy, but I wished to "realize" my stock-in-trade, by P—Q5), KR—Q1; *14.* Kt—Kt5, Q—K2; *15.* Q—K2, B—Kt1; *16.* P—Q5, P x P; *17.* Q x Q, Kt x Q; *18.* B x Kt, P x B; *19.* P x P, B—K4 *!*; *20.* QR—Kt1, and the QP not only managed to maintain himself, but also in the whole further course of the game formed a counterweight to Black's majority on the Q-side which was not to be underestimated. Tartakover did underestimate it, and lost.

The game from which Diagram 176 was taken did not run so comfortable a course for the possessor of the hanging Pawns. The game proceeded *17.* Q—R3, Kt—K5; *18.* R—Q3, KR—Q1; *19.* KR—Q1, Q—K3; *20.* Kt—Q2, Q—QKt3; *21.* Kt—B1, Kt—B3; *22.* Kt—Kt3, QR—B1; *23.* P—KR3, P—KR3; *24.* Kt—K2, R—Q2; *25.* Kt—B3, Q—K3; *26.* Q—R5, P—Q5 *!* (he is tired of the eternal threats and seeks to substitute for the "hanging position" the "blockaded security" of which we have so often spoken, but it nearly costs him dear); *27.* P x P, P x P; *28.* Kt—Kt5 (how is the newly arisen isolani now to be saved?), Q—B4 *!* (there followed some dexterous parries);

DIAGRAM 176

Bernstein—Teichmann
Carlsbad 1923
**Some elegant pirouetting by Black
is seen**

29. Q—R4 *!*, R—B8 *!*; *30.* R x R, Q x R; *31.* R—B8 *ch*, K—R2; *32.* Q—B2, Q x Q; *33.* R x Q, P—Q6 *!*; *34.* R—Q2 (the QP still seems to be in danger), Kt—K5 *!*; *35.* R—Q1, R—Kt2 (final liquidation!); *36.* Kt—B3, Kt x Kt; *37.* P x Kt, R—Kt7; *38.* R x P, R x RP. Draw. The student should observe the way in which the QP was indirectly protected. This strategem furnishes the defending party with one more chance to emerge from the distress of his hanging Pawn position to more settled circumstances.

The "hanging condition" must be regarded as a passing one and what we have to do is to find the proper moment for liquidating it. In general the defending party proceeds to this a move or two too soon, he does not hold tight long enough, perhaps because the consciousness of being "in the air" is not greatly to the taste of the human psyche. But if you have it in mind to realize your hanging Pawns, do not do it unless you can sense behind the "blockaded security" which you crave, a glimmer of an initiative. Never let yourself be drawn into a dead blockaded position; rather remain "in the air."

Other games illustrating this chapter are Nos. 36 and 37.

4. The Two Bishops

§ 1. Introductory. Relative strength of Bishop and Knight.

THE two Bishops are, in the hands of a skillful fighter, a terrible weapon; yet I confess that for a moment I dallied with the blasphemous thought of omitting them from any detailed examination in my book. My system, so I said to myself, only recognizes two things worthy of thorough investigation: the elements, and strategical devices. For instance, we regarded the isolani, which seemed to us in some way to have grown out of the problem of restraint, as a strategical device. Under what heading, however, were the proud Prelates to be placed?

This question which we have thrown out must not be dismissed without further to-do as an idle or a trifling one, rather does it appear to me to be one of decided theoretical interest. It would lead us too far to develop here the grounds on which my views on this are based, so I will content myself with giving the result. I have arrived at the conclusion that the advantage of the two Bishops can be called neither an element nor a stratagem. To me the two Bishops are, and can be, nothing else than a kind of weapon. The examination of the various kinds of weapons and the determination of their applicability to given cases lies wholly outside the plan of my book. Moreover, Berger has made this the leitmotif of his book on the End Game. Nevertheless, the reader has naturally the right to expect that I should enlighten him, as far as I can, on the dangers in which a pair of enemy Bishops may involve him. And this I will proceed to do.

The superiority of the Bishop over the Knight is strikingly shown in one of the two positions given below. Each player has one or more passed Pawns (see Diagram 177) which are supported by their own King. The Bishop wins because he is wonderfully good at holding up the advance of passed Pawns, or at slowing it down.

DIAGRAM 177

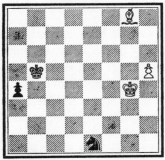

Superiority of the long-striding B over the short-winded Kt. Black's game could not be saved even if his Kt were at QB6 or Q5 or KB1

DIAGRAM 178

White succumbs under the weakness of his white squares. The Bishop is seen here at his most ineffectual

On the other hand the play in Diagram 178 shows up the principal weakness of the Bishop, namely that if his wish is to defend a terrain, he is usually helpless, for how shall a black-squared Bishop protect white squares? Black's advance in Diagram 178 which puts the Bishop to shame would develop somewhat as follows: *1. . . . . Kt—R4 ch; 2. K—B3, K—R5; 3. B—B2, Kt—B3; 4. B—K3, Kt—R2; 5. B—B2, Kt—Kt4 ch; 6. K—Q3, K—Kt6;* and there will presently follow a Kt check at QKt7 or QKt5 whereby the Black King will win the point QB5, etc.

We ask the reader to regard the cases in the positions on Diagrams 177 and 178 as the two poles between which all other cases move. That he can take long strides is the advantage which a Bishop has; his serious disadvantage lies in the weakness of the squares of an opposite color to his.

Another point. In the position, White: B at KKt2, P at QB5. Black: Kt at QKt1, P at QB3 (with other Pawns and pieces *ad lib*), the advantage of the Bishop is as little demonstrable, as is its apparent inferiority in the position White: B at QKt4; P at QB5; Black: Kt at K3, P at QB3. In both cases it is the strategical preponderance (the advantage of an active over a passive position of the pieces, which we analyzed in its place) which makes itself felt, *not any possibly inherent superiority of the class of weapon in question.*

We repeat, the principal weakness of the Bishop consists in the defenselessness of the squares of opposite color, its main strength in the fact that it is long-striding. And now it suddenly becomes plausible why two Bishops are held to be so strong. The reason is clear, their strength appears doubled, the weakness which we underlined is neutralized by the presence of the "other" Bishop. It is scarcely possible to set down on paper all the many and varied situations in which two Bishops may make themselves unpleasant; we will, however, attempt to note the most important.

§ 2. *The Horwitz Bishops.*

Two Bishops when they rake two neighboring diagonals (*e.g.,* B at QKt2, B at Q3), and thus united bombard the enemy

DIAGRAM 179

Q—K4 forces Black's KKtP to move and thus smooths the road for the B at B2

King's position, are sometimes called the Horwitz Bishops. Their effect is often devastating: One Bishop forces an enemy Pawn move, which smooths the road for the second Bishop. For instance in Diagram 179 *1.* Q—K4 forces the move . . . . P—Kt3 which loosens up Black's position, on which the B at B2 intervenes with decisive effect. Events took a similar course in the following game. *1.* P—K4, P—K4; *2.*

P—Q4, P x P; 3. P—QB3, P x P; 4. B—QB4, P x P; 5. B x P, B—Kt5 ch; 6. Kt—B3, Kt—KB3; 7. Kt—K2, Kt x P; 8. O—O, Kt x Kt; 9. Kt x Kt, B x Kt; 10. B x B, O—O. He has castled and feels himself safe against Q—Kt4 (. . . . P—KKt3) as also against Q—Q4 (. . . . Q—Kt4), overlooks however the combined play which is characteristic of the Horwitz Bishops. 11. Q—Kt4 !, P—Kt3, and only now 12. Q—Q4 and mate cannot be averted. The co-operation of the B at B4 lies obviously in the pinning of Black's P at KB2.

The Bishops in Diagram 180, I should regard as a variety of Horwitz Bishops, one, indeed, of the nobler sort. Of an attack on the King there is here no talk. Yet the attack on Black's P at QR2 (I have only included the most important pieces) though, it is true, not very intensive, is at all events unpleasant, and will, in the end, force the enemy to take up the position P at QR2, P at QKt3, P at QB4, whereupon the road will have been smoothed for the other Bishop; for there then follows White's P—R4 and P—Kt3, and the stations QR6, QKt5, and particularly QB4 are made available for the White Bishop. And now Black's majority appears crippled. A stratagem of this kind is not seldom to be found in Maróczy's games.

§ 3.   *The effective support afforded by the two Bishops to an advancing Pawn-mass. The hemming-in of the enemy Knights.*

A Pawn-mass, which need not by any means be a "majority," guided by a pair of Bishops can roll forward fairly far, and thus lead to the imprisoning of the enemy Knights. The well known game Richter—Tarrasch may serve as an example. (See Diagram 181.) The game went on: 19. . . . . P—QB4; 20. Kt—KKt3, P—KR4; 21. P—KB3 (he does not show great expertness in the defense; if the Kts are not to go under altogether, they must fight for stations for themselves. Hence 21. P—QR4 followed by Kt—B4 would seem to be indicated), B—Q2; 22. R—K2 ?, P—Kt4 !; 23. QR—K1, B—KB1 !; 24 Kt(Kt3)—K4, R —KKt1 (in order to

DIAGRAM 180

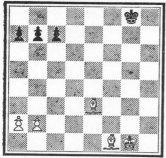

Two Bishops attack a Pawn-mass
with the intention of winning stations for themselves

DIAGRAM 181

Tarrasch (as Black) hems in the enemy Knights by appropriate Pawn
moves

play . . . . P—B4); 25. Kt—QKt3, R—B1; 26. Kt(K4)—Q2, B—Q3;
27. Kt—K4, B—B1; 28. Kt(K4)—Q2, P—B4; 29. R—K5, B—Q3; 30.
R(K5)—K2 (or R—Q5 ?, R—Kt3), R—QR1 (now the QRP is to
advance); 31. Kt—R5, QR—Kt1 (else after Kt—Kt7 his hemming
labor would have been vain); 32. Kt(R5)—Kt3, P—R5; 33. K—R1,
R—KKt3; 34. K—Kt1, B—K3 (the barricading of the K file
effected by the B at Q2 and B at Q3 has been up to this excellent move more of an "ideal" nature. With 34. . . . . B—K3
this is changed into a "material" one, corresponding to the
process we have before noted, where the "ideal" restraint of a
passed Pawn gave place to a mechanical stopping [= block-
ade]. So much on the strategic-theoretical meaning of the
maneuver chosen. The practical significance of the move lies,
however, as Dr. Tarrasch himself very rightly notes, in the fact
that fresh possibilities are opened up: (i) . . . . K—K2—Q2,
(ii) . . . . P—R3, R—QB1, then . . . . B—Kt1—R2, and
finally . . . . P—QB5. I may add this remark that . . . . P—
QB5 must be regarded as without question the strategical plan
indicated in the position. Why it is will appear in the note to
White's 38th move); 35. R—B2, R—QR1 ? (He is untrue to his

main plan, ... P—QB5, and again tries to make . . . . P—R4
possible; and he succeeds, but only because his opponent neglects a subtle resource. Of course it is a fine thing to put into
execution . . . . P—R4 and drive back the enemy forces completely; but one should not go so far as to subordinate a plan
indicated by the position to the idea of a broader decorative
effect. But then the pseudo-classical school had an incredible
weakness for such embroideries!); 36. R(B2)—K2 ? (A bad mistake. How could anyone allow . . . . P—R4 to be played without a fight! In answer to 36. Kt—R5 Dr. Tarrasch gives the line
36. . . . . B—B2; 37. Kt—Kt7, B—KB5, winning time for . . . .
R—QB1 and . . . . P—QB5 by the threat . . . . B—K6. But
he overlooks a hidden resource: 37. . . . . B—KB5; 38.
Kt x P !, B—K6; 39. P—QB4 ! and Black cannot win, as the
White's Q wing is strong and the black squares, e.g., QB5 for
the Kt, not less so. A plausible variation would be 39. . . . . .
P x P; 40. P x P, R—QB1; 41. P—QKt4 !, R—B2; 42. K—B1,
B x R; 43. K x B and White stands well), P—R4; 37. Kt—Kt1,
P—R5; 38. Kt(Kt3)—Q2. See Diagram 182. (And now the
break-through follows, and there is nothing logically surprising
in this, for, as we know, Black
has a decided "qualitative majority," as would show up even
more obviously if we imagined
added to the position a White
and Black KP at their 4th. Here
the possibility of a break-through
is still further enhanced by the
miserable position of the White
Kts, and by the large surface of
friction, by which I mean the
four-Pawn front), P—QB5; 39.

DIAGRAM 182

The hemming-in accomplished

Kt —B1, R—QB1; 40. K—R1, P—B6; 41. P x P, P x P; 42. Kt—K3,

P—QKt5; etc. (The game plays itself. White resigned on his 47th move.)

§4.　*Fight against a Pawn majority with simultaneous hemming-in of the enemy Knights.*

The hemming-in of the Knights with simultaneous fight against a Pawn majority is a very different problem, one would say, to the solving of which outstanding technical ability will be needed. But this is not so. Anyone who is moderately versed in the art of restraining and blockading Pawn-complexes, will soon find to his satisfaction that in the class of positions in question the hemming in of the Kts is more easily compassed than in the case considered under § 3. We can say with some justice that the restraint of the Pawn-majority once in operation carries with it automatically the hemming-in of the Kts; that is to say the blockaded Pawns may easily develop into obstructions to their own Kts. An example is found in the following game.

Harmonist—Tarrasch, Breslau, 1889. *1.* P—K4, P—K4; *2.* Kt—KB3, Kt—QB3; *3.* B—Kt5, Kt—B3; *4.* O—O, Kt x P; *5.* P—Q4, Kt—Q3; *6.* B x Kt, QP x B; *7.* P x P, Kt—B4; *8.* Q x Q *ch*, K x Q; *9.* B—Kt5 *ch* ?, K—K1; *10.* Kt—B3, P—KR3; *11.* B—B4, B—K3 (White's majority has but slight mobility); *12.* QR—Q1, R—Q1; *13.* Kt—K4, P—B4; *14.* R x R *ch*, K x R; *15.* R—Q1 *ch*, K—B1; *16.* P—KR3, P—QKt3; *17.* K—B1, B—K2; *18.* P—R3, R—Q1; *19.* R x R *ch*, K x R (the exchange of Rooks has sensibly increased the radius of action of Black's King); *20.* P—B3, B—Q4; *21.* Kt(B3)—Q2, K—Q2; *22.* K—K2, P—KKt4; *23.* B—R2, Kt—R5; *24.* P—KKt3, Kt—Kt3; *25.* P—KB4, K—K3; *26.* K—K3, P—B5; *27.* Kt—B3, P x P *ch*; *28.* P x P, P—QB4; see Diagram 183. (In the position now reached White's pieces are fairly well shut in. This gratifying state of affairs has followed almost automatically from Black's successfully executed blockade of White's P at K5 and in particular his P at KB4. This cannot surprise us; for have we not often experienced how the whole situation may be favorably affected, as if by a miracle, by successful blockade?) 29. Kt—Kt3, Kt—R5; 30. Kt x Kt, B x Kt; 31. Kt—K4, B—K2; 32. B—Kt1, B—QB3 (the intention is . . . . K—Q4 followed by . . . . B—Q2—B4, driving the Kt yet further back); 33. B—B2, B—Q2; 34. B—Kt3 (Kt—Q6 offered the possibility of a draw, by playing for B's on opposite color), K—Q4; 35. Kt—B2, P—KR4; 36. K—B3, B—B4 (Blockade!); 37. K—K3, P—Kt4; 38. K—B3, P—R4; 39. K—K3 (White is "stalemated"), P—Kt5; 40. K—B3,

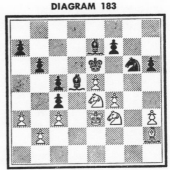

DIAGRAM 183

Harmonist—Tarrasch
Breslau, 1889

K—B3; 41. RP x P (White is lost), BP x P; 42. P x P, P x P; 43. Kt—K4, K—Q4; 44. Kt—Q6, B x Kt; 45. P x B, P—B6; 46. P x P, P—Kt6; 47. Resigns.

§ 5. *The two Bishops in the end game.*

We regard as the ideal the transmutation of an advantage founded only in the class of weapon employed to one which is clearly and perceptibly strategical; for instance, that of the aggressive position of our pieces as opposed to the passive one of our opponent's. (See I. vi. § 2.) Combined play with two B's, leading to such a transmutation as we have mentioned, comes out in the following example. See Diagram 184, Michel-Tartakover, 1925. White's position is well consolidated, the weakness of the black squares QB3, Q4, does not appear important. The continuation was:—40. K—Kt1, K—Kt2; 41. K—B1, B—B3; 42. Kt—Kt1, P—Kt4; 43. Kt—B3, P—R4. (The two Pawns advance, since they feel themselves to be a qualitative majority owing to the exalted protection which they enjoy, supported as they are by two Bishops.) 44. B—K2, R—K5 !; 45. B—Q3, R—KB5; 46. K—

K2, P—KKt5; 47. P x P, P x P; 48. Kt—R2, P—Kt6 !; 49. Kt—B3
(Black has quite rightly not pursued any further the advantage
to be got from hemming in the Kt; what he now has got is
more valuable: White's P at KKt2 has become a mark for attack, and the White pieces, particularly the Kt at B3, are from

DIAGRAM 184

Tartakover (as Black) realizes one
after the other various chances
given him by his B's

DIAGRAM 185

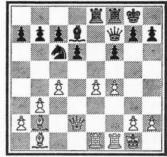

Black's position appears to be defensible; the Bishops are less formidable than they look

now on forced to keep perpetual watch over him. This strategical advantage very soon brings a decision), P—Q5; 50. R—KB1,
P—Kt5; 51. Kt—Q2, R—R5; 52. Kt—B3, R—R1; (from here he
threatens at once the point KR7 and the K file); 53. K—Q2 (For
—with apologies to Goethe and his translator—where of good
moves there's a failing, a botch steps promptly in as deputy!),
R—R7 !; 54. Kt x R, P x Kt; 55. R—KR1, B—K4; 56. B—B1, B—K5
(a charming situation!); 57. K—Q1, K—B3; 58. K—Q2, K—Kt4;
59. K—Q1, K—Kt5; 60. *Resigns.*

We have now done enough for the glorification of the
Bishops, and a few words may be added on situations in which
they do not cut such a good figure. These are wholly, or half
closed positions, see for example Games No. 15 and 38; while
they are astonishingly weak against an unassailable, centrally
posted Kt. Even in the position on Diagram 185 it would seem

to me that Black can maintain himself against the Horwitz Bishops. In the next chapter we shall pass to "over-protection."

An excellent example of play with two Bishops will be found in Game No. 41, Lasker—Burn. See also No. 47, Gregory—Nimzovich.

5. Over-Protection

§ 1. *Why we should systematically over-protect our own strong points.*

A short chapter, which in particular may serve to illustrate the various forms under which "over-protection" can appear. In II. i. § 3 we have already attempted to explain the spirit and inner significance of over-protection. We will therefore only repeat here that the contact established between the strong point and the "over-protector" can only be of advantage to both parties; to the strong point because the prophylactic induced by such a process affords it the greatest imaginable security against possible attack; to the over-protector, since the point serves him as a source of energy, from which he may continually draw fresh strength.

Over-protection clearly represents a maneuver, which from its very essence must have developed in close connection with position play. Nevertheless even in the "Elements" we came across traces of over-protection; for example in the open file. White: R, Q1; Kt, QB3; P, K4. Black: Pawns, QB2, Q3. The outpost Kt (after Kt(QB3)—Q5) must, as was emphasized in I. ii. § 6, be protected not only by a Pawn but also by a Rook. What can this compulsion signify other than the necessity of over-protecting the strategically important outpost!

Again, in the domain of the Pawn-chain over-protection is a strategem which deserves every preference. Turn to the game Nimzovich—Giese (II. i. § 3, Diagram 126), and notice in particular how the over-protection was not even intended for the base of the Pawn-chain, however awesome the respect this inspired in us, but rather for a more humble candidate for that position; for we over-protected the P at K5 since we had always to reckon with an eventual and inevitable QP x P, when the P at K5 would be promoted to be the base.

The wonderful vitality of the over-protector may here be demonstrated by two further examples:

Nimzovich—Rubinstein, Carlsbad, 1911.

1. P—K4, P—K3; *2.* P—Q4, P—Q4; *3.* P—K5, P—QB4; *4.* P—QB3, Kt—QB3; *5.* Kt—B3, Q—Kt3; *6.* B—Q3, P x P; *7.* P x P, B—Q2; *8.* B—K2, KKt—K2; *9.* P—QKt3, Kt—B4; *10.* B—Kt2 (at the moment the P at Q4 is barely protected, not more), B—Kt5 *ch;* *11.* K—B1, P—KR4; *12.* P—KKt3, R—QB1; *13.* K—Kt2, P—Kt3; *14.* P—KR3, B—K2 (intending to answer a possible P—KKt4 by . . . . Kt—R5 *ch*); *15.* Q—Q2 *!,* P—R4; *16.* R—QB1, B—B1; *17.* Q—Q1 *!,* B—R3; *18.* R—B3, O—O; *19.* P—KKt4, Kt(B4)—K2; *20.* Kt—R3 *!* (only now will it be clear why White delayed with the development of this Kt. An honorable post had been contemplated for him, namely as over-protector of the P at Q4), Kt—Kt5; *21.* Kt—B2 (there now follows a surprising and effortless unravelling of the skein of White pieces on the Q's Wing), R x R; *22.* B x R, Kt x Kt; *23.* Q x Kt, R—B1; *24.* Q—Kt2 *!* (whatever happens, the P at Q4 shall stay over-protected), B—QKt4; *25.* B x B, Q x B; *26.* B—Q2 *!* (the over-protector shows his teeth!), B—B1; *27.* R—QB1, P x P; *28.* P x P, R—B3; *29.* Q—R3 (over-protector No. 2 won't take a back place to No. 1—see the last note), R x R. (A pity! for on *29.* . . . . Kt—B4, White intended to offer a Queen sacrifice: *30.* R x R, B x Q; *31.* R—B8 *ch,* K—Kt2; *32.* P x Kt with a strong attack. An excellent index to the inherent elasticity of an over-protector.) *30.* Q x R, with the superior game.

Nimzovich—Spielmann, Stockholm, 1920.

1. P—K4, P—K3; *2.* P—Q4, P—Q4; *3.* P—K5, P—QB4; *4.* Kt—KB3, Kt—QB3; *5.* P—B3, Q—Kt3; *6.* B—K2, P x P; *7.* P x P, Kt—R3; *8.* Kt—B3 (P—QKt3, as in the last example, is more prudent),

Kt—B4; 9. Kt—QR4, Q—R4 *ch;* 10. B—Q2, B—Kt5; 11. B—B3, B—Q2 (Preferable would have been *11. . . . . B x B ch; 12. Kt x B, Q—Kt5 [if . . . . Q—Kt3 then Kt—QR4 !]; 13. B— Kt5, O—O; 14. B x Kt, Q x KtP; 15. Kt—QR4, Q—Kt5 ch; 16. Q—Q2.* White would then have had the point QB5, Black a backward Pawn plus); 12. P—QR3, B x B *ch;* 13. Kt x B, P—R4; 14. O—O, R—QB1 (see Diagram 186); 15. Q—Q2, Q—Q1 (threatening . . . . P—KKt4); 16. P—R3 (in order to parry . . . . P—KKt4 by the riposte P—KKt4, *e.g.,* 16. . . . . P— KKt4; 17. P—KKt4, P x P; 18. P x P, Kt—R5; 19. Kt x Kt, R x Kt; 20. K—Kt2 followed by R—R1 with advantage to White), Kt—R4; 17. QR—Q1, Q—Kt3; 18. KR—K1 (the P at Q4 and to a certain degree the P at K5 are now systematically over-protected, and this strategy makes it possible later to be automatically, so to speak, master of the situation, whatever complications may arise), Kt—B5; 19. B x Kt, R x B; 20. Kt—K2, B—R5; 21. R—QB1 (notice how available an over-protector is for service in all directions, *e.g.,* the R at Q1 at QB1 and the Kt at KKt3), B—Kt6; 22. R x R, B x R; 23. Kt—Kt3, Kt—K2; and White

DIAGRAM 186

White develops his pieces in the sense of a systematic over-protection of the P at Q4

stands rather the better. (He won the game on the 61st move. See *Die Blockade,* p. 69.)

So much on the over-protection of the base; the over-protection of the following points is also of importance.

(*a*) Over-protection of the central points. We have already on a previous opportunity emphasized the fact that the very common neglect of the central theater of war is reprehensible. But we have here to do rather with a detail, or more accurately, with the examination of a quite definite, and, for the hypermodern style of play, typical situation. As is generally known, the hypermodern knows admirably how to resist the temptation to occupy the center with Pawns, at any rate not until a really favorable opportunity presents itself. If such offers, he casts aside all shyness, and the Pawns, supported by the fianchettoed Bishops, rush wildly forward, seize the center, and strive to crush the enemy. Against this threatened evil the over-protection of certain central points provides a thoroughly proven remedy, which cannot be too strongly recommended. Let us glance at the following opening of the game Réti—Yates, New York, 1924: *1.* Kt—KB3, P—Q4; *2.* P—B4, P—K3; *3.* P—KKt3, Kt—KB3; *4.* B—Kt2, B—Q3; *5.* P—Kt3, O—O (Why this hurry? To put the center in order was much more pressing: therefore . . . . P—B3, ... QKt—Q2, and . . . . P—K4 was his proper line); *6.* O—O, R—K1; *7.* B—Kt2, QKt—Q2; *8.* P—Q3 ?, P—B3; *9.* QKt—Q2, P—K4 (the position now reached is undoubtedly more favorable for Black; White ought to have played 8. P—Q4); *10.* P x P, P x P; *11.* R—B1, Kt—B1; *12.* R—B2, B—Q2; *13.* Q—R1, Kt—Kt3; *14.* KR—B1. (See Diagram 187.) White's Q maneuver is significant; he intends to undermine the enemy center by P—Q4 when opportunity offers and if Black reply . . . . P—K5, then Kt—K5. Hence Black's duty is to over-protect his P at K4, even to excess. His best course was first *14.* . . . . P—Kt4 aiming at White's Q's Wing which is compromised by the position of his Q; if then *15.* Kt—B1, there would follow *15.* . . . . Q—Kt1 ! (=over-protection of K4); *16.* Kt—K3, P—QR4 and Black has the better game. This line of play which I pointed out in

Black to move. What point is worthy of over-protection?

Kagan's Neueste Schachnachrichten, 1924, met at the time with little approbation. Nowadays things are different.

For a game which took a most instructive course, and in which I employed the same Queen maneuver (. . . . Q—Kt1) with the same idea as that indicated above, see No. 38.

(*b*) The over-protection of the center as a measure of defense for our own King's wing.

The case which is about to be discussed in detail differs from that considered above under (*a*) in its general tendency, and is therefore treated here as an independent maneuver, not as a subdivision of that case. In II. i. § 6, under Diagram 124, a position was discussed which comes under the classification of the case now to be considered. Game No. 15 is also instructive in the same sense. In this game after the 13th move a position was reached which is shown in Diagram 188. Black's last

DIAGRAM 188

White parries every attempt at an attack on his King by over-protection of a central point. How does he do it?

DIAGRAM 189

Consultation game. Three Amateurs —Nimzovich. Black is confronted with this problem: how can he over-protect his strong point Q4?

move was *13. . . . . P—Kt5 !* To the reply *14.* P x P, P x P; *15.* Q x P, he had planned . . . . R x B followed by . . . . B x P *ch* and . . . . B x P. White, however, played *14.* R—K1, and in doing something for his center he at the same time strengthened the power of resistance of his position against flank attacks as well. There followed *14. . . . . K—B1; 15. Kt—B3 !* (the prelude to a blockading maneuver), *Q—K2; 16. B x Kt, P x B; 17. Q—K3, R—R3; 18. Kt—K2, P—B4; 19. Kt—B4,* and White has the better game, for the two B's have little to say in view of the strength of the unassailable Kt; moreover, the collective mobility of Black is quite small, for though the P at QB4 and the P at Q4 have a certain measure of mobility, the rest are blockaded.

Of quite special interest in the same sense is the position shown in Diagram 189 which is taken from Game No. 39. It was Black's move. That the Kt at Q4 was the pride of Black's position is beyond all doubt. It was, however, not easy to devise a suitable plan. White was preparing one, though it is true it presented no great danger; namely Q—Q2 followed by Kt— K1—Q3—B5. The train of thought which I followed in the game brought me on the track of a hidden maneuver, which to this day I consider a good one. The separate links in this chain of ideas are these: (i) the Kt at Q4 is strong, therefore (ii) the over-protectors, the Q at Q2 and R at Q1 are also strong, but (iii) the R at Q1 has a duty in connection with the K's position, which has a bearing on his strength in the center, therefore (iv) the KR must come to Q1! Accordingly there followed *14. . . . . K—Kt1; 15. Q—Q2, R—B1 !; 16. Kt—K1, B—K2; 17. Kt— Q3, KR—Q1.* The deed is done! The R at Q1 now feels that he can devote his whole attention to the center, since his colleague at QB1 is looking after the King. The further adventures of the R at Q1 will be found in Game No. 39.

We could name many more "points" that are worthy of over-protection, but will limit ourselves to the few examples we have here given. Before, however, passing on to the next stra-tegical device, we must once more stress the fact that only strategically valuable points should be over-protected, not a sickly Pawn, nor a K's wing which rests on a weak foundation. Over-protection must in no sense be regarded as an act of

Christian meekness and loving-kindness! The pieces over-protect a point because they promise themselves strategical advantages to be gained from contact with it. We must there-fore seek to establish connection with strong points. A weak Pawn is only in a single exceptional case justified in claiming over-protection, and that is when he is engaged in looking after a potential giant of his species. For instance: White: Pawns, Q4, K5. Black: Pawns, Q4, K3. The P at Q4 as the base of White's Pawn chain is nurse to the strategically important P at K5; so that the over-protection of the P at Q4 seems indicated.

§ 2. *How to get rid of weak Pawns.*

We are not concerned here with the actual way by which we may get rid of weak Pawns, but rather with the question what Pawns deserve to have this hardly kind treatment meted out to them.

The situation is always the same: an otherwise sound Pawn complex which, however, has to acknowledge a weakling in its body. We distinguish two cases:

(*a*) the weakness of the Pawn is patent.

(*b*) the weakness would only appear after a Pawn advance, whether of our own or of the enemy.

We shall give an example of each of these two cases.

(*a*) See Diagram 190. The game proceeded 36. R—B5, B—Q2 (or 36. . . . . B—Q6 *ch;* 37. K—B1, R—Q2; 38. R—B8 *ch* and 39. R—Kt8); 37. R x P. White is therefore now a Pawn to the good. 37. . . . . K—B1; 38. K—B2, P—Kt6 *ch;* 39. K—B3, K—K2 (White is in a position to bring his own flock of Pawns, K, KB, KKt, under one shelter, and to do this he has only to play P—K4. Everything will then be beautifully protected, and the shepherd, the R at Q5, can, with a clear conscience, turn his attention to other matters. Not quite! for that stupid little sheep, the P at KR4, would scamper away from the shepherd —for at some time there would be threatened, for instance in

DIAGRAM 190   DIAGRAM 191

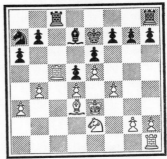

Nimzovich—Jacobsen 1923   Tarrasch—Barthmann

a Rook ending, the maneuver . . . . R—QR8—KR8 x P, therefore he shall be cast out of the company of the righteous!); 40.
P—R5 !, B—K3; 41. R—QB5, K—Q3; 42. R—B6 ch, K—Q2; 43.
P x P, RP x P (That's done!); 44. Kt x B !, P x Kt; 45. R—B5 followed by R—KKt5 and P—B4 with an easily won Rook end
game. (The position reached after Black's 41st move has already been considered under another aspect in I. vi. § 4 under
Diagram 81.)

(b) Tarrasch—Barthmann, played when Dr. Tarrasch was
still a youth. (See Diag. 191.) Black played here 21. . . . . R—
B3; and there followed 22. KR—QB1, KR—QB1; 23. P—Kt4,
P—KKt3; 24. P—B5, KtP x P; 25. P x P, R—KKt1 ? (He ought not
to have allowed P—B6 ch at any price, hence 25. . . . . P x P
was essential, e.g., 26. Kt—B4, B—K3; 27. R—KKt1, with a
hard fight ahead); 26. P—B6 ch, K—B1; 27. R—KKt1, KR x R; 28.
Kt x R, K—Kt1; and Black's KRP is a very serious weakness
in Black's game. This drawback could have been avoided had
Black on his 21st move played . . . . P—KR4 with the idea of
only allowing P—B6 (as in the game) on the stipulation that
both the KKt and KRP's should disappear in the exchange. The
continuation might have been: 21. . . . . P—KR4; 22. P—R3,
P—KKt3 (not 22. . . . . P—R5 ?, because of 23. Kt—Kt1 fol-

lowed by Kt—B3); and Black, after a few moves, would have obtained a more favorable position than he did in the game.

Whereas case (*a*) does not make very great demands on the player, the right handling of the strategical weapon discussed under (*b*) is extremely difficult. It demands, above everything, a pretty thorough knowledge of the various forms under which an advance of a compact Pawn-mass, and particularly on a wing, may run its course. Many pages, however, of this book have been devoted to this advance with all its consequences, and to deal with it we may therefore leave the kind reader to his own, as we hope, not less kind fate. Only let him keep well in view that the strategical necessity of ridding himself of a troublesome Pawn of his own may arise in the case of an advance of his Pawns, just as much as in that of an enemy advance. When the black sheep of the family should be cast out, whether before the operation begins, or during it (when the advance of the Pawn-mass is under way); this question can only be decided on the merits of each case.

For a very instructive game illustrating over-protection see No. 39.

6. Maneuvering Against Weaknesses

Maneuvering against an enemy weakness. The combined attack on both wings

§ 1. *The logical components which go to make up a maneuvering action against a weakness.*

A s an introduction to the following analysis I should like to try to present a scheme for the operation which is to be considered. I picture the course of a maneuvering action to myself somewhat as follows: An enemy weakness can be attacked in at least two ways; each of these attempts at attack would be met by an adequate defense. In order that in spite of this we may in the end conquer the enemy weakness, we take advantage of the greater freedom of movement which is ours, due to certain conditions of the terrain, so as to attack it in turn by different ways (maneuvering action), and thus oblige the enemy pieces to take up uncomfortable positions for its defense, whence an obstruction to the defense or something of the kind will intervene, and the "weakness" will be proved untenable.

As we can see from this scheme, it would be quite a mistake to label this type of maneuvering as mere purposeless moving to and fro. On the contrary: every move has set before it a clearly prescribed end, has the conquest of a quite definite weakness in view. The ways which lead to this conquest are, it is true, of a complicated nature. That is why such maneuvering play requires foresight, tenacity, patience, elasticity of outlook. The modern master is noted above all for his virtuosity in maneuvering technique.

§ 2. *The terrain. The conception of the pivot round which the maneuvering turns.*

The terrain over which any maneuvering action takes place must, if our plan is to succeed, be strongly built up. A characteristic of such action is that the different troop movements always cross a quite definite square (or line of demarcation). An example is seen in Diagram 192. Here it is the point Q5 which the White pieces will wish to occupy, making it a base for further maneuvering. Accordingly the point Q5 might be described as a fortified post in the lines of communication; and it is therefore right and proper to regard it as the pivot round which the whole maneuvering action turns. It is by virtue of this fortified post Q5 that the whole operation is accomplished: every piece, even the R at Q1, strives to get there at some time or other. The law governing this maneuvering action moreover demands that Q5 shall be occupied by different pieces in turn, for this will always create new threats and thus help to embarrass the enemy. The relationship between the White pieces and the pivot Q5 exactly corresponds, too, to the "contact" between over-protectors and a strategically important point, which was discussed in the previous chapter. That in this case the pieces strive to establish contact with Q5 speaks plainly for the strength of that point. Notice, too, the device by which pieces exchange stations in, *e.g.*, the sequence of White moves Kt—K3, Q—Q5, Kt—QB4, an operation which may serve the purpose of the general plan of the maneuvering action right well.

We will now give some typical examples of this type of maneuvering.

(*a*) A Pawn weakness which is to be brought under bombardment from the 7th rank.

Rubinstein—Selesniev. Diagram 193. There occurred *1.* . . . . P—Kt3 (*1.* . . . . P—Q5 deserved the preference. For

DIAGRAM 192

DIAGRAM 193

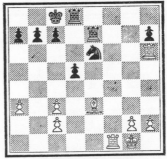

White maneuvers against the P at
Q3 using the point Q5 as the pivot
round which the operation turns

Rubinstein—Selesniev
White maneuvers cleverly against
the weak King's Rook Pawn

instance, 2. P x P, Kt x P; 3. B—Kt5, Kt—K7 *ch*; 4. K—B2 ! [else
4. . . . . R—B2], R—B1 *ch*; 5. R—B6, R x R *ch*; 6. B x R,
R—K3); 2. B—B2, R—B1; 3. R—K1, R(K2)—B2; 4. R(R6) x Kt,
R x B; 5. R—K8 *ch*, K—Kt2; 6. R x R, R x R; 7. R—K7 (and now
begins some magnificent maneuvering against Black's P at
KR2), R—KR1; 8. K—B2, K—B3; 9. P—Kt4, K—Q3; 10. R—B7,
P—QR4; 11. P—Kt5, P—R5; 12. P—R4, P—Kt4; 13. K—Kt3, P—B4
(Black now threatens to make a passed Pawn for himself by
. . . . P—Kt5, so Rubinstein attacks the weakness at KR2,
from the other side); 14. R—B6 *ch* !, K—B2; 15. R—KR6, P—Kt5;
16. BP x P, P x P; 17. P x P, R—R1; 18. R x P *ch* ! (the "weakness"
has fallen), K—Kt3; 19. R—KB7, P—R6; 20. R—B1, P—R7; 21.
R—QR1, K—Kt4; 22. P—Kt6, K x P; 23. P—R5, *Resigns*. The pivot
is here to be thought of as in the lines K7 to KR7 and KR6 to
KR8. The student should seek to determine why the change of
front of the 14th move could not take place earlier.

The following case is much more complicated, for it requires
maneuvering on a much wider scale.

(*b*) Two Pawn weaknesses (see Diagram 194), here White's
P at QB3 and P at KR3. The pivotal point, round which action
against the P at KR3 turns (Black's KB5), seems to be threat-

DIAGRAM 194

Dr. W. Kalashnikov—Nimzovich 1914

ened, but is rescued, and actually by a timely attention paid to the weak P at QB3 on the other side of the board; so that we see here the two separated theaters of war logically connected the one with the other. The play follows:

Kalashnikov—Nimzovich: Black played 36. . . . . K—K2. If White would only do nothing Black would get the advantage by a direct attack, by . . . . K—B2—Kt3 followed by . . . . P—KB4. White would then have to defend with P—B3, and would thereby give his opponent the handle, to clutch which he has long wanted, namely (after, of course, moving the Kt at B5 out of the way) the posting of his B at Kt6, when the threat to the whole of White's line of defense could not be parried. But White did not sit still; instead he did his best to hinder his opponent in the execution of his plan, and played 37. Kt— Kt2 !; with this he hopes to bring off a general exchange which would lead to a clear draw, thus:—38. B x Kt, and if 38. . . . . Kt x B, then 39. Kt x Kt, B x Kt; and there is nothing left. The pivotal point KB5 thus threatened could not now be held but for the maneuvering chance on the other side of the board, so there followed 37. . . . . R—R8 ch; 38. R—B1, R—R7 !; 39. Kt— K1 ! (the relief expedition carried out by Black with his 37th and 38th moves has succeeded, for now with the R at QR7 White's intended exchange would lead to his own disadvantage: 39. B x Kt, B x B !; 40. R—Q1, B—Q7; 41. Kt—K2, Kt— B5 ! and after the sequel 42. Kt[Kt2] x Kt, P x Kt; 43. K—Kt2, R—B7, Black develops a remarkable appetite), K—B2. So Black has gained a tempo! But now the same game starts anew. 40.

R—B2, R—R6 !; 41. Kt—Kt2, R—R8 ch; 42. R—B1, R—R7 !; 43. Kt—K1, K—Kt3; 44. R—B2, R—R6; 45. P—B3 (this weakening move could not have been permanently avoided; otherwise . . . . P—KB4 would follow, and if P x P ch then . . . . K x P and . . . . P—Kt5 yielding a passed RP), P—KB4. It is accomplished! The end was peaceful: 46. K—B2, K—B3 (to make room for the Kt); 47. B—B1, R—R8; 48. K—K3, Kt—Kt3; 49. Kt—Q3, B—Kt6 (cf. the note to Black's 36th move); 50. Kt—K2 Kt(K3)—B5; 51. Kt—Kt1, Kt x Kt; 52. K x Kt, B—B5 !; 53. Kt—K2, B x B; 54. Kt x B, Kt—B5 ch; 55. K—K3, Kt x P. After a heroic defense the fortress (P at KR3) falls. There followed only 56. Kt—K2, P—B5 ch; and White resigned since . . . . R—KB8 wins another Pawn.

(c) The King as a "weakness." (See Diagram 195.) For the terrain there function here two possibilities of a driving action; as pivot we have a line of demarcation.

Nimzovich—Kalinsky, 1914. In this very piquant position there occurred first 1. B—Kt3 (the reply to 1. B—B2, P—B7; 2. R—Q1 would be . . . . K—K3, and White cannot win), P—Q5; 2. B—Q5, R—Kt5 (not at once . . . . P—B7 because of B x KP, etc.); 3. R(R1)—R5, P—B7; and now White doubles his Rooks in the KB file with a gain of tempo. 4. R—B6 ch, K—K2; 5. R(R5)—B5, R—Kt8 ch; 6. K—R2, P—Q6. We shall use the position now reached as a touchstone of the correctness of our thesis. We explained in its place that a maneuvering action is only possible if certain conditions are fulfilled. These were: (a) the presence of a pivot; (b) a diversity of threats which might be directed against the weakness. The test turns out in our favor. Although this time the weakness is an ideal one, and no concrete Pawn weakness, yet the circumstances (favoring a maneuvering action) are identical with those which we have laid down as typical; here, too, the variety of threats leaves nothing to be desired, for White plans by their means not only

DIAGRAM 195

Nimzovich—Kalinsky 1914

to force the King to the edge of the board, but purposes also to arrange, when opportunity serves, a pretty hunt, which shall drive him into the middle of the board. Nor is the requisite pivot wanting, for the KB file (=line of demarcation across which the King cannot pass) serves this purpose. Thus visualized, the following movements back and forth will be intelligible, indeed will gain in animation and in color. The game proceeded (after 6. . . . . P—Q6) 7. R—K6 *ch*, K—Q2; 8. R—B7 *ch*, K—Q1; 9. R(K6)—KB6, P—Q7 (the border position now reached cannot yet be taken advantage of, for 10. R—R7 would fail against P—B8(Q), and 10. R—KR6 obviously won't do, so he maneuvers further); 10. R—B8 *ch*, K—K2; 11. R(B6)—B7 *ch*, K—Q3; 12. B—Kt3, B—Kt3 ? (Perhaps . . . . P—R3 giving a loophole for the King to creep through was preferable); 13. R—B6 *ch! !* Now the King has to face the choice; either he may return to the side of the board, where his position will now be untenable, or he must go out into the open, where fate in another form will overtake him. There followed 13. . . . . K—K4 (if 13. . . . . K—K2; then 14. R(B8)—B7 *ch*, K—Q1; 15. R—R6 and wins); 14. R—K6 *ch!*, K—Q5; 15. R x P!, P—Q8(Q); 16. B x Q, R x B; 17. R—K2 ! and won the Pawn and the game.

§ 3.   *Combined play on both wings, with weaknesses which though for the moment wanting are yet latent.*

Von Gottschall—Nimzovich, Hanover, 1926. (See Diagram 196.) A logical analysis of the position reveals the following data. White's P at QB5 is, in view of the insecure position of the B at KB2, to be regarded as a Pawn weakness. On the other·

hand I cannot agree under any circumstances in branding the Pawn-mass P at KKt3, P at KR3 as a "weakness," and this for the reason that here, on the King's wing, "terrain" is lacking. Black chose the following maneuver which at first sight looks a most unintelligible one. 39. . . . . K—K4; 40. R—Kt4, K—Q4. The explanation of this combination which sacrifices a tempo lies in the following: With these moves a position is reached where White is in a *Zugzwang*,

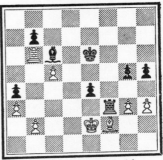

DIAGRAM 196

v. Gottschall—Nimzovich
Hanover 1926

Combined attack on both wings. The White weaknesses are the P at QB5 and as becomes evident later the P at KR3

for if the Rook goes back to Kt6 (and he has no other plausible move, for *41*. R—Q4 *ch* fails against . . . . K x P; *42*. R x KP *dis. ch* ?, R x B *ch*, etc., while as we shall see *41*. P—R4 would provide just that "terrain" which before was so sadly missed) —if the Rook goes back to Kt6, there will follow after the break through *41*. . . . . P—R5; *42*. P x P, P x P; *43*. B x P, the intermezzo *43*. . . . . K x P threatening the Rook; so White decided after all on *41*. P—R4, there followed *41*. . . . . P x P; *42*. P x P, R—R6 !; *43*. R—Q4 *ch*, K—K3; *44*. R—Q8, B—Q4; and now Black began systematically to maneuver against the P at KR4, with the point KKt5 as his pivot, and in fact by way of this point succeeded in breaking into his opponent's game.

The meaning of the strategy employed here appears out of the following scheme which is applicable to all analogous cases. We maneuvered first against the obvious weakness, the P at QB5. By means of the *Zugzwang* (with a slight mixture of threats) we succeeded in inducing our opponent to make a deployment (P—R4). This, however, only led to a weakness, which before P—R4 was merely latent, becoming patent and moreover easily assailable. To recapitulate: Play on two wings is usually based on the following idea. We engage one wing, or the obvious weaknesses in it, and thus draw the other enemy wing out of its reserve, when new weakness will be created on that reserve wing, and so the signal is given for systematic maneuvering against two weaknesses, as in the game Kalashnikov—Nimzovich which we gave above.

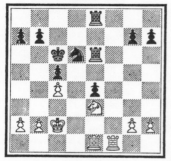

DIAGRAM 197

This is the rule. As an interesting exception to the rule, I may call attention to the case where we may act as if the exposure of the weakness on the other wing had already taken place.

The following is an example of such an exposure. Von Holzhausen—Nimzovich, Hanover, 1926.

See Diagram 197. Black here hastened to bring about the exposure and moved 32. . . . . R—R3. True, the real fight was to take place on the Q-wing; but I knew that after I had succeeded in opening up the game (by . . . . P—QKt4, etc.) the advanced position of White's King side Pawns could only serve my ends. There followed 33. P—KR3, R—Kt3; 34. R—K2, P—QR3; 35. R—B4, P—Kt4; 36. P—QKt3, R—Kt4; 37. P—KKt4, R(Kt4)—K4; 38. K—B3, P—QR4! (The weakness P at KR3 in conjunction with the possible chance of getting the P at K5 unblocked made Black peremptory in his demand for "terrain" with the pivot to go with it; it is for this that Black was fighting with his last moves); 39. R(K2)—KB2, P—R5 (now . . . . RP x P is threatened, followed by . . . . P x P allowing an invasion by the Rooks via the QR and QKt files); 40. P x P, P x BP!; 41. R—B8, R(K4)—K2; 42. R x R, R x R; 43. Kt x P, Kt x Kt; 44. K x Kt, R—QR1 (the desired terrain is now won; it consists of the QR, QKt, and Queen files.

I should call Q5 the pivot); 45. R—B7 (or 45. K—Kt3 ?, K—Q4 !), R x P ch; 46. K—Kt3 (K—B3 was rather better), R—Kt5 ch !; 47. K—B3, R—Kt2; 48. R—B5, R—R2; 49. K—B4, R—R5 ch; 50. K—Kt3, R—Q5 (the pivot!); 51. R—K5, K—Q3; 52. R—K8, R—Q6 ch; 53. K—B4, R x P (the proper use made of the "terrain" has not failed to yield fruit; the weakness has fallen); 54. R x P, R—R6; 55. R—K2, R—R5 ch; 56. K—Kt5, R x KtP; 57. P—R4, R—Kt5 ch and won on the 71st move.

DIAGRAM 198

Teichmann—Nimzovich
San Sebastian 1911

In Diagram 198 an elegant mating threat is used merely as an instrument to carry out with gain of tempo a weakening attack on the enemy's Q's-wing. 31. . . . . Kt—K3 (threatening . . . . R x Kt ch; Kt x R, R x Kt ch; K x R, Q—B7 ch; K—R3, B—B5 and wins); 32. R—K2 (parries the threat, but now there follows. with gain of tempo), Kt—Q5. The game went on: 33. R(K2)—K1 (if 33. R—B2, ... B—K6 !), Q—Kt2 !; (. . . . R—QB1 cannot be warded off now except by a sacrifice); 34. R x Kt (or 34. P—B3 ?, P x P; 35. P x P, Q—Kt7 ch and wins), P x R and Black won after a hard struggle. (See game No. 40)

We will now give two end games which illustrate in miniature the combined attack on two wings. As the position on Diagram 199 shows, Black (Nimzovich) has first made a gesture as if he were going to attack the Q's-Wing, but then has chosen the K's-Wing for his field of operations. White has taken up a tough defensive position. It was my move, and after a little reflection I played 1. . . . . P—Kt4 ! ! Great astonishment among the spectators! On the Q's Wing Black has surely no troops for the attack. However, the sequel was 2. P x P, R—R7; 3. Kt x R, R x Kt; 4. B—B1, B x P ! Now we have daylight. The advance on the Q's wing was conceived as a diversion against the King-wing. *5. B x B, Kt—R6 ch; 6. K—B1, Q x R; 7. Q—K1, Q—Kt8 ch; 8. K—K2, Q x P ch;* and mate in two moves.

The next example also, Diagram 200, is characteristic of a surprising co-operation of two separate "diversions." It is taken from a game played in a tournament of the lighter genre in Leipzig, 1926. The game proceeded. *1. . . . . P—KR5; 2. Kt x R, RP x Kt; 3. R—Q2,* and now there followed a thrust on the other wing. *3. . . . . P—R4.* My opponent parried with *4. P—Kt5,* but

DIAGRAM 199

Vestergaard—Nimzovich
from a simultaneous display
against 25 opponents

DIAGRAM 200

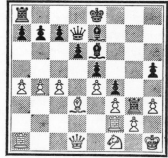

Seifert—Nimzovich
Black's King-side attack will get unexpected support

after *4. . . . . B x RP; 5. P x B, Q x P ch; 6. K—Kt1, P—Q4 ! !* (the point) he resigned since the effect of the check at B4 is catastrophic. His correct move was *4. B—B1, e.g., 4. . . . . P x P; 5. R—Kt2, P—B4,* with a drawish position.

For further games illustrating this Chapter, see Nos. 40–45.

§ 4. *Maneuvering under difficult conditions, our own center lacking protection.*

In conclusion we will give a game inspired with the true spirit of this form of maneuvering. (See Diagram 201.) Black's cramped King's position is here a glaring weakness, and as such must Black's P at Q3 be regarded. But his own weakness at K4 forces a certain reserve on White. The terrain bearing on the weak P at Q3 has little elasticity: the PQ3 can only be attacked by the R at Q1 and from the diagonal. Somewhat more varied seem the possibilities of an advance on the K's Wing, for Queen and Rook can at any time change places on the KKt and KR files. To make these not precisely impressive possibilities the basis of an effective operation demands the highest skill of a Master. Lasker displayed it as follows in his game against Salve. In the Diagram position the game continued 27. . . . . Q—K1; 28. Q—B2 ! (if Kt—B4, the parry . . . . Kt—R3 would be possible), R—B1; 29. Q—Q2 (watches the P at Q3 and hence makes the parry just alluded to impossible), Q—Kt1; 30. K—R1, R(B1)—K1; 31. R—Kt4 !, R—Kt1 (if 31. . . . . Kt—R3, then 32. Kt x BP with advantage to White); 32. R—Q1 ! (because the pressure was taken off the KP); Q—Kt5 (with this the Queen eventually gets out of play. 32. . . . . Q—K1 was decidedly preferable; but it was at this moment difficult to foresee that the circle of influence of

DIAGRAM 201

Lasker—Salve 1909
Masterly maneuvering

the Queen entering the enemy game would be so convincingly localized); 33. Q—KB2, Q—B6; 34. Q—R4 (now this old position taken up anew is stronger than ever), Kt—R3; 35. R—B4, Kt—B2; 36. K—R2, R(Kt1)—K1; 37. Q—Kt3, R—KKt1; 38. R—R4, P—Kt4 (the threat was Kt—B4, Kt—R3; R x P); 39. P x P e.p., R x KtP; 40. Q—B2, P—B4 (to be rid of the weakness at KB3); 41. Kt—B4, R—B3; 42. Kt—K2, Q—Kt7; 43. R—Q2, Q—R8; 44. Kt—Kt3, K—Kt1 (White threatened 45. P x P, B x P; 46. Kt x B, R x Kt; 47. R x P ch); 45. P x P, B x P; 46. Kt—Q4 !, P x Kt; 47. Kt x B, K—B1; 48. Q x P, Q x Q; 49. Kt x Q, Kt—K4; 50. R—R5,

R(K2)—KB2; *51.* P—B5, P x P; *52.* R x Kt, P x Kt; *53.* R x P, R—B7; *54.* R—Q8 *ch,* K—Kt2; *55.* R—QR5 and won.

The way in which Lasker conducts the game is impressive. How he manages, in spite of the small variety of threats at his disposal, to dominate the whole board, and almost wholly to eliminate his own weakness, is worthy of all admiration. The student may learn from this game that the presence of a variety of objects for attack, *i.e.,* enemy weaknesses, can up to a certain point compensate for a lack of variety in threat-bearing lines of play.

With this magnificent example of master play we take leave of our readers.

THIRD PART

Illustrative Games

Illustrative Games

1. FRENCH DEFENSE

Illustrating the consequences of Pawn-snatching in the opening.

Riga, 1913

WHITE	BLACK
A. *Nimzovich*	S. *Alapin*
1. P—K4	P—K3
2. P—Q4	P—Q4
3. Kt—QB3	Kt—KB3
4. P x P	Kt x P

Surrender of the center.

| 5. Kt—B3 | P—QB4 |

To "kill" the Pawn (see I. i. § § 6, 6a, on the surrender of the center). "Restraint" might have been effected by, say, ... B—K2, ... O—O, ... P—QKt3, ... B—Kt2.

| 6. Kt x Kt | Q x Kt |
| 7. B—K3 | . . . . |

It was to be able to make this move, which combines development and attack (the threat is P x P winning a Pawn), that White exchanged Knights. (See I. i, § 4.)

| 7. . . . . | P x P |

Disappearance of tempo spells loss of time.

| 8. Kt x P | P—QR3 |
| 9. B—K2 | Q x KtP |

Stealing a Pawn. The consequences are grievous.

| 10. B—B3 | Q—Kt3 |
| 11. Q—Q2 | P—K4 |

The crisis. Black means to be rid of the unpleasant Knight, so that he may in some measure catch up in development.

| 12. O—O—O ! | P x Kt |
| 13. B x QP | . . . . |

White's advantage in development is now too great.

| 13. . . . . | Kt—B3 |
| 14. B—B6 ! | . . . . |

Travels by express. Any other Bishop move could have been answered by a developing move, whereas now there is no time for this; Black must take.

| 14. . . . . | Q x B |
| 15. KR—K1 *ch* | . . . . |

Play in the King and Queen files at the same time. The danger of a break-through is great.

| 15. . . . . | B—K2 |

or 15. . . . . B—K3; 16. Q—Q7 mate!

16. B x Kt *ch*   K—B1

or 16. . . . . P x B; 17. Q—Q8 mate.

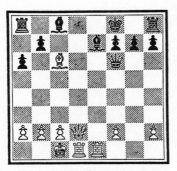

17. Q—Q8 *ch !*   B x Q
18. R—K8 mate

2. PHILIDOR'S DEFENSE

White obtains a free, mobile center Pawn in his KP; Black keeps it in restraint by means of the resources which he has in the King file, succeeds quite properly in killing the "criminal" (See I. i. 6a, p. 15), but then comes to grief. The end game is instructive as an example of the problems of restraint in the wider sense.

Carlsbad, 1911

WHITE	BLACK
R. Teichmann	A. Nimzovich
1. P—K4	P—K4
2. Kt—KB3	P—Q3
3. P—Q4	Kt—KB3
4. Kt—B3	QKt—Q2

The Hanham Variation; makes development more difficult, but holds the center. To call the move "ugly" would be a question of—aberration of taste. *Cf.* Game No. 40 between the same opponents.

5. B—QB4	B—K2
6. O—O	O—O
7. Q—K2	P—B3

By which at least Black establishes a sort of Pawn majority in the center, though it is true White for the time calls the tune.

8. P—QR4   . . . .

The close character of the game allows of Pawn moves in the opening.

8.	Q—B2
9. B—Kt3	P—QR3

In order to be able eventually to advance the QBP.

10. P—R3   P x P

Giving up the center must not be regarded as illogical here; was happiness no happiness, because it endured for but a short time?—One cannot always be happy.

11. Kt x P   R—K1

Restraint strategy, directed against the KP. (*Cf.* Diagram 10, p. 16).

12. B—KB4   B—B1

13. P—B3   Kt—B4

The attentive student will here have expected Black to take possession of an advanced post at K4; but he wishes first to exchange; a commendable stratagem in cramped positions.

14. B—QR2   Kt—K3 !
15. B x Kt   B x B
16. Q—Q2   QR—Q1
17. KR—K1   B—B1
18. QR—Q1   Kt—Q2 !

And now having harmoniously completed his development (though for harmony there was in truth not much room to spare in his cramped quarters), Black occupies the advanced post.

19. Kt—B5   Kt—K4

Commands the field. Large radius of attack. Any attempt to drive him away by P—KB4 would weaken the KP.

20. Kt—Q4   P—B3

Observe the gradual paralyzing of the KP.

21. K—R1   Q—B2
22. Q—B2   Q—Kt3
23. P—QKt3   Kt—B2

And now . . . . P—KB4 is prepared for. The student will perhaps ask, What has the Kt at K4 accomplished? Quite enough, since White could undertake nothing.

24. K—R2   R—K2
25. Kt(Q4)—K2   P—KB4 !

"Killing the paralyzed Pawn."

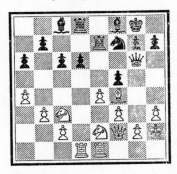

26. Kt—Kt3   P x P ?

Overhasty; . . . . QR—K1 should have been played: 26. . . . . QR—K1; then 27. P x P, B x P; 28. Kt x B, Q x Kt; 29. B—Kt3, R x R; 30. R x R, R x R; 31. Q x R, Q x QBP.

27. Kt(B3) x P   . . . .

After P x P the isolated KP would have been a bad weakness.

27. . . . .   P—Q4
28. Kt—QB5   QR—K1
29. Kt—Q3   R x R

Black has now got an equal game. 29. . . . . Kt—Q3 would surrender his K4 square (30. B—K5)

30. R x R   R x R
31. Q x R   Q—K3
32. Q x Q   B x Q

33. **B—K3** . . . .

This good move puts Black's Pawn majority on the Q side under restraint. Black should now have contented himself with a draw; he wished to get more and lost the game as follows:—*33.* . . . . **B—Q3;** *34.* **P—KB4, K—B1;** *35.* **K—Kt1, P—KKt3;** *36.* **K—B2, P—KR4;** *37.* **Kt—QB5, B—B1;** *38.* **P—R5, Kt—R3;** *39.* **P—Kt4, K—B2;** *40.* **P—B3, Kt—Kt1** (. . . . Kt— B4 would have drawn); *41.* **K— B3, Kt—B3;** *42.* **B—Q4, B x Kt;** *43.* **B x B, B—K3;** *44.* **B—Q4, Kt—K5;** *45.* **Kt—K2 !** (Not *45.* Kt x Kt, P x Kt *ch;* *46.* K x P because of . . . . B—Q4 *ch* followed by . . . . B x P), **B—B4** (It is no use, Black is in effect a Pawn down; his majority is paralyzed, White's is mobile); *46.* **P—Kt4, P x P** *ch;* *47.* **P x P, Kt—Q7** *ch* (It would have been much better to keep the Bishop at home, thus: . . . . B—Q2); *48.* **K—Kt3, B—B7;** *49.* **Kt—Kt1, K—K3;** *50.* **K—R4, B— Q8;** *51.* **Kt—R3, Kt—K5;** *52.* **P—B5** *ch !* (ingeniously turns his majority to account!), **P x P** (If *52.* . . . . K—B2 then 53. P x P *ch,* K x P; *54.* Kt—B4 *ch* would have been unpleasant); *53.* **Kt— B4** *ch,* **K—B2;** *54.* **P—Kt5 !, B—Kt5;** *55.* **P—Kt6** *ch,* **K—K2;** *56.* **P—Kt7, K—B2;** *57.* **Kt—Kt6, Resigns.**

3. QUEEN'S PAWN OPENING

An excellent example of play in the open file. Black by this alone builds up a superior position and without the establishment of any outpost forces his way to the enemy's base.

Ostend, 1907

WHITE	BLACK
L. Van Vliet	*E. Znosko-Borovsky*
1. P—Q4	P—Q4
2. P—K3	P—QB4
3. P—QB3	P—K3
4. B—Q3	Kt—QB3
5. P—KB4	. . . .

The Stonewall, a very close opening

5.	Kt—B3
6. Kt—Q2	Q—B2
7. KKt—B3	. . . .

Overlooks the threat involved in . . . . Q—B2; 7. Kt—R3 followed by Q—B3 would have been the better course.

7. . . . .   **P x P** *!*

(*See Diagram*)

8. **BP x P** . . . .

Positionally the right move here would usually be KP x P (White then has the King file with an outpost station at K5, while the P at QB3 closes the opponent's QB file, see I. ii. 4, p.

Position after 7. . . . . P x P !

26), but here this move would lose a Pawn: 8. KP x P, Q x P. Nevertheless it was preferable to the text move; for 8. KP x P, Q x P; 9. Kt—B4, Q—B2 (. . . . Q—Kt5, 10. Kt—K3 !); 10. Kt(B4)—K5, B—Q3; 11. Q—K2, and White has a fairly well protected outpost in the King file, which Black cannot disturb even by 11. . . . . . B x Kt; 12. BP x B, Kt—Q2; 13. B—KB4, P—B3 ?; for then 14. P x P, Q x B; 15. P x P, KR—Kt1; 16. Q x P ch would win for White. So long as the King file with the outpost Kt at K5, or its full equivalent, a P at K5 (after Pawn recaptures), remains in White's possession he stands excellently, despite the Pawn minus.

8.	Kt—QKt5
9. B—Kt1	B—Q2
10. P—QR3	R—B1 !

It is only by this subtle Rook move that the somewhat beginner-like Kt maneuver gets a meaning.

11. O—O	B—Kt4 !
12. R—K1	Kt—B7
13. B x Kt	Q x B
14. Q x Q	R x Q

The 7th rank, seconded by the Bishop's diagonal QKt4 to KB8 and the point K5 for the Kt.

15. P—R3	B—Q3
16. Kt—Kt1	Kt—K5

No outpost in our sense (the open file behind is wanting); but a good substitute.

17. Kt(B3)—Q2	B—Q6
18. Kt x Kt	B x Kt

18. . . . . P x Kt with the B established at Q6 would also have been good.

19. Kt—Q2	K—Q2
20. Kt x B	P x Kt
21. R—Kt1	KR—QB1
22. P—QKt4	R(B1)—B6
23. K—B1	K—B3 !
24. B—Kt2	R—Kt6
25. R—K2	R x R
26. K x R	K—Kt4
27. K—Q2	K—R5
28. K—K2	P—QR4

The decisive break-through. The position of Black's Rook, holding the White KP under a continual threat, was also too

strong to be withstood. The rest
is readily understandable. **29.
K—B2, P x P; 30. P x P, K x P; 31.
K—K2, K—Kt4; 32. K—Q2, B—R6;
33. K—B2, R x B** *ch;* **34. R x R,
B x R; 35. K x B, K—B5; 36. P—
Kt4, K—Q6; 37. P—Kt5, K x P; 38.
Resigns.**

4. INDIAN DEFENSE

File—Outpost—7th Row.

Ostend, 1907

WHITE	BLACK
F. J Lee	*A. Nimzovich*

The opening moves have already been discussed (I. i.
§ 6a); they were:

1. **P—Q4, Kt—KB3;** *2.* **Kt—KB3,
P—Q3;** *3.* **QKt—Q2, QKt—Q2;** *4.*
P—K4, P—K4; *5.* **P—B3, B—K2;** *6.*
B—B4, O—O; *7.* **O—O, P x P;** *8.*
P x P, P—Q4; *9.* **B—Q3, P x P;** *10.*
Kt x P, Kt x Kt; *11.* **B x Kt, Kt—B3;**
12. **B—Q3, Kt—Q4;** *13.* **P—QR3,
B—B3.**

14.	Q—B2	P—KR3
15.	B—Q2	B—K3
16.	QR—K1	P—B3
17.	B—K3	Q—Kt3
18.	P—R3	QR—Q1
19.	R—B1	R—Q2

Quietly building up the position; the QP cannot move, so
why get excited?

20.	KR—K1	KR—Q1
21.	Q—K2	Q—B2

22.	B—Kt1	Kt—K2

His work done (for the
Knight has been working), a
change of air is good. The
Knight aims to get to KB4.

23.	Kt—K5	B x Kt
24.	P x B	Q x P
25.	B x QRP	Q x Q
26.	R x Q	R—Q8 *ch*

Black now invades the enemy
position via the Q file.

27.	R—K1	R x R(B8)
28.	R x R	R—Q7

Now play in the 7th rank begins.

29.	P—QKt4	Kt—Q4
30.	B—K4	Kt—B3
31.	B—B2	Kt—Q4
32.	B—K4	R—R7 *!*

Allowing Bishops on opposite
color.

33.	B x Kt	B x B
34.	R—B3	P—KB4 *!*

All according to my system.
Black seeks an object of attack
in the 7th rank; against the QRP
nothing further can be done, so
the second player intends to lay
bare White's KKtP. This will be
brought about by a compact advance of the King's wing forces.

(See Diagram)

35.	K—R2	K—B2
36.	B—B5	P—KKt4

Position after 34. . . . . P—KB4!

37. R—Q3	P—Kt4
38. B—Q4	B—K5
39. R—QB3	B—Q4
40. B—B5	K—Kt3
41. R—Q3	P—R4
42. B—Kt6	P—B5
43. B—Q4	K—B4
44. P—B3	. . . .

White stood very badly, the threat was . . . . P—Kt5 followed by . . . . P—Kt6 *ch;* P x P, R x P *ch.*

44.	P—Kt5
45. RP x P *ch*	P x P
46. K—Kt1	R—K7

The 8th rank (White's 1st rank) is also weak (. . . . P—Kt6 is threatened when opportunity arises) and White has not a plethora of moves at his command either.

47. P x P *ch*	K—K5 !

48. R—Q1	B—Kt6
49. R—KB1	K x B

And *Black won* in a few moves.

In the two games which follow, the Knight as outpost is the chief actor. In the first he is exchanged, but finds full compensation in the recapturing Pawn. In the second his capacity to maneuver is exemplified.

5. FRENCH DEFENSE

Riga, 1913

WHITE	BLACK
Dr. v. Haken	*Giese*
1. P—K4	P—K3
2. P—Q4	P—Q4
3. P x P	P x P
4. Kt—KB3	B—Q3
5. B—Q3	Kt—KB3
6. P—KR3	O—O
7. O—O	P—KR3

In the Exchange Variation of the French Defense with both KKts developed at their KB3 the pinning move B—KKt5 furnishes one of the leading motives for both sides. Here, however, this motif is ruled out by the moves of the KRP's, and, except for a moment, we see, and hear of, nothing but the King file.

8. Kt—B3	P—B3

9. Kt—K2	R—K1
10. Kt—Kt3	Kt—K5

The outpost.

11. Kt—R5	Kt—Q2
12. P—B3	QKt—B3
13. Kt—R2	Q—B2
14. Kt x Kt *ch*	Kt x Kt
15. Kt—B3	Kt—K5
16. B—B2	B—KB4 *!*

All pieces are directed towards the strategical point; this is also called emphasizing one's strength (here the Knight at K5).

17. Kt—R4	B—R2
18. B—K3	P—KKt4
19. Kt—B3	P—KB4
20. R—K1	R—K2

The pressure in the file grows more acute move by move.

21. Kt—Q2	P—B5
22. Kt x Kt	P x Kt

The place of the outpost Knight is now worthily taken by a "half-passed" Pawn.

23. B—Q2	QR—K1
24. P—B4	P—B4
25. B—B3	B—Kt3 *!*

In order to be able to play . . . . K—R2 and . . . . P—K6; a timely advance against the P at KR3 is also threatened by . . . . P—KR4, ... P—Kt5, an echo of the pin motif! (I. vii. § 1).

26. Q—Kt4	P x P
27. B x QP	B—K4
28. B x B	R x B

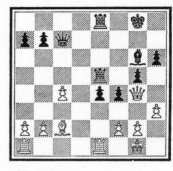

29. Q—Q1	. . . .

If 29. QR—Q1 then 29. . . . . . P—K6; 30. B x B, P x P *ch*; 31. K x P, Q—B4 *ch*; 32. K—B1, Q x P *ch*; 33. K—B2, Q—B4 *ch*; 34. K—B1, Q—Kt4 *ch*; 35. K—B2, Q x P *ch*; 36. K—B1, Q—Kt4 *ch*; 37. K—B2, Q—Kt3 *ch*; 38. K—B1, Q—R3 *ch*; 39. K—B2, Q x P *ch*; 40. K—B1, Q—R3 *ch*; 41. K—B2, Q—Kt3 *ch*; 42. K—B1, followed by the double exchange at K8 and . . . . Q x B. A fine illustration of the theme: the win of a Pawn with a check (see also I. iii. § 3, Diagram 33).

The game continued 29. . . . . R—Q1; 30. Q—Kt1, R—Q7; 31. B x P, Q—B4 *!*; 32. B—Q5 *ch*, K—Kt2; 33. Q—B1, Q x P *ch*; 34. K—R1, R(4) x B; White resigns.

The above game provides a

transparent, therefore, a good, illustration to the outpost theme.

6. RUY LOPEZ

A game from the early days of chess science.

Breslau, 1889

WHITE   **BLACK**
Dr. S. Tarrasch   *J. Berger*

After the opening moves:—*1.* **P—K4, P—K4;** *2.* **Kt—KB3, Kt—QB3;** *3.* **B—Kt5, P—QR3;** *4.* **B—R4, Kt—B3;** *5.* **Kt—B3, B—Kt5;** *6.* **Kt—Q5, B—K2;** *7.* **P—Q3, P—Q3,** Tarrasch with *8.* **Kt—Kt4, B—Q2;** *9.* **Kt x Kt, B x Kt;** *10.* **B x B** *ch,* **P x B,** gave Black a doubled Pawn, whose weakness, however, must be considered for the present as problematical.

The game proceeded:—

11. O—O	O—O
12. Q—K2	P—B4 *?*

This move would be considered bad today. The weakness of the doubled Pawn appears when Black advances; while an advance by White (in the center) would not reveal it; on the contrary, after P—Q4, P x P, Black's Pawn at QB3 would attack White's outpost station in the Q file! (One can see how much easier thinking is made by the system.) Right was, therefore, ... R—K1 and . . . . B—B1 awaiting events.

13. P—B3   . . . .

To be able at any cost to play P—Q4 as quickly as possible. We know today that the central attack is by no means the only one to bring happiness. The right course was Kt—Q2—B4, followed after due preparation by P—QKt4 or P—KB4, leaving the center passive.

13.	Kt—Q2
14. P—Q4	KP x P
15. P x P	B—B3
16. B—K3	P x P
17. B x P	R—K1
18. Q—B2	B x B
19. Kt x B	Kt—B4

On this position of the Knight the whole fate of the game now hangs. If this Knight is driven away, Black's QBP may become weak.

20. P—B3	Q—B3
21. KR—Q1	KR—Kt1

White has the Queen file with a point at Q5. The King file is of no value to Black, partly because of White's protected KP, partly, however, because his Rooks have been told off to stop P—QKt4.

22. QR—Kt1	P—QR4
23. K—R1(*!*)	. . . .

The idea of this subtle move is to use the center as a weapon of attack. The threat is now 24.

P—K5, Q x P; 25. Kt—B6, which before would have failed because of . . . . Q—K6 *ch.* Of positive value, however, there is little in this King move, for in any case Black would have to play . . . . R—Kt2, if only to double the Rooks. (We see that Black operates in the QKt file against the thrust P—QKt4.)

23. . . . .   R—Kt3

Not good, for White suddenly becomes strong in the Q file (the outpost station at Q5 will now be occupied with attack on the R at Kt3). More in place would be 23. . . . . R—Kt2 (given by Steinitz) or some passive move (say . . . . P—R3). For instance: 23. . . . . P—R3; 24. P—K5, P x P; 25. Q x Kt, P x Kt; 26. R x P, P—R5 (Black's QKt file is telling); 27. R—QKt4, Q—Q3, equalizing comfortably. Or 23. . . . . R—Kt2; 24. Kt—K2, QR—Kt1; 25. Kt—B3; and now 25. . . . . P—R5, and the QKt file makes itself felt.

24. Kt—K2   Kt—K3
25. Kt—B3   R—B3

It is intelligible that Berger should regard Kt—Q5 as not conducive to his comfort; nevertheless, it would have been better to retreat in good order with 25. . . . . Q—Q1; 26. Kt—Q5,

R—Kt2; followed by . . . . QR—Kt1.

26. Q—R4   R—B4
27. Kt—Q5   Q—Q1
28. QR—B1   . . . .

White's maneuver (Q—R4, QR—B1) is clear as daylight. White wishes to control the QB file, which is still in dispute, in order at the proper moment to play his trump Q—B6.

28. . . . .   R x R
29. R x R   P—QB4

Puts his QB2 out of danger, but now his Pawn at Q3 has become a delicate child. Black, however, already stood unfavorably; he had in fact neglected the QKt file.

30. R—Q1   Kt—Q5

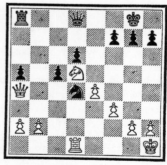

31. Q—B4 !   . . . .

White wishes to exchange the Kt say by Kt—B3—K2, in order then to be able to attack the QP to his heart's content. This at-

tack must succeed, for the protecting pieces can easily get into
uncomfortable positions (*e.g.*,
Black: R, Q2; Q, K2; White: R,
Q5; Q, Q3), on which the KP
will attack for the 3rd time and
the Black QP will be won. From
our point of view it is of interest
to notice how the White pieces
have their eyes fixed on the point
Q5 (*31. Q—B4 !*).

What happens is that if one is
in possession of such a point as
Q5 here is, one embarks on pro-
tracted maneuvering with the
point in question as base. That is
to say one's own pieces come
and go over the point Q5, the
poor Black QP is attacked now
in one way, now in another, and
at last Black loses his wind, that
is, he cannot keep pace with this
tacking to and fro; which is intelligible enough since he not
only has no base on which to
pivot, but is in addition cramped
for space (see II. v. on maneuvering against an enemy weakness). True, in this game it does
not come to the sort of struggle
we have sketched, for Black
makes a mistake, which takes the
game out of the path of its logical development.

31.	. . . .	R—Kt1
32.	P—QKt3	R—B1 ?
33.	R x Kt	P x R
34.	Kt—K7 *ch*	. . . .

Not *34.* Q x R *?,* Q x Q; *35.*

Kt—K7 *ch,* because then the QP
would Queen.

34.	. . . .	Q x Kt
35.	Q x R *ch*	Q—B1
36.	Q x Q *ch*	K x Q

And *White won* the Pawn
ending by means of the "remoter" passed Pawn. The ending is used as an illustration to I.
iv. § 6 on privileged passed
Pawns. See Diagram 64.

7. QUEEN'S INDIAN DEFENSE

Baden-Baden, 1925

WHITE	BLACK
E. Rabinovich	*A. Nimzovich*
1. P—Q4	Kt—KB3
2. P—QB4	P—K3
3. Kt—KB3	P—QKt3
4. Kt—B3	B—Kt2
5. B—Kt5	P—KR3
6. B—R4	B—K2
7. P—K3	P—Q3
8. B—Q3	QKt—Q2

Black has a solid but cramped
game; as a rule such a game can
only be slowly opened up.

| 9. O—O | O—O |
| 10. Q—K2 | P—K4 |

Slower, therefore more true to
type, would be . . . . Kt—R4.

| 11. P x P | B x Kt *!* |

Not *11.* . . . . Kt x P; *12.*

Kt x Kt, P x Kt; *13.* KR—Q1; with pressure in the Q file.

12. P x B	Kt x P
13. B x Kt	B x B
14. B—K4	R—Kt1

White with his Queen file and a Knight outpost at Q5 will be able to force . . . . P—B3, that is already clear. True, the Black QP will not be difficult to defend, for it stands on a square of the same color as his Bishop; but what is going to happen in the KKt file? This we shall soon see.

15. QR—Q1	Kt—Q2 *!*
16. Kt—Q5	Kt—B4
17. B—Kt1	P—QR4

No outpost, yet strong. The student should learn by careful practice how to establish Knights so that they cannot be driven away.

| 18. K—R1 | P—Kt3 |

This would in any event be forced by Q—P2.

19. R—Kt1	B—Kt2
20. R—Kt3	P—QB3 *!*
21. Kt—B4	R—Kt2 *!*

The situation in the KKt file may now be regarded as so far cleared up, that it is evident that the threat consists in a sacrifice at Kt6 (*i.e.*, the "revolutionary"

attack). The slow undermining operations by P—KR4—R5 would be, on the other hand, difficult to carry through.

| 22. Q—B2 | Q—B3 |
| 23. P—Kt3 | . . . . |

He might have gone in for the combination 23. Kt—R5, Q x P; *24.* R x KtP, P x R; *25.* Q x P; but the attack would hardly have succeeded.

| 23. . . . . | R—K1 |
| 24. Kt—K2 | . . . . |

In order to bring the Knight to Q4. White's dilemma consists in having two files, the Queen and KKt; he cannot quite make up his mind which to use, and on this indecision his game goes to pieces.

24.	R—Q2 *!*
25. R—Q2	R(K)—Q1
26. Kt—B4	K—B1
27. Q—Q1	P—R4 *!!*

Not merely to make B—R3 possible, but also because the KRP has a great rôle to play.

| 28. Q—Kt1 | B—R3 |
| 29. Kt—K2 | P—Q4 |

Gets rid of the weakness at Q3 and soon commands the Queen file.

| 30. P x P | R x P |

| 31. R x R | R x R |
| 32. P—B4 | . . . . |

If 32. Kt—Q4, then 32. . . . . B—B5. For instance: 32. Kt—Q4, B—B5; 33. P x B, Q x Kt; 34. P—B5, P—KR5 !; 35. R—Kt4, Q—B6; and the P at KB3 is hard to defend.

| 32. . . . . | B—Kt2 |

The decision to abandon the diagonal KR3 to KB5, a difficult one to have to make, becomes comparatively easy to one who knows that there will be impediments (here very likely a Knight at Q5) to be bombarded. I did not like . . . . R—Q7 at once (instead of . . . . B—Kt2) because of the reply 33. Kt—Q4, B x P; 34. R—B3.

| 33. Q—QB1 | . . . . |

I had expected here (at last!) the sacrifice at KKt6 and had in anticipation prepared a real problem in reply; namely 33. B x P, P—KR5 !; 34. R—Kt4, P x B; 35. R x KtP, Q—B4; 36. R x B, Q—K5 ch; 37. Q—Kt2 (forced), R—Q8 ch; 38. Kt—Kt1, and now the point 38. . . . . P—R6; 39. Q x Q, Kt x Q; threatening mate at B7.

| 33. . . . . | Q—Q3 |

The exploitation of the Queen file which now follows is all according to book (I mean my book), but is here embellished by a pretty feature.

34. B—B2	Kt—K5
35. R—Kt2	P—KR5
36. Kt—Kt1	. . . .

I was glad to be rid of the Knight and played

| 36. . . . . | Kt—B6 |

This Knight maneuver makes possible the invasion of the enemy's base (here his 1st and 2nd ranks).

| 37. P—R4 | . . . . |

If 37. P—QR3 then . . . . Kt—R7 winning the QRP.

| 37. . . . . | Kt—R7 |
| 38. Q—B1 | Kt—Kt5 |

Here I had the unpleasant feeling that I had let the Bishop escape, had allowed him elbow-room.

39. B—K4   R—Q8

My first thought was: What a pity! now the Queen will also find her way into the open; but then I saw the mating specter loom up, the same one which I had known well ever since the 33rd move.

40. Q—B4   P—KB4
41. B—B3   P—R6
42. R—Kt3   Kt—Q6
43. Q—B2   R—QB8

and here I rejoiced over the Queen's involuntary return home.

44. Q—K2   R—QKt8

45. **Resigns,** for the turning move . . . . R—Kt7 will be deadly in effect.

The impression we get from this game is that the system supports combinative play most effectively.

Final Position

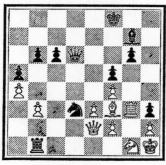

And now a short game which is especially interesting since the outpost appears only as a threat, as a mere ghost, and yet its effect is enormous.

8. QUEEN'S INDIAN DEFENSE

Copenhagen, 1923

WHITE	BLACK
F. Saemisch	A. Nimzovich
1. P—Q4	Kt—KB3
2. P—QB4	P—K3
3. Kt—KB3	P—QKt3
4. P—KKt3	B—Kt2
5. B—Kt2	B—K2
6. Kt—B3	O—O
7. O—O	P—Q4
8. Kt—K5	P—B3

Safeguards the position.

9. P x P   BP x P
10. B—B4   P—QR3 *!*

Protects the outpost station QB5, *i.e.,* by . . . . P—QR3 and . . . . P—QKt4.

11. R—B1   P—QKt4
12. Q—Kt3   Kt—B3

The ghost! With noiseless steps he presses on towards QB5.

13. Kt x Kt   . . . .

Saemisch sacrifices two tempi (exchange of the tempo-eating Kt at K5 for the Kt which is almost undeveloped) merely to be rid of the ghost.

13.	B x Kt
14. P—KR3	Q—Q2
15. K—R2	Kt—R4

I could have supplied him with yet a second ghost by . . . . Q—Kt2, and . . . . Kt —Q2—Kt3—B5, but I wished to turn my attention to the King's side.

16. B—Q2	P—B4 !
17. Q—Q1	P—Kt5 !
18. Kt—Kt1	B—QKt4
19. R—Kt1	B—Q3
20. P—K4	BP x P !

This sacrifice, which has a quite surprising effect, is based upon the following sober calculation: two Pawns and the 7th rank and an enemy Queen's wing which cannot be disentangled—all this for only one piece!

21. Q x Kt	R x P
22. Q—Kt5	QR—KB1
23. K—R1	R(B1)—B4
24. Q—K3	B—Q6

| 25. QR—K1 | P—R3 ! ! |

A brilliant move which announces the *Zugzwang*. White has not a move left. If, *e.g.*, K—R2 or P—Kt4, then . . . . R(B4)—B6. Black can now make waiting moves with his King, and White must, willy-nilly, eventually throw himself upon the sword. So 26. **Resigns.**

9. KING'S INDIAN DEFENSE

Copenhagen, 1922

WHITE	BLACK
A. *Nimzovich*	*Pritzel*
1. P—Q4	P—KKt3
2. P—K4	B—Kt2
3. Kt—QB3	P—Q3
4. B—K3	Kt—KB3
5. B—K2	O—O
6. Q—Q2	. . . .

In order to exchange Black's KB by B—KR6.

6.	P—K4
7. P x P	P x P
8. O—O—O	. . . .

The plan chosen by White is seductive in the simplicity of the means to be employed. He intends after allowing the exchange of Queens, to get some advantage in the Queen file.

| 8. . . . . | Q x Q *ch* |
| 9. R x Q | . . . . |

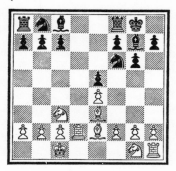

9. . . . .   P—B3

Moves which weaken such important points (as Q3) should be avoided if in any way possible; and in fact a piece soon settles itself on this square. The important point to be observed by the student is that before . . . . P—B3 the Queen file was only under pressure, whereas after this move it is clearly weakened. It would, therefore, have been better to forgo . . . . P—B3 and to play instead 9. . . . . Kt—B3; for instance, the continuation might be: 10. P—KR3 (in order to be able to play Kt—B3 without the fear of the reply . . . . Kt—KKt5), Kt—Q5 ! ?; 11. Kt—B3 ! (but not 11. B x Kt, P x B; 12. R x P, Kt—Kt5 !), Kt x B or Kt; 12. R or B x Kt, and White stands better.

Nevertheless, 9. . . . . Kt —B3 was the correct move, only after 10. P—KR3 Black must continue with . . . . B—

K3. For example: 10. P—KR3, B—K3; 11. Kt—B3, P—KR3; 12. KR—Q1, P—R3. In the position here reached White has unquestionably full possession of the Queen file; since, however, neither an invasion of the 7th rank by R—Q7 nor the establishment of an outpost by Kt—Q5 lies within the realm of possibility, the value of the file would seem to be problematical. White's KP is, in fact, in need of protection and this circumstance has a not inconsiderable crippling effect. Black has two courses open for consideration: (a) to play at once . . . . KR—Q1, with the idea R x R ch, R x R; R x R ch, Kt x R; Kt x P, Kt x P; though this variation must be prepared for by . . . . K—R2 or . . . . P—KKt4, so as to safeguard the KRP; else after the double exchange of Rooks and Kt x P, Kt x P, there would follow Kt x Kt, B x Kt, QB x P. (b) the slow maneuver . . . . KR—B1, followed by . . . . K—B1—K1, and finally the challenge of the Rooks by . . . . R—Q1. The fact that this last line of play is possible is significant proof of the small activity of White in the Queen file.

10. P—QR4   . . . .

Apparently compromising, in reality well thought out; for firstly . . . . P—QKt4, which would be an indirect and therefore unwelcome attack on the P at K4, must be prevented, and secondly Black's Queen's wing is to be besieged. We feel ourselves justified in pursuing this ambitious plan since now that 9. . . . . P—B3 has been played our positional advantage in the center is unquestionable, and should have a real effect even on the wings; a proposition which may be thus formulated: *a superior position in the center justifies a thrust on an extreme flank.*

10.	Kt—Kt5
11. B x Kt	B x B
12. KKt—K2	Kt—Q2

In unusual situations ordinary moves are, it would seem, seldom suitable. The proper system of development here was . . . . Kt—R3, ... KR—K1, and . . . . B—KB1. The weakness at Q3 would then have been covered and the position would have been perfectly tenable.

13. KR—Q1	Kt—Kt3
14. P—QKt3	B—B3
15. P—B3	B—K3
16. P—R5	Kt—B1
17. Kt—R4	. . . .

It is now clear that the suggested development by 12. . . . . Kt—R3 etc. would have wasted less time than that in the

text (. . . . Kt—Q2—Kt3—B1). White has now a strong position on the extreme left and threatens to get a grip on the enemy with Kt—B5. We now see that 10. P—QR4 ! was not so very valueless as an attacking move.

17. . . . .   P—Kt3

An excellent parry. If 18. P x P, P x P; 19. B x P, then naturally . . . . B—Kt4.

18. R—Q3 !   . . . .

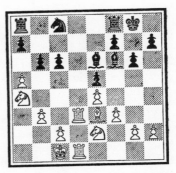

The "restricted" advance in a file, which here is revealed in a singularly plastic form, in that the Rook is brought from the Q to the QB file and thence to the QR file.

18. . . . .   P x P

Bad. The right move was . . . . R—Kt1 and Black's position still had life in it.

19. R—B3   Kt—K2

| 20. R—B5 | KR—Kt1 |
| 21. Kt(2)—B3 | .... |

The QRP won't run away.

21.	P—QR3
22. R x RP	K—Kt2
23. Kt—Kt6	R—R2
24. Kt(3)—R4	....

The one Kt made room for the other.

24.	R(R)—Kt2
25. R x RP	Kt—B1
26. Kt x Kt	R x Kt
27. Kt—B5	R(2)—B2
28. R—Q6	....

Now at last is the point seized which Black weakened by his 9th move; but its occupation had always been in the air.

| 28. .... | R—Q1 |
| 29. R x B | Resigns |

In the notes to this game we have become acquainted with the resources at the disposal of the defender of a file. Since a knowledge of these is of the greatest practical value in the conduct of a game, we give another example which will be found instructive in the same sense.

10. QUEEN'S PAWN OPENING (in effect)

Breslau, 1925

| WHITE | BLACK |
| A. Nimzovich | Dr. S. Tarrasch |

1. Kt—KB3	Kt—KB3
2. P—B4	P—B4
3. Kt—B3	P—Q4

Playable; but 3. .... P—K3 seems better (3. .... P—K3; 4. P—Q4, P x P; 5. Kt x P, B—Kt5) or even 3. .... Kt—B3. For example 3. .... Kt—B3; 4. P—Q4, P x P; 5. Kt x P, P—KKt3, and now White could, it is true, try by means of 6. P—K4 slowly to tie up his opponent, but this attempt could be adequately parried by 6. .... B—Kt2; 7. B—K3, Kt—KKt5 ! (Breyer's move); 8. Q x Kt, Kt x Kt; 9. Q—Q1 !, Kt—K3 ! (suggested by me). The position reached after 9. .... Kt—K3 is fairly rich in resources for Black, e.g., (i) .... Q—R4, (ii) . . . O—O followed by .... P—B4, (iii) .... P—Kt3 and .... B—Kt2. The student should examine for himself these lines of play.

| 4. P x P | Kt x P |
| 5. P—Q4 | P x P |

Best for Black would appear to be 5. .... Kt x Kt; 6. P x Kt, P x P; 7. P x P, P—K3.

| 6. Q x P | P—K3 |
| 7. P—K3 | . . . . |

A very cautious move, on
which I determined because I
recognized the more enterprising
continuations 7. P—K4 and 7.
Kt x Kt, P x Kt; 8. P—K4, as
leading to little. For instance 7.
P—K4, Kt x Kt !; 8. Q x Kt
(after Q x Q *ch* and P x Kt he
would have a sick QBP in an
open file to tend), Kt—B3; 9.
P—QR3, Q—R4 !; or 9. B—
QKt5, B—Q2; with an equal
game. Or, 7. Kt x Kt, P x Kt; 8.
P—K4, P x P !; 9. Q x Q *ch*,
K x Q; 10. Kt—Kt5, B—Kt5 *ch*;
11. B—Q2, B x B *ch*; 12. K x B,
K—K2; with an equal game.
The student who is interested in
problems of development should
test the following variation: 7.
Kt x Kt, P x Kt; 8. P—K4, Kt—
B3 (instead of . . . . P x P ! as
given by us). After 9. Q x QP,
Q x Q; 10. P x Q, Kt—Kt5; there
would follow B—Kt5 *ch*, and
Black would have difficulty in
finding a good continuation.

7.	Kt—QB3
8. B—Kt5	B—Q2
9. B x Kt	B x B
10. Kt—K5	Kt x Kt
11. Kt x B	Q x Q
12. Kt x Q	Kt—Q4
13. B —Q2	. . . .

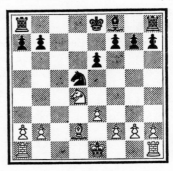

The position here shown is for
all its harmless appearance full
of poison. White threatens to
take possession of the QB file;
moreover he has at his disposal
a convenient square for his K
(K2), whereas Black enjoys this
last advantage in only a restricted fashion (see note to
move 17). In such positions the
defense must be played very
carefully.

| 13. . . . . | B—B4 |

In order to drive the Kt away
from the center; but as the Kt
moves to Kt3 in order to promote
his QB5 into an outpost station,
. . . . B—B4 proves to be pleasant for White. Best appears to
be 13. . . . . B—K2, intending
. . . . B—B3. For example, 13.
. . . . B—K2; 14. P—K4, Kt—
Kt3; 15. R—QB1, O—O; 16
K—K2; and now White is full
of pride in his developed King,
whereas his Black Majesty can
in this case give up all thought

of development since the B at
K2 is a crafty minister, who likes
to keep the reins of government
in his own hands. For instance:
*16. K—K2, B—B3 !; 17. B—K3,
KR—B1; 18. P—QKt3, B x Kt;
19. B x B; and now . . . . Kt—
Q2*, or else *19. . . . . R x R* (instead of . . . . Kt—Q2); *20.
R x R, R—QB1; 21. R x R ch,
Kt x R; 22. K—Q3*, and though
it is true that the White King is
now able to make his influence
felt, it is questionable whether
Black will not overtake his opponent, *e.g., 22. . . . . P—B3;
23. K—B4, K—B2; 24. K—Kt5,
P—R3 ch !* (else the Bishop sacrifice); *25. K—B5, K—K2;* followed by . . . . K—Q2 with a
draw. It follows that *13. . . . .
B—K2* was the right defense.

14. Kt—Kt3   B—Kt5

Either . . . . B—Kt3 or . . . .
B—K2 would have been de-
cidedly better. . . . . B—Kt3
would have safeguarded QB2
against invasion, and this is an
imperative duty in the defense.
After *14. . . . . B—Kt3; 15.
P—K4, Kt—K2;* White's advantage would have been infinitesimal.

15. R—QB1   R—Q1
16. B x B   Kt x B
17. K—K2   K—K2

Black has cleared a square for
himself, but at what a cost of

valuable time! (. . . . B—B4—
Kt5).

18. R—B4   Kt—R3

An unpleasant retreat. If *18.
. . . . Kt—B3;* then not *19.
Kt—B5* because of the answer
. . . . Kt—R4 and . . . . P—
QKt3, but rather a doubling of
the Rooks, and Black's position
would not be favorable.

19. KR—QB1   R—Q2

Black's position still makes an
impression which inspires confi-
dence in it, and this at a moment
when it carries the seeds of death
in itself. The next two moves of
White reduce Black's Q file to
passivity, that is to say take away
from it any potential attacking
value.

20. P—B4 !   KR—Q1
21. Kt—Q4   P—B3

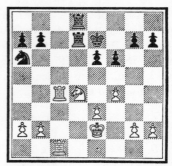

Black intends . . . . P—K4. Is
this a threat? If not, find a
sensible waiting move for
White.

22. P—QR4 ! . . . .

Even a full advance of a Pawn can imply a waiting policy. White does not fear . . . . P—K4 in the least, for after 22. . . . . P—K4; 23. P x P, P x P; Black's KP would be weak. The more energetic 22. P—QKt4 was, however, also to be considered.

22. . . . . P—K4

In a cramped position the attempt to hit out is explicable on psychological grounds, even if it be not always equally justified if viewed dispassionately. So, too, here. It is true that in any case Black stands badly.

23. P x P	P x P
24. Kt—B3	K—K3
25. P—QKt4	P—QKt3
26. R(B1)—B2 !	. . . .

One, of those unpretentious moves which are more disagreeable to a cramped opponent who is threatened on all sides than the worst direct attack. The move is a defending and a waiting move, and moreover involves a threat; though this from the nature of things is but a small one, and is in fact of but secondary importance. The (slight) threat is Kt—Kt5 ch and Kt—K4, and then P—Kt5, driving the Kt back to Kt1.

26. . . . . P—R3

27. P—R4 ! **R—Q3**
28. P—KR5 . . . .

As a result of 26. R—B2 entirely new attacking possibilities have arisen. Black's P at KKt2 has become backward. The maneuver R—Kt4 would, however, not only help to expose the weakness of the KtP, but, what is more important, put the Black King in an extremely disagreeable situation. All this fell like ripe fruit into White's lap, simply and solely as the logical (or psychological) result of the waiting move 26. R(B1)—B2. The finest moves are after all waiting moves!

28.	R—Q4
29. R—Kt4	R(Q4)—Q2
30. R—B6 *ch*	R—Q3

If 30. . . . . K—B4 ? then 31. R(B6)—Kt6 followed by mate. On 30. . . . . K—Q4; 31. R(B6)—KKt6, P—K5 !; there would follow 32. Kt—Q2, Kt x P; 33. Kt x P, with advantage to White.

31. R—Kt6 *ch* . . . .

The possession of the points QB6 and KKt6 insures the complete investment of the enemy King. Observe how the QB file has been used as a jumping off place to get into the KKt file.

31. . . . . K—K2

On *31. . . . .* K—Q4 there
would have followed a pretty
little catastrophe: *32.* R(B6) x
R *ch,* R x R; *33.* P—K4 *ch!,* K—
B3; *34.* P—-Kt5 *ch,* and the Kt,
who had felt so thoroughly safe
at R3, to his intense surprise
meets his doom!

32.	R x P *ch*	K—B1
33.	R x R	R x R
34.	R x P	Kt x P
35.	Kt x P	R—K3

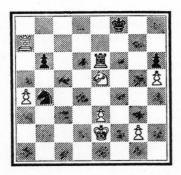

White wins. To make effective
use of a superiority in material is
one of the most important things
which a student has to learn. He
cannot practice himself enough
in it.

White has now won two
Pawns. A glance at the position
shows (i) that White commands
the 7th row; (ii) that White's
KP is isolated and his KKtP
backward. The policy, therefore,
is, taking full advantage of the
7th row, to assemble (unite) our

isolated or badly placed detachments. To this end the Kt will be
brought, with gain of tempo, to
KB5.

36.	Kt—Kt6 *ch*	K—Kt1 *!*
37.	Kt—K7 *ch*	K—B1
38.	Kt—B5	Kt—Q4
39.	P—Kt4	. . . .

The Kt at KB5 has the effect
planned for him; he protects the
KP, attacks the KRP and makes
K—B3 possible.

39.	. . . .	Kt—B5 *ch*
40.	K—B3	Kt—Q6

In order if R—R7 to protect
the RP by . . . . Kt—K4 *ch*
and . . . . Kt—B2.

41.	R—R8 *ch !*	K—B2
42.	R—R8	Kt—B4
43.	R—R7 *ch*	. . . .

*On revient toujours à sa pre-
mière amour!*

43.	. . . .	K—Kt1

For if . . . . K—B1 then *44.*
Kt x P, and White gets a mating
attack, or else the advance of
his KtP cannot be stopped.

44.	R x P	R x R
45.	Kt x R *ch*	K—B1
46.	Kt—B5	Kt x P
47.	P—R6	K—Kt1
48.	P—Kt5	K—R2
49.	K—Kt4	Kt—B4
50.	K—R5	. . . .

According to the motto, the line will advance! See I. vi. § 3.

50.	Kt—K3
51. P—Kt6 *ch*	K—Kt1
52. P—R7 *ch*	K—R1
53. K—R6	Resigns

In the following game we come to the "restricted advance" (of a Rook) in an open file, in which the file does not show up sporadically like summer lightning, but throughout dominates the field. The student may learn from this game how closely the "elements" are allied to the higher technique of the game. A thorough knowledge of the elements takes us more than half the road to mastership.

11. ALEKHINE'S DEFENSE

Baden-Baden, 1925

WHITE	BLACK
Sir G. A. Thomas	*Dr. A. Alekhine*
1. P—K4	Kt—KB3
2. P—Q3	P—B4
3. P—KB4	Kt—B3
4. Kt—KB3	P—KKt3
5. B—K2	B—Kt2
6. QKt—Q2	P—Q4
7. O—O	O—O
8. K—R1	P—Kt3
9. P x P	Q x P
10. Q—K1	B—Kt2
11. Kt—B4	. . . .

The position of this Kt is all the (poor) consolation White has for the want of harmony in his position (B at K2). Black stands much the better. White at his 5th move or even earlier ought to have played P—QB4.

11.	Kt—Q5

Outpost in the Queen file.

12. Kt—K3	Q—K3
13. B—Q1	Kt—Q4

See the remarks on this position in I. ii. § 2.

14. KKt x Kt	P x Kt
15. Kt x Kt	Q x Kt
16. B—B3	Q—Q2
17. B x B	Q x B

White has eased his position by the exchanges, but the open QB file forces the next disorganizing move. (See again I. ii. § 2.)

18. P—B4	P x P e.p.
19. P x P	QR—B1
20. B—Kt2	KR—Q1
21. R—B3	B—B3
22. P—Q4	. . . .

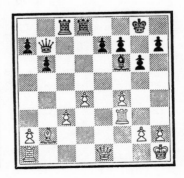

We have now arrived at a well known position in the QP opening only with the colors reversed. Compare the following, the opening of a consultation game, Nimzovich *v.* Professor Kudriavtsev and Dr. Landau, Dorpat, 1910. *1.* P—Q4, P—Q4; *2.* Kt—KB3, Kt—KB3; *3.* P—B4, P—K3; *4.* Kt—B3, P—B4; *5.* P x QP, KP x P; *6.* B—Kt5, P x P; *7.* KKt x P, B—K2; *8.* P—K3, O—O; *9.* B—K2, Kt—B3; *10.* Kt x Kt, P x Kt; and now with colors reversed we have the same Pawn configuration as in the game Thomas—Alekhine; the game went on: *11.* O—O, B—K3; *12.* R—B1, R—Kt1; *13.* Q—B2, B—Q2; *14.* KR—Q1. The well known theme of the isolated Pawn couple now comes up for discussion. *14.* . . . . . Kt—K1; *15.* B x B, Q x B; *16.* Kt—R4, Kt—B3; *17.* Kt—B5, R—Kt3; *18.* R—Q4 *!*, R(B)—Kt1; *19.* P—QKt3, B—K1; *20.* B—Q3, P—KR3; *21.* Q—B3, B—Q2; *22.* R—QR4, with marked advantage in position.

(*See Diagram*)

We will now revert to the Thomas—Alekhine game:

22.	. . . .	Q—Q4
23.	Q—K3	Q—QKt4
24.	Q—Q2	R—Q4
25.	P—KR3	P—K3

Position after White's 22nd move in the game Nimzovich —the Allies.

26.	R—K1	Q—R5
27.	R—R1	P—QKt4
28.	Q—Q1	R—B5

The restricted advance, or else the QB file used as a jumping off place for the QR file. See I. ii. § 5. Observe the similarity of the maneuver in this game and the consultation game quoted above.

29.	Q—Kt3	R—Q3
30.	K—R2	R—R3

The Q file is also used as a jumping off place!

31.	KR—B1	B—K2
32.	K—R1	R(5)—B3 *!*

Very fine play! The regrouping . . . . Q—B5, ... R—R5 and . . . . R(3)—R3 is planned.

| 33. | KR—K1 | B—R5 |
| 34. | R—KB1 | . . . . |

White dare not weaken his own base by, say, R—K5; *e.g.*, 34. R—K5 ?, Q x Q; 35. P x Q, R x R *ch;* 36. B x R, R—R3; 37. B—Kt2, R—R7 and wins.

| 34. | . . . . | Q—B5 *!* |
| 35. | Q x Q | R x Q |

The exchange is grist to Black's mill, for now White's QRP has become very weak. The student should notice that the exchange is the direct, almost automatic consequence of the quiet seizing of strategically important points. The beginner seeks to bring about an exchange in other ways; he pursues the piece, which tempts him, with offers to elope (exchange), only to have them refused. *The master occupies the strong points* and the exchange which seems desirable to him falls like ripe fruit into his lap. See I. v.

36.	P—R3	B—K2
37.	KR—QKt1	B—Q3
38.	P—Kt3	K—B1
39.	K—Kt2	K—K2

Bringing the K to the center, see I. vi. § 1.

40.	K—B2	K—Q2
41.	K—K2	K—B3
42.	R—R2	R(B)—R5
43.	R(Kt)—QR1	K—Q4

Centralization is now complete.

44.	K—Q3	R(3)—R4
45.	B—B1	P—QR3
46.	B—Kt2	P—R4

A new attack and yet the logical consequence of the play on the extreme Queen's wing; for the White Rooks are chained to the QRP, and even if we assumed the Black Rooks to suffer from a like immobility, (which is not the case since they can be brought into play via their QB5 against the QBP) yet there remains to Black an indubitable advantage in the more enterprising position of his King. And that this advantage should weigh in the balance at all, we have once more only to thank the fact that as a consequence of Black's diversion the White Rooks have lost their wind; for if they were mobile, Black's advantage derived from his K's position would be illusory. Thus the attack on the extreme flank has not immaterially increased the importance of the mobility of Black's King. The strategic contact between the two seemingly separated theaters of war is now made clear. And now on the King's wing . . . . P—R4 is intended to provoke P—R4, so that, with White's P at KKt3 exposed, ... P—K4 may exercise its full effect.

A very instructive case which the student is recommended to study.

| 47. | P—R4 | P—B3 |
| 48. | B—B1 | P—K4 |

The break-through which sets the seal on White's downfall.

49.	BP x P	P x P
50.	B—Kt2	P x P
51.	P x P	P—Kt5 !

Obvious though this move be, it must yet delight every connoisseur, that the sole purpose of the break-through was to get the disturbing White QBP out of the way.

52.	P x P	R x R
53.	P x R	R x B
54.	Resigns	

The "restricted advance" has been carried out with great virtuosity in this game.

12. PHILIDOR'S DEFENSE

San Sebastian, 1912

WHITE	BLACK
P. S. Leonhardt	*A. Nimzovich*
1. P—K4	P—K4
2. Kt—KB3	P—Q3
3. P—Q4	Kt—KB3
4. Kt—B3	P x P

Surrender of the center. Black will seek to keep White's KP under restraint. (*Cf.* Game No. 2.)

5.	Kt x P	B—K2
6.	B—K2	O—O
7.	O—O	Kt—B3
8.	Kt x Kt	P x Kt

This exchange creates advantages for both sides. Black gets a more compact Pawn formation in the center, safeguards for instance his Q4 against its possible occupation as an advanced post by a White Kt; but the QRP is isolated, and, moreover, as in the game, his QB4 may become a weak point.

| 9. | P—QKt3 | P—Q4 |

Very playable here would also have been . . . . R—K1 and . . . . B—B1, directed against White's KP to keep it in restraint.

| 10. | P—K5 | Kt—K1 |
| 11. | P—B4 | P—KB4 |

Otherwise P—B5 with a strong attack.

| 12. | B—K3 | P—Kt3 ! |

White's KP is to be blocked; it is, however, by no means indifferent whether this blockade is effected by Kt or B. The latter would be inelastic, and its range of action small, at best as far as Kt5 (should White play P—KKt4 to attack the opposing Pawn minority), while it would also be more attackable, *e.g.*, by a Kt at QB5, which could not be driven off. On the other hand a Kt at K3 would be not only an excellent, because unassailable, blockader, but also a very aggressive one; among other things preparing for . . . . P—KKt4. It is often of the greatest importance to find the right blockading piece.

13. Kt—R4 !   Kt—Kt2
14. Q—Q2   Q—Q2

In order to follow with . . . . R—Q1 as soon as possible.

15. Q—R5   . . . .

Combines continued pressure on Black's QB4 (*Cf.* note to Black's 8th move) with play against the weak, isolated QRP.

15. . . . .   Kt—K3
16. QR—Q1   R—Q1
17. Kt—B5 ?   . . . .

A positional mistake. White should seek to keep the Kt as a potential blockader, or at any rate only exchange him for a Kt. The situation is this: the two Knights are the chief actors (because the most effective in blockade) and whoever gives up his proud horseman for a prelate gets in this case the worst of the bargain. 17. B—B5 was the right move.

17. . . . .   B x Kt
18. B x B   B—Kt2

19. R—B3   K—B2
20. R—R3   K—Kt2
21. R—KB1   R—K1
22. R(3)—KB3   QR—Q1

Since Q x RP is forbidden on account of . . . . R—QR1; 24. Q x B, R(K)—QKt1. There is little that White can undertake.

23. R—Q1   P—QR3
24. P—QKt4   K—R1
25. Q—R3   R—KKt1
26. Q—B3   R—Kt2
27. K—R1   R(Q)—KKt1

Black plans . . . . P—Kt4, and in this the blockading Kt at K3 would render priceless service. A comparison between the two blockading pieces, the Black Kt at his K3 and the White B at QB5, is here all in favor of the Kt. The B, it is true, does his work as a blockader pure and simple well enough, but otherwise his effective range of action is very small.

28. B—K3   P—B4 !

The advance which we have so often discussed! The Bishop's diagonal is opened by the Pawn sacrifice. But it may be objected that the QBP is here neither a passed Pawn nor a "candidate." True, and yet logically he must be filled with that ambition to expand, for otherwise White would not have kept him under a blockade for so long. But now he takes vengeance for the restraint he has had to suffer.

The Pawn's ambition to expand comes to fruition.

29. R—Kt3   . . . .

Best, as given by Schlechter, would be 29. P x P, P—Q5; 30. R x P, Kt x R; 31. B x Kt, B x R; 32. B x B, with two Bishops and two Pawns for two Rooks.

29.	P—Q5
30. Q—R3	P—Kt4 *!*
31. B—B4	P x BP

. . . . B—Q4 would have been good, if only to preserve the Kt.

32. B x Kt   . . . .

(*See Diagram*)

32. . . . .   B x P *ch !*

Now the Bishop runs amok! The death of the Kt makes him utterly reckless.

33. K—Kt1   . . . .

How is Black to pursue his plan of breaking through ?

But behold he still lives, the saucy fellow! and indeed after 33. K x B (R x B ? Q—B3), Q—B3 *ch;* 34. K—B1, P x R; 35. B x R, KtP x P; he would have been bloodily avenged.

33. . . . .   Q x B

He who would regard . . . . B x P *ch* as a bolt from a clear sky, shows thereby that he has not fully grasped the logic which lay in this sudden irruption of the B, who had been kept under restraint for such a long time.

| 34. B x BP | B—Kt2 |
| 35. P x P | Q—Q4 |

and won. 36. **P—B6,** B x P; 37. **K—B2,** R x R; 38. P x R, Q—Kt7 *ch,* 39. **K—K1,** B—B6; 40. **Q x P,** Q—Kt8 *ch;* 41. **Resigns.**

13. QUEEN'S GAMBIT DE-CLINED (*in effect*)

An instructive example of the method of dealing with the supports of a blockader. In the end game they are usually driven away, in the middle game on the other hand—kept busy. See I. iv. § 4.

Breslau, 1925

WHITE	BLACK
A. Nimzovich	*H. von Gottschall*
1. Kt—KB3	P—K3
2. P—Q4	P—Q4
3. P—K3	Kt—KB3
4. P—QKt3	QKt—Q2

He should have played . . . . P—QB4 and . . . . Kt—QB3.

5. B—Q3	P—B3
6. O—O	B—Q3
7. B—Kt2	Q—B2

In order to play . . . . P—K4 and thus open up the game. To prevent this, White undertakes a counter attack.

8. P—B4	P—QKt3

If now 8. . . . . P—K4, the continuation would be 9. P—B5, B—K2 (9. . . . . P—K5, 10. P x B, Q x P; 11. B—R3 etc.); 10. P x P, Kt—Kt5; 11. P—Kt4, QKt x KP; 12. Kt x Kt, Kt x Kt; 13. P—B4, Kt x B; 14. Q x Kt, and White commands the diagonal QKt2 to KKt7.

9. Kt—B3	B—Kt2
10. R—B1	R—QB1
11. P x P	KP x P
12. P—K4	. . . .

White opens all the lines.

12.	P x P
13. Kt x P	Kt x Kt
14. B x Kt	O—O
15. P—Q5	P—QB4

The two Bishops have now a clear line of fire to the enemy King's wing. Impressed by this the second player is inclined to underestimate the fact that the QP is now passed; in fact to overlook it altogether. And indeed what possible rôle could this most carefully blockaded passed Pawn play? Why, a reserve blockader is already stationed at Q2! But things turn out quite otherwise.

16. R—K1	Q—Q1
17. B—Kt1	. . . .

This attack leads to the instructive results that the blockading pieces, the B at Q3 and Kt at Q2 are either cut off or killed off.

17.	R—K1
18. Q—Q3	. . . .

First R x R *ch* would have been more precise.

19.	Kt—B1

. . . . R x R *ch* would have been better.

19. R x R	Q x R
20. Kt—R4 *!*	P—B3
21. Kt—B5	R—Q1

Black is about to try to show up the weakness of White's QP, when he is wakened from his dream by the flash of a sacrifice.

| 22. B x P *!* | B x P *ch !* |

In order not to lose a Pawn Black must submit to this indirect exchange of his B. If 22. . . . . P x B then 23. Kt x B, R x Kt; 24. Q—Kt3 *ch.*

| 23. K x B | P x B |

What a change! the B at Q3 has disappeared and the reserve blockader, the Kt at Q2 will soon land at KKt3. The QP is therefore free!

| 24. Q—Kt3 *ch* | Kt—Kt3 |
| 25. P—B4 | . . . . |

To allow R—K1; the passed Pawn is indirectly protected.

| 25. . . . . | K—R1 |

Not 25. . . . . B or . . . . R x P because of 26. R—K1, and 27. Kt—K7 *ch* etc.

| 26. R—K1 | . . . . |

(*See Diagram*)

| 26. . . . . | Q—B1 *!* |

If 26. . . . . Q—Kt1, the passed Pawn would have come into his own in a most interesting

Position after 26. R—K1

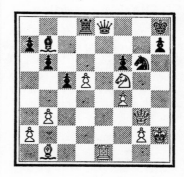

manner; namely as follows: 27. Kt—K7, Kt x Kt; 28. R x Kt (7th rank), Q x Q *ch;* 29. K x Q, R—Kt1 *ch;* 30. K—B2, R—Kt2. Apparently the 7th rank is now neutralized, but the passed Pawn has something to say to that. 31. P—Q6, R x R; 32. P x R, B—B3; 33. B—K4, B—K1; 34. P—B5 *!*, K—Kt2; 35. B—Q5, and now the P at K7 is unassailable. 35. . . . . K—R3; 36. K—B3, K—Kt4; 37. K—K4, and Black is powerless against the threat B—Kt7, K—Q5, and B—B6, and the blockader must die.

| 27. P—Q6 *!* | R—Q2 |

Why not . . . . B—B1, would not this have led to the winning of the passed Pawn? The answer is no, for the continuation would be 28. Kt—K7 (By his P—Q6 White has provided an outpost station at K7), 28. . . . . Q—R3 *ch* (best); 29. K—Kt1, Kt x P; and now 30. Kt x B, R x Kt; 31. P—Q7 and wins.

28. Q—QB3 . . . .

Threatening 29. R—K8 *!*, Q x R; 30. Q x P *ch*, K—Kt1; 31. Kt—R6 mate.

Accordingly the 8th rank must be safeguarded by the retreat . . . . R—Q1. But in this case the 7th rank will be left without protection and White wins by R—K7. Note that the winning moves R—K7 or Kt—K7 (as in the last note), must be regarded as a direct consequence of the passed Pawn's advance.

28. . . . . R x P

A desperate expedient. If 28. . . . . R—KB2, then 29. P—Q7, R x P; 30. R—K8 *!* would have been immediately decisive.

29. Kt x R   Q x Kt
30. B x Kt   P x B
31. R—K8 *ch*   K—Kt2
32. Q—Kt3 and White won:

32. . . . . B—B3; 33. R—K3, B—Q2; 34. P—B5 *!*, Q x Q *ch*; 35. K x Q, B x P; 36. R—K7 *ch*, K—R3; 37. R x P, B—Kt8; 38. R—R6, P—QKt4; 39. P—R4, P x P; 40. P x P, K—Kt4; 41. R—Kt6, B—K5; 42. P—R5, P—B4; 43. P—R6, P—B5; 44. P—R7, P—B6; 45. R—Kt3, P—B5 *ch*; 46. K—B2, P—B7; 47. R—QB3, Resigns.

14. GRECO COUNTER GAMBIT

Riga, 1919

WHITE	BLACK
A. *Nimzovich*	C. *Behting*

1. P—K4   P—K4
2. Kt—KB3   P—KB4

According to C. Behting's view, which I am inclined to share, this move is quite playable. At any rate I do not know a refutation of it.

3. Kt x P   Q—B3
4. P—Q4   P—Q3
5. Kt—B4   P x P

Does the blockading move Kt— K3 appear justified?

Theory (the practice of the other Masters) now recommends 6. Kt—B3, Q—Kt3; 7. P—B3, but after 7. . . . . . P x P; 8. Q x P, Kt—KB3; 9. B—Q3, Q—Kt5; 10. Q—K3 *ch*, B—K2; 11. O—O, Kt—B3; 12. P—Q5,

Kt—Kt5; *13.* R—B4, Q—Q2; *14.* Kt—Kt6, RP x Kt; *15.* R x Kt the game is even.

6. Kt—K3 *!*   . . . .

Against this move speak (1) tradition, which rather demands 6. Kt—B3; (2) the principle of economical development, *i.e.*, not to let one piece go a-wandering; (3) the apparently small threat effect of the blockader. And yet 6. Kt—K3, taken with the move next following, is in every respect a master-move. And even if all the rest of the world play here 6. Kt—B3, I yet hold my move Kt—K3 to be more correct, and this for reasons based on the "system."

6. . . . .   P—B3
7. B—B4 *! !*   . . . .

The point. In order to be able to castle, Black must now play . . . . P—Q4, but this move will hold out another field for the Kt (after B—Kt3 and P—QB4).

7. . . . .   P—Q4
8. B—Kt3   B—K3

Or 8. . . . . P—QKt4; 9. P—QR4, P—Kt5; *10.* P—QB4, etc.

9. P—QB4   Q—B2
10. Q—K2   Kt—B3
11. O—O   . . . .

Not Kt—B3 because of . . . . B—QKt5. White wants to bring the maximum pressure to bear on Black's QP. If we look at the blockading Kt at K3 more closely, do we find that he meets the requirements asked of a blockader? Yes, for (1) he establishes a strong blockade, hindering the approach of enemy pieces (to *e.g.*, his KKt4); (2) exercises threats from where he is stationed; (3) is very elastic, as we shall see later. In short, the Kt at K3 is an ideal blockader.

11. . . . .   B—QKt5 *!*
12. B—Q2   B x B
13. Kt x B   O—O
14. P—B4   . . . .

Intending P—KB5 in order to win the QP.

14. . . . .   QP x P
15. Kt(Q2) x BP   Q—K2
16. P—B5   B—Q4

Black seeks to maintain the point Q4.

17. Kt x B   P x Kt
18. Kt—K3   . . . .

Hardly has the Kt at K3 disappeared than a new Kt stands in his place. Against such "elasticity" not even Death can prevail!

18. . . . .   Q—Q2
19. Kt x P *!*   . . . .

The threat effect of the blockader from his post culminates in this decisive sacrifice.

19.	Kt x Kt
20. Q x P	R—Q1
21. P—B6 !	. . . .

The point of the combination and at the same time a further illustration of the Pawn's lust to expand (the KBP was a "candidate").

21.	P x P

If 21. . . . . . Kt—B3, then 22. P—B7 *ch*, K—R1; 23. B x Kt, Q x B ?; 24. Q x Q, R x Q; 25. P—B8(Q) *ch* etc. And if 22. . . . . K—B1, then 23. B x Kt, Q x B; 24. Q x P, and wins.

22. R—B5	K—R1
23. R x Kt	R—K1

If 23. . . . . Q—K1, then 24. B—B2 ! wins a whole Rook.

24. R x Q	R x Q
25. R—Q8 *ch*	K—Kt2
26. R—Kt8 *ch*	K—R3
27. R—KB1	Resigns

And now a companion picture to the previous game.

15. FRENCH DEFENSE

Vilna, 1912

WHITE	BLACK
A. Nimzovich	*S. von Freymann*
1. P—K4	P—K3
2. P—Q4	P—Q4
3. P—K5	P—QB4
4. Kt—KB3	P x P

4. . . . . Q—Kt3 seems to be better.

5. Kt x P	Kt—QB3
6. Kt x Kt	P x Kt
7. B—Q3	Q—B2
8. B—KB4	P—Kt4

Not quite sound but leading to interesting play. The resulting position is discussed under Diagram 188 in II. v.

9. B—Kt3	B—KKt2
10. Q—K2	Kt—K2
11. O—O	P—KR4
12. P—KR3	Kt—B4
13. B—R2	. . . .

13. B x Kt, P x B; 14. P—K6, would be obviously bad because of 14. . . . . P—B5; 15. P x P *ch*, K x P.

13.	P—Kt5

The pretty point of the attack started by 8. . . . . P—Kt4.

14. R—K1	. . . .

The answer to *14.* P x P, P x P; *15.* Q x P, would have been *15. . . . .* R x B; *16.* K x R, B x P *ch;* followed by . . . . B x P.

14.	K—B1
15. Kt—B3	. . . .

This Kt proposes to make his way to KB4 (after the Black Kt at B4 is exchanged off).

15.	Q—K2
16. B x Kt	P x B
17. Q—K3	R—R3
18. Kt—K2	P—B4
19. Kt—B4 *!*	. . . .

This Kt is to be regarded as primarily the blockader of Black's P at KB4 and its adherent mass of Pawns; but in addition he acts as an "anti-blockader" for his own aspiring P at K5.

19.	P—Q5
20. Q—Q3	Q—Q2
21. Q—B4	Q—B3
22. P x P *!*	. . . .

The necessary prelude to Kt—Q3. If at once *22.* Kt—Q3 there would have followed *22. . . . .* P x P; *23.* Q x P *ch,* Q x Q; *24.* Kt x Q, R—KKt3; *25.* P—KKt3, and White stands badly.

22.	B—R3

(*See Diagram*)

23. Q—Q5 *! !*	Q x Q

Position after 22. . . . . B—R3

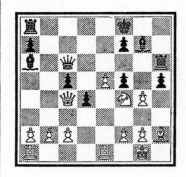

Most interesting would have been *23. . . . .* RP x P; the result would have been a triumphant march of the KP to K8. For instance, *23. . . . .* RP x P; *24.* P—K6 (with attack on the Queen), *24. . . . .* Q x Q; *25.* P—K7 *ch,* K—K1; *26.* Kt x Q, followed by check at QB7. (The "unexpected advance of the unstopped Pawn.")

24. Kt x Q	B—B5

If *24. . . . .* RP x P, then again P—K6, winning the exchange.

25. Kt—B6	RP x P
26. B—B4	R—Kt3

27. **Kt—Q7** *ch* and won the QBP and, after twenty further moves, the game.

What interests in the above game is above all the rôle which the Kt at B4 has played. As a blockader he was strongly posted and excellently supported (by the B at KR2). Again he had a crippling effect on Black's B at KKt2 and R at KR3, etc. Further, his "threat effect" was considerable, particularly on the points Q5 and K6. (The mobility of White's KP affords a piquant antithesis to the immobility of Black's P at KB4.) And lastly, his elasticity was striking, for he could composedly go on his travels, leaving the Bishop to take his place.

The three following games show the connection between the "pin" and the "center."

16. FOUR KNIGHTS' GAME

San Sebastian, 1911

WHITE	BLACK
A. *Nimzovich*	P. S. *Leonhardt*
1. P—K4	P—K4
2. Kt—KB3	Kt—QB3
3. Kt—B3	Kt—B3
4. B—Kt5	B—Kt5
5. O—O	O—O
6. B x Kt	QP x B
7. P—Q3	. . . .

White has now a solid position, since the enemy Queen file "bites on granite" (the protected P at Q3). This solidity, however, also finds expression in the fact that White's KP can never be troubled by an advance of

Black's QP; in other words, the center cannot be opened.

7.	B—Kt5

The pin.

8. P—KR3	B—KR4
9. B—Kt5	. . . .

9. P—Kt4 would have been premature, because of 9. . . . . Kt x KtP; 10. P x Kt, B x P; followed by . . . . P—KB4.

9.	Q—Q3
10. B x Kt	Q x B
11. P—Kt4	. . . .

The "question" is here indicated, since the Bishop will be driven into a desert, which, because of the impossibility of . . . . P—Q4, can never be transformed into a "flowering garden." (See I. vii. § 3a.) Observe how the KR and KKt Pawns slowly develop into storm troops.

11.	B—Kt3
12. K—Kt2	QR—Q i
13. Q—K2	B x Kt

Else Kt—Q1—K3—B5 would have followed.

14. P x B	P—B4
15. Kt—Q2	. . . .

White now intends to bring his Kt to KB5 via QB4 and K3; on the other hand he proposes to prevent the embarrassing move . . . . P—B5 for as long as possible without the aid of P—QB4, since this move would leave the outpost position in the Queen file (at his Q4) unguarded.

15.	Q—K2
16. Kt—B4	P—Kt3
17. Kt—K3	P—KB3

In order at length to free the Bishop; this move, however, invites P—Kt5 when an opportune moment comes.

18. R—KKt1	Q—Q2
19. K—R2	K—R1
20. R—Kt3	Q—Kt4
21. Q—K1	Q—R5
22. Q—QB1	R—Q2
23. P—R4	B—B2
24. P—QB4	. . . .

Black has succeeded in provoking P—QB4; in the meantime, however, White has got the King's wing beautifully arranged to suit himself.

24.	B—K3
25. Q—Kt2	P—QR4
26. QR—KKt1	Q—B3
27. R(Kt1)—Kt2 ! !	. . . .

White quietly makes his last preparations for a worthy reception of the enemy Queen at her Q5, for which point she is striving. Observe how the first player has succeeded in combining the defense of the center

with his plans for a King-side attack.

| 27. . . . . | Q—Q3 |
| 28. Q—B1 | Q—Q5 ? |

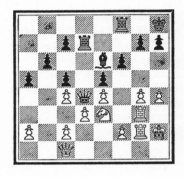

| 29. Kt—Q5 ! | . . . . |

Traps the Queen. This "trap" was everywhere applauded. That it was subordinate to the strategic ends which I had set myself in this game was taken into consideration by no one. The aim of my strategy was, however, to prevent a breakthrough or any maneuvering in the center and to make possible the ultimate advance P—Kt5 with the attack. There followed 29. . . . . R x Kt; 30. P—QB3, Q x QP; 31. KP x R (31. BP x R was more precise), 31. . . . . Q x P(B5); 32. P x B, Q x KP; 33. Q—B2, P—B5; 34. Q—B5, Q x Q; 35. P x Q and *White won.*

The student may see from the laborious and tedious defense

which White adopted (see moves 21, 22, 25, 28) that he fully recognized the fact that the disposition of his King-side Pawns (P at KR3, P at Kt4) demanded a closed center.

This game elucidates the problem of the "Question" in an instructive manner.

17. GIUOCO PIANO

Played by correspondence in 1913.

WHITE	BLACK
A. Nimzovich	*Dr. G. Fluss*
1. P—K4	P—K4
2. Kt—KB3	Kt—QB3
3. Kt—B3	Kt—B3
4. B—B4	B—B4
5. P—Q3	P—Q3
6. B—KKt5	P—KR3
7. B—R4	. . . .

Of course 7. B—K3 is also playable.

7. . . . .   P—KKt4

Here . . . . B—K3 was probably better. *Cf.* I. vii. § 4(d), p. 122, the game Nimzovich—Capablanca.

8. B—KKt3	B—KKt5
9. P—KR4	Kt—KR4
10. P x P	. . . .

As already remarked (I. vii. p. 119). White ought here to have given more attention to the problem of the center. For instance 10. Kt—Q5, Kt—Q5; 11. P—B3 and White's game for choice.

10. . . . .   Kt—Q5

And here Black by 10. . . . . . Kt x B; 11. P x Kt, Kt—Q5; could utilize the center which White has neglected. As we have already said (I. vii. § 4a under Diagram 96) 12. Kt—Q5 would not be sufficient, since Black has the Queen sacrifice at his disposal (namely 12. . . . . . B x Kt; 13. P x B, Q x P; 14. P—KKt4, P—QB3; 15. R—R5, P x Kt, etc.), nor would the sacrificial combination 12. B x P *ch*, K x B; 13. Kt x P *ch*, P x Kt; 14. Q x B be enough, for after 14. . . . . Q x P; 15. Q—Q7 *ch*, K—Kt3; Black would be safe. Hence 10. P x P instead of the central thrust 10. Kt—Q5, which we indicated, would seem to be a decisive mistake, of which Black could take advantage with 10. . . . . Kt x B, followed by 11. . . . . Kt—Q5.

11. B x P !   . . . .

A disconcerting evasion. White gives up his Bishop, but leaves Black with a Knight in the air and his King in much the same state.

11. . . . .   B x Kt

If immediately . . . . P x B then 12. B x P *ch*, K x B; 13. Kt x P *ch*, K—Kt1; 14. Q x B wins.

| 12. | P x B | P x B |
| 13. | R x Kt | R—KKt1 |

On the surface White's position is by no means an enviable one, for the Kt at Q5 exerts pressure and the KKtP seems lost.

| 14. | P—B4 ! | . . . . |

The saving move.

| 14. | . . . . | KP x P |
| 15. | Q—Kt4 | . . . . |

The point. White is not afraid of 15. . . . . Kt x P *ch* etc., which is a mere flash in the pan.

| 15. | . . . . | Kt x P *ch* |
| 16. | K—Q2 | Kt x R |

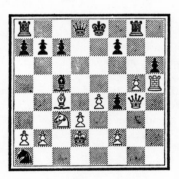

17. B x P *ch !*   **Resigns**

for if 17. . . . . K x B, then 18. Q—B5 *ch*, K—K1; 19. Q—K6 *ch*, K—B1; 20. P—Kt6, and wins; or 19. . . . . Q—K2; 20. Q x R *ch*, Q—B1; 21. Q—R7, Q—K2; 22. P—Kt6, Q x Q; 23. P x Q, B—Q5; 24. Kt—Kt5 ! or 22. . . . . B—Q5; 23. Kt—Kt5 !,

Q—Kt5 *ch;* 24. K—Q1 and wins.

18. INDIAN DEFENSE

Introduces a whole assortment of pins, poisonous and harmless ones following in quick succession.

Marienbad, 1925

WHITE	BLACK
A. Rubinstein	A. Nimzovich
1. P—Q4	Kt—KB3
2. Kt—KB3	P—QKt3
3. P—KKt3	P—B4
4. B—Kt2	B—Kt2
5. P x P	P x P
6. P—B4	. . . .

The line of play chosen by White is certainly not to be blamed. He holds the Q file with the outpost station belonging to it at Q5, whereas Black's majority in the center (the QB, Queen, and King Pawns against the QB and King Pawns) gives evidence of but slight mobility.

6.	. . . .	P—Kt3
7.	P—Kt3	B—Kt2
8.	B—Kt2	O—O
9.	O—O	. . . .

Each side castles now with a clear conscience, for not even the most hypermodern pair of masters can produce more than four Bishops developed "askew"!

| 9. | . . . . | Kt—B3 |

A normal move which, however, has a deeper meaning. The Kt is better placed at QB3 than at QKt3 (. . . . Kt—Q2—Kt3), for White is clearly planning the configuration Kt at QB3, Q at QB2, P at K4. Black therefore relies on the counter configuration Kt at QB3, P at Q3, P at QR4, followed by . . . . Kt—Q5 and (when opportunity comes) . . . . P—R5, thus sheltering his QP behind the Kt at Q5.

10. Kt—B3	P—QR4
11. Q—Q2	P—Q3
12. Kt—K1	. . . .

The start of a tiring journey: Kt—K1—B2—K3—Q5. More natural would seem to be 12. Kt—Q5. For instance, 12. Kt—Q5, Kt x Kt; 13. B x B, K x B; 14. P x Kt.

12.	Q—Q2
13. Kt—B2	Kt—QKt5 !
14. Kt—K3	B x B
15. K x B	. . . .

To retake with the Kt would mean straying off the road to the goal of the journey (Q5).

| 15. . . . . | Q—Kt2 *ch* |
| 16. P—B3 | . . . . |

If 16. K—Kt1, then 16. . . . . Kt—K5; 17. Kt x Kt, Q x Kt; and . . . . P—R5 becomes an actual menace.

| 16. . . . . | B—R3 |

A pin of the harmless order, since obviously this last move implies a serious weakening of his own (Black's) King's wing.

| 17. QKt—Q1 | . . . . |

Now the threat is 18. B x Kt, P x B; 19. Q x P.

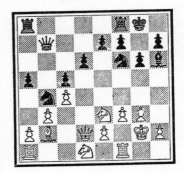

| 17. . . . . | P—R5 |

See the note to 9 . . . . . Kt—B3.

| 18. P x P | KR—K1 *! !* |

This purely defensive move (against the aforesaid threat B x Kt etc.) is the more surprising, since, after the energetic thrust at move 17, which had been so eagerly looked forward to for so long, anything but a defensive move was to be expected. This amalgamation of attack and defense stamps the combination as a truly original one.

| 19. B x Kt | P x B |

20. K—B2   . . . .

Now White plans to break the pin by P—B4, after which he would at last be in a position to take possession of the point Q5 for good and all.

20. . . . .   P—B4 *! !*

Revealing his subtle plan. Against the double threat of 21. . . . . P—B5; 22. P x P, B x P, with an enduring pin on the one hand, and 21. . . . . B—Kt2, followed by . . . . B—Q5 with an equally chronic pin on. the other, White is defenseless.

21. Q x P   B—Kt2 *!*
22. R—QKt1   B—Q5

Threatening . . . . Kt—Q6 *ch.*

23. K—Kt2   . . . .

The poor Knights! At the 17th move they had to break their journey, and now they actually both have to die without reaching their journey's end.

In reply to 23. R—Kt3, Black, with 23. . . . . R—K3; 24. Q—B4, Q—K2 (threatening Kt—B7); 25. K—Kt2, QR—K1, would have pushed forward the siege in the most energetic way.

23. . . . .   B x Kt
24. Kt x B   R x Kt
25. Q x P   . . . .

Now it is White's turn to pin.

25. . . . .   R x P *ch*

26. R—B2   R x R *ch*
27. Q x R   . . . .

Forced, for 27. K x R, Kt—Q6 *ch;* followed by . . . . Kt x Q, thus protecting his own Queen at Kt2, would lose at once.

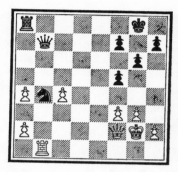

27. . . . .   R x P *!*

The "immediate unpinning" by . . . . Q—K2 is avoided, for White can get no profit out of the pin.

28. P—QR3   . . . .

If 28. Q—Kt2, then 28. . . . . Q—B1 *!;* for this is the only feasible retreat for the piece behind the pinned one. That 28. . . . . R x P *? ?* would be a gross mistake (because of 29. Q x R, Kt x Q; 30. R x Q) is obvious.

28. . . . .   R x P
29. Q—K2   R—R1

Now he goes back home, tired but happy.

30. P—B5	Q—R3

Unpinning.

31. Q x Q	Kt x Q
32. R—QR1	. . . .

A last pin.

32.	Kt—B2

A last unpinning.

33. R x R *ch*	Kt x R

And White *resigned* on the 38th move.

There follow six games illustrating the Pawn-chain.

19. FRENCH DEFENSE

Nuremberg, 1888

Illustrates the fight against a Pawn-chain (siege).

WHITE	BLACK
L. Paulsen	*Dr. S. Tarrasch*
1. P—K4	P—K3
2. P—Q4	P—Q4
3. P—K5	P—QB4
4. P—QB3	Kt—QB3
5. Kt—B3	Q—Kt3
6. B—Q3	. . . .

More natural would have been B—K2, for the P at Q4 is the "base," and as such should be protected as thoroughly as possible. B—K2 "protects" more thoroughly than B—Q3.

6.	P x P
7. P x P	B—Q2
8. B—K2	KKt—K2

9. P—QKt3	Kt—B4
10. B—Kt2	B—Kt5 *ch*
11. K—B1	. . . .

Forced (see I. ix. § 5a, Diagram 118, p. 147).

11.	B—K2

In order to keep up the pressure on the QP (*12*. P—KKt4, Kt—R5); but as shown in Diagram 120 Black should have played to take direct advantage of White's spoiled King's wing, by *11*. . . . . O—O *!*, etc.

12. P—Kt3	P—QR4 ?

In order to exploit the new "weakness" White's P at QKt3. The only pity is that this point is no weakness; he should have gone for the weak King's position.

13. P—QR4	R—QB1
14. B—Kt5	. . . .

The point QKt5 now becomes a good pivot for White's pieces.

14.	Kt—Kt5

15. B x B *ch* ?   . . . .

Quite wrong. With *15.* Kt—B3 (see the next game) White could have overcome all difficulties. For instance:—*15.* Kt—B3, B x B *ch;* *16.* Kt x B, Kt—B7; *17.* R—B1, KKt—K6 *ch;* *18.* P x Kt, Kt x P *ch;* *19.* K—K2, Kt x Q; *20.* R x R *ch,* K—Q2, *21.* R x R, Kt x B; *22.* R—QB1 and wins.

15.	K x B
16. Kt—B3	Kt—B3
17. Kt—QKt5	Kt—R2
18. Kt x Kt ?	. . . .

Never in this life ought White to have relinquished his QKt5; *18.* Q—Q3, Kt x Kt; *19.* P x Kt would have after all sufficed. We can see what harm Black's QRP has done him.

| *18.* . . . . | Q x Kt |
| *19.* Q—Q3 | Q—R3 ! |

Now we shall see how a weakened "base" becomes a weakness in the end game.

20. Q x Q	P x Q
21. K—Kt2	R—B7
22. B—B1	R—QKt1
23. R—QKt1	R—B6
24. B—Q2	R(B) x P
25. R x R	R x R
26. B x P	. . . .

Now White is happily rid of his weakness at QKt3 (in an open file!), but his Q4 and QR4 are hard to defend.

| *26.* . . . . | R—Kt7 |

Not . . . . R—R6 because of R—QB1, but now the answer to R—QB1 would be . . . . Kt —K6 *ch,* followed by . . . . Kt—B5.

| *27.* B—Q2 | B—Kt5 |
| *28.* B—B4 | P—R3 |

There's no harm in this; Black's position can stand this little weakening (the KRP is now a possible objective).

29. P—Kt4	Kt—K2
30. R—R1	Kt—B3
31. B—B1	R—B7
32. B—R3	R—B5

32. . . . . B x B would have been simpler.

33. B—Kt2	B—B6
34. B x B	R x B
35. R—QKt1	K—B2
36. P—Kt5	R—B5

At last!

37. P x P	P x P
38. P—R5	R—R5
39. K—Kt3	. . . .

A last despairing attempt to continue the attack begun by P—Kt5.

| *39.* . . . . | R x RP |

And *Black won:* *40.* K—Kt4, R—R6; *41.* R—Q1, R—Kt6; *42.* P—

R4, Kt—K2; *43.* Kt—K1, Kt—B4; *44.* Kt—Q3, P—R4; *45.* Kt—B5, R—QB6; *46.* R—QKt1, Kt x QP; *47.* Kt—R6 *ch,* K—Q1; *48.* R—Kt8 *ch,* R—B1; *49.* R—Kt7, K—K1; *50.* Kt—B7 *ch,* K—B1; *51.* Kt—Kt5, Kt x Kt; *52.* R x Kt, R—R1, etc. We advise the reader to study this well played ending by Dr. Tarrasch.

20. FRENCH DEFENSE

San Sebastian, 1912

WHITE   BLACK
A. Nimzovich   Dr. S. Tarrasch

The first 14 moves (with transposition) are as in Game No. 19.

15. Kt—B3 *!*   Kt—QR3

For *15.* .... B x B; *16.* Kt x B, Kt—B7; see note to move 15 in the last game.

16. K—Kt2	Kt—B2
17. B—K2	B—Kt5
18. Kt—R2	Kt—QR3
19. B—Q3	Kt—K2
20. R—QB1	Kt—B3
21. Kt x B	Kt(R3) x Kt
22. B—Kt1	....

White has now overcome the difficulties of development, the base (Q4) is thoroughly protected; and so the game can now take another turning. White opens an attack against the Black King's wing which is cramped by the P at K5.

22.	P—R3
23. P—Kt4	....

To make castling appear unhealthy; but R—-B3—K3 was also good, perhaps even better.

23.	Kt—K2
24. R x R *ch*	B x R
25. Kt—K1	R—B1
26. Kt—Q3	P—B3
27. Kt x Kt	Q x Kt
28. P x P	R x P

29. B—B1	....

The courage required deliberately to let oneself be kept under pressure for hours, simply for the sake of a remote chance of attack, now has its reward. White gets a direct attack. Note the Bishop which has been roused to activity.

29.	Kt—B3
30. P—Kt5	P x P
31. B x P	R—B1
32. B—K3	Q—K2
33. Q—Kt4	Q—B3

34.	R—Kt1	R—R1
35.	K—R1	R—R5
36.	Q—Kt3	R x P

Despair! B—Kt5 was threatened as also Q x P.

37.	B x R	Kt x B
38.	Q x P	Q—B6 *ch*
39.	Q—Kt2	Q x Q *ch*
40.	R x Q	Kt x P
41.	P—R4	Resigns

Burn remarks on this game: "An excellent game on the part of Herr Nimzovich, well illustrating his strategic skill. Dr. Tarrasch, himself one of the greatest masters of strategy, is completely outplayed." Flattering as this praise is I must, nevertheless, remark that it is probably not so very difficult to maneuver well if one has a complete system to fall back upon. P—K5, as I even then knew, seriously cramps Black's King's wing, and if White succeeds in holding his Q4 without any counterbalancing disadvantage elsewhere, a moment must sometime come when fortune will smile on him; in the form, that is, of an attack with his pieces on the Black King in his cramped position, or else a vigorous onslaught on the chain by P—KB4 —B5 x KP, etc. To-day all this rings plausible; at the time this game was played it seemed nothing short of revolutionary.

21. FRENCH DEFENSE

The following game illustrates my idea of the two theaters of war in a particularly striking manner.

Breslau, 1925

WHITE	BLACK
A. Becker	A. Nimzovich
1. P—K4	P—K3
2. P—Q4	P—Q4
3. Kt—QB3	Kt—QB3

The "odds-giving style" to use Dr. Lasker's expression. Lasker means by this that one chooses a variation which one considers inferior, with the idea of setting the opponent a difficult problem to solve. Lasker plays this style by preference—and with inimitable virtuosity. It is this that might make people believe that the heel of Achilles lay for Lasker in his treatment of the opening. But such a judgment rests on an entire misconception.

The move 3. . . . . Kt—QB3 was introduced by Alapin. It obstructs the QBP, however, and therefore in the event of P—K5 there is a very dark side to Alapin's innovation.

4. Kt—B3	B—Kt5
5. P—K5	B x Kt *ch*
6. P x B	Kt—R4
7. P—QR4	. . . .

Not very intelligible. Better

was 7. Kt—Q2, Kt—K2; 8. Q—
Kt4, Black would then have had
to defend laboriously by 8.
. . . . Kt—B4; 9. B—Q3, R—
KKt1; 10. Q—R3, P—KR3.

| 7. . . . . | Kt—K2 |
| 8. B—Q3 | P—QKt3 |

Preparing to attack the White
Base (Q4) by . . . . P—QB4.

| 9. Kt—Q2 ! | P—QB4 |
| 10. Q—Kt4 | . . . . |

How is Black to defend his
KKtP?

| 10. . . . . | P—B5 |

The answer is: not at all; for
all direct defenses would here be
compromising.

| 11. B—K2 | . . . . |

If 11. Q x KtP then . . . . KR
—Kt1 and . . . . P x B.

| 11. . . . . | Kt—B4 |

The KKtP is protected, but
the pressure on White's Q4 is
removed and White now again
gets a free hand to make play on
the right wing.

| 12. Kt—B3 | P—KR3 |

In order to be able to maintain the Kt at B4. The threat was
13. B—Kt5, Q moves; 14. Kt—
R4. Lasker prefers, and rightly,
the elastic defense 12. . . . . . Kt
—B3 and if 13. B—Kt5, then
13. . . . . P—B3. An interest-

ing possibility would be 12. . . . .
Kt—B3; 13. P—R5 ! P, Kt x RP;
14. B—Kt5, P—B3; 15. P x P,
P x P; 16. B—R4, for now 16.
. . . . Kt x B would fail against
17. Q—Kt7 !; on the other hand
16. . . . . Q—K2 would seem
to consolidate the position sufficiently.

| 13. Q—R3 | . . . . |

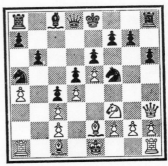

*How can Black counter the fol-
lowing elegant threat to break
through?—i.e., the threat 14.
P—Kt4, Kt—K2; 15. P—Kt5,
P—R4; 16. P—Kt6, Kt x P;
17. Kt—Kt5, followed by R—
KKt1.*

| 13. . . . . | K—Q2 ! |

My King likes going for walks.

| 14. P—Kt4 | Kt—K2 |
| 15. Kt—Q2 | . . . . |

Threatening Q—B3 followed
by Q x BP or Kt x P !

| 15. . . . . | Q—K1 |

The Queen takes possession
of the throne, which the King
has vacated!

Moreover, she has her eye on
the QRP for which she seems to
have a fancy.

16. **P—B4**   . . . .

The scene shifts! The old
theater of war vanishes as in a
flash, and new plans of attack
appear. White intends to attack
the base of the chain by P—B5.

16. . . . .   **K—B2**

The King proceeds on his
walk.

17. **B—R3**   **B—Q2**
18. **Q—B3**   **P—R4** *!*

White's King's wing provides
him with a terrible instrument of
attack. To blunt this was the
object of Black's last move. *18.*
. . . . B—B3, to counter the
other threat (Kt x P) would,
however, not have sufficed. E.g.,
18. . . . . B—B3; *19.* P—B5,
followed by P—B6, and the
wedge would have been unen-
durable.

19. **Kt x P** *!*   . . . .

If *19.* P x P then Kt—B4, and
the King's wing, which had been
all ready to march to the attack,
is crippled. But if *19.* P—R3,
then *19.* . . . . P x P; *20.* P x P,
R x R *ch*; *21.* Q x R, Q—R1,
and White finds all his attention
occupied.

19. . . . .   **Kt x Kt**
20. **B x Kt**   **P x P**

Naturally not . . . . *20.* P x
B *? ?* because of *21.* B—Q6 *ch*
and *22.* Q x R *ch*.

21. **Q—Kt2**   **Kt—B4**
22. **B—Q3**   . . . .

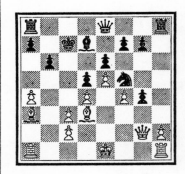

22. . . . .   **B x P** *! !*

A lunch under dangerous conditions!

23. **B x Kt**   **P x B**
24. **Q x QP**   . . . .

24. P—B4 would also have
been difficult to parry. The defense would be found in *24.*
. . . . Q—B3; *25.* Q x QP (but
not *25.* P x P, Q—B6 *ch*), Q x
Q *!*; *26.* P x Q, B—Kt4 *! !*; for
then the establishment of the
Bishop at Q4 (via B5) could not
have been prevented.

24. . . . .   **B—B3**

Black's King's position is

threatened on all sides, but the situation is not hopeless.

| 25. | Q—Q6 *ch* | K—B1 |

Having regard to the planned combination; but 25. . . . . . K—Kt2; 26. P—Q5, B—Kt4 was also possible.

| 26. | P—Q5 | R—R3 |
| 27. | P—K6 | . . . . |

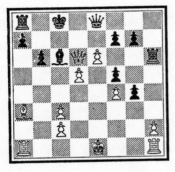

| 27. | . . . . | B x P *!* |

This was afterwards pronounced the "only move." Black had, however, another one, namely 27. . . . . . R x P *ch;* 28. P x R, B x R; 29. O—O—O, B—B6 *!* (not . . . . B—K5; 30. P—K7 and then 31. Q—K5 and the White Queen has now new squares for decisive operations); 30. P x P, Q x P; 31. Q—Q8 *ch,* K—Kt2; 32. R—Q7 *ch,* K—R3, and Black is safe.

| 28. | Q x B | Q x P *ch* |
| 29. | Q x Q *ch* | R x Q *ch* |

White now has a piece for two Pawns, but his own Pawns are weak.

30.	K—Q2	K—Kt2
31.	QR—K1	R—R1
32.	R x R *!*	P x R
33.	R—K1 *!*	R x P *ch*
34.	K—Q3	P—Kt6

Anything but a passive Rook position (. . . . R—R3 *?*).

| 35. | R—KKt1 | . . . . |

After 35. R x P, P—KKt4 *!;* 36. P x P, P—Kt7; White's P at KKt5 would prove an obstruction.

| 35. | . . . . | R—R6 |

Much better than . . . . P—Kt7 for, as will shortly appear, it is important to have a clear road to QB7.

36.	K—Q4	K—B3
37.	R—Kt2	P—R4
38.	P—B4	R—R7 *!*
39.	R x P	R x P

Cf. the last note.

40.	R x P	R—K7
41.	B—B1	R—K5 *ch*
42.	K—Q3	P—Kt4
43.	P x P *ch*	K x P
44.	B—K3	K—B3
45.	R—B7	P—R5
46.	R—B8	P—R6
47.	R—QR8	P—K4
48.	R—R6 *ch*	K—Kt4
49.	R—Kt6 *ch*	. . . .

Prof. Becker is absolutely bent on winning, and so it comes about that in the end he loses. The game continued 49. . . . . **K—R4; 50. R—KB6, P—R7; 51. B—Q2** *ch,* **K—Kt4; 52. B—B3, R—Q5** *ch.* After six hours of hard fighting to get such a problem check is hardly pleasurable! **53. K—K2 ?** (Right was 53. K—B2, R—B5; 54. K—Kt2, R x B; 55. R x P), **R x P; 54. R—B8, K—B5; 55. B—R1, R—K5** *ch; 56.* **K—Q2, P —B5.** Now White may be said to be lost. 57. **R—B8** *ch,* **K—Q4; 58. R—Q8** *ch,* **K—K3; 59. R—K8** *ch,* **K—B4; 60. R—KKt8, P—B6; 61. Resigns.**

The following game shows how an advance on the wrong wing should be punished.

22. NIMZOINDIAN DEFENSE

Marienbad, 1925

WHITE	BLACK
C. *Opocensky*	A. *Nimzovich*
1. P—Q4	Kt—KB3
2. P—QB4	P—K3
3. Kt—QB3	B—Kt5
4. Q—B2	P—QKt3
5. P—K4	B—Kt2

The expansive power of White's center Pawns is less than might at first sight appear.

6. B—Q3	Kt—B3
7. Kt—B3	B—K2 !

By this unexpected retreat. which threatens . . . . Kt— QKt5, Black manages to muzzle White's mass of Pawns in the center while still keeping his valuable KB.

8. P—QR3	P—Q3
9. O—O	P—K4
10. P—Q5	. . . .

Now the center is stabilized.

10.	Kt—QKt1
11. P—QKt4	QKt—Q2

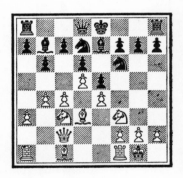

12. B—Kt2	. . . .

The Pawn-chain P at K4, P at Q5; P at K4, P at Q3; called for the play P—B5, of course after due preparation. For of the two theaters of war resulting from P—Q5 (see our remarks in I. ix. § 1) only one is available, namely attack on Black's base, the P at Q3. The other theoretically possible plan, *i.e.,* an advance with pieces against the wing cramped by P—Q5, must be regarded as nipped in the bud by the presence of an obstruction at QB4.

The only plan of campaign feasible here (P—B5) could, however, have been prepared for by 12. P—R3, followed by 13. B—K3. For instance 12. P—R3, P—KR3 ! (the best chance); 13. B—K3, P—KKt4; 14. Kt—KR2. Black will try to attack White's King's wing, but White's attack (Kt—QR4, P—B5) is quickly put in motion, while his castled position is defendable. Hence 12. P—R3 and 13. B—K3 was the right continuation.

| 12. . . . . | O—O |
| 13. Kt—K2 | . . . . |

White's pieces desert the Queen's wing in order to demonstrate on the other. By this movement, however, the effect of his own center is weakened. For with the Kt still at QB3, ... P—B3 could be answered by P x P, while this Kt, too, casts a threatening eye on the point Q5 as an outpost station. If, however, the Kt at QB3 is gone on a journey, the thrust . . . . P—B3 gains in effect. True, this thrust is not a present threat, for on the Queen's wing Black is the weaker; however in the end he will come to it.

The way in which the theater disdained by White is made a base of operations by his opponent makes the game of fundamental interest to the student.

| 13. . . . . | Kt—R4 |
| 14. Q—Q2 | . . . . |

The answer to P—Kt4 would have been . . . . Kt—B3. Black *wants* to be attacked on the King-side, since he regards that theater as unavailable. See note to move 12.

14.	P—Kt3
15. P—Kt4	Kt—Kt2
16. Kt—Kt3	P—QB3 !

What sense can there be in this move? If in the end . . . . P x P is played, then the answer BP x P would attain nothing other than the exposure of his own base Q3. Black then in this case would have worked for his opponent, for (let us suppose Black's Pawn still at QB2) the strategic advance indicated for White, namely P—QB5 x QP, leads, after . . . . P x P, to exactly the same Pawn configuration, and that the one which is the object of White's efforts!

This calculation contains, however, two logical errors. Firstly White in advancing P—B5 will certainly not content himself with P x QP; this is only one threat. The insertion of a wedge (in other words the transference of the attack by P—B6) would be by long odds the sharper threat. Secondly, White by B—Kt2, Kt—K2—Kt3, etc., has been untrue to his Queen's wing; the just punishment will lie in Black's becoming strong there!

| 17. | Q—R6 | R—B1 |
| 18. | QR—B1 | . . . . |

18. . . . .   P—R3 *!!*

A very difficult move. The answer to 18. . . . . P x P could be 19. KP x P, and Black, it is true, would get two powerful Pawns by 19. . . . . P—B4; 20. P x P, P x P; but after 21. K—R1, and 22. R—KKt1, Black would stand badly; the mobility of his KP and KBP would in fact prove to be illusory, whereas White's King's side attack would be a very real one. Black intends to play . . . . P x P at a moment when KP x P is not feasible.

19.	KR—Q1	R—B2
20.	P—KR4 ?	P x P
21.	BP x P	. . . .

Since P—KR4 has still further weakened White's position (the point KKt4), 20. . . . . P x P seems to be in place. The answer to 21. KP x P would be . . . . Kt—B3 as in the game; moreover, the threat to break through by . . . . P—QKt4 would be in the air.

21.	. . . .	R x R
22.	R x R	Kt—B3
23.	Kt—R2	K—R1

The White Queen goes in danger of her life. For instance 24. P—B4 ?, Kt—Kt1. If White had played 23. Kt—Kt5 then 23. . . . . Q—Q2; 24. P—B3, R—B1, and the Bishop threatens danger to her at KB1.

24.	Q—K3	Kt—Q2
25.	Kt—B3	Kt—B3
26.	Kt—R2	Kt—Kt1
27.	P—KKt5	P—B3
28.	Kt—B3	P x P
29.	P x P	B—B1
30.	R—B6	. . . .

A clever resource, which is extraordinarily difficult to parry. Observe, too, that in the position now arrived at it looks for all the world as if White had all the time exclusively operated on the Queen's wing (by P—B4—B5 x

QP, on which . . . . P x P had followed), whereas Black had sought salvation by a counter-attack directed against the base of the Pawn-chain, White's P at K4.

| 30. . . . . | B—Q2 |
| 31. B x RP | . . . . |

31. R x KtP would have been answered by 31. . . . . R x Kt. The sacrifice of the exchange is very promising.

31.	B x R
32. P x B	Q—B2
33. P—Kt5	. . . .

| 33. . . . . | P—R3 *!* |

This Pawn sacrifice yields Black freedom to maneuver; without this, sacrifices at Q6 or K5 would have been possible for White. Take, for instance, the following variation: 33. . . . . Kt—K3 (instead of the text move); 34. P—R4, B—Q1; 35. B—R3, Q—B2; 36. B x P *!*, Q x

Kt; 37. B x P *ch*, Kt—Kt2; 38. Q x Q followed by 39. P—B7.

34. P x P	Kt—K3
35. P—R4	B—Q1
36. B—R3	Q—B2

For now 37. B x P, Q x Kt; 38. B x P *ch* would be answered simply by . . . . K—R2.

37. Kt x P	P x Kt
38. B x R	Q x B
39. P—R5	Kt x P

Black has his 33rd move to thank for the possibility also of the Knight's intervention.

40. P x P	Kt—Kt5
41. P—B7	Kt x Q
42. P—B8 (Q)	Q—B6 *!*
43. P x Kt	Q x Kt *ch*

44. Resigns for Black will take the KP with a check and then the KtP.

23. ENGLISH OPENING

Carlsbad, 1911

WHITE	BLACK
A. *Rubinstein*	O. *Duras*
1. P—QB4	P—K4
2. Kt—QB3	Kt—KB3
3. P—KKt3	B—Kt5
4. B—Kt2	O—O
5. Kt—B3	R—K1
6. O—O	Kt—B3

The exchange . . . . B x Kt. was to be considered.

7.	Kt—Q5	B—B1
8.	P—Q3	P—KR3
9.	P—Kt3	P—Q3
10.	B—Kt2	Kt x Kt
11.	P x Kt	Kt—K2
12.	P—K4	P—QB4

In the long run something must be done for the QBP.

13.	P x P e.p.	Kt x P
14.	P—Q4	B—Kt5
15.	P—Q5	Kt—K2

We have now got our Pawn chain, and the Black base, the P at Q3, already seems exposed (from the side), just as if the typical attack had been made on it by P—B4—B5 x QP, BP x P.

| 16. | Q—Q3 | Q—Q2 |
| 17. | Kt—Q2 | . . . . |

The Kt is already being sent forward to the attack on the exposed base.

| 17. | . . . . | B—R6 |
| 18. | P—R4 | . . . . |

To safeguard the Kt position at QB4.

18.	. . . .	B x B
19.	K x B	KR—Kt1
20.	Kt—B4	P—QKt4
21.	P x P	Q x P
22.	R—R3	. . . .

In this and similar positions the question arises, which Pawn

is the weaker, White's QKtP or Black's QRP? In the present case this problem could be solved by logical deduction. Since Black's P at Q3 is weaker than White's P at Q5, a like relation must exist throughout what remains of the Queen's wing. Were this not the case then White's P—QR4 must have been wrong, and that is unlikely. Was he in fact not justified in supporting his own important Kt at QB4? But that would be absurd. No, Kt—B4 was indicated, similarly P—QR4; hence . . . . P—QKt4 must have led to a less favorable position for Black. And the course of the game proves the correctness of this judgment.

| 22. | . . . . | Kt—Kt3 |

. . . . Kt—B1 would perhaps have been better.

23.	KR—QR1	P—R3
24.	B—B1	R—Kt2
25.	B—K3	P—B3

26. P—B3 . . . .

If Black could manage to play . . . . P—B4, his position would not be so bad. But this is out of the question, and Black is besieged.

26. . . . .   Kt—K2
27. Q—B1   . . . .

Threatening Kt x QP.

27. . . . .   Kt—B1
28. Kt—Q2   Q—Kt5
29. Q—B4   Q x Q
30. Kt x Q   R(R)—Kt1
31. Kt—Q2   R—QB2
32. R x P   . . . .

The masterly and varied uses made of the points Q2 and QB4 should be noted.

32. . . . .   R—B7
33. R(R6)—R2   R x R
34. R x R   . . . .

The rest of the game, which consists of bringing the King to the center followed by an advance in close order of the fighting unit Bishop, Kt and King is easily intelligible. There followed 34. . . . . **B—K2; 35. K—B2, K—B2; 36. K—K2, K—K1; 37. K—Q3, K—Q2; 38. K—B3, B—Q1; 39. Kt—B4** (QB3 is our shelter), **B—B2; 40. P—KKt4, B—Q1; 41. R—R6, B—B2; 42. P—R4, B—Q1; 43. P—R5, B—B2; 44. P—Kt4, R—Kt2; 45. R—R8, K—Q1; 46. K—Kt3, R—Kt1; 47. R x R, B x R; 48. P—**

QKt5, Kt—K2; 49. P—Kt6, P—B4 (there is nothing left to hope for); **50. KtP x P, Kt—Kt1; 51. B—B2, Kt—B3; 52. B—R4, Resigns.**

In the following game the transference of the attack from one point to another is carried out in classic style.

24. QUEEN'S GAMBIT DECLINED

Barmen, 1905

WHITE	BLACK
G. *Maroczy*	H. *Suechting*
1. P—Q4	P—Q4
2. P—QB4	P—K3
3. Kt—QB3	Kt—KB3
4. B—Kt5	QKt—Q2
5. P—K3	B—K2
6. Kt—B3	O—O
7. Q—B2	P—B3
8. P—QR3	Kt—R4

Hardly in place; better was . . . . R—K1 or . . . . P—KR3.

9. P—KR4   P—KB4

. . . . P—B3 would be answered by B—Q3 !

10. B—K2   QKt—B3
11. Kt—K5 !   B—Q2
12. Q—Q1   B—K1
13. P—B5   . . . .

Weaving the chain.

13. . . . .   Q—B2

| 14. P—QKt4 | P—R4 |
| 15. P—Kt3 ! | . . . . |

No one knows better than Maroczy how to prevent freeing moves (here . . . . P—B5).

15.	P x P
16. P x P	R x R
17. Q x R	Kt—K5
18. P—Kt4 !	Kt x Kt
19. Q x Kt	Kt—B3
20. B—KB4 !	. . . .

Threatens Kt—Kt6 and thus gains time for P—KKt5.

20.	Q—B1
21. P—KKt5	Kt—Q2
22. Kt—Q3 !	. . . .

To exchange would make it more difficult to break through.

22.	B—B2
23. K—Q2	B—Q1
24. R—R1	. . . .

Only now does play begin in the real theater. The idea is naturally attack on the base (P at QB3) by P—Kt5.

24.	B—B2
25. R—R7	R—K1
26. B x B	Q x B
27. P—B4	. . . .

Stops all attempts to break through by . . . . P—K4.

| 27. . . . . | R—Kt1 |
| 28. P—Kt5 | . . . . |

At last!

| 28. . . . . | Q—B1 |

Or 28. . . . . . P x P; 29. Kt—Kt4, etc.

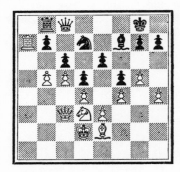

29. P—QKt6 !   . . . .

With this White transfers the attack to the new base, the P at QKt2. Play against the base P at QB3 could have been pursued by 29. Kt—Kt4 followed by, say, Q—R3—R4; but the transference of the attack to Black's QKt2 is still stronger, and above all safer. Suechting is now helpless.

29.	B—K1
30. Kt—B1	Kt—B1
31. Kt—Kt3	P—K4 !

The only way of saving the QKtP, otherwise there would have come 32. Kt—R5, 33. Kt x KtP and if 33. . . . . R x Kt 34. B—R6.

32. QP x P	Kt—K3
33. B—Q3 !	P—Kt3
34. P—R5	B—B2

35. Kt—R5   Kt—Q1
36. P—K6 !   . . . .

Our sacrificing advance of the unblockaded passed Pawn. The pieces to the rear come to life. (See I. iv. § 2a.)

36. . . . .   Q x P
37. P—R6   P—Q5
38. Q x P   Q—R7 *ch*

and White won: 39. **K—K1, Kt—K3**; 40. **Q—K5, R—K1**; *41.* **Kt x KtP, Q—Kt6**; 42. **B—K2, Q—Kt8** *ch;* 43. **K—B2, Q—KR8**; 44. **Kt—Q6, Q—R5** *ch;* 45. **K—Kt2, Kt x P** *ch;* 46. **Q x Kt, B—Q4** *ch;* 47. **B—B3, B x B** *ch;* 48. **K x B, Resigns.**

25. NIMZOVICH ATTACK

Illustrates the idea of collective mobility, and touches also on the problem of prophylactic.

Semmering, 1926

WHITE   BLACK
A. *Nimzovich* Dr. W. *Michel*

1. Kt—KB3   P—Q4
2. P—QKt3   Kt—KB3
3. B—Kt2   P—B4
4. P—K3   P—K3

A new idea. Black avoids developing the Kt at QB3, since it might be pinned by B—Kt5.

5. Kt—K5   QKt—Q2
6. B—Kt5   P—QR3 ?

. . . . B—Q3 was much better here than the text move,

firstly with regard to his development, and secondly because White threatens to make strong use of the diagonal QKt2 to KKt7, taking advantage of it to support his outpost at K5. A prophylactic measure was urgently needed. For instance 6. . . . . B—Q3 *!*; 7. Kt x Kt, B x Kt; 8. B x B *ch*, Q x B; 9. B x Kt, P x B; and the doubled Pawn has both its dark and its bright side. (See II. ii.) Further we consider 6. . . . . B—K2 also better than the text move (. . . . P—QR3).

7. B x Kt *ch*   Kt x B
8. Kt x Kt   B x Kt
9. O—O   P—B3

An admission of weakness in the long diagonal. There came under consideration also 9. . . . . B—Q3; 10. Q—Kt4, Q—B2, followed by . . . . O—O.

10. P—QB4   P x P

The threat was 11. P x P, P x P; 12. Q—R5 *ch*, followed by Q x QP.

11. P x P   B—Q3
12. Q—R5 *ch*   P—Kt3
13. Q—R6   B—KB1
14. Q—R3 *! !*   . . . .

The best place for the Queen and one difficult to find. . . . . P—K4 would now only surrender the point Q4 to White. For instance *14*. . . . . P—K4; *15*. Q—Kt3 (threatening B x P), B—Kt2; *16*. P—K4, followed by P—Q3 and Kt—B3—Q5 with advantage in position for White.

14.	B—K2
15. Kt—B3	O—O
16. P—R4 *!*	. . . .

White plans the configuration P at K4, P at KB4, etc., which would leave his QP backward. As he thus sacrifices the effective power of his QP, he must necessarily first paralyze the three Black Queen-side Pawns. Hence the text move.

16.	B—Q3
17. P—B4	Q—K2
18. P—K4	B—B3
19. P—Kt4	. . . .

A "Pawn roller" which can hardly be rendered innocuous.

| *19*. . . . . | P—B4 |

If Black does nothing, White has the choice between a direct attack on the one hand and play against the QBP on the other. The latter could be carried out in some such way as say *19*. . . . . QR—K1; *20*. Q—K3 and then P—R5 and B—R3, finally driving away the defending B at Q3 by P—K5. After the text move a mating attack wins the game straight off.

| *20*. KtP x P | KP x P |

Or . . . . KtP x P; *21*. K—B2, etc.

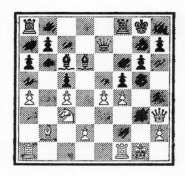

| *21*. P—K5 | . . . . |

The following variation may be dedicated to those who love combinative complications. *21*. Kt—Q5 (instead of P—K5), Q x P; *22*. QR—K1, Q x QBP; *23*. Kt—K7 *ch*, B x Kt; *24*. R x B, R—B2; *25*. R x R, Q x R; *26*. Q—QB3, K—B1 *!*; and Black, it would appear, has a sufficient defense.

| *21*. . . . . | B—B2 |
| *22*. Kt—Q5 | B x Kt |

If on his 21st move Black had played his Bishop back to Kt1, he would now have been able to answer the entry of the Kt by . . . . Q—K3; but this would have availed nothing. For example: *21*. . . . . B—Kt1; *22*. Kt—Q5, Q—K3; *23*. Kt—B6 *ch*, R x Kt; *24*. P x R, Q—K5 (his one chance); 25. P—B7 *ch*, and White wins by 25. . . . . K x P; 26. Q x RP *ch*, K—B1; 27. Q—Kt7 *ch*, K—K1; 28. QR—K1, etc.

| 23. P x B | Q—Q2 |
| 24. P—K6 ! | Resigns |

For if 24. . . . . Q x QP; 25. Q—R6 forces mate, or the loss of a Rook, and if 24. . . . . Q—K2, the fatal Queen plays to her QB3 and there is no answer.

The following game shows how easily the early surrender of the center can lead to disaster. Nevertheless, this procedure seems to us to be in itself quite practicable, provided we bring to bear on the problem all the tenacity which we possess, and do not allow ourselves to be forced down an inclined plane.

If we do this our prospects for the future are good. As examples we may point to Rubinstein's games of this kind which he won at St. Sebastian in 1911, and further to Game No. 28 in this book. We now proceed to

26. FRENCH DEFENSE

Berlin, 1916

WHITE	BLACK
Dr. S. Tarrasch	*J. Mieses*
1. P—K4	P—K3
2. P—Q4	P—Q4
3. Kt—QB3	P x P

Gives up the center, but opens the Queen file and the long diagonal QKt2 to KR8 for pressure on White's center.

4. Kt x P	Kt—Q2
5. Kt—KB3	KKt—B3
6. B—Q3	Kt x Kt

Better would be . . . . P—QKt3, but the text move is playable.

| 7. B x Kt | Kt—B3 |
| 8. B—Q3 | . . . . |

If 8. B—Kt5, B—K2; 9. B x Kt, then best 9. . . . . . P x B.

8.	P—QKt3
9. B—Kt5	B—Kt2
10. O—O	B—K2
11. Q—K2	O—O

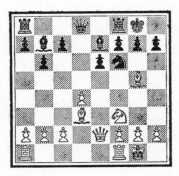

| 12. QR—Q1 | P—KR3 ? |

The tenacity of purpose so necessary to tournament play fails him here. Why not . . . . Q—Q4? If then 13. P—B4, Q—R4 followed presently by . . . . QR—Q1; and the pressure is already sensible. If, however, *13.* P—B4, Q—R4; *14.* P—Q5, then *14.* . . . . QR—K1 *!*, with strong counter-threats. For instance *15.* P x P *?*, B x Kt; followed by . . . . Q x B. Why the mere contact with the point Q4 must bring a blessing is evident. This point in the first place is the outpost station in the Queen file, and in the second the same thing in the diagonal QKt2 to KR8, while lastly, Q4 is a blockading point. The enormous strategical importance to Black of the point Q4 makes it clear that any, even the most passing, contact with it must work wonders.

13. **B—KB4**   **Q—Q4**

Now this move is unfavorable, since the QBP is in the air. The inclined plane makes its appearance.

14. **P—B4**   **Q—QR4**
15. **B x BP**   **B x Kt**

15. . . . . QR—B1 was to be considered here, and after *16.* B—K5, KR—Q1, the advance of White's Pawn majority is very much hindered.

16. **P x B** *!*   **Q x P** *?*

Black will not resign himself to the loss of a Pawn, runs risks in seeking compensation, and thus loses the Queen.

With *16.* . . . . KR—B1; *17.* B—K5, Kt—Q2 *!* (with a view

to the threatened K—R1 and R—KKt1), he could still have put up a resistance. For if then *18.* B—K4, then *18.* . . . . Kt x B; *19.* B x R, Kt—Kt3, and Black threatens . . . . Kt—B5 leading to mate or win of the Queen.

17. **R—R1**   **Q—Kt6**
18. **B—B2**   **Q—Kt5**
19. **R—R4**   **Resigns**

The Queen is prettily trapped.

27. QUEEN'S GAMBIT

In a situation very similar to that in the preceding game Tartakover succeeds in making the point Q4, which Mieses so badly neglected, the basis of an undertaking which he carries out with great virtuosity.

Semmering, 1926

WHITE	BLACK
E. Gruenfeld	Dr. S. Tartakover
1. P—Q4	P—Q4
2. P—QB4	P x P
3. Kt—KB3	B—Kt5
4. Kt—K5	B—R4
5. Kt x QBP	. . . .

The best answer to 5. Kt—QB3 would be 5. . . . . Kt—Q2, and the proud Kt at K5 will be forced to declare his intentions.

| *5.* . . . . | P—K3 |
| *6.* Q—Kt3 | . . . . |

Threatening both Q x KtP and
Q—Kt5 *ch.*

| 6. . . . . | Kt—QB3 |
| 7. P—K3 | R—Kt1 *!* |

He does not hesitate at employing the Rook to protect the
modest Pawn!

8. Kt—B3	Kt—B3
9. B—K2	B x B
10. Kt x B	B—Kt5 *ch*
11. Kt—B3	O—O

Both sides have now com-
pleted their development, and
the game is about equal. But
White's center, which is otherwise well protected, betrays a
striking measure of immobility.
My System, however, teaches
that every immobile complex
tends to become a weakness.
The truth of the proposition will
here be shortly manifested.

| 12. O—O | Kt—Q4 *!* |

He feels himself here as if at
home, for P—K4 is not possible
because of . . . . Kt x P.

| 13. Kt x Kt | . . . . |

If *13.* Kt—K4, the result
would be the mobilization of
Black's Queen side by *13.* . . . . .
P—QKt4; *14.* Kt—K5, Kt x Kt;
15. P x Kt, P—QB4; *16.* P—
QR3, P—B5, etc.; or *14.* Kt(B4)
—Q2, P—K4, etc. and White's
game is disorganized.

| 13. . . . . | Q x Kt *!* |
| 14. Q—B2 | P—K4 |

White's center is already being demolished.

15. Kt x P	Kt x Kt
16. P x Kt	Q x KP
17. B—Q2	B x B
18. Q x B	KR—Q1
19. Q—B2	R—Q4 *!*

He makes use of the point Q4
in excellent fashion.

20. QR—Q1	QR—Q1
21. R x R	R x R
22. R—Q1	P—KKt3
23. R x R	Q x R
24. P—QR3	P—QB4

Black has a decided advantage for the end game. Pawn majority on the Queen side, the
Queen file, and last but not least
the central position of his Queen.
This advantage is, however, still
only a small one.

| 25. P—R3 | P—QKt4 |

Centralization proceeds apace! White's Pawn majority is much less easily realizable than Black's (if, for instance, 26. P—B3, then 26. . . . . P—B4, and White's K4 is in bondage), and this is sufficient to explain the loss of the game.

26. P—B4	P—B5
27. Q—B3	Q—K5 !
28. K—B2	P—QR4

The whole ending is played by Tartakover with wonderful precision and truly artistic elegance. Tartakover is, in my opinion, without question the third best end game artist of all living masters.

| 29. P—KKt4 | P—R3 |
| 30. P—KR4 | Q—R8 ! |

Only now, and this tardiness is to his credit, does he give up the central position in favor of a diversion.

31. K—Kt3	Q—Kt8
	ch
32. K—B3	Q—R7 !
33. P—Kt5	P—R4
34. K—K4	Q x RP
35. Q x RP	Q—R8 ch
36. K—K5	Q—B3 !

In order on 37. Q—K1 to put in operation the following maneuver: 37. . . . . Q—B4 ch;

38. K—K4, Q—B4 ch followed by . . . . Q—B7 and wins.

| 37. Q—R7 | P—R5 |
| 38. P—B5 | . . . . |

White is already at his last gasp.

38.	P x P
39. K x P	Q—B6 ch
40. K—K5	P—R6
41. K—Q4	Q—Kt5
	ch

42. Resigns

The following game illustrates the plan of action "center file *v.* flank attack."

28. INDIAN DEFENSE

New York, 1913

| WHITE | BLACK |
| *H. Kline* | *J. R. Capablanca* |

1. P—Q4	Kt—KB3
2. Kt—KB3	P—Q3
3. P—B3	QKt—Q2
4. B—B4	P—B3
5. Q—B2	Q—B2
6. P—K4	P—K4
7. B—Kt3	B—K2

White has now the attacking position in the center. This is unquestionably an advantage. But here the weakness of his P at K4 (we shall quickly see why K4 is weak) will soon force White to surrender this advantage; that is to say he will find himself obliged to equalize with P x P.

8. B—Q3	O—O
9. QKt—Q2	R—K1 !
10. O—O	Kt—R4

In order to exchange the B.

11. Kt—B4	B—B3
12. Kt—K3	Kt—B1
13. P x P	. . . .

Since the B is needed at Q3 for the protection of the KP, the QP can only be protected against a Kt at K3 by exchanging him. The student should consider carefully the motif here used, aimed at forcing the opponent to declare himself (whether for P x P or for P—Q5).

13.	P x P
14. B—R4	Q—K2
15. B x B	Q x B
16. Kt—K1	Kt—B5 ?

With this move a diversion is put *en train* which may be said to run counter to the spirit of the opening. The right line of play consisted in . . . . B—K3 and doubling the Rooks in the Q file. By this means advantage could have been taken of the rather uncomfortable position of White's B at Q3. Black's simplest course would have been to play . . . . B—K3 on his 14th move.

| 17. P—KKt3 | Kt—R6 *ch* |

18. K—R1	P—KR4
19. Kt(K3)—Kt2	P—KKt4
20. P—B3	Kt—Kt3
21. Kt—K3 !	P—R5

| 22. P—KKt4 ? ? | . . . . |

The entry of the Kt at KB5 would, according to my analysis, have decided the game in White's favor. See the Diagram.

The retreat of the Black Kt at R6 is cut off. The attempt at a rescue undertaken by means of a reckless advance of the K side Pawns gives the opportunity, often occurring in such a position, for a decisive counter stroke, by an invasion in the center, in the present case by Kt—B5.

For instance 22. Kt—B5, P x P; 23. P x P, B x Kt; 24. P x B, Kt—K2; 25. K—Kt2, K—Kt2 (is the P sacrifice 25. . . . . P—Kt5; 26. P x P, Kt—Kt4 any better?); 26. K x Kt, R—R1 *ch* (or 26. . . . . Kt—Q4; 27. Q—

K2); 27. K—Kt2, Q—R3; 28.
K—B2, Q—R7 *ch;* 29. Kt—Kt2,
R—R6; 30. K—K1, R x P; 31.
Kt—K3, etc. Moreover, as a su-
perabundance, 26. R—R1 is also
playable, which I showed to be
a win for White in an analysis I
published in the *Rigaer Rund-
schau.*

22. . . . .   Kt(R6)—B5

Now the Kt rejoices in his re-
discovered freedom, and Black,
after this doubtful excursion,
which could easily have ended
fatally for him, takes up the
right line, play in the Q file, and
pursues it with complete mas-
tery to victory. What remains
needs but few remarks. The continuation was: 23. **R—B2, Kt x B;**
24. **Kt x Kt, B—K3;** *25.* **R—Q1,**
KR—Q1; *26.* **P—Kt3, Kt—B5;** *27.*
Kt—KKt2, Kt x Kt(Q3); *28.* **R x Kt,**
R x R; *29.* **Q x R, R—Q1** (why not
. . . . B x KKtP ?); *30.* **Q—K2,**
P—R6; *31.* **Kt—K3, P—R4;** *32.* **R—**
B1, P—R5; *33.* **P—QB4, R—Q5** *!;*
34. **Kt—B2, R—Q2;** *35.* **Kt—K3, Q—**
Q1; *36.* **R—Q1, R x R** *ch;* *37.*
Kt x R, Q—Q5 (Q file and cen-
tralization); *38.* **Kt—B2, P—Kt4** *!;*
39. **BP x P, RP x P;** *40.* **RP x P, B x**
QKtP (threatening . . . . Q—
R8 *ch*); *41.* **Kt x P, B—Q8;** *42.*
Q—B1, P x P; *43.* **K—Kt2, P—Kt5;**
44. **Q—Kt5, P—Kt6;** *45.* **Q—K8** *ch,*
K—Kt2; *46.* **Q—K7, P—Kt7;** *47.*
Kt x P, B—Kt6 and wins.

The next game illustrates the
plan of action: play in a file
against the enemy center: First
restrain, then blockade, and
lastly destroy!

29. FRENCH DEFENSE

Carlsbad, 1911

WHITE	BLACK
A. *Rubinstein*	G. *Levenfish*
1. P—K4	P—K3
2. P—Q4	P—Q4
3. Kt—QB3	Kt—KB3
4. B—Kt5	B—K2
5. P—K5	KKt—Q2
6. B x B	Q x B
7. Q—Q2	O—O
8. P—B4	P—QB4
9. Kt—B3	P—B3

It would be more in the spirit
of a correct attack on a Pawn-
chain first to play 9. . . . .
P x P; *10.* KKt x P, and not till
then . . . . P—B3. But after
10. . . . . P—B3; *11.* P x P, Q x
P; the position arrived at is after
all similar to that of the text.

10. P x KBP	Q x P
11. P—KKt3	Kt—B3
12. O—O—O	P—QR3
13. B—Kt2	Kt—Kt3

The diagonal attacking range
KKt2 to Q5 is a necessary element in White's plan of operations; for this, after KP x B*P*,
holds up the freeing thrust

. . . . P—K4 better than any other possible disposition could.

14.	KR—K1	Kt—B5
15.	Q—B2	P—QKt4
16.	P x P *!*	. . . .

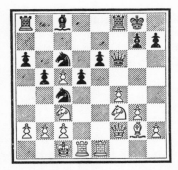

Bravo! The flank attack . . . . Kt x P has no terrors for him, since a flank attack by itself can never ruin a strongly centralized game. And White's game is centralized, for he holds the center files and pressure in them is already making itself felt, and further he has the prospect of occupying the central points Q4 and K5. Observe now how Black's wing attack is thrown back by action in the center.

16.	. . . .	Kt x P
17.	K x Kt	P—Kt5
18.	Kt—Q4 *!*	P x Kt *ch*
19.	K—R1	. . . .

The QBP will be gobbled up presently by a Rook.

| 19. | . . . . | Kt x Kt |

If *19*. . . . . B—Q2, then *20*. Kt x KP, B x Kt; *21*. R x B, followed by B x P.

| 20. | Q x Kt | R—Kt1 |
| 21. | R—K3 | P—Kt4 |

Now he has a go on the other wing.

22.	R x BP	P x P
23.	P x P	B—Q2
24.	P—B6	Q x Q
25.	R x Q	B—K1
26.	B—R3	R—B3
27.	P—B7	. . . .

It would have pleased me even better if the decision had been brought about in a Bishop ending instead of through the somewhat "tacked on" action of the passed P at B7; for instance from such a position as White: K, K5; B, KR3; Pawns, QR2, QB3, KB4, KR2. Black: K, K2; B, KB2; Pawns, QR3, Q4, K3, KR2; with the continuation P—B5, P x P; B x P, and White wins the QP and the game. We should then have the general idea more markedly brought out, namely first to keep the KP and QP under restraint, then to blockade them and only at the end to destroy them. But as played the game was instructive enough! (*e.g.*, moves 13, 16 and 18).

| 27. | . . . . | R— QB1 |

| 28. R x P | R x QBP |
| 29. B x P *ch* | Resigns |

The following game is instructive for the way in which Black turns his majority in the center to account despite disturbing counter-measures.

30. ENGLISH OPENING

London, 1927

WHITE	BLACK
E. Bogolyubov	A. Nimzovich
1. P—QB4	P—K3
2. Kt—QB3	Kt—KB3
3. P—K4	P—B4

Since P—K5 did not seem to be dangerous.

| 4. P—KKt3 | . . . . |

There was also to be considered 4. Kt—B3, Kt—B3; 5. P—Q4, P x P; 6. Kt x P, B—Kt5; 7. Q—Q3 (Bogolyubov's suggestion).

4.	P—Q4
5. P—K5	P—Q5
6. P x Kt	P x Kt
7. QP x P	. . . .

An interesting idea. He, so to speak, sacrifices a P, in that he makes his Pawn majority on the Q side of no value; but he hopes, by occupying certain central points, to be able to bring counter-pressure to bear. *Cf.* the next note.

7.	Q x P
8. Kt—B3	P—KR3
9. B—Kt2	B—Q2 *!*
10. Kt—Q2	. . . .

White's command of the diagonal KKt2 to QKt7 coupled with that of the point K4 is no small embarrassment to Black. If now 10. . . . . Q—K4 *ch ?*, then 11. Kt—K4 and 12. B—B4.

10.	B—B3
11. Kt—K4	Q—Kt3
12. Q—K2	B—K2

Not 12. . . . . P—B4 because of the reply 13. B—B3 followed by Kt—Q2 and Black's K4 will remain a weak point.

| 13. O—O | O—O |

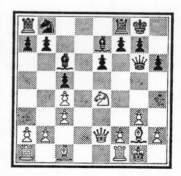

| 14. P—KR4 | . . . . |

An ingenious move, which, however, brings about a disturbance of the equilibrium which up to now may be said to have existed. Better was 14. P—B4 *!*,

Kt—Q2; *15.* B—Q2, K—R1 *l*;
16. QR—K1, Kt—B3; *17.* B—
B1. After the text move the balance weighs in Black's favor.

14.	P—B4
15. Kt—Q2	B x B

Not *15.* . . . . . B x P because
of *16.* Kt—B3 *!*

16. K x B	Kt—B3
17. Kt—B3	P—B5

Otherwise B—B4, and the balance is readjusted.

18. R—K1	R—B3
19. Q—K4	. . . .

The game is already lost for White, for the occupation of the point K4 which seems to consolidate the position proves to be deceptive. White's KKt3 is in fact sick unto death.

19.	P x P
20. P x P	B—Q3
21. P—KKt4	Q x Q
22. R x Q	QR—KB1
23. R—K3	R—B5
24. P—Kt5	. . . .

24. R x P, R x P *ch; 25.* K—B2, Kt—K4 would lead to a *débâcle.*

24.	R—Kt5 *ch*
25. K—R1	. . . .

Or *25.* K—B2, Kt—K4; *26.* K—K2, R—Kt7 *ch; 27.* K—B1, R—Kt6 winning a piece.

25.	P x P
26. P x P	K—B2
27. Kt—Kt1	. . . .

If *27.* P—Kt6 *ch*, K—B3 (not
. . . . K—K2 because of *28.*
Kt—R2, R—KR1; *29.* R—K2,
R(Kt)—R5 *? ?; 30.* B—Kt5 *ch*).

27.	R—R1 *ch*
28. Kt—R3	K—K2
29. P—Kt3	B—B5
30. R—B3	Kt—K4
31. Resigns	

31. SICILIAN DEFENSE
(in effect)

In which seven White Pawns show greater collective mobility than eight Black ones. Thus does mind (*i.e.*, dynamic effect) triumph over mere matter.

Copenhagen, 1924

WHITE	BLACK
A. Nimzovich	*A. Olson*
1. P—KB4	P—QB4
2. P—K4	Kt—QB3
3. P—Q3	P—KKt3
4. P—B4	B—Kt2
5. Kt—QB3	P—Kt3
6. Kt—B3	B—Kt2
7. P—KKt4	. . . .

The collective mobility of White's King's side Pawns already makes itself quickly felt.

7.	P—K3
8. B—Kt2	KKt—K2

9. Kt—QKt5 !   . . . .

In order to provoke . . . . P—QR3, after which the lack of protection under which the QKtP will suffer is to form the basis of a sharp combination.

9.	. . .	P—Q3
10.	O—O	P—QR3
11.	Kt—R3	O—O
12.	Q—K2	Q—Q2
13.	B—K3	Kt—Kt5

Else there would follow QR—Q1 and P—Q4 with advantage to White.

14.	Kt—B2 !	B x P
15.	QR—Kt1	B—B6
16.	Kt x Kt	B x Kt

Or 16. . . . . . P x Kt; 17. B x P. *Cf.* the note to White's 9th move.

17. B—B1 !   . . . .

White has succeeded in wresting the long diagonal from his opponent.

17.	. . .	P—B3
18.	B—Kt2	P—K4
19.	P—Kt5	. . .

The connection between "sacrifice" and "blockade" would have stood out in even sharper relief had the continuation been 19. P—B5, P—KKt4, 20. P—KR4 with an enduring attack,

while Black's Pawn plus would have but an illusory value.

19.	. . .	Kt—B3

or 19. . . . . P x KtP; 20. Kt x KtP (threatening B—KR3), Kt—B3; 21. P—B5.

20.	P x BP	Q—Kt5
21.	P x P	P x P
22.	Q—K3	Q—R4

To protect the KP.

23.	Kt—Kt5	B—B1
24.	P—B7 *ch*	K—Kt2
25.	Q—B4	K—R3

Forced.

26.	Kt—K6 *ch* !	P x Q
27.	B—Kt7 mate	

In the following game we have an instance of a "mysterious" Rook move, also a striking example of the difference between a true and a false freeing move. As this game in addition illustrates very clearly our conception of prophylactic strategy, it is inserted here.

32. VAN'T KRUYS OPENING

St. Petersburg, 1914

WHITE	BLACK
J. H. Blackburne	*A. Nimzovich*
1. P—K3	P—Q3
2. P—KB4	P—K4
3. P x P	P x P
4. Kt—QB3	B—Q3

The best move, for the early development of the Kts advocated by Lasker would not get at the root of the matter here. This root lies rather in the Pawn configuration and in the prevention of any freeing Pawn moves.

| 5. P—K4 | B—K3 |

Preventing B—B4.

| 6. Kt—B3 | P—KB3 |

Black plays (as will become evident at his 8th move) to prevent the advance of the QP to his fourth which would in a certain sense have a freeing effect; since it would make White's majority in the center felt. Black, as he plays it, succeeds in completely crippling the enemy majority in the center. And now the reader may ask, why does Black give White the opportunity of playing P—Q4 on his 7th move?

| 7. P—Q3 | . . . . |

White forgoes the advance, and rightly, for 7. P—Q4 would here be the typical false liberating move, which merely creates new weaknesses. *E.g.*, 7. P—Q4, Kt—Q2 *!*; 8. P—Q5 (otherwise ultimately . . . . P x P with play against White's isolated KP), B—B2 followed by the occupation of the point QB4 by Bishop or Knight.

| 7. . . . . | Kt—K2 |
| 8. B—K3 | P—QB4 *!* |

With the aid of the resources he has in the Q file Black now succeeds in forcing his opponent to act on the defensive. See Black's 9th and 10th moves.

9. Q—Q2	QKt—B3
10. B—K2	Kt—Q5
11. O—O	O—O
12. Kt—Q1	Kt(K)—B3
13. P—B3	. . . .

The reward which Black's systematic scheme of operations has earned for him. White's P at Q3 is now a weakness.

| 13. . . . . | Kt x B *ch* |
| 14. Q x Kt | . . . . |

See diagram 157, p. 201.

14. . . . .   R—K1 *!*

The "mysterious" Rook move, which in the event of White playing P—Q4 threatens to make things uncomfortable for him in the K file. In addition to this it makes room for the B at KB1 to which square the latter wishes to go.

15. Kt—R4   B—KB1
16. Kt—B5   K—R1 *!*

White has made pertinent use of the open KB file, his one advantage. Black's move for all its unpretentiousness has its significance in position play. Black insures the eventual possibility of playing . . . . P—KKt3 and . . . . P—B4 without being disturbed by a check at R6.

17. P—KKt4   Q—Q2 *!*

Renders possible a parry to the ever threatening advance P—Kt5. For example: *18.* P—Kt5, P—KKt3; *19.* Kt—Kt3, P—B4 *!*; with an excellent game. *Cf.* the previous note.

18. Kt—B2   P—QR4

White's QRP is constantly threatened, and if P—Kt3, ... P—R5 will now be possible. It is evident that White's Q wing is sympathetically affected by the weakness of his center.

19. P—QR3   ᴰ—QKt4

. . . . B—Kt6 would have been a strong move here, although by it Black would have to forgo the parry he had planned to P—Kt5. Nevertheless, ... B—Kt6 could have composedly been played (one should not be a slave to one's parries): *19.* . . . . B—Kt6; *20.* P—Kt5, P x P; *21.* B x KtP, P—B5 *!* (Lasker's suggestion); *22.* P x P, Q—K3; *23.* Kt—K3, Q—Kt3; *24.* Q—Kt4, B—B4 *!*, and wins. Or *23.* Q—B3 *!*, B x P; *24.* KR—Q1, and Black has a slight advantage.

20. QR—Q1   QR—Kt1

Some tempi could have been saved by playing . . . . P—Kt5 at once.

21. R—Q2   P—Kt5
22. RP x P   RP x P *!*

If . . . . BP x P; *24.* P—Q4 *!*

23. P—B4

Black ought now to play out his trumps.

(*See Diagram*)

23. . . . .   R—R1 *?*

Black had brought about a strategically won position, only he should not have delayed any longer playing out his trumps. These consisted of . . . . Kt—Q5, which would lead to B x Kt, and of . . . . P—Kt3 and . . . .

Position after 23. P—B4

B—R3, in order to dominate the diagonal. Thus: 23. . . . . P—Kt3 (instead of . . . . R—R1); 24. Kt—Kt3, Kt—Q5 !; 25. B x Kt, BP x B, followed by B—R3. Or 25. Q—Q1 (instead of exchanging), R—R1, followed by . . . . Q—R5; the exchange of Qs will be forced and Black has a good end game. He could also play out his trumps in the reverse order; 23. . . . . . Kt—Q5; 24. B x Kt, BP x B; 25. Q—B3 (best), P—Kt3; 26. Kt—Kt3, Q—K2; 27. Kt—Q1, B—R3; 28. R—Kt2, B—Kt4 ! followed by . . . . R—R1—R8, etc.

24. Q—B3   R—R7 ?

There was still time for . . . . Kt—Q5, etc.

25. P—Kt5   . . . .

Thanks to a tactical sally (White's 26th move) this thrust which was thought to have been prevented, is now after all possible.

25. . . . .   P—Kt3
26. Kt—Kt4 !   . . . .

Robs Black of the fruits of his deep plan of campaign.

There followed 26. . . . . . **P x Kt;** 27. **Kt x BP, Kt—Q5;** 28. **Q—B2** (Q—R5 would have won more quickly), **Q—B3;** 29. **Kt x R, Q x Kt;** 30. **B x Kt, KP x B;** 30. **P x P,** and *White won* easily.

What we have to learn from this game is the ability to distinguish between true and false freeing moves. The manner in which Black was able to hold in check the thrusts P—Q4 and later (until the moment of aberration) P—Kt5 is worthy of special notice. See II. ii. § 3.

The following game illustrates the effect of preventive measures and the idea of collective mobility.

33. ENGLISH OPENING

Dresden, 1926

WHITE	BLACK
A. Nimzovich	A. Rubinstein
1. P—QB4	P—QB4
2. Kt—KB3	Kt—KB3
3. Kt—B3	P—Q4
4. P x P	Kt x P
5. P—K4	. . . .

A novelty which at the price of a backward QP aims at securing other advantages.

5. . . . .   Kt—Kt5

Preferable was . . . . Kt x Kt; 6. KtP x Kt, P—KKt3.

6. B—B4 !   P—K3

It was not possible here to take immediate advantage of White's weakness at Q3. For instance, 6. . . . . Kt—Q6 ch; 7. K—K2 !, Kt—B5 ch; 8. K—B1, with the threat P—Q4. Or 6. . . . . Kt—Q6 ch; 7. K—K2, Kt x B ch; 8. R x Kt, Kt—B3; 9. B—Kt5, B—Q2; 10. B x Kt, followed by P—Q4 with the superior end game.

7. O—O   QKt—B3

I should prefer . . . . P—QR3 here, though it is true that even then White with 8. P—QR3, KKt—B3; 9. P—Q3 and B—K3, would have an excellent game. See II. i. 4, p. 169.

8. P—Q3   Kt—Q5

P—QR3 was threatened.

9. Kt x Kt   P x Kt
10. Kt—K2   . . . .

White now stands very well; any weakness which may exist at Q3 is covered up, the collective mobility of White's K side (P—B4 !) is considerable, and, most important, the apparently blocked KB plays from the background a preventive rôle (directed against . . . . P—K4) which goes far to turn the scale in White's favor.

10. . . . .   P—QR3

Directed against the threat 11. B—Kt5 ch, B—Q2; 12. Kt x P.

11. Kt—Kt3   B—Q3

12. P—B4   . . . .

Q—Kt4 would have been very strong here: 12. Q—Kt4, O—O; 13. B—KKt5 !, B—K2; 14. B—R6, B—B3; 15. B x KtP, B x B; 16. Kt—R5; or else 13. . . . . P—K4; 14. Q—R4, with the sacrifice at Kt7 to follow (Kt—R5 x KtP). The best answer to Q—Kt4 would have been . . . . Q—B3; for instance, 12. Q—Kt4, Q—B3; 13. P—B4; but even in this case White's superiority in position would have been very great

After the less incisive text move Black can approximately equalize.

| 12. . . . . | O—O |
| 13. Q—B3 | . . . . |

A direct mating attack is no longer feasible. For example: *13.* P—K5, B—B2 *!; 14.* Q—Kt4, K—R1; *15.* Kt—R5, R—KKt1; *16.* R—B3, P—B4 *!; 17.* P x P *e.p.*, P x P; *18.* Q—R4, R—Kt3; *19.* R—R3, Q—K2; and Black threatens to consolidate his position by . . . . B—Q2 and . . . . QR—KKt1.

13.	K—R1
14. B—Q2	P—B4
15. QR—K1	Kt—B3

Rubinstein has defended himself skillfully, but White has always a trump in hand: the K file.

| 16. R—K2 | Q—B2 |

Not good. In cramped positions one should never give away the slightest future possibility of a move. But . . . . Q—B2 gives away the possibility of playing . . . . Q—B3, after P x P, P x P. The right move was therefore *16*. . . . . B—Q2, and if then *17.* P x P (best), P x P; *18.* KR—K1, then *18.* . . . . Q—B3, and Black stands much better at any rate than he does in the game.

| 17. P x P | P x P |

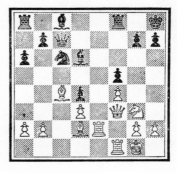

| 18. Kt—R1 *!* | . . . . |

The Kt starts on a long journey with KKt5 as his goal, in order to support with all the means at his disposal the KB who now wakes up and throws off his preventive rôle for one of direct activity. And meanwhile White's K file, thrown, so to speak, on its own resources, makes a desperate but successful struggle for existence. This vitality of the K file gives point to the Kt maneuver.

18.	B—Q2
19. Kt—B2	QR—K1
20. KR—K1	R x R
21. R x R	Kt—Q1

We see now that *21.* . . . . R—K1 would be met by *22.* Q—Q5.

| 22. Kt—R3 | B—B3 |

And here *22.* . . . . R—K1 would lead to a combination full of pleasantries, *e.g., 22.* . . . . .

R—K1; *23.* Q—R5 *!*, R x R; *24.* Kt—Kt5, P—R3; *25.* Q—Kt6, P x Kt; *26.* Q—R5 mate.

23. Q—R5	P—KKt3
24. Q—R4	K—Kt2
25. Q—B2 *!*	. . . .

Black's castled position was still too strongly defended, so White intends first to force a re-grouping of the enemy forces.

25.	B—B4

Or *25.* . . . . Q—Kt3; *26.* P—Kt4 and *27.* B—B3 *!*

26. P—QKt4	B—Kt3
27. Q—R4	. . . .

The switch-back theme, such as usually only occurs in problems. *27.* Q—K1 would, however, also have been good: *27.* Q—K1, B—K5; *28.* Kt—B2, winning a P by Kt x B, etc.

27.	R—K1

The answer to . . . . R—B3 would have been *28.* Kt—Kt5, P—R3; *29.* Kt—R7 winning at once.

28. R—K5 *!*	Kt—B2

If *28.* . . . . P—R3 there would follow *29.* P—Kt4 with a very strong attack. Thus: *29.* P—Kt4, P x P; *30.* P—B5, Q x R; *31.* P—B6 *ch*, Q x P; *32.* Q x P mate. Or *29.* P—Kt4, P— Kt4 *?*; *30.* P x KtP, threatening

mate at R6. After the text move White forces an elegant win.

29. B x Kt	Q x B

If *29.* . . . . R x R; then *30.* P x R, Q x B; *31.* Kt—Kt5, Q— Kt1; *32.* P—K6, B—Q4; *33.* Q—B4, with an easy win.

30. Kt—Kt5	Q—Kt1
31. R x R	B x R
32. Q—K1 *!*	. . . .

A remarkable position; Black is lost. In spite of the scanty material a mating attack is in the air. Some pretty play now follows.

32.	B—B3

If *32.* . . . . K—B1, White wins by *33.* Q—K5, B—Q1 (best; the reply to *33.* . . . . Q x P would be *34.* Q—B6 *ch*, K—Kt1; *35.* Kt—K6; or *34.* . . . . B—B2; *35.* Kt x B and *36.* Q x B); *34.* Kt—K6 *ch*, K— K2; *35.* Q—B5 *ch !*, K—Q2; *36.*

Kt—B8 *ch* ! Observe how White on his 35th move forgoes the discovered check and how the Black King has got tangled up with his own pieces.

33. Q—K7 *ch*   K—R1

If . . . . K—R3, then obviously 34. Kt—K6.

34. P—Kt5 *!*   . . . .

Pulls the noose taut!
If 34. . . . . P x P, then 35. Kt—K6, P—R4 *!*; 36. Q—B6 *ch*, K—R2; 37. Kt—Kt5 *ch*, K—R3; 38. B—Kt4 leads to a mate.

34. . . . .   Q—Kt2

Desperation.

35. Q x Q *ch*   K x Q
36. P x B and wins

34. NIMZOVICH ATTACK

Illustrates the restraint of a double complex in an extraordinarily striking manner.

Baden-Baden, 1925

WHITE	BLACK
A. Nimzovich	S. Rosselli del Turco

1. Kt—KB3	P—Q4
2. P—QKt3	P—QB4
3. P—K3	Kt—QB3
4. B—Kt2	B—Kt5
5. P—KR3	B x Kt
6. Q x B	P—K4
7. B—Kt5	Q—Q3
8. P—K4	. . . .

We have here to do with the remarkable situation which we have already had occasion to notice (see II. ii. § 2, Diagram 151), namely the one in which we do not at once cause the doubled Pawns by B x Kt *ch*, P x B, but rather bring this about by a roundabout way. As a matter of fact after 8. B x Kt *ch ?*, P x B, we should never be able to force our obstinate opponent to accommodate us by playing . . . . P—Q5, *e.g.*, 8. B x Kt *ch*, P x B; 9. P—K4, Kt—B3; etc.

8. . . . .   P—Q5
9. Kt—R3   . . . .

Threatening 10. Kt—B4, Q—B2; 11. B x Kt *ch*, P x B; and the weakness of the doubled Pawns is evident.

9. . . . .   P—B3
10. Kt—B4   Q—Q2
11. Q—R5 *ch*   . . . .

The maneuver of the Q is intended to help prevent Black's castling on the Q side; not on the K side as one might at first sight think.

11. . . . .   P—Kt3
12. Q—B3   Q—QB2

Not . . . . O—O—O because of Kt—R5 and the covering move . . . . KKt—K2 is ruled out because of Q x P.

13. Q—Kt4 *!*   . . . .

Now she rejoices in the observation post she has won for herself. This Q maneuver has quite a hyper-modern air to it.

13. . . . .   K—B2

White threatened 14. Q—K6 *ch*, K—Q1 (or . . . . B—K2; 15. Kt—R5); 15. B x Kt, and the unpleasant doubled Pawn is a fact.

14. P—B4   P—KR4
15. Q—B3   P x P

16. B x Kt   . . . .

At the right moment, for the Q dare not retake. For instance, 16. . . . . Q x B; 17. Q x P, R— K1; 18. O—O *! !*, Q x P (. . . . R x P; Kt—K5 *ch*); 19. Q—B7 *ch ! !* and wins (19. . . . . Q— K2; 20. Kt—Q6 *ch* followed by 21. Kt x R).

16. . . . .   P x B

At last White has achieved his end, at the cost it is true of a P; but here this plays but a subordinate rôle.

17. O—O   P—Kt4

For (see the previous note) Black's position can be broken up. (Obviously White must not allow Black to safeguard his position by . . . . Kt—K2— Kt3—K4.) To break up Black's game three Pawn moves are necessary, (i) P—B3, (ii) P—K5, and (iii) P—KR4. If White contented himself with only two of these his work were but half done. In the game all three are brought about.

18. P—B3 *!*   R—Q1

Now this R is happily tethered! (to his P at Q5).

19. QR—K1 *!*   Kt—K2
20. P—K5   Kt—B4
21. P x QP *!*   Kt x P

If 21. . . . . P x QP; then 22. P x P, K x P; 23. Q—K4, and . . . . Kt—Kt6 is impracticable on account of B x P *ch*.

22. Q—K4   B—K2

The reply to . . . . P—B4 would have been Q—Kt1, an attacking move in the best modern spirit. For example, 22. . . . . P—B4; 23. Q—Kt1, K—K3 (to protect the KBP); 24. Q—Q3 *!* and 25. Kt—Q6 *!* with a decisive attack.

23. P—KR4 !   . . . .

Now the undermined Black position tumbles like a house of cards.

23.	Q—Q2
24. P x BP	B x P
25. P x P	Resigns

For after 25. . . . . B—Kt2; 26. Kt—K5 *ch,* B x Kt; 27. Q x B, Black's King is a pathetic figure in his helplessness.

35. NIMZOINDIAN DEFENSE

Illustrates a position held under complete restraint, and may serve as a pendant to my game (No. 8) against Saemisch.

Dresden, 1926

WHITE	BLACK
P. Johner	A. Nimzovich
1. P—Q4	Kt—KB3
2. P—QB4	P—K3
3. Kt—QB3	B—Kt5
4. P—K3	O—O

Black intends to bring into existence the double complex only under conditions favorable to himself. *Cf.* No. 34.

5. B—Q3	P—B4
6. Kt—B3	Kt—B3
7. O—O	B x Kt
8. P x B	P—Q3

The prognosis for the complex P at QB4, P at QB3, etc., is in a

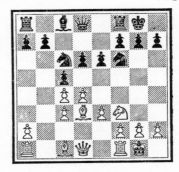

measure (but not pronouncedly) in favor of Black. Yet after 9. P—K4, P—K4; 10. P—Q5, Kt —QR4; Black would not have bought the barricade which he has achieved altogether cheaply, for his QBP would then have been much better placed if it were still at QB2. (See the remarks on the double complex in II. ii. § 2 my game against Janowski; Diagram 150, p. 191.)

9. Kt—Q2 !   . . . .

A fine idea. In reply to 9. . . . . P—K4; 10. P—Q5, Kt— QR4, the intention is by 11. Kt—Kt3 to bring the aggressive Black Kt at R4 to reason.

9. . . . .   P—QKt3
10. Kt—Kt3 ?   . . . .

There was time enough for this. P—B4 should first have been played. If then 10. . . . . P—K4, there would follow 11. BP x P, QP x P; 12. P—Q5, Kt—

QR4; *13*. Kt—Kt3, Kt—Kt2; *14*. P—K4, Kt—K1, and the weak point QB4, which is now attackable also from Black's Q3, will be protected by Q—K2, while White for his part can use the KB file together with P—QR4—R5 as a base of operations. The game would then stand about even.

10. . . . .   P—K4
11. P—B4   . . . .

For the reply to *11*. P—Q5 would now be P—K5 ! Thus: *11*. P—Q5, P—K5; *12*. B—K2, Kt—K4 *!*; or *12*. P x Kt, P x B; with advantage to Black.

11. . . . .   P—K5

11. . . . . Q—K2 was also possible, for if, say, *12*. BP x P, QP x P; *13*. P—Q5, then *13*. . . . . Kt—Q1; *14*. P—K4, Kt—K1; and Black by . . . . Kt—Q3 and . . . . P—B3 gets a strong defensive position. (*Cf.* the note to move 10.)

12. B—K2   Q—Q2 *!*

Black sees in White's K side Pawns (KB, KKt and KR) a qualitative majority. The text move involves a complicated system of restraint. A simpler one could have been brought about by *12*. . . . . Kt—K1. For example: *12*. . . . . Kt—K1; *13*. P—Kt4 (or *13*. P—B5,

Q—Kt4), P—B4; *14*. QP x P *!* (observe the "dead" B at QB1 and consider further how ineffectively posted the White pieces are for an attack to be launched in the KKt file), QP x P; *15*. Q—Q5 *ch*, Q x Q; *16*. P x Q, Kt—K2; *17*. R—Q1, Kt—Q3; and Black has rather the better game.

13. P—KR3   Kt—K2

14. Q—K1   . . . .

If *14*. B—Q2, Black would still get the advantage. For instance: *14*. B—Q2 (to threaten B—K1—R4) *14*. . . . . Kt—B4; *15*. Q—K1 (best; Black threatened . . . . Kt—Kt6 and to exchange the B, when White's QB4 would become very weak), *15*. . . . . P—Kt3; and if now *16*. P—Kt4, Kt—Kt2; *17*. Q—R4, then . . . . Kt(B)—K1, and the Pawn movement is strangled at birth; for now would follow at the next move

the powerful . . . . P—B4. So
we always get the same picture.
The awkwardness of White's
pieces as a result of the doubled
Pawns renders more difficult by
far the carrying out of any action
on the K side however planned.

| 14. . . . . | P—KR4 ! |
| 15. B—Q2 | . . . . |

Q—R4 will not do because of
15. . . . . Kt—B4; 16. Q—Kt5,
Kt—R2; 17. Q x RP, Kt—Kt6.

| 15. . . . . | Q—B4 ! |

The Q is bound for—KR2 !
Where she will be excellently
placed, for then the crippling of
White's K side by . . . . P—R5
will at once be threatened. It
must be conceded that the restraint maneuver . . . . Q—Q2
—B4—R2 represents a remarkable conception.

| 16. K—R2 | Q—R2 ! |
| 17. P—QR4 | Kt—B4 |

Threatening 18. . . . . Kt—
Kt5 ch; 19. P x Kt, P x P ch; 20.
K—Kt1, P—Kt6; etc.

| 18. P—Kt3 | P—R4 ! |

In this position the backward-
ness of the QKtP is easy to put
up with.

19. R—KKt1	Kt—R3
20. B—KB1	B—Q2
21. B—B1	QR—B1

Black wishes to force P—Q5
in order to operate undisturbed
on the K side.

| 22. P—Q5 | . . . . |

Otherwise . . . . B—K3 would
follow and P—Q5 would be
forced after all.

| 22. . . . . | K—R1 |
| 23. Kt—Q2 | R—KKt1 |

And now comes the attack. So
was . . . . Q—Q2—B4—R2 actually an attacking maneuver?
Yes and no. No, since its whole
idea was to restrain White's K
side Pawns. Yes, since every restraining action is the logical
prelude to an attack, and since
every immobile complex tends
to be a weakness and therefore
must sooner or later become an
object of attack.

24. B—KKt2	P—KKt4
25. Kt—B1	R—Kt2
26. R—R2	Kt—B4
27. B—R1	. . . .

White has very skilfully
brought up all his defensive
forces.

| 27. . . . . | QR—KKt1 |
| 28. Q—Q1 | P x P |

Opens the KKt file for himself, but the K file for his opponent. This move, therefore,
demanded deep deliberation.

| 29. KP x P | B—B1 |

| 30. Q—Kt3 | B—R3 |
| 31. R—K2 | . . . . |

Seizes his chance. Black's KP now needs to be defended. If he had limited himself to purely defensive measures, as, say, 31. B—Q2, a pretty combination would have resulted; namely, 31. B—Q2, R—Kt3 *!;* 32. B—K1, Kt—Kt5 *ch;* 33. P x Kt, P x P *ch;* 34. K—Kt2, B x P *!;* 35. Q x B, and now follows the quiet move 35. . . . . P—K6; and Q—R6 mate can only be parried by Kt x P, which move, however, would cost White his Q.

| 31. . . . . | Kt—R5 |

| 32. R—K3 | . . . . |

Here I had naturally expected Kt—Q2 for Black's obligation to defend the important KP furnished White's only counter chance, as has already been observed. But a result of that move would have been a delightful Q sacrifice, namely: 32. Kt—Q2, B—B1; 33. Kt x P, Q—B4; 34. Kt—B2, Q x P *ch;* 35. Kt x Q, Kt—Kt5 mate. The point, moreover, lies in the fact that the moves . . . . B—B1 and . . . . Q—B4 cannot be transposed. *E.g.,* 32. Kt—Q2, Q—B4 *?* (instead of B—B1); 33. Q—Q1 *!,* B—B1; 34. Q—B1, and everything is protected; whereas if 32. . . . . B—B1; 33. Q—Q1, the move . . . . B x P *!* wipes out the corner stone of White's building. (*34.* K x B, Q—B4 *ch;* etc.)

32.	B—B1
33. Q—B2	B x P *!*
34. B x P	. . . .

34. K x B, Q—B4 *ch;* 35. K—R2 would have led to mate in three.

| 34. . . . . | B—B4 |

Best, for . . . . P—R5 can no longer be withstood. After the fall of White's KRP the defense is hopeless.

35. B x B	Kt x B
36. R—K2	P—R5
37. R(Kt)—Kt2	P x P *ch*
38. K—Kt1	Q—R6
39. Kt—K3	Kt—R5
40. K—B1	R—K1 *!*

A precise finish, for now there is threatened *41.* . . . . Kt x R;

42. R x Kt, Q—R8 *ch; 43.* K—
K2, Q x R *ch;* and against this
threat White is defenseless. If
41. K—K1, then, *41.* . . . . . Kt—
B6 *ch; 42.* K—B1 or Q1, Q—R8
ch would lead to mate. Hence
White resigns.

One of the best blockading
games that I have ever played.

36. QUEEN'S GAMBIT DECLINED

Illustrates the isolated QP.

St. Petersburg, 1913

WHITE	BLACK
A. *Nimzovich*	S. *Taubenhaus*
1. P—Q4	P—Q4
2. Kt—KB3	Kt—KB3
3. P—B4	P—K3
4. P—K3	P—B4
5. B—Q3	Kt—B3
6. O—O	QP x P
7. B x BP	P x P
8. P x P	B—K2
9. Kt—B3	O—O
10. B—K3	. . . .

10. P—Q5 would be bad because of . . . . Kt—QR4; *11.*
P—QKt3, B—Kt5; nor would
10. B—KKt5 be good: *10.* . . . . .
P—QKt3, etc.

10. . . . .   P—QKt3

. . . . P—QR3 and . . . . P—
QKt4 would unnecessarily weak-
en the point QB4.

11. Q—K2   B—Kt2

12. KR—Q1	Kt—QKt5
13. Kt—K5	R—B1
14. QR—B1	QKt—Q4
15. Kt—Kt5	. . . .

A strategically noteworthy
conception. White says to himself: in the center I am strong,
therefore a strategical diversion
is justified; moreover, I have no
particular wish after say *15.* B—
QR6 or Q3 to be saddled with
hanging Pawns. The right move
was, nevertheless, B—QR6. For
example: *15.* B—QR6, Kt x Kt;
16. P x Kt, Q—B2; *17.* B x B,
Q x B; *18.* P—QB4 with eventually P—QR4—R5.

15.	P—QR3
16. Kt—R7 *!*	R—R1

If . . . . R—B2, then B x P.

17. Kt(R)—B6	Q—Q3
18. Kt x B *ch*	Q x Kt
19. B—Q3 *!*	Kt x B

There was no occasion for this.
Other lines of play to be considered were, (i) *19.* . . . . . P—
QR4 and . . . . KR—B1, or
(ii) *19.* . . . . KR—Q1 followed
by . . . . Kt—Q2—B1; for
(iii) . . . . Kt—K1, see the remarks on Diagram 169 in II. iii.
§ 4, p. 216.

20. P x Kt	P—QKt4

Weakens the point QB4. After
20. . . . . . P—QR4 (instead of
the text move) and . . . . KR—

B1, there would not be much wrong with him.

21. R—B5

By occupying this outpost station White gets play in the QB file.

21.	KR—B1
22. R(Q1)—QB1	P—Kt3
23. P—QR3	. . . .

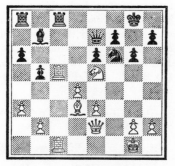

What now follows could serve as a text book example for play in an open file. The slowness with which White step by step gains in terrain is also of significance from the point of view of position play.

| 23. . . . . | Kt—K1 |
| 24. P—QKt4 | Kt—Q3 |

If . . . . Q—Kt4, then Kt x BP *!*

| 25. Q—KB2 *!* | P—B4 |

In order to relieve the KBP and to make . . . . Q—Kt4 possible.

| 26. Q—B4 | Kt—K1 |

Black can undertake nothing.

| 27. B—K2 *!* | Kt—Q3 |
| 28. B—B3 | . . . . |

Breaks down the opposition in the QB file.

| 28. . . . . | R x R |
| 29. QP x R | Kt—K1 |

If 29. . . . . Kt—K5; then 30. P—B6 *!*, P—KKt4; 31. P x B, R—KB1; 32. R—B8 and wins.

| 30. R—Q1 | Kt—B3 |
| 31. P—B6 | . . . . |

The QBP, the fruit of the operations on the QB file, now brings the decision.

31.	B—B1
32. P—B7	R—R2
33. R—Q8 *ch*	K—Kt2
34. R x B	R x P
35. Kt x P	Resigns

37. QUEEN'S GAMBIT DECLINED

Is dedicated to hanging Pawns, and is characteristic of these, though only in a quite special sense. It shows the frightful dangers to which hanging Pawns are exposed at birth. Infant mortality is very high among them, and appreciably exceeds the mortality of grown-up hanging Pawns, who if the worst comes to the worst can seek refuge in "blockaded security."

St. Petersburg, 1909

WHITE	BLACK
A. Rubinstein	*Znosko-Borovsky*
1. P—Q4	P—Q4
2. P—QB4	P—K3
3. Kt—QB3	Kt—KB3
4. B—Kt5	B—K2
5. P—K3	QKt—Q2
6. Kt—B3	O—O
7. Q—B2	P—QKt3

. . . . P—B4 is possible here. For instance, 7. . . . . P—B4; 8. P x QP, Kt x P; 9. B x B, Q x B; 10. Kt x Kt, P x Kt; 11. P x P, Kt x P; and the isolani does not look so bad.

8. P x P	P x P
9. B—Q3	B—Kt2
10. O—O—O	Kt—K5
11. P—KR4	P—KB4
12. K—Kt1	P—B4

The correctness of this move stands or falls by that of the Pawn sacrifice recommended in the next note. Sound and good is, instead of P—B4, 12. . . . . R—B1 as given by Dr. Lasker. For instance, 13. Q—Kt3, Kt x Kt *ch*, followed by . . . . P—B4. Not quite so good, yet by no means bad would seem to be 12. . . . . P—KR3; 13. B—KB4, B—Q3; 14. B x B, P x B.

13. P x P	P x P

13. . . . . R—B1 was possible here. If then 14. P x P, QKt x P Black would have attacking chances; the answer to 14. Kt—Q4 could be . . . . QKt x P. The outcome of the game would have been doubtful in either case, whereas now there is no doubt whatever. It may be observed that if 13. . . . . QKt x P, then 14. Kt x QP *!*, B x Kt; 15. B—QB4 wins.

14. Kt x Kt	BP x Kt
15. B x P	P x B
16. Q—Kt3 *ch*	K—R1
17. Q x B	P x Kt
18. R x Kt	Q—K1
19. R x B	Q–Kt3 *ch*
20. K—R1	QR—Kt1

The gale has not only blown away the hanging Pawns but has also taken a piece along with them. Black's desperation attack is warded off easily.

21. Q—K4	. . . .

Lasker praises this move, but 21. Q—Q5 seems to do as well. *E.g.,* 21. . . . . P x P; 22. Q x KtP, Q—B7; 23. B—B6 ! True, many roads lead to Rome.

21.	Q x Q
22. R x Q	P x P
23. R—KKt1	R x BP
24. R—KB4	R—B7

If 24. . . . . R(Kt1) x P; then R—B8 *ch !* and wins outright.

25. P—Kt3	P—KR3

There followed 26. **B—K7, R—K1; 27. K—Kt1, R—K7; 28. B x P, R—Q1; 29. B—Q4, R—QB1; 30. R—Kt4, Resigns.**

38. RETI OPENING

This game took an instructive course. It was played in a simultaneous exhibition. White: Schurig with, up to the 12th move, K. Laue of Halle.

Leipzig, 1926

WHITE	BLACK
The Allies	*A. Nimzovich*
1. Kt—KB3	P—K3
2. P—KKt3	P—Q4
3. B—Kt2	P—QB3
4. P—Kt3	B—Q3
5. B—Kt2	Kt—B3
6. P—Q3	QKt—Q2
7. QKt—Q2	Q—B2

7. . . . . P—K4 was also possible. With the text move an original maneuver begins. Black plans an attack on the extreme Q's wing; but before launching it wishes to safeguard his center against the possible threat of P—K4—K5; and accordingly first sees to the over-protection of his K4. Further, from where she stands his Q has at her disposal a reserve square in QKt1 to which she can withdraw if need arise, should the QB file be opened.

8. O—O	P—QR4
9. P—B4	P—QKt4

The question whether a flank attack is admissible or not can only be solved by reference to the actual position in the center. If this be secure a flank attack cannot be wholly amiss. So, too, here. And what matters it that the K has not yet castled? As it is he is unassailable.

10. P x KtP	P x P
11. R—B1	Q—Kt1

The withdrawing room.

12. Q—B2	. . . .

P—K4 seems more to the point.

12.	O—O
13. P—K4	B—Kt2
14. Kt—Q4	R—B1
15. Q—Kt1	R x R
16. R x R	P—Kt5
17. Kt—B6	. . . .

A bit premature in my opinion.

| 17. . . . . | B x Kt |
| 18. R x B | P—R5 |

Every free moment is used to the strengthening of the position on the extreme Q's wing.

19. P—Q4   . . . .

This move must be credited to Black's strategy in over-protecting his K4. The valuable diagonal QKt2 to KB6 is now obstructed; but by no other means could the thrust P—K5 have been effected. Those engaged in this over-protection have once more stood the test excellently. Moreover, they have had to put up with no inconveniences, but have made themselves felt in all directions.

One variation should be mentioned, namely 19. P—B4 in order to keep the QP at Q3. The continuation might have been 19. . . . . B—B4 *ch !*, and White has after all to submit to playing 20. P—Q4, and after 20. . . . . B—B1; 21. P—K5 we should have arrived at the position in the text.

| 19. . . . . | B—B1 |
| 20. P—K5 | Kt—K1 |

The White Bishops have now small possibilities of action.

21. P—B4   Q—Kt4

. . . . P—R6 at once would have been more precise.

| 22. Q—B2 | P—R6 |
| 23. B—QB1 | . . . . |

It was essential to interpolate here B—KB1.

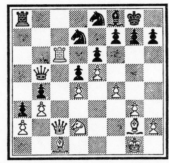

Black with the move forces his way into the enemy game by means of a sacrifice of the exchange, and wins the entrenched QRP. How does he do it?

23. . . . .   B—B4

This interesting combination should begin with . . . . Kt—B4 (not . . . . B—B4). The difference will soon be manifest.

| 24. R x B | Kt x R |
| 25. P x Kt ? | . . . . |

The interpolation here of B—B1 (which would not have been possible if Black had played 23. . . . . Kt—B4) would have yielded him an extra tempo for the end game.

25. . . . .   R—B1

We can see by his face that White's QRP is marked out for death.

26. Kt—Kt1	Q x P ch
27. Q x Q	R x Q
28. B x RP	. . . .

Or 28. B—Q2, R—B7; 29. B—KB1, R x P; 30. B x P, R—Kt7 ch !, and wins. If White had had one tempo more (see note to White's 25th move) this combination would have been impossible. There followed: 28. . . . . P x B; 29. Kt x P, R—R4; 30. Kt—B2, R x P; 31. Kt—Q4, R—Kt7; 32. P—B5, Kt—B2; 33. P x P, Kt x P; 34. Kt—B6, P—Q5, and White *resigned*.

39. NIMZOVICH DEFENSE

Illustrates over-protection and also the problem of the isolated QP.

Played in 1921

WHITE	BLACK
Three Swedish	*A. Nimzovich*
Amateurs	
1. P—K4	Kt—QB3
2. P—Q4	P—Q4
3. P—K5	P—B3
4. B—QKt5	. . . .

P—KB4 is held to be better.

| 4. . . . . | B—B4 |
| 5. Kt—KB3 | Q—Q2 |

| 6. P—B4 | B x Kt ! |

With this exchange, which is anything but obvious, Black plans to win the square Q4 for his Kt.

| 7. R x B | O—O—O |
| 8. P x QP | . . . . |

If P—B5, then . . . . P—Kt4. A fight would then take place for possession of the point K4. For example, 8. P—B5, P—Kt4; 9. Q—K2 (to threaten P—K6 shutting Black in), 9. . . . . . Q—K3; 10. P—KR3, Kt—R3, followed by . . . . Kt—B2, or else . . . . Kt—QKt1. In either case Black would not stand badly.

8.	Q x P
9. B x Kt	Q x B
10. O—O	P—K3
11. B—K3	Kt—K2
12. Q—K2	Kt—Q4

We may with a clear conscience regard White's QP as isolated. His weakness (for the end game!) is evident; further Black has in his Q4 a very strong point. As regards any compensating advantage for what we have called his isolated QP White has the outpost station QB5 which will serve some purpose; on the other hand his K5 is of no use to him as a station for his Kt. The game is about equal.

13. KR—B1	Q—Q2

It is very questionable whether P x P would not have been better for White than the R move. True his opponent would have had the KKt file and a centrally posted B at Q3, but the K file must not be despised, at any rate as a counter weight. The curious over-protection which is built up in moves 13–18 has been discussed in II. iv, 1, p. 242, under Diagram 189.

14. R—B4	K—Kt1
15. Q—Q2	R—B1
16. Kt—K1	B—K2
17. Kt—Q3	KR—Q1
18. Q—B2	P—KB4

Having consolidated his position, Black passes to the attack, which indeed is by no means easy to conduct since for one thing objectives are wanting and for another White himself has some attacking chances.

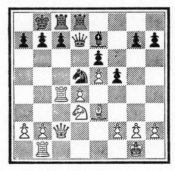

19. R—QB1	. . . .

Without question 19. P—QKt4 should have been played here; with the intention of playing when opportunity offered Kt—B5, B x Kt; KtP x B. The question now arises, is Black's position strong enough to bear weakening? Two moves in particular come under consideration in answer to 19. P—QKt4, namely 19. . . . . . P—QKt3, and 19. . . . . . P—QKt4. If 19. . . . . . P—QKt3, then 20. Kt—B5 ! can be played, but after 20. . . . . . B x Kt !; 21. KtP x B, P—B3, Black would stand very well. However, he must emphatically not accept the Kt sacrifice as the following combination proves. (See diagram.) 19. P—QKt4 !, P—QKt3; 20. Kt—B5 !, P x Kt; 21. P x P ch, K—R1 ? (the return sacrifice . . . . Kt—Kt3 was essential); 22. P—B6, Q—K1; 23. R—R4 (threatening R x P ch), Kt—Kt3; 24. P—Q5 ! !, R x P; 25. R x P ch, K x R; 26. Q—R4 ch, K—Kt1; 27. B x Kt, P x B; 28. R x P ch, K—B2; 29. R—Kt7 ch, K—Q1; 30. P—B7 ch !, R x P; 31. R—Kt8 ch, R—B1; 32. R x R ch, and Q x Q ch and wins. A true Morphy combination.

We may quietly note the fact that his over-protected central position is so strong that Black can here without a qualm leave himself unprotected and yet remain master of the situation as he was before, for he is in a position laughingly to evade any enemy combination, be it ever so diabolical.

We have still to show what would happen if Black played 19. . . . . P—QKt4 in reply to 19. P—QKt4. In this case, too, Black would not fare badly: 20. R—B6, K—Kt2; 21. Kt—B5 *ch*, B x Kt; 22. R x B, Kt—Kt3; followed by . . . . P—B3; Black is strong on the white squares.

19.	P—KKt4
20. Kt—B5	B x Kt
21. R x B	R—Kt1
22. Q—K2	P—KR4 !
23. B—Q2	. . . .

23. Q x P *?*, P—Kt5 and . . . . R—R1.

23.	P—R5
24. P—R4	P—Kt5
25. P—R5	P—R3 *!*
26. P—Kt4	P—B3

White has at last spent his fury.

27. R—Kt1	Q—KB2
28. R—Kt3	P—B5
29. Q—K4	P—B6 *!*

For White would not be able to hold out after 30. P x P, P x P *ch;* 31. K—B1, QR—B1 (stronger than . . . . R—Kt8 *ch*).

| 30. R—B1 | P x P |

| 31. K x P | QR—B1 |

Note with what surprising ease the Black Rooks are brought into action, a further proof, to my mind, of the enormous vitality of over-protecting pieces.

32. R—B1	P—Kt6 *!*
33. RP x P	P x P
34. P—B4	. . . .

After R x P, R x R *ch* the King would be exposed.

34.	Kt—K2
35. B—K1	Kt—B4
36. R—R1	R—Kt5
37. B x P	Q—Kt3
38. Q—K1	Kt x B

Decisive, though so simple and even insipid. It wins the Pawns which are so conveniently exposed in the 4th rank.

39. R x Kt	R(B1) x P
40. R(R1)—R3	R x P
41. Q—B2	R x R *ch*
42. R x R	Q—K5 *ch*
43. K—R2	Q x P
44. K—Kt2	Q—Q4 *ch*
45. Resigns	

One of my favorite games.

40. PHILIDOR'S DEFENSE

The Hanham Defense. Illustrates combined play on both wings. The fearlessness with which Black is able up to a certain point to ignore his own weakness at Q3 is notable.

San Sebastian, 1911

WHITE	BLACK
R. *Teichmann*	A. *Nimzovich*
1. P—K4	P—K4
2. Kt—KB3	P—Q3
3. P—Q4	Kt—KB3
4. Kt—B3	QKt—Q2
5. B—QB4	B—K2
6. O—O	O—O
7. Q—K2	P—B3
8. B—KKt5	. . . .

P—QR4 would have been preferable here.

8.	P—KR3
9. B—R4	Kt—R4
10. B—KKt3	Kt x B

10. . . . . B—B3 was also to be considered.

| 11. RP x Kt | P—QKt4 |
| 12. B—Q3 | P—R3 ! |

Black's Pawn-mass is now of such a constitution (I mean inner structure), that they must inspire respect. Notice the twofold possibility of deployment by . . . . P—QB4 or, on occasion, ... P—Q4.

| 13. P—R4 | . . . . |

He tries to nip the latent strength of Black's Pawns in the bud.

13.	B—Kt2
14. QR—Q1	Q—B2
15. RP x P	RP x P
16. P—KKt4	KR—K1
17. P—Q5	. . . .

To get out of the way of his *vis-à-vis* on the King file.

17.	P—Kt5
18. P x P	B x P
19. Kt—Kt1	Kt—B4
20. QKt—Q2	Q—B1

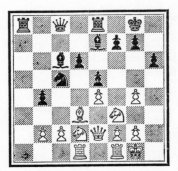

White's attempt to pick a quarrel, *sit venia verbo,* must be regarded as having failed, for Black's P at Q3 is easily defendable while the two Bishops in conjunction with the QR file and the threatening diagonal QB1 to KKt5 exercise no mean influence.

| 21. B—B4 | . . . . |

A witty defense of the KKtP (. . . . Q x P ? ?; B x P *ch*).

21.	P—Kt3
22. P—KKt3	K—Kt2
23. Kt—R2	B—KKt4 !

The weakness at Q3 is here of but slight importance.

| 24. P—KB3 | . . . . |

If 24. P—B4 ?, then 24. . . . . . P x P; 25. P x P, B—B3, winning a P.

| 24. . . . . | Q—B2 |

Threatening . . . . Kt—R5, and if R—Kt1 then . . . . B x Kt and . . . . B x P.

| 25. KR—K1 | R—R1 |
| 26. Kt(Q2)—B1 | P—R4 |

The moves now following lead to the occupation of the important files and diagonals.

27. P x P	R x P
28. B—Q5	QR—R1
29. B x B	Q x B
30. Q—B4	Q—Kt3 !
31. K—Kt2	. . . .

A weakness has now slowly crystallized out; namely that of White's base. With the Black Kt placed at Q5 the invasion of White's 2nd rank would be decisive.

| 31. . . . . | Kt—K3 |

He has his eye on Q5 but at the same time threatens the K's wing by . . . . R x Kt ch; Kt x R, R x Kt ch; K x R, Q—B7 ch;

K—R3, B—B5 ! See Diagram 198, p. 255.

| 32. R—K2 | . . . . |

But for the threat just referred to White could perhaps find an adequate defense by 32. Q—Q5, Kt—Q5; 33. P—KB4.

| 32. . . . . | Kt—Q5 |

But now this move takes place with the win of a tempo.

| 33. R(K2)—K1 | . . . . |

Or R—B2 ?, B—K6 !

| 33. . . . . | Q—Kt2 |

. . . . R—QB1 can no longer be parried; a good example this of how one can devote one's attention to several weaknesses at the same time.

| 34. R x Kt | . . . . |

After 34. P—B3, P x P; 35. P x P, Q—Kt7 ch, the weakness of White's 2nd rank would have been shown up.

| 34. . . . . | P x R |
| 35. Kt—Kt4 | . . . . |

or 35. Q x P ch, B—B3; 36. Q x QP, R—Q1.

35.	Q—Kt3
36. P—B4	B—K2
37. R—Q1	P—B4
38. Kt—B2	P x P
39. Q x P ch	Q x Q
40. R x Q	P—Q4

41.	P—Kt4	B—B4 !
42.	R—Q1	R—R5
43.	R x P	B x Kt
44.	K x B	R x P

Black in order to maintain his advantage had always to try to combine attack on the K with play in the center. (*Cf.* his 40th and 41st moves.)

45.	K—K3	R—QB1

And now the Q's wing is brought in too.

46.	K x P	R—B5 *ch*
47.	K—Q3	R(B) x KBP

Now things go easier. 48. Kt—K3, R—Kt6; 49. R—K5, K—B3; 50. R—K8, K—B2; 51. R—K5, R—B3; 52. P—B4, P—Kt6; 53. K—K4, R—K3; 54. R x R, K x R; 55. Kt—Q5, P—Kt4 and White **resigned**.

41. RUY LOPEZ

A most complicated game in the strategical sense. Lasker maneuvers on one wing and breaks through on the other. The why and the wherefore of this procedure will be found explained in the notes.

St. Petersburg, 1909

WHITE	BLACK
Dr. E. Lasker	*A. Burn*
1. P—K4	P—K4
2. Kt—KB3	Kt—QB3
3. B—Kt5	P—QR3

4.	B—R4	Kt—B3
5.	O—O	B—K2
6.	R—K1	P—QKt4
7.	B—Kt3	P—Q3
8.	P—B3	Kt—QR4
9.	B—B2	P—B4
10.	P—Q4	Q—B2
11.	QKt—Q2	Kt—B3
12.	Kt—B1	O—O ?

Black ought to have tried to force White to declare his intentions in the center; therefore 12. . . . . BP x P; 13. P x P, B—Kt5.

13. Kt—K3	. . . .

Intending to invade the center with Kt—Q5.

13.	B—Kt5
14. Kt x B	. . . .

The reply to 14. Kt—Q5 would have been 14. . . . . . Q—R2; 15. Kt x B *ch*, Kt x Kt ! With the text move Lasker plays for the advantage of the two Bishops.

14.	Kt x Kt
15. P—KR3	Kt—B3
16. B—K3	Kt—Q2
17. Q—K2	B—B3
18. QR—Q1	Kt—K2
19. B—Kt1	Kt—QKt3
20. P—R3	Kt—Kt3
21. P—KKt3	KR—K1

Black has consistently kept his end in mind, that is to prepare for . . . . P—Q4; so now Lasker finds himself forced to play P—Q5 thus blocking his own B. The game now enters a new stage.

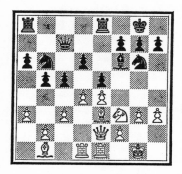

| 22. | P—Q5 | Kt—Q2 |
| 23. | K—Kt2 | Q—Q1 |

Instead of this he should have played . . . . P—B5 followed by . . . . Kt—B4. The Kt would then have been well posted and, more important, would have a preventive effect, for White was preparing for P—KB4 *inter alia*.

24.	P—KR4	B—K2
25.	P—R5	Kt(3)—B1
26.	R—R1	P—R3
27.	QR—Kt1	Kt—R2

Black's KKt4 seems now strongly fortified.

28.	K—B1	K—R1
29.	R—R2	R—KKt1
30.	Kt—K1	. . . .

If Kt—R4, Black would simply exchange (. . . . B x Kt; R

x B), and the game would then take on a somewhat rigid aspect. Lasker, therefore, wisely avoids Kt—R4 and seeks to preserve whatever latent dynamic force there is in the position, little though this be.

30.	. . . .	R—Kt1
31.	Kt—B2	P—R4
32.	B—Q2	B—B3
33.	P—B3	Kt—Kt3
34.	R—KB2	. . . .

White intends to play Kt—K3 and wishes to hold the move P—KB4 in readiness should Black play . . . . B—Kt4 (Lasker).

34.	. . . .	Kt—QB1
35.	K—Kt2	Q—Q2
36.	K—R1	Kt—K2
37.	R—R2	R—Kt2
38.	R—KB1	R—K1
39.	Kt—K3	Kt—Kt1
40.	P—KB4	B—Q1
41.	Q—B3	. . . .

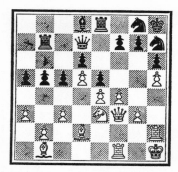

Lasker has succeeded in car-

rying out P—B4 under circumstances favorable to himself; but there was no direct advantage to be got by the move. However, Black's pieces which have to keep on the look-out against the threat of an invasion by Kt—B5, are less well posted in case of an attack on the Q's wing. And so we may say that Lasker has laid the K's wing under siege in order to bring the enemy pieces out of contact with their own Q's wing, and will now roll up this (left) wing and thus score a double advantage; definite weaknesses are to be created, and in addition his B's are to get room for maneuvering; for instance, by P—B4, P—Kt5; B—B2 followed by Q—Q1 and B—R4.

41.	. . . .	P—B5
42.	P—R4	B—Kt3
43.	P x KtP	Q x P?

The decisive error. The right course, as Lasker pointed out in the book of the Congress, was 43. . . . . B x Kt; 44. B x B, Q x P followed by . . . . P—R5 and . . . . R—R1, and Black's game is tenable.

| 44. | Kt—B5 | Q—Q2 |
| 45. | Q—Kt4 | P—B3 |

The Kt at B5 can no longer be driven away by, say, ... Kt—K2. Black has now evident weak-nesses on both wings and Lasker exploits them without any particular trouble.

46.	B—B2	B—B4
47.	R—R1	KR—Kt1
48.	B—B1	Q—QB2
49.	B—R4	Q—Kt3
50.	R—Kt2	R—KB2
51.	Q—K2	Q—R3
52.	B—B6	. . . .

Threatening P—QKt4.

| 52. | . . . . | Kt—K2 |

At last he manages to oust the intruder at his KB4, but meanwhile White is grown too strong on the Q's wing.

| 53. | Kt x Kt | R x Kt |
| 54. | R—R4 | P x P |

Desperation.

There followed: 55. P x P, P—B4; 56. P—K5, Kt—B3; 57. R x BP, Kt—Kt5; 58. R x B, Q x Q; 59. R x Q, P x R; 60. P—Q6, R—R2; 61. P—K6, R—R3; 62. P—K7, Kt—B3; 63. P—Q7, Kt x QP; 64. B x Kt, Resigns.

This fine game is instructive as illustrating, *inter alia*, the struggle of united Bishops for open country in which to maneuver.

The following game won a brilliancy prize in the New York tournament, 1927.

42. INDIAN DEFENSE

New York, 1927

WHITE	BLACK
A. Nimzovich	*F. J. Marshall*
1. P—QB4	Kt—KB3
2. P—Q4	P—K3
3. Kt—KB3	P—B4
4. P—Q5	P—Q3
5. Kt—B3	P x P
6. P x P	P—KKt3
7. Kt—Q2	. . . .

To establish himself at QB4.

7.	QKt—Q2
8. Kt—B4	Kt—Kt3
9. P—K4	B—Kt2
10. Kt—K3	. . . .

Planning P—QR4—R5 and to post the Kt anew at QB4. Black would have done better to exchange Kts on his 9th move. White now gets the advantage.

10.	O—O
11. B—Q3	Kt—R4
12. O—O	B—K4
13. P—QR4	Kt—B5
14. P—R5	Kt—Q2
15. Kt—B4	Kt x B
16. Q x Kt	P—B4
17. P x P	R x P
18. P—B4	. . . .

The prelude to a complicated attacking operation which was the more unexpected since Kt—K4 gave a good game without any effort. But for once I wanted to go in for a combination.

18.	B—Q5 *ch*
19. B—K3	B x Kt
20. Q x B	Kt—B3
21. Q—Kt3 !	. . . .

White gets compensation for the QP. Note, *inter alia*, that Black's Queen-side is difficult to develop.

21.	R x QP

The answer to . . . . Kt x P would have been QR—K1 *!!*, for . . . . B—K3 would have been prevented because of B x P. Black would then have been quite helpless, and White could have won by, *e.g.*, B—Q2 followed by the doubling of the Rooks in the K file.

22. P—B5 *!*	P x P
23. B—Kt5	. . . .

There is a peculiar point in this move.

If, that is to say, 23. . . . . B—K3, and it is with this parry that White has above all things to reckon, then 24. Q x P (threatening B x Kt and the win of a piece), R—B1; 25. QR—K1 *!*, and the B must give up the defense of either of the Rooks on which B x Kt would lead to the win of whichever is left defenseless.

23.	R—Q5
24. Kt—Kt6 *ch*	P—B5
25. Q—QB3	P x Kt
26. Q x R	K—Kt2
27. QR—K1	. . . .

The quickest road to the win.

27.	P x P
28. R—K8 *!*	. . . .

Violent but intelligible.

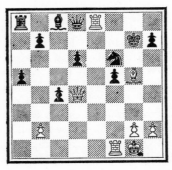

28.	Q x R
29. Q x Kt *ch*	K—Kt1
30. B—R6	Resigns

43. ALEKHINE'S DEFENSE

Semmering, 1926

WHITE	BLACK
A. *Nimzovich*	Dr. A. *Alekhine*
1. P—K4	Kt—KB3
2. Kt—QB3	P—Q4
3. P—K5	KKt—Q2
4. P—B4	P—K3
5. Kt—B3	P—QB4
6. P—KKt3	Kt—QB3
7. B—Kt2	. . . .

Black's King's wing seems somewhat boxed in, but as compensation his center is the more mobile.

7.	B—K2
8. O—O	O—O
9. P—Q3	Kt—Kt3

9. . . . . P—Q5 would have been bad because of Kt—K4 and the Knight is centrally established. On the other hand 9. . . . . P—B3 was well worth consideration. For instance, P x P, B x P and Black controls the center.

10. Kt—K2	P—Q5 *! ?*

Black wants to score the Kt move as an error, for now the Kt can no longer get to K4. This is, however, a mistake and therefore it would have been much better to play . . . . P—B3 instead of . . . . P—Q5. For example: 10. . . . . P—B3; 11. P x P, B x P; 12. P—B3, P—K4;

13. P x KP, Kt x P, and Black would not stand badly.

    11. **P—KKt4**   **P—B3**

This move, which Black has twice passed over, leads now, thanks to the weakness of his K5 to a result which promises little fruit. The "prophylactic" defense, *11.* . . . . R—K1; *12.* Kt—Kt3, B—B1; *13.* Kt—K4, Kt—Q4 (putting a stop to P—B5), would therefore have deserved the preference.

    12. **P x P**   **P x P**

There was also no true joy to be got out of *12.* . . . . B x P; *13.* Kt—Kt3, P—K4; *14.* P—B5.

    13. **Kt—Kt3**   **Kt—Q4**

Black seeks to defend his threatened wing from the center, but this plan should not here have been sufficient to save the situation.

    14. **Q—K2**   **B—Q3**
    15. **Kt—R4**   . . . .

To threaten *16.* B x Kt and *17.* Kt—B5.

    15. . . . .   **Kt(B)—K2**
    16. **B—Q2**   . . . .

Kt—R5 would have been sharper here. *E.g.*, *16.* Kt—R5, Kt—Kt3; *17.* B x Kt, P x B; *18.* Kt—B5 with a winning attack.

    16. . . . .   **Q—B2**
    17. **Q—B2**   . . . .

Kt—R5 was still preferable.

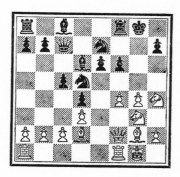

    17. . . . .   **P—B5 !**
    18. **P x P**   **Kt—K6 !**

With this ingenious diversion Dr. Alekhine succeeds in bringing his opponent's attack to a standstill for some time. The game up to this point is discussed in II. i. § 6, p. 178, in connection with "centralization."

    19. **B x Kt**   **P x B**
    20. **Q—B3**   **Q x P**

The position is in a measure cleared up. Black has a passed Pawn which, it is true, is very sick, but very highly insured against death. We mean to say that the Bishop diagonals QB3—KR8 (after . . . . B—Q2—B3) and QB4—KKt8 are compensation. Instead of chasing after the dubious win of the Pawn it would have been more to the purpose had White gone on with his King-side attack; and this by

P—Kt5. Neglect of this move throws White back.

21. Kt—K4	B—B2
22. P—Kt3	Q—Q5
23. P—B3	Q—Kt3
24. K—R1	. . . .

White has localized the enemy thrust.

24.	Kt—Q4

. . . . B—Q2 was certainly better.

25. P—B5	. . . .

Here he misses his opportunity to play P—Kt5, which would have won. For instance: 25. . . . . P x P; 26. Kt x P, R x P; 27. Q—R5; or 25. . . . . P—B4; 26. Q—R5, P x Kt, 27. B x P, etc.

25.	Kt—B5 !
26. KR—Q1	K—R1

Better, according to H. Wolf, would have been 26. . . . . P—K7; 27. R—Q2, Q—Kt4 followed by . . . . Q—K4.

27. B—B1	P x P
28. P x P	B—K4
29. R—K1	B—Q2

The game proceeds as was indicated in the note to the 20th move. White wins the P, but Black keeps the pressure by means of his two Bishops.

30. R x P	B—B3

31. QR—K1	Kt—Q4

With . . . . R—KKt1 Black could have increased the pressure.

32. R—Q3	Kt x P

Pretty but insufficient. True the acceptance of the sacrifice would have been ruinous (33. R x Kt, B x R; 34. Q x B, Q—B7), but White has a truly startling counter-combination at his disposal.

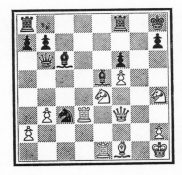

33. Kt—Kt6 ch !	P x Kt
34. Q—Kt4 ! !	. . . .

The point. To strike at once would have been bad, e.g., 34. P x P, K—Kt2; 35. Q—R3, R—R1; 36. R—Q7 ch, B x R; 37. Q x B ch, K x P, and White is threatened with mate.

34.	R—B2 ?

. . . . R—KKt1 was imperative The continuation would

have been 35. P x P, K—Kt2;
36. R—Q7 ch, B x R; 37. Q x B
ch, K x P; 38. B—Q3 !, K—R3;
39. Q—R3 ch, K—Kt2; 40. R—
Kt1 ch, Q x R ch !, and the win
is still far away.

35. R—R3 ch	K—Kt2
36. B—B4 !	B—Q4
37. P x P	Kt x Kt
38. P x R ch	K—B1
39. R x Kt	. . . .

A simpler win would have
been 39. Q—Kt8 ch, K—K2; 40.
P—B8 (Q) ch, R x Q; 41. R—
R7 ch, K—K1; 42. Q x B.

39.	B x R ch
40. Q x B	K—K2
41. P—B8 (Q) ch	. . . .

The passed Pawn's lust to expand!

| 41. . . . . | R x Q |
| 42. Q—Q5 | Q—Q3 |

42. . . . . Q—B3 would have
led not to the exchange of
Queens but to the loss of his
Queen, namely 43. R—R7 ch,
K—K1; 44. B—Kt5.

43. Q x P ch	K—Q1
44. R—Q3	B—Q5
45. Q—K4	R—K1
46. R x B	Resigns

44. FRENCH DEFENSE

Illustrates in an instructive
manner the connection between
play in the center on the one
hand, and diversions undertaken
on the wings on the other. The
dependence of a flank attack for
success on the "state of health"
of the center is very clearly
brought out.

One of four simultaneous consultation games.

Upsala, 1921

WHITE	BLACK
E. Andersson	A. Nimzovich
R. Enström	
O. Oeberg	
1. P—K4	P—K3
2. P—Q4	P—Q4
3. Kt—QB3	. . . .

The right move is 3. P—K5.

| 3. . . . . | B—Kt5 |
| 4. B—Q3 | Kt—QB3 |

A new train of thought.

5. Kt—K2	KKt—K2
6. O—O	O—O
7. P—K5	. . . .

Looks very good.

| 7. . . . . | Kt—B4 |
| 8. B—K3 | P—B3 |

Black has now got over the
difficulties of the opening.

| 9. B x Kt | P x B |
| 10. P—B4 | B—K3 |

Obedient to the law that a passed Pawn must be blockaded.

| 11. Kt—Kt3 | B x Kt *!* |
| 12. P x B | Kt—R4 *!* |

It was only reluctantly and after much deliberation that I determined on this diversion on the extreme flank; it looks risky, since the situation in the center is by no means secure. For one of my leading principles lays down that a flank attack is only justified if the center is secure. Yet in the present case White cannot force his opponent to play . . . . P x P, and if he take the KBP himself, he gets, it is true, the point K5 (after . . . . R x P), but Black by bringing up his reserves can mitigate this danger.

13. Q—Q3	Q—Q2
14. R—B3	P—KKt3
15. Kt—K2	R—B2 *!*
16. P—KR4	P—R4
17. K—R2 *!*	QR—KB1

The reserves; see the last note.

| 18. R—Kt3 | K—R2 |
| 19. Kt—Kt1 *!* | . . . . |

Aiming for KKt5 or K5. It will be seen that the consulting players are thoroughly exercised in the art of maneuvering, and are opponents to be taken seriously.

| 19. . . . . | R—Kt2 |
| 20. Kt—B3 | Q—R5 |

At last Black proceeds with the attack to which his 11th move was the prelude. This slowness is all to his credit.

21. P x P	R x P
22. Kt—Kt5 *ch*	K—Kt1
23. B—Kt1	Kt—B5
24. R—K1	B—Q2 *!!*

This simple strategical retreat reveals my plan of defense. As my system lays down, the ideal aimed at by every operation in a file is the entry into the 7th and 8th ranks. However, here the points of invasion, K7 and K8 are safeguarded, and the R at Kt3 cannot co-operate since he is deprived of the square K3.

25. Kt—B3	B—Kt4
26. Q—Q1	Q x RP
27. Q—K2	. . . .

| 27. . . . . | Kt—Q3 *!!* |

With this retreat a maneuver is started which is designed to neutralize the enemy's apparently strong hold on the K file. Less good would have been 27. . . . . Q—R6 with the idea of getting home safely with the booty by means of 28. . . . . Q—Q3, thus: 27. . . . . Q—R6; 28. Kt—K5, Q—Q3; 29. Kt x Kt, B x Kt; 30. Q—B2, R—K3; 31. R—K5 ! and White still has drawing chances, whereas the phlegmatic maneuver in the text wins.

28. Q—K5   Kt—K1 !

With this the regrouping . . . . R—Q3 and . . . . Kt—B3 is threatened, whereby the R and Kt will have exchanged stations. If White prevents this by 29. Kt—Kt5 (29. . . . . R—Q3 ?; 30. Q x Kt ch and mate next move), White will be undoubtedly strong in the K file, yet the distinctive characteristic of the position, namely the spearhead station of White's Q, will prevent him from taking full advantage of the file. For instance, 29. Kt—Kt5, B—B3; 30. R(Kt)—K3, Q x P; or 30. R—K2, Q—B5 (Blockade!); 31. R(Kt)—K3, P—R4, and wins, for Kt—K6 ? is impossible because of . . . . R—K2, and he has no other effective move in the K file at his disposal. In the game the continuation was:—

29. Kt—Q2   R—Q3
30. P—B4   B—Q2

31. R—QB3   Kt—B3

And now this difficult regrouping maneuver (under enemy fire) has been successfully carried out.

32. P x P ? ?   . . . .

A gross mistake, but even after 32. Q—K2, R—K3; 33. Q—Q1, R(Kt)—K2, White's game would have been hopeless.

32. . . . .   Kt—Kt5 ch
33. Resigns

In the following game two armies out of contact with one another operate in the center and on a flank. It is interesting to see how contact is finally established between them.

45. SICILIAN DEFENSE

London, 1927

WHITE	BLACK
F. D. Yates	A. Nimzovich
1. P—K4	P—QB4
2. Kt—KB3	Kt—KB3

The innovation introduced by me in 1911 at San Sebastian.

3. P—K5   Kt—Q4

The relationship between the Alekhine Defense (1. P—K4, Kt—KB3) introduced in 1921 and my treatment of the Sicilian will be noted. (Cf., too, Bogolyubov's application of the idea in 1. P—Q4, Kt—QB3.)

| 4. B—B4 | Kt—Kt3 |
| 5. B—K2 | Kt—B3 |

White has lost a tempo with his B, on the other hand the Kt at Kt3 is not particularly well placed, so that the Bishop maneuver is not to be criticized.

| 6. P—B3 | P—Q4 |
| 7. P—Q4 | . . . . |

We should have given 7. P x P *e.p.* the preference.

7.	P x P
8. P x P	B—B4
9. O—O	P—K3
10. Kt—B3	B—K2
11. Kt—K1	. . . .

If the attack planned by this move, namely P—B4 with P—KKt4 and P—B5 should really prove possible to carry out, this would be a proof of the incorrectness of 8. . . . . B—B4, and that would be an absurdity. In point of fact the matter stands thus: No particular result is achieved by 11. Kt—K1, and this diversion would better have been abandoned in favor of a systematic utilization of the QB file. For example, 11. B—K3, O—O; 12. R—B1, followed by P—QR3, P—QKt4 and Kt—Q2—Kt3—B5, when the establishment of an outpost advocated by my system would have been attained.

| 11. . . . . | Kt—Q2 *!* |

| 12. B—Kt4 *!* | . . . . .. |

Cleverly played. The answer to 12. P—B4 would have been, of course, ... Kt x QP; Q x Kt *? ?*, B—B4. 12. B—K3 would also have been unfavorable because of 12. . . . . Kt (Q2) x P; 13. P x Kt, P—Q5; 14. B—Q2, P x Kt; 15. B x P, Q—B2, with advantage in position for Black. By the text move (12. B—Kt4) Yates is able in a quite startling manner to make the advance, P—B4, at which he was aiming.

12.	B—Kt3
13. P—B4	Kt x QP
14. Kt x P *!*	Kt—QB3

If 14. . . . . B—QB4, then 15. P—QKt4 would have been strong. 14. . . . . . P x Kt would have also been bad because of B x Kt *ch*, followed by Q x Kt.

| 15. Kt x B | Q—Kt3 *ch* |
| 16. K—R1 | Kt x Kt |

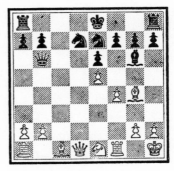

| 17. Q—R4 | . . . . |

A typical sin of omission!

In the face of Black's obvious plan to occupy the central points, White should, by himself centralizing, have disputed them with his opponent, thus: *17. Q—K2* (intending B—K3), Kt—Q4; *18. B—B3*, Q—B4; *19. B—Q2*, Kt(Q2)—Kt3; *20. R—B1*, Q—K2, and White has more of the center than Black. And even if such a "more" were not attainable, what matter! Even in this case White ought to have fought for it. As it is a just punishment now overtakes him.

| 17. . . . . | P—KR4 |
| 18. B—R3 | . . . . |

Forced, for if B—B3, then Kt—B4 with a further gain of terrain in the center; moreover, there would then be a mating threat in the air, namely . . . . P—R5 and . . . . Kt—Kt6 *ch.*

| 18. . . . . | B—B4 |
| 19. Q—R3 | Q—Kt4 |

Making room for the Kt at Q2, which is aiming for Q4 via QKt3.

20. K—Kt1	Kt—QKt3
21. Q—KB3	Kt(Kt3) Q4
22. P—QKt3	Q—Kt3 *ch*
23. R—B2	. . . .

(*See Diagram*)

| 23. . . . . | R—QB1 |

This move in conjunction with

Position after 23. R—B2

the one following leads to a decentralization of his King's Rook and so to a defect in his position which has been so harmoniously constructed. On the other hand the continuation *23. . . . . O—O—O !* held out the promise of untroubled harmony; for after *24. . . . . K—Kt1* and *25. . . . . P—Kt3* nothing stood in the way of employing the two Rooks centrally: *e.g., 26. . . . . R—Q2; 27. . . . . R—QB1.*

However, *23. . . . . B—Kt5* seems to be still better. For instance, *24. B x B*, P x B; *25. Q x P*, R x P; *26. Q x KtP*, O—O—O; *27. K x R,* Q x R; *28. Kt—Q3*, Q—K7, and Black must win. Or, lastly, it was also possible to combine the two plans, thus: *23. . . . . O—O—O; 24. B—R3* and now *24. . . . . B—Kt5.* If then perhaps *25. R—B1 ch,* K—Kt1; *26. B—*

B5, then 26. . . . . Q x B; 27. R x Q, B x Q; 28. R x B, R—QB1 with a victorious incursion via the QB file.

24. B—Q2   R—R3

Interesting, for when all is said and done, Black's position, centralized even to the extent that it is, can support an adventurous raid; yet 24. . . . . O—O with . . . . P—Kt3 and . . . . KR—Q1 was certainly more correct.

25. R—Q1	B x B
26. Q x B	Kt—B4
27. Q—Q3	R—Kt3
28. Kt—B3	R—Kt5
29. P—KR3	R—Kt6
30. P—QR4	Kt—R5

Black's structure suffers from an inner discord. The position of the cut off R makes a mating attack seem desirable; but the disposition of the rest of the army is rather directed towards the end game, in which the Kt at Q4 would have enormous effect, while the white squares would be in Black's undisputed possession.

31. K—B1   R—B3

To draw the sting of the threat Q—R7 and Q—Kt8 *ch*, the R runs away betimes. Black has in fact to maneuver very cautiously.

| 32. P—R5 | Q—Q1 |
| 33. K—Kt1 | Kt—B4 |

33. . . . . Kt x Kt *ch*; 34. R x Kt, R x R; 35. Q x R, P—KKt3, would not have been good because of 36. P—B5.

| 34. K—R2 | P—R3 |
| 35. Q—Kt1 | . . . . |

To threaten Kt—Q4.

35. . . . .   Q—K2

He does not mind the threat, has his eye, moreover, on his QB4 (. . . . Q—B4).

36. Kt—Q4 ?   . . . .

Loses; R—QB1 was better.

36. . . . .   Q—R5 !

As the detachments which have been cut off cannot get back to the army, the latter comes to them.

37. B—K1   . . . .

If 37. Kt x R, then . . . . R x RP *ch* and mate in two moves.

37. . . . .   Kt x P

Again threatening mate, this time by . . . . R x KtP *ch*, etc.

38. R x Kt   R x RP *ch*

Simplest.

39. P x R   Q x R *ch*

40. K—Kt2	Kt—K6 *ch*

And *mate* in two moves.

For this game I was awarded the special prize of £10, "for the best played game" in the tournament.

There follow five games of historical interest.

46. FRENCH DEFENSE

A most instructive game from A to Z, one which I regard as the first in which my new philosophy of the center was exhibited. See I. ix. § 4, p. 142.

Carlsbad, 1911

WHITE	BLACK
A. Nimzovich	*G. Salve*
1. P—K4	P—K3
2. P—Q4	P—Q4
3. P—K5	P—QB4
4. P—QB3	Kt—QB3
5. Kt—B3	Q—Kt3
6. B—Q3	. . . .

See note to this move in Game No. 19.

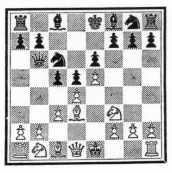

6.	B—Q2

A very plausible move.

Since White still delays P x P, Black intends to force his hand with . . . . R—B1. The right course was 6. . . . . P x P; 7. P x P and thus to pass into quite other channels. See Games Nos. 19 and 20.

7. P x P *! !*	B x P
8. O—O	P—B3

Black swells in triumph and throws himself hungrily on the last remaining member of the once so proud chain-family, to destroy him. His war cry is "Room for the KP!" But it happens quite otherwise.

9. P—QKt4	. . . .

In order to be able to provide his K5 with an enduring defense. 9. Q—K2 would also have been a defense, but no enduring one, for there would follow 9. . . . . P x P; 10. Kt x P, Kt x Kt; 11. Q x Kt, Kt—B3 and the blockading Q at K5 will be easily driven away.

9.	B—K2
10. B—KB4	P x P

Again we have the exchange operation which we have so often discussed; this time, however, it is not really justified, for the new blockader, the B at K5, proves to be a stout fellow.

| 11. | Kt x P | Kt x Kt |
| 12. | B x Kt | Kt—B3 |

For the otherwise desirable .... B—KB3 would fail against *13.* Q—R5 *ch,* P—Kt3; *14.* B x P *ch,* P x B; *15.* Q x P *ch,* K—K2; *16.* B x B *ch,* Kt x B; *17.* Q—Kt7 *ch.*

| 13. | Kt—Q2 | . . . . |

That the win of a Pawn by *13.* Q—B2 *?,* O—O, etc. is a snare, has been pointed out under Diagram 115, p. 142.

| 13. | . . . . | O—O |
| 14. | Kt—B3 *!* | . . . . |

The blockading forces are to be reinforced by the Kt.

| 14. | . . . . | B—Q3 |

14. .... B—Kt4 would yield little profit, for *15.* B—Q4, Q—R3; *16.* B x B, Q x B; *17.* Kt—Kt5, would win a Pawn.

| 15. | Q—K2 | . . . . |

That *15.* B—Q4 would be premature has been pointed out under Diagram 116.

15.	. . . .	QR—B1
16.	B—Q4	Q—B2
17.	Kt—K5	. . . .

The immobility of the KP is now greater than ever. White has utilized his resources very economically. The possibility of a successful occupation of the points Q4, K5, hung on a hair, on taking minute advantage of the terrain (the points Q4, K5, QB2, and K2).

17.	. . . .	B—K1
18.	QR—K1	B x Kt
19.	B x B	Q—B3
20.	B—Q4	. . . .

In order to force Black's QB, who also has his eye on R4, to come to a decision.

| 20. | . . . . | B—Q2 |
| 21. | Q—B2 | . . . . |

The decisive re-grouping.

21.	. . . .	R—KB2
22.	R—K3	P—QKt3
23.	R—Kt3	K—R1
24.	B x RP *!*	P—K4

24. .... Kt x B loses because of Q—Kt6.

25.	B—Kt6 *!*	R—K2
26.	R—K1	Q—Q3
27.	B—K3	P—Q5
28.	B—Kt5	R x P

29. R x R   P x R
30. Q x P and White won:

30. . . . . K—Kt1; *31*. P—QR3, K—B1; *32*. B—R4, B—K1; *33*. B—B5, Q—Q5; *34*. Q x Q, P x Q; *35*. R x R, K x R; *36*. B—Q3, K—Q3; *37*. B x Kt, P x B; *38*. P—KR4, Resigns.

47. INDIAN DEFENSE

Of special interest historically as being the first game in which what has been called the "Ideal Queen's Gambit" was played, where Black forgoes altogether the occupation of the center by his Pawns.

St. Petersburg, 1913

WHITE	BLACK
B. Gregory	*A. Nimzovich*
1. P—Q4	Kt—KB3
2. Kt—KB3	P—K3
3. B—Kt5	. . . .

In answer to 3. P—B4 I had intended . . . . P—QKt3. The point Q4 is to remain permanently unoccupied.

3.	P—KR3
4. B x Kt	Q x B
5. P—K4	P—KKt3

Black has the two Bishops, and in what follows is concerned to keep them.

6. Kt—B3	Q—K2

In order after . . . . P—Q3

not to be exposed to the move P—K5, which would open the game.

7. B—B4	B—Kt2
8. O—O	P—Q3
9. Q—Q3	O—O
10. QR—K1	P—R3
11. P—QR4	P—Kt3
12. Kt—K2	. . . .

The mobility of White's center must be rated as very slight, for any thrust would be intercepted without any trouble: *12*. P—K5, P—Q4 *!*; or *12*. P—Q5, P—K4 *!*

12.	P—QB4

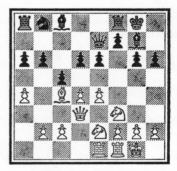

The critical position

A strategical device, which every Hypermodernist may care to note, makes its appearance here. I mean the continuity of an attack directed against a Pawn-mass. This is to be understood thus: the threatened advance must first have its sting drawn (in this game this was done by . . . . Q—K2). It is only when this has happened that we may regard the mass as semi-mobile, and attack it; for only those objects which have been made immobile should be chosen as a target.

13. P—B3	B—Q2
14. P—QKt3	....

14. Kt—Q2 was to be considered. For instance, 14. . . . . B x RP; 15. P—B4 with definite chances.

14.	Q—K1
15. Q—B2	P—QKt4
16. P x KtP	P x KtP
17. B—Q3	Q—B1
18. P x P	P x P
19. P—K5	Kt—B3
20. B x QKtP	....

If 20. Kt—Kt3 then 20. . . . . . P—Kt5 and if 21. P—B4, B—K1 with the superior game.

20.	Kt x P
21. Kt x Kt	B x B
22. Kt—B3	Q—Kt2
23. Kt—Q2	B—QB3
24. P—B3	KR—Kt1

Now the Bishops assert their rights.

25. Kt—Kt3	Q—R2
26. R—B2	B—Q4
27. K—B1	Q—R7
28. Q x Q	R x Q
29. P—QB4	B—Q5

30. R(B2)—K2	B—QB3
31. R—Q1	R—Kt7
32. R—B1	P—R4
33. K—K1	R—R1

Threatens complete paralysis by . . . . R(R1)—R7, since R—Kt1 is then impossible because of . . . . R x R *ch* and . . . . R—R8.

34. Kt—R1 !	R(R1)—R7
35. Kt—B2	R x Kt
36. R x R	R x R
37. K x R	B x Kt

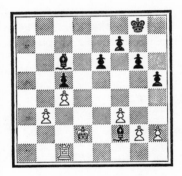

The win is still some considerable way off. In what follows Black maneuvers against the QBP, but also keeps before himself the possibility of an incursion of his K at KKt6, as for instance at the 70th move. However, this by itself would not suffice, Black has also still to play out the duel on the K's wing with his Pawn-majority, and in doing so his position will become broken up; and with all this the QBP is not to be joked with.

38. R—QKt1	K—B1
39. P—QKt4	P x P
40. R x P	K—K2
41. R—Kt8	B—Q5
42. R—QB8	B—Q2
43. R—QR8	P—K4
44. K—B2	B—B3
45. R—QB8	B—R5 *ch*
46. K—Q3	B—Q2
47. R—B7	K—Q3
48. R—Kt7	B—Kt8
49. P—R3	P—R5

The point KKt6 now looks ripe for an invasion by Black.

50. R—Kt8	B—K3
51. R—QR8	B—Kt3
52. R—R8	B—B7
53. R—R8	B—B4 *ch*
54. K—K2	B—Kt3
55. R—R8	P—Kt4
56. R—KKt8	P—B3
57. R—KB8	K—K2
58. R—QKt8	B—Q5
59. R—Kt5	B—KKt3
60. R—R5	B—KB4
61. R—R6	B—B1
62. R—B6	B—Q2
63. R—R6	B—QB4
64. K—Q3	B—B4 *ch*
65. K—K2	P—K5 *!*

At last the fitting moment has arrived.

66. R—B6	B—Q5
67. R—R6	B—K3
68. R—R4	P—K6 *!*
69. K—Q3	B—B4

Now the King threatens to journey to his KKt6.

70. R—R6	B x P *ch*
71. Resigns	

This game aroused lively interest at the time, and the idea was tried at the same tournament by other masters, though with indifferent success. I continued my studies of the opening, and employed it the next year, 1914, in the St. Petersburg Tournament, and against Janowski and Bernstein. The first 18 moves of the former game were given and discussed in II. ii. § 2, p. 191. Against Bernstein (White) the game ran: 1. P—Q4, Kt—KB3; 2. Kt—KB3, P—K3; 3. P—B4, P—QKt3; 4. Kt—B3, B—Kt2; 5. P—K3, B—Kt5; 6. Q—Kt3, Q—K2; 7. P—QR3, B x Kt *ch;* 8. Q x B, P—Q3; 9. P—QKt4, QKt—Q2; (Black now has an excellent game; the mobility of the White center is slight, and the diagonal QKt2 to K5 is an important asset). 10. B—Kt2 P—QR4 (even better was . . . . Kt—K5 and . . . . P—KB4); 11. B—K2, P x P; 12. P x P, R x R *ch;* 13. B x R,

O—O; *14.* O—O, Kt—K5; *15.*
Q—B2, P—KB4; *16.* Kt—Q2,
Kt x Kt (now *16.* . . . . P—B4
with its hypermodern savor
would seem to be more in keeping here). *17.* Q x Kt, R—R1;
18. B—QB3, Q—K1 (with *18.*
. . . . Kt—B3, in order to
anticipate P—Q5, Black's game
would still have been good); *19.*
P—Q5 *!,* P—K4 (if *19.* . . . .
P x P *?; 20.* B—B3); *20.* P—
KB4, B—B1; and, after a sequence of highly dramatic complications, the game ended in a
draw.

In the same tournament Alekhine adopted my innovation—
the "Ideal Queen's Gambit"—
and with success.

48. SICILIAN DEFENSE

This is the first game in which
the thesis of the relative harm-
lessness of the "Pawn-roller"
was stated.

San Sebastian, 1911

WHITE	BLACK
R. *Spielmann*	A. *Nimzovich*
1. P—K4	P—QB4
2. Kt—KB3	Kt—KB3

This set Spielmann thinking.
After some minutes I raised my
eyes from the board and saw
that my dear old companion in
arms was quite disconcerted.
He looked at the Kt, now confidently, now suspiciously, and

after much hesitation gave up
the possible chase started by
P—K5 and played the more
circumspect Kt—B3. Next year
I tried *2.* . . . . Kt—KB3 on
Schlechter, and in the Book of
the Congress we find the following note to this move by Tarrasch: "Not good, since the Kt
is at once driven away, but Herr
Nimzovich goes his own road in
the openings; one, however,
which cannot be recommended
to the public."

Ridicule can do much, for instance embitter the existence of
young talents; but one thing is
not given to it, to put a stop
permanently to the incursion of
new and powerful ideas. The old
dogmas, such as the ossified
teaching on the center, the wor-
ship of the open game, and in
general the whole formalistic
conception of the game, who
bothers himself to-day about
these? The new ideas, however,
those supposed by-ways, not to
be recommended to the public,
these are become to-day high-
ways, on which great and small
move freely in the consciousness
of absolute security.

My game against Schlechter
ran as follows: *1.* P—K4, P—
QB4; *2.* Kt—KB3, Kt—KB3; *3.*
P—K5, Kt—Q4; *4.* P—Q4.
Why, asks Dr. Tarrasch, should
not P—B4 be played here? The
Black Kt would then certainly

be driven on to unfavorable squares. Alas, no; even in the case of *1. P—K4, Kt—KB3* (Alekhine's Defense) the effect of driving the Kt by *2. P—K5, Kt—Q4; 3. P—QB4, Kt—Kt3; 4. P—Q4* is merely to compromise White's game.

In my game against Schlechter the continuation was: *4. .... P x P; 5. Q x P, P—K3; 6. B—QB4, Kt—QB3; 7. Q—K4, P—Q3 !; 8. P x P* (or *8. B x Kt, P x B; 9. Q x P, P x P;* with two Bs and a compact Pawn majority), *Kt—B3; 9. Q—R4, B x P; 10. Kt—B3, Kt—K4 !;* and Black obtained a certain freedom for maneuvering in the middle of the board.

To return to my game with Spielmann:

3.	Kt—B3	P—Q4
4.	P x P	Kt x P
5.	B—B4	P—K3
6.	O—O	B—K2
7.	P—Q4	Kt x Kt
8.	P x Kt	O—O
9.	Kt—K5	Q—B2

What now follows is play against the hanging Pawns which will soon come into existence.

10.	B—Q3	Kt—B3
11.	B—KB4	B—Q3
12.	R—K1	P x P *!*

This exchange in conjunction with .... Kt—Kt5 is the point of the proceedings started by *9. .... Q—B2.*

13.	P x P	Kt—Kt5
14.	B—Kt3	Kt x B
15.	Q x Kt	P—QKt3
16.	P—QB4	B—R3

The hanging Pawns, which come under heavy fire, prove, however, in the end to have a lot of vigor. The game is about equal.

17.	QR—B1	QR—B1
18.	Q—Kt3 *!*	P—B3
19.	Q—R4 *?*	. . . .

19. P—B5, B x Kt; 20. P x B would have led to a draw.

19.	. . . .	P x Kt
20.	P x P	B—R6 *!*
21.	Q x KB	B x P
22.	R—K4	Q—Q2
23.	P—R3	B—Q4

With his B thus posted Black's advantage is clear.

24. R—K2	Q—Kt2
25. P—B4	Q—KB2
26. R(K2)—QB2	R x R
27. R x R	Q—Kt3
28. Q—QB3	. . . .

White cannot well give up the QB file; if, however, 28. R—B3 then 28. . . . . P—KR4; 29. P—R4, R x P.

28.	B x RP *!*
29. B—R4	B—Q4
30. B—K7	R—K1
31. B—Q6	Q—K5
32. Q—B7	P—KR3
33. R—B2	Q—K8 *ch*
34. R—B1	Q—K6 *ch*
35. R—B2	P—QR4
36. B—K7	Q—K8 *ch*
37. R—B1	Q—K6 *ch*
38. R—B2	K—R1

Directed against B—B6.

39. B—Q8	Q—K8 *ch*
40. R—B1	Q—K6 *ch*
41. R—B2	Q—K8 *ch*
42. R—B1	Q—Kt6
43. R—B2	R—B1
44. Q x P	R x P
45. B—K7	P—R5

A passed Pawn plus a mating attack, a wicked affair.

46. K—B1 *?*	. . . .

But he was lost whatever he did.

46.	Q x P *ch*
47. Resigns	

49. FRENCH DEFENSE

This being the first game in which my idea of a sacrifice for the sole purpose of establishing a blockade was illustrated.

San Sebastian, 1912

WHITE	BLACK
A. *Nimzovich*	R. *Spielmann*
1. P—K4	P—K3
2. P—Q4	P—Q4
3. P—K5	P—QB4
4. Kt—KB3	Kt—QB3
5. P x P	B x P
6. B—Q3	KKt—K2
7. B—KB4 *!*	. . . .

The over-protection of the strategically important P at K5.

7.	Q—Kt3
8. O—O	Q x P

This was no ordinary Pawn sacrifice for the attack. Its motive was simply and exclusively this, to maintain the point K5, in order to use it as a base for a blockading action. We know this motive in checkers, where a man is sacrificed in order to make it possible to lock up an enemy majority by our minority. To have translated this idea to the field of chess was a revolutionary act.

9.	QKt—Q2	Q—Kt3
10.	Kt—Kt3	Kt—Kt3
11.	B—Kt3	B—K2
12.	P—KR4	. . . .

This, too, is no attacking move in the ordinary sense; its meaning is: "Get away from the Key Square K5."

12.	. . . .	Q—Kt5
13.	P—R4	P—QR3
14.	P—KR5	Kt—R5
15.	Kt x Kt	B x Kt
16.	P—QB3	Q—K2
17.	B—R2	P—B4

This move, which throws open all lines of approach to his opponent, he has got to make in order to give himself air; and with it White's attack first appears in evidence.

| 18. | P x P e.p. | P x P |
| 19. | Kt—Q4 | P—K4 |

20. B—B5 with a strong attack, and White *won* on the 44th move. For the balance of the game, see the play following Diagram 83.

My game against Leonhardt (Black) in the same tournament took much the same course: 1. P—K4, P—K3; 2. P—Q4, P—Q4; 3. P—K5, P—QB4; 4. Kt—KB3 (later I discovered the still more revolutionary Q—Kt4, see No. 50), Q—Kt3; 5. B—Q3, P x P: 6. O—O, Kt—QB3; 7. P—QR3, KKt—K2; 8. P—QKt4, Kt—Kt3; 9. R—K1, B—K2; 10. B—Kt2, P—QR4. Black now has to give up the Pawn again; after 10. . . . . P—QR3 !, we should have had the state of affairs we have discussed, namely Pawn plus vs. a cramping policy.

The same strategical device appeared in a particularly plastic shape in a game played in 1923, when the position shown in the diagram was reached.

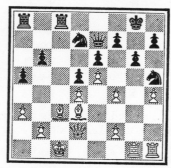

Brinckmann—Nimzovich

The game continued 19. . . . . P—QKt4 ! !; Black sacrifices a P in order to exchange

White's KB, after which the blockade of White's position by .... Kt—KB4 becomes effective. There followed, *20.* **B x QKtP, QR—Kt1;** *21.* **B—K2, Kt—Kt3** (more precise was .... Kt—Kt2 at once; for if P—R5, then .... Kt—Kt3, followed by the forced exchange at B5 and finally by the occupation of his KB4 by the Kt, with a positional winning advantage for Black); *22.* **K—Q1** (he could have saved himself by *22.* B x Kt, Kt—B5; *23.* Q—B2, Kt x RP; *24.* Q—Q2), **Kt—B5;** *23.* **B x Kt(B4), R x B;** *24.* **R—Kt5, Kt—Kt2;** *25.* **P—R5, Kt—B4;** *26.* **P x P, BP x P;** and Black **won** without difficulty.

50. FRENCH DEFENSE

From a match; the first game in which appears my idea of a Pawn sacrifice in the opening, not to obtain an attack, but merely, with gain of a tempo, to overprotect a strategical point with a view to cramping the enemy forces.

Kristianstad, 1922

WHITE	BLACK
A. Nimzovich	A. Hakansson
1. P—K4	P—K3
2. P—Q4	P—Q4
3. P—K5	P—QB4
4. Q—Kt4	. . . .

My innovation.

4.	P x P
5. Kt—KB3	Kt—QB3
6. B—Q3	P—B4
7. Q—Kt3	KKt—K2
8. O—O	Kt—Kt3
9. P—KR4	Q—B2
10. R—K1	. . . .

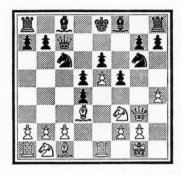

White's plan is now clear. He has given up a Pawn, careless when, if ever, he recovers it provided his PK5 is maintained as an instrument to cramp Black's game. There is no idea of attack in *9.* P—KR4, its object is solely to pave the way to the removal of some of the pressure on the P at K5. The Pawn sacrifice clearly comes within the category of sacrifice for the sake of blockade, *cf.* Game No. 49.

10. . . . .   B—Q2

.... B—B4 was essential here so as to leave the KB square free for the Kt to retreat to after P—R5.

| 11. P—R3 | O—O—O |
| 12. P—Kt4 | . . . . |

White could, of course, have won the exchange here by 12. P—R5, Kt—K2; 13. Kt—Kt5, R—K1; 14. Kt—B7, R—Kt1; 15. Kt—Q6 *ch;* but with his un-developed Q side and his un-protected P at R5 he would have had some difficulties to contend with. The text move is the logi-cal continuation.

| 12. . . . . | P—QR3 |

Rather better was 12. . . . . K—Kt1; 13. P—B3 *!*, P x P; 14. Kt x P, Kt x KtP; 15. P x Kt, Q x Kt; 16. B—K3, Q x B; 17. B x P *ch,* K—B1; 18. KR—B1 *ch,* B—B3; 19. P—Kt5 *!*, Q x P; 20. Kt—Q4 with complications, which, of course, White, had he been so minded, could have avoided by simply playing 13. B—Kt2.

13. P—R5	KKt—K2
14. B—Q2	P—R3
15. P—R4	P—KKt4
16. P—Kt5	P—B5
17. Q—Kt4	. . . .

The Q is well placed here.

| 17. . . . . | Kt—QKt1 |
| 18. P—QB3 | R—K1 |

His only move. It will be noted that the over-protector, the R, K1, now has the QB file opened for him without any trouble to himself. In order to avoid loss of material Black has to submit to a curious regroup-ing of his forces.

19. BP x P	K—Q1
20. R—QB1	Q—Kt3
21. P—R5	Q—R2
22. P—Kt6	Q—R1

The Q finds herself in a posi-tion to which as a rule she would only be consigned in a problem.

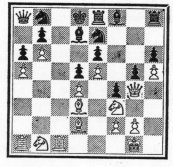

23. R—B7	Kt—B4
24. Kt—B3 *!*	B—K2
25. Kt x QP	Kt x P
26. Kt x Kt	P x Kt
27. Q x B	*ch*—and mates

next move.